THE FORMS AND FUNCTIONS OF TORT LAW

FOURTH EDITION

By

KENNETH S. ABRAHAM

David and Mary Harrison
Distinguished Professor of Law
University of Virginia

CONCEPTS AND INSIGHTS SERIES®

FOUNDATION PRESS
2012

THOMSON REUTERS™

© 1997, 2002 FOUNDATION PRESS
© 2007 THOMSON REUTERS/FOUNDATION PRESS
© 2012 By THOMSON REUTERS/FOUNDATION PRESS

    1 New York Plaza, 34th Floor

    New York, NY 10004

    Phone Toll Free 1–877–888–1330

    Fax 646–424–5201

    foundation–press.com

Printed in the United States of America

ISBN 978–1–60930–053–1

Mat #41181370

For Vincent Blasi and Andrew Delbanco

PREFACE TO THE FOURTH EDITION

This book is designed to provide a concise analysis of the conceptual foundations of tort liability. Although the book is designed to be used mainly by first-year law students, it is also of use to upper-class students and practitioners seeking an overview of particular areas of tort law. Having taught courses in Tort Law for almost forty years, I have come to recognize students' need for something beyond the typical casebook to help them understand what is going on in the cases and in class. Yet the kind of books that are traditionally available do not always satisfy this need. Books of rules don't explain what lies behind the rules; and treatises are both too long and, often, not sufficiently analytical. What first-year students need is a book that helps them to think about "what the Professor was getting at" without spoon-feeding it to them. I hope that this book does exactly that.

The organization and strategy of the book are as follows. I have found that students often are much better able to understand the cases they study during their first few weeks in law school if they appreciate something about the procedure that has brought the case to the point where it can be decided on appeal. In addition, often some part of the earliest classes is devoted to discussion of the purposes served by the imposition of tort liability. Therefore, Chapter One provides a primer on procedure and discusses the functions of tort liability. Thereafter the book follows the pattern of most of the major casebooks, beginning with material on intentional physical injury and then moving on to negligence, causation, defenses, products liability, affirmative and limited duty, and damages. This material pretty well coincides with what is taught in the typical one semester course in Torts. There follow Chapters on subjects that are usually taken up in a second-semester or Torts II course, on tort reform and alternative compensation systems, defamation, invasion of privacy, misrepresentation, and interference with contract and prospective contractual advantage.

My strategy throughout the book is to provide a brief summary of the rules that govern a particular area, but then to devote the majority of the analysis to an examination of the purposes the rules serve and the arguments that can be made for and against the rules as they stand. Where some knowledge of the way the law has developed over time can help the reader to appreciate the current state of the law, I have tried to provide a capsule history that puts things in context. In short, the reader will find a conceptual analysis of virtually all the major issues in tort law. Ideally, the student who has read the material on a particular subject before he or she goes to class will be prepared to discuss not only what the cases hold, but their implications as well. Although I have discussed most of what would be covered in two semesters of tort law, inevitably there have been a few omissions. I have barely talked about the torts of trespass to land and conversion of property, for example, and have entirely omitted malicious prosecution.

I have dedicated this book to two people who have meant a lot to me, both intellectually and personally. The greatest help I have had in writing this book has come from my friend and former colleague, Vincent Blasi. Over the years we have had countless discussions about torts, as we both taught first-year torts classes, and for a decade as we co-taught a seminar on Tort Theory. He has pushed, stimulated, and puzzled me with his questions and insights, and he gave me very detailed comments on the fourth edition of this book. I am grateful not only for his help, but for the way he has single-handedly raised the level of my intellectual satisfaction. Andrew Delbanco has been a great professional and personal friend, acquainting me with ways of thinking that would never have occurred to me, and providing me with emotional sustenance both on and off the golf course. We have smiled at fate together, agonized about our children together, and, most importantly, consistently laughed out loud together. Both Vince and Andy have enriched my life.

KENNETH S. ABRAHAM

Charlottesville, Virginia
October, 2011

TABLE OF CONTENTS

THE FORMS
AND
FUNCTIONS
OF TORT LAW

1

THE NATURE AND FUNCTIONS OF TORT LAW

The law of torts (a name derived from the Latin word for "twisted" and from the French word for injury or "wrong") mainly concerns the rights of private parties to obtain monetary compensation from those who have caused them injury or damage. Most of tort law is "common law," that is, law made by courts rather than legislatures. Legislatures enact statutes, whereas courts decide individual cases. A series of judicial decisions based on the same principle—usually at the appellate level—then comes to stand for a rule of law. Most tort law is made by state rather than federal courts. So although reference often is made to "the" law of torts, in fact there are fifty separate state regimes of tort law. These different bodies of state tort law are nonetheless sufficiently similar in important respects to constitute one body of law with variations within it.

It is useful to begin at a general level before addressing particular areas of tort law and specific legal doctrines. This Chapter starts with a brief discussion of the nature of tort law in order to introduce the subject. As in many areas of the law, however, it is impossible to obtain the fullest appreciation of substance if one does not understand the procedural setting in which a substantive rule has been made. The Chapter therefore turns next to the procedural context in which tort law is made, surveying the points of procedure that arise most frequently in tort cases. Finally, the Chapter takes up the functions of tort law, surveying briefly the different functions that have been attributed to tort law and that figure prominently in the Chapters that follow this one.

I. Introduction

Courses in Torts often begin with the question, "What is a tort?" Students give puzzled responses until the correct answer, "A civil wrong not arising out of contract," eventually emerges. This answer is a good enough starting point, but it is both overinclusive and underinclusive. Not all civil wrongs that do not arise out of contract are torts. For example, many statutory schemes that create civil liability, such as Civil Rights statutes, involve neither contract nor tort liability, although they resemble tort in an attenuated way. And some torts actually do "arise" of out contract, at least in a loose sense. Certain legal actions for bodily injury or property damage caused by defective products, as well as claims for bad-faith breach of contract, are examples. But these are, so to speak, exceptions that prove the rule. For the most part tort law is in fact a residual category of civil liability. Legally cognizable wrongs that are not part of another discrete field of law tend to fall under the rubric of tort law.

Tort law itself can be subdivided into two general categories, based on the "standard of care" whose breach may result in liability. What might be called *accident law* is comprised of cases imposing strict liability or negligence liability, usually for physical injury—bodily injury or property damage. Strict liability is imposed without regard to the degree of care that the defendant, or "tortfeasor," exercised. Negligence liability is imposed only upon proof of some kind of carelessness—technically, the failure to exercise reasonable care under the circumstances. In contrast, in what are sometimes called the *intentional torts*, liability is not imposed for negligence, but only upon proof of the defendant's intention to invade the legally protected interest of another. The intentional torts involve a wide variety of non-accidental behavior. Some of this behavior obviously merits the name "intentional" in the sense of an intention to cause harm. A good deal of what falls in the category of the intentional torts, however, does not necessarily require or involve an intent to cause harm. Certain forms of defamation and some invasions of privacy, to give just two examples, can result in liability even in the absence of intent to cause harm, as long as the defendant intended to take the action that caused the plaintiff harm. Nonetheless, this rough distinction between the torts that fall in the general area of accident law and those informally classified as intentional is worth recognizing.

The distinction between tort liability for accidental and intentional harm, however, goes only to the standard of care at issue. Proof that the defendant violated the applicable standard of care is not enough to warrant the imposition of tort liability. Breach of the standard of care is merely one element of any "cause of action"—basis for imposing liability—in tort. There must be proof that the plaintiff suffered actionable harm, and that the defendant's conduct in breaching the applicable standard of care caused that harm. Combining these requirements yields the four elements of any cause of action in tort: 1) Duty (i.e., the legal duty to comply with a particular standard of care); 2) Breach of Duty (i.e., failure to

2

comply with the applicable standard of care); 3) Causation; and 4) Damages.

Although tort liability is imposed, under various circumstances, for bodily injury, property damage, emotional harm, and economic loss, liability for bodily injury and property damage dominates tort law in practice. Consequently, it also dominates introductory courses in tort law. The reason is that tort liability is much more likely to be imposed when conduct causes physical harm than when only emotional or only economic loss occurs. Bodily integrity is central to people's ability to benefit from all the other goods of life. Greater obligations of safety therefore attach to conduct that risks bodily injury, and tort law affords greater protection against such risks. It would be much harder to justify also affording greater protection against the risk of damage to property, except for the fact that conduct that risks property damage typically simultaneously risks bodily injury. It is often a matter of serendipity whether the conduct results in bodily injury, property damage, or both.

Tort law in the United States has four features that are so fundamental to its operation, even though their existence is not logically necessary to it, that they are worth noting at the outset:

Jury Trial. In all state and federal courts there is a right to a trial by jury in almost all tort cases. This produces a body of rules about the allocation of authority between courts and juries. Much of tort law emerges in decisions about this allocation of authority. In addition, there is more potential for emotion and sympathy for the plaintiff to influence the outcome, and less concern for consistent treatment of similar cases, than there would be if ultimate decisions were made by professional judges rather than by lay juries. It is worth noting, however, that over ninety percent of all tort suits are settled. Settlements typically are reached in anticipation of what would happen at trial. But many routine, small and medium-sized claims are handled in a somewhat bureaucratic fashion by lawyers and liability insurance companies, without careful consideration of factual and legal nuances that would be relevant at trial.

Liability Insurance.[1] Beginning in the second half of the nineteenth century there was a significant increase in the incidence of accidental injuries. This resulted from industrialization, the mechanization of transportation and a consequent increase in the risk

---

1. A brief, introductory primer on insurance, including liability insurance, is set out at the beginning of Chapter Twelve. Interested readers may wish to review these paragraphs now.

3

of injury from railroads, trolley cars, and airplanes, and a political and cultural shift that favored the greater socialization of risk generally. In part to respond to the increased liability that resulted, late in the nineteenth century liability insurance was introduced. It has grown exponentially since then. Today, virtually all defendants in bodily injury and property damage suits, and many defendants in other kinds of suits, have at least some liability insurance. The availability of liability insurance influences the decision whether to sue and whom to sue. Moreover, over a period of more than a century, the availability of insurance and the scope of tort liability have influenced each other. The more tort liability expanded, the more liability insurance became available. And often tort liability expanded at least in part because liability insurance was, or could be expected to become, available.[2]

The Contingent Fee System. Plaintiffs' attorneys almost always take cases on a "contingent-fee" basis. That is, the plaintiff's attorney receives a percentage of the plaintiff's recovery if the suit is successful, and charges nothing if the suit is unsuccessful. The result is that plaintiffs are not required to be able to pay their attorneys in order to bring suit. In addition, the contingent fee approach affects the selection of cases in which suit is brought, because plaintiffs' attorneys are heavily influenced by their prospects of success and by the magnitude of the plaintiff's alleged losses.

The "American Rule" for Costs. In our tort system, each party pays its own costs, including counsel fees, win or lose. In contrast, in many other systems, a loser-pays approach is applied. Under our system, plaintiffs are less discouraged from bringing suit, because they do not risk incurring a sizeable personal cost if they lose their suits, and defendants must pay their own counsel fees and costs even if they win. Obviously, fewer suits would be brought, whether involving strong or weak claims, and some suits might be more vigorously defended, under a loser-pays system.

These four features of tort law and liability have heavily influenced its development. Together they help to account for the great transformation of tort law that took place in the twentieth century. From a comparatively obscure field of law with little economic importance even in the late nineteenth century, the scope and incidence of tort liability expanded substantially. Tort law had become a major legal specialty of considerable economic importance by the beginning of the twenty-first century. That is one reason

2. *See* Kenneth S. Abraham, THE LIABILITY CENTURY: INSURANCE AND TORT LAW FROM THE PROGRESSIVE ERA TO 9/11 (2008).

that virtually every law school requires the study of tort law in the first year. The other reason is that tort law is a near-perfect vehicle for studying the legal process. And that is where we now turn.

II. Procedure in a Tort Suit: Where Tort Law Comes From

Tort law does not simply spring spontaneously out of the mouths of judges. Tort law is created through rulings that courts make in lawsuits. These rulings are made when a lawyer for the plaintiff or defendant requests that a judge do or not do something as part of a lawsuit—e.g., when a lawyer makes a motion, objects to the admissibility of evidence, or requests a particular instruction to the jury. Often the substantive rules of tort law determine the proper procedure to be followed by a court in ruling on such requests, and the applicable rule of tort law can be inferred from a court's procedural ruling. Thus, to understand substance, one must understand procedure; and to understand procedure, one must understand substance. Turning your mind off when you encounter a procedural issue in the course of examining a judicial opinion usually is a big mistake, for it is in the resolution of procedural issues that substantive law emerges.

There are five major phases of a tort suit: pleadings; pre-trial motions; discovery; trial; and appeal. The pleadings initiate the suit. Pre-trial motions raise legal issues that may clarify or narrow the range of the dispute. Discovery is the process by which, prior to trial, the parties obtain information about each side's position and about the facts as they will be presented at trial. At trial evidence is introduced, the judge instructs the jury about the relevant legal rules, the jury makes findings of fact, and the jury applies the rules about which it has been instructed to its factual findings, yielding a verdict from the jury and a consequent judgment issued by the trial court either for the plaintiff or for the defendant. On appeal the party who was unsuccessful at trial identifies what it contends were legal errors committed by the trial judge, and the appellate court determines whether any of these errors were committed.

A. *Initial Pleadings*

Tort suits proceed much like other civil actions. A lawsuit, or action, is commenced when the injured party, or *Plaintiff*, files a *Complaint* or *Declaration*, alleging facts giving rise to a *cause of action*. The Complaint is said to contain "allegations" because the assertions in it do not count as facts unless and until the defendant admits them, or a jury finds them to be true at trial. A "cause of action" is the plaintiff's legally actionable claim, the basis upon which he asserts a right to damages or other relief. Typically a cause of action is the name of a particular tort, such as negligence, battery, or defamation.

The *Defendant* is then served with the Complaint and a summons requiring the filing of an *Answer*, which admits or denies the allegations of the Complaint. The answer also may state what are known as *Affirmative Defenses*—defenses that the defendant is required to raise specifically and prove at trial. Commonly the defendant admits some of the plaintiff's allegations, denies others, and indicates that it possesses insufficient information as to still others. By comparing the Complaint and the Answer the parties can determine what is initially disputed and what is not. All the documents mentioned thus far, as well as pre-trial motions filed later, are typically referred to as the *Pleadings*.

B. *Discovery*

In the *Discovery* stage of the suit the parties are permitted to seek information from each other about the nature of their positions and the evidence supporting them. Through written *Interrogatories* the parties may propound questions to be answered in writing, and through oral *Depositions* witnesses (including the plaintiff and the defendant) may be examined under oath to determine the scope and details of their possible testimony at trial. The information sought in discovery need not be admissible in evidence to be discoverable, as long as it has the potential to lead to admissible evidence. For example, through discovery the defendant may learn the precise nature of the injuries the plaintiff claims to have suffered, and the basis for the plaintiff's claim that the defendant was negligent. Similarly, the plaintiff may learn what features of her claim the defendant contests and the basis for the defendant's contentions. Discovery reduces the element of surprise at trial, thereby permitting the parties to prepare and focus only on the issues actually in dispute, and promotes settlement before trial by helping to inform the parties of the strengths and weaknesses of each side's position.

In the simplest of cases there is little discovery, but these days discovery is an important part of virtually all cases. A single deposition may take a day, two days, or even occasionally a week, and may be preceded or followed by written interrogatories. Even in a simple auto accident case discovery can take some time if there are eye witnesses and medical experts who are in the possession of potentially relevant information. On the other hand, in a complicated tort suit discovery may take months or even years, if there are large numbers of documents to be obtained and many witnesses to be deposed. For example, think of how many people may have information that is potentially relevant when the manufacturer of a prescription drug is sued for negligently failing to warn of a side effect that injured the plaintiff. Research scientists, marketing personnel, financial analysts, and management officials all may know something relevant to the decisions that led to the failure to warn. The plaintiff is likely to depose many, and perhaps all, of these individuals.

C. *Pre–Trial Motions*

Pre-trial motions may be made before or after discovery. This is the first stage at which the court makes important "procedural" decisions. For our purposes the important pre-trial motions are the *Motion to Dismiss* and the motion for *Summary Judgment*. The former tends to be made before discovery and the latter after discovery.

The function of a motion to dismiss the plaintiff's complaint is to test the legal sufficiency of the plaintiff's allegations. For purposes of the motion the plaintiff's allegations are accepted as true. By making the motion the defendant asserts that, even if the allegations are true, the plaintiff does not have a valid, legally cognizable claim. For example, suppose that the plaintiff alleged that he was walking down the street when the defendant frowned at him, and that as a result he experienced emotional pain and suffering. The defendant's motion to dismiss for failure to state a cause of action (or as it is described in the federal system, for "failure to state a claim upon which relief can be granted") would in effect admit that the defendant frowned at the plaintiff, and admit that the plaintiff experienced emotional pain and suffering as a result, but would deny that this behavior is actionable—i.e., deny that this behavior constitutes a tort.[3]

These motions are made prior to discovery. In contrast, after discovery a motion for *Summary Judgment* by either side asserts that 1) there is no genuine issue of material fact, and 2) based on the undisputed facts, the party making the motion is entitled to

---

3. A similar motion in some states is known as a *Demurrer*. But demurrers can be filed by either side, and simply test the legal sufficiency of the pleading to which they respond. For instance, a defendant's demurrer to the plaintiff's complaint is in effect a motion to dismiss; a plaintiff's demurrer to a defendant's answer is in effect a motion to strike the answer as a legally insufficient defense.

judgment "as a matter of law." For example, if discovery reveals no dispute between the parties that while driving blindfolded down Main Street the defendant struck and injured the plaintiff, the plaintiff would move for summary judgment. The only question would be whether the defendant was negligent "as a matter of law" or, on the contrary, a jury could legitimately conclude on the basis of the undisputed facts that the defendant was not negligent. In all probability the plaintiff would be granted summary judgment under these circumstances. Thus, whereas typically a motion to dismiss or a demurrer tests the legal sufficiency of mere *allegations*, a motion for summary judgment tests the legal sufficiency of a party's position based on undisputed and therefore established *facts*. But in other respects the two kinds of motions function in a very similar way: they take certain facts to be established, and then assert that on the basis of these facts (and sometimes notwithstanding these facts) the party making the motion is entitled to prevail as a matter of law, without the need for decision by a jury.

From these examples it should be obvious that these motions are not "mere" procedure. Rather, their proper resolution depends on the applicable substantive rule of tort law. The motion to dismiss a suit claiming damages for injury caused by being frowned at cannot be granted or denied without knowing whether frowning under those circumstances constitutes a tort (which of course it does not). And the motion for summary judgment cannot be granted or denied without identifying the applicable rule governing the role of the jury in determining whether driving blindfolded down Main Street is negligent. If the question whether the defendant was negligent must always be decided by a jury, then the plaintiff's motion for summary judgment must be denied. But if there are cases in which it can be said "as a matter of law" that the defendant is negligent (and as we shall see in Chapter Three there are such cases), and this is one of those cases, then summary judgment should be granted. Much of tort law, in fact, is made and applied through rulings on motions such as these.

D. *Trial*

If a ruling on a pre-trial motion has not disposed of the case and the parties have not settled, then the case proceeds to trial. At trial the allocation of decision-making authority between the court (i.e., the trial judge) and the jury is of crucial significance: courts *only* decide issues of law; juries *only* decide issues of fact. When there is a trial without a jury—a "bench trial"—the trial judge wears two hats. Then the trial judge both rules on the law and serves as the "trier of fact."

1. Fact–Finding by the Jury

There are two different kinds of fact-finding that juries perform. One is making "pure" findings of fact. This requires answering *empirical* questions about the world, past, present, or future: did the defendant strike the plaintiff, how long had the banana peel been lying on the supermarket aisle before the plaintiff slipped on it, would the plaintiff have chosen to use the defendant's product if he had been warned of the risks it posed, how much suffering has the plaintiff experienced as a result of her injury, what medical treatment will the plaintiff need in the future? I do not mean to minimize how difficult it sometimes is to answer merely empirical questions. Predicting how much an injured person will suffer from her injury twenty years from now is a pure empirical question, but that does not make it any easier to answer.

In contrast, a second kind of "finding of fact" that juries are required to make involves what are sometimes called *mixed questions of fact and law*. In answering these questions the jury does not make empirical findings. Rather, it evaluates or characterizes empirical facts that it has already found, or applies the law to these facts. To do this the jury makes such determinations as, was the defendant negligent, did the plaintiff assume the risk of harm, was the defendant's product defective because of its design?

These two kinds of findings of fact are made at the close of a trial in which evidence has been introduced directed at proving the facts relevant to the four necessary elements of the plaintiff's case: 1) duty (a legal issue that sometimes depends on facts); 2) breach of duty; 3) causation; and 4) damages. Typically the plaintiff bears the *burden of proof* on all factual elements of the claim. That burden in turn consists of two parts. The "burden of production" requires the plaintiff to introduce evidence from which the jury "could" find that each element of the case has been proved. Introducing evidence that satisfies this standard constitutes making out a *prima facie* case. For instance, in an intersection collision case the plaintiff might testify that he was proceeding through the intersection when the defendant's vehicle, which was required to stop at a stop sign, collided with his own vehicle, breaking his arm. Ordinarily this testimony would make out a *prima facie* case. That is, if the jury believed the testimony, it *could* find, but would not be required to find, that the defendant had failed to yield the right of way, that the defendant was negligent in failing to do so, and that this negligence caused damage to the plaintiff's vehicle and a broken arm.

The second feature of the burden of proof, the "burden of persuasion," requires the plaintiff actually to persuade the jury by a *preponderance of the evidence*, of the truth of the facts relevant to each element of his or her claim. To satisfy this preponderance standard, the jury must be persuaded that it is "more probable than not" that the alleged facts relevant to each element of the claim are true. Whether the plaintiff satisfied this standard would depend on whether the jury believed his testimony, what the defendant and other witnesses testified, and whether the jury believed them.[4] If the evidence on any element on which a party bears the burden of persuasion is in "equipoise," or evenly balanced, then the party bearing that burden has not satisfied it.

2. Legal Rulings by the Court

What the court does in a tort suit follows from the fundamental point that courts do not find facts, but *only* make decisions of law. The legal function of the judge and the fact-finding function of the jury operate (and interact) at trial in connection with the court's rulings on the admissibility of evidence, on motions such as a motion for a directed verdict, and in the court's instructions to the jury. First, when oral or documentary testimony is offered into evidence, the court rules on its admissibility. The principal rule governing admissibility is that evidence which is irrelevant to the issues to be decided is not admissible. This rule does not rule evidence in, since not all relevant evidence is admissible, but it rules evidence out. This is a simple enough, but very important rule: nothing irrelevant is admissible. By applying the substantive rules of tort law, the court can determine whether evidence is or is not irrelevant and therefore whether it is automatically inadmissible. For example, if intent to cause physical harm to the plaintiff is not a necessary element of the tort of battery, then testimony by the defendant that he did not intend to cause the plaintiff harm when he slapped him on the back after telling a joke would be inadmissible, because this evidence would be irrelevant. On the other hand, if failure to comply with a safety statute enacted by the legislature is negligence, then evidence that the defendant violated the statute is obviously relevant and (absent special circumstances) will be admissible. A number of the rules of tort law are reflected in, and can be deduced from, rulings on the admissibility of evidence of this sort.

4. On certain affirmative defenses (e.g., that the plaintiff is barred from recovery because she assumed the risk of the defendant's negligence) and in a few unusual situations, the defendant rather than the plaintiff bears the burden of proof.

Second, the court decides a legal question when it applies the rule that a factual contention may only be submitted to the jury for decision if there is evidence to support it. If there is no evidence to support a contention whose proof is essential for a party to prevail, then that party has not met the burden of production, and the opposing party prevails. But if there is evidence to "make out a jury question" on all the elements of the case, then the case is submitted to the jury. The significance of the decision to submit an issue to the jury cannot be emphasized enough: submitting an issue to the jury means that the jury may decide the issue for or against the plaintiff, for or against the defendant. The same issue, submitted to different juries, might be decided differently. That is why the standard for making out a jury question is often said to be whether "reasonable people could disagree" about the question. If reasonable people could disagree, the case goes to the jury; if reasonable people could not disagree, then either the plaintiff wins as "a matter of law" (having prevailed on all the elements as a matter of law) or the defendant wins because, as matter of law, the plaintiff failed to provide evidence sufficient to make out a jury question on one or more of the necessary elements of his case.

The question whether an issue poses a question for the jury may be raised at the close of either party's evidence, when the opposing party moves for a *directed verdict* (or in the federal system, a motion for judgment as a matter of law or "JML"). This phrasing is a holdover from the time when, if the motion was granted, the court literally "directed" the jury to bring in a verdict for the party whose motion prevailed. But the granting of a motion for a directed verdict today means that the court determines as a matter of law, rather than the jury finding as a matter of fact, which party wins. Ordinarily plaintiffs' counsel do not move for directed verdicts, on the theory that if their case is strong enough to warrant a directed verdict, the jury will very likely find in the plaintiff's favor anyway. The granting of a motion for a directed verdict in such a situation might afford the defendant a basis for appeal that it would not otherwise have. So typically motions for directed verdicts are made by defendants. There is necessarily some judgment involved when a trial court decides whether reasonable people could disagree about a particular question of fact. Nonetheless, because the court rather than the jury makes that decision it is considered a question of law, even though it requires a conclusions about facts. The consequence is that this decision is subject to legal review on appeal, as described below.

Rules of tort law are embedded in and reflected by rulings on motions for directed verdicts, just as they are embedded in rulings on the admissibility of evidence. For example, there is liability in tort for injuries caused by defective products, as the discussion of products liability in Chapter Nine indicates. Suppose that the plaintiff is injured when she dives into an above-ground swimming pool with aluminum sides. She submits evidence of the dangers that this product design poses (as well as proof of causation and damages). The defendant then moves for a directed verdict on the ground that the plaintiff submitted no evidence that an alternative safer design of the product was feasible. The court would grant the motion in a state where the rule is that a product design is not defective unless an alternative safer design was feasible. On the other hand, the court would deny the motion in a state where the rule is that such proof is not required in order to show that a product's design is defective. In effect, the motion for a directed verdict is the trial equivalent of the pre-trial motion to dismiss for failure to state a viable claim or cause of action. Whereas the motion to dismiss tests the legal sufficiency of the plaintiff's *allegations* by assuming them to be true and contending that the plaintiff nevertheless is not entitled to recover, a defendant's motion for a directed verdict tests the legal sufficiency of the plaintiff's *evidence* by assuming it to be true and contending that the plaintiff nevertheless is not entitled to recover. By the same token, a plaintiff's motion for a directed verdict tests the legal sufficiency of the defendant's position by assuming the defendant's evidence to be true and contending that the plaintiff is nevertheless entitled to recover as a matter of law.

Sometimes courts decline to grant directed verdicts even when they believe that doing so would be proper, so as to obtain a record of what the jury verdict is in the event that, contrary to what the court expects, the case does pose a question for the jury. For example, suppose the court concludes that the plaintiff is entitled to a directed verdict. The court nonetheless submits the case to the jury for decision. If the jury finds for the plaintiff, the court enters a judgment in the plaintiff's favor. But if the jury finds for the defendant, the court then grants the plaintiff's motion for *judgment notwithstanding the verdict*—also known as a "j.n.o.v.", which stands for judgment *non obstante veredicto* (or in the federal system, "judgment as a matter of law"). The court thereby has on record the decision of the jury if it turns out on appeal that the court was correct to submit the case to the jury—i.e., that it would have been incorrect to grant a directed verdict for the plaintiff and was incorrect to grant the plaintiff's motion for a j.n.o.v. In this manner the same issue that is raised by a motion for a directed verdict can be decided, but without the burden of a new trial if granting the motion would have been error. The appellate court either affirms the trial court, or reverses and enters a judgment for the party in whose favor the jury brought back its verdict, without the need for a new trial simply to see what the jury would have decided had it only been given the chance to decide. It was given that chance.

The third way in which the allocation of authority between court and jury operates is through the court's *instructions* to the jury at the close of the evidence. In its instructions the court describes the rules of tort law to be applied by the jury. The judge identifies the factual disputes the jury should resolve and the rules of law the jury should apply to its factual findings, in order to determine whether to bring back a verdict for the plaintiff or the defendant. The substantive rules of tort law are thus expressed in these instructions. For example, in a negligence case the judge will explain the concept of negligence; the meaning of the requirement that the defendant's negligence, if any, have caused the plaintiff injury; the rules governing the assessment of damages; and the way in which the jury is to determine whether any defenses interposed by the defendant should prevail. The jury then retires to deliberate and bring back its verdict.

3. Verdicts

In most cases the jury is asked to return a *general verdict*, simply indicating whether it finds for the plaintiff or defendant, and if the former, the amount of damages awarded. In most states, however, the court has discretion to ask the jury to return a *special verdict*, answering each of the specific questions posed by the instructions as to whether there was proof of each element of the plaintiff's case and any defenses available. There are number of differences between these two approaches. Since instructions typically are given orally and except in very lengthy cases jurors do not take notes, jurors must try to remember the instructions given to them when they are asked to return a general verdict. In contrast, when a jury is asked to return a special verdict, the jury normally is given a written list of the questions to be answered. The jury can therefore use this list of questions, or "special verdict form," to guide its deliberations.

In addition—and perhaps more importantly—when the jury is required to bring in a special verdict, the court can examine the verdict to determine whether the jury's answers are internally consistent. For example, after being properly instructed, if the jury indicates on its special verdict form that it finds that the defendant was negligent but that the defendant's negligence did not cause the plaintiff any injury, yet the jury still makes an award of damages to the plaintiff, the court will detect this inconsistency: the jury found that the plaintiff did not meet her burden of proving causation, but the jury nonetheless imposed liability on the defendant. The court will therefore grant the defendant's motion for judgment notwithstanding the verdict. If the jury had made a similar mistake in its deliberations prior to returning a general verdict in favor of the plaintiff, the mistake would not be detected. Indeed, asking the jury to return a general verdict not only forfeits the opportunity to detect honest mistakes, but in a sense gives the jury the power deliberately to ignore the instructions.

The natural question to ask at this point is why special verdicts are not used more often, or universally required, in order to preclude the jury's inadvertent or even deliberate circumvention of the court's instructions. One possible answer is that using special verdicts more frequently would in fact be a good idea, and that the prevalence of the general verdict procedure simply reflects the stubborn conservatism of the law. But there is something more going on here than the mere stubborn refusal of the law to change. Tort law has undergone a great deal of change over the years, after all, much of it in the hands of the very judges who continue to employ general verdict rather than special verdict procedure. It makes more sense to infer that there is something desirable about the insulation of jury deliberations from judicial review that results from asking juries only for general verdicts.

What might that be? The answer, I think, is that tort law is ambivalent about the relationship between its rules and the function of the jury. On the one hand, the trial judge must strictly apply the rules of tort law in making decisions about the admissibility of evidence, in ruling on motions, and in formulating instructions to the jury. On the other hand, rules are rigid things. We have juries in tort cases not because we need fact-finding robots, but because they can bring the common sense of the community into the courtroom. Asking juries for general verdicts reflects the recognition that not everything that is relevant to the outcome of a lawsuit can be fully captured by a judge's oral summary of a set of legal rules. The request for a general verdict implicitly permits jurors to take other factors into account, not because they are told that they are permitted to do so, but because under a general verdict approach there is no way to police such behavior. At its extreme, of course, this approach permits *jury nullification* of the law. But in its more moderate manifestations, this approach permits juries to soften the hard edges of rules, without paying painstaking attention to the precise verbal formulations in which the rules are embodied.

14

Under a special verdict approach, that is much more difficult, because the jury's task is defined and contained by a set of specific questions whose answers are supposed to be the jury's only concern. To oversimplify only a bit, the request for a special verdict seeks specific answers; but the request for a general verdict seeks justice.

E. *Appeal*

After a judgment is entered, the losing party may appeal. The party appealing is referred to as the "appellant" (sometimes the "petitioner") and the opposing party is referred to as the "appellee" (sometimes the "respondent"). The key point to understand about appeal, whether in tort or other cases, is that the only basis for any appeal is that the trial judge committed an "error." This fundamental point follows from what appellate courts can and cannot do. Like trial judges, appellate courts make decisions of law only. Appellate courts have no authority to make factual findings. There is no new evidence introduced on appeal, there is no jury, and there is no fact-finding. Rather, appellate courts accept the factual findings made by juries at trial, or accept as fact the findings that logically must be inferred from general verdicts returned by juries.[5]

It follows from the fact that appellate courts make only legal decisions that they review only the decisions of the trial judge, because only the trial judge has made legal decisions at trial. In tort cases, this means that appellate courts review the "procedural" moves of the trial court, which of course reflect the substantive rules of tort law: rulings on the admissibility of evidence, disposition of the parties' motions, and the formulation of instructions to the jury. Thus, the following are examples of typical issues raised on appeal: "Did the trial court err in admitting evidence that the defendant did not intend to cause the plaintiff harm?"; "Did the

5. This latter point is worth a bit of explanation. Suppose that in a negligence case the plaintiff testifies as follows. He was a passenger in the defendant's car when he said to the defendant, "Slow down." The defendant then nodded his head up and down. However, the defendant testifies that the plaintiff never said those words to him. The contention that the defendant failed to heed the plaintiff's warning is the only evidence of negligence in the case. The jury finds for the plaintiff. At this point it is therefore established as a fact that the defendant heard and failed to heed the plaintiff's warning and that this failure was negligent, because that failure was the only evidence of negligence. On appeal, the appellate court is not permitted to hold that, although the jury found that the plaintiff did warn the defendant by saying "Slow down," the appellate court (unlike the jury) believes the defendant's testimony and doubts that such a warning was given. On the contrary, the appellate court must accept it as established that, for purposes of the legal issues that the court has authority to decide, there was such a warning.

trial court err in denying the defendant's motion for a directed verdict?"; and "Did the trial court err in instructing the jury that the defendant could not be held liable for battery if he did not intend to harm the plaintiff?"An appellate court has three alternatives available to it: affirm, reverse, or reverse and remand for further proceedings, such as a new trial.

Just as at trial each of the court's "procedural" moves reflects a particular substantive rule of tort law, so too on appeal the appellate court's decision reviewing the correctness of the trial court's actions reflects a substantive rule. Suppose that in a battery case the evidence was that the defendant intended to touch the plaintiff without permission, but that the defendant did not intend to cause harm in doing so. The trial court then instructed the jury that if the defendant did not intend to cause the plaintiff harm, liability cannot be imposed. The jury then found for the defendant. The plaintiff appealed, arguing that this instruction was incorrect, because a defendant can be held liable for battery if he touches the plaintiff without permission, even without intending to cause harm. The appellate court will then apply the correct rule governing liability for battery to determine whether the trial court's instruction was or was not correct.[6] This ruling will be embodied in a written opinion explaining the basis for the appellate court's decision and indicating whether the court's instruction was or was not correct in light of the substantive rules of battery.

III.   The Nature of Tort Law

Fields of law normally do not come labeled with a self-designated character or set of goals. As a field that is predominately common law—law made by courts adjudicating individual disputes over a period of centuries—the law of torts has grown and evolved, state-by-state, without any central, self-conscious authority to make it responsive to a clear set of express goals. Although much of modern tort law scholarship has been concerned with analysis of and debate about the nature and proper functions of tort law, they remain contested. Some scholars argue that tort law is, and should be, rights-based. On this view, tort law is about redressing, or providing recourse for, wrongs. It is about the relationship between a wrongdoer and a victim. Others see tort law's function as more instrumental: to prevent wrongs, or to compensate those who suffer loss. For many instrumentalists, tort law is, or should be, concerned

---

6. For an appellate opinion addressing this issue, see *Vosburg v. Putney*, 80 Wis. 523, 50 N.W. 403 (1891).

among other things with the effect that imposing liability will have on others beside the plaintiff and defendant. It is about the external effects of imposing, or not imposing, liability. And still others see tort law as a mixed system that performs a combination of these and other functions.

A. *Corrective Justice*

One important rights-based understanding of the function of tort liability is corrective justice. When one party wrongs another, correction of the wrong may help to restore the moral balance between them. In tort law, when bodily injury has occurred, the injurer cannot literally rectify the injury. Liability is therefore imposed for monetary compensation, though it is admittedly often a poor substitute for prior good health. In cases involving only economic loss the correction can be more nearly adequate and complete. The case of the intentional wrongdoer is most obviously an occasion for corrective justice. But in many cases of negligence and even sometimes when there has been neither intention to cause harm nor negligence, corrective justice may have appeal as a justification for the imposition of liability.

The way in which correction actually occurs, however, may affect the strength of the appeal of corrective justice as a justification for imposing tort liability. The core of the notion of corrective justice envisions an individual injurer who directly compensates an individual victim, with the injurer's own money. Here the correction of the wrong by the injurer is direct and close. In contrast, as the connection between injurer and victim becomes less direct, corrective justice seems less relevant. For example, if the injurer is protected by liability insurance, she does not pay her victim directly. Instead, she has paid premiums for this insurance that may or may not bear a close relation to the degree of risk that her activities pose. Similarly, if the injurer is a corporation, then ultimately the shareholders, employees, or customers of the corporation may bear the cost of compensating the victim. In these situations an injustice still is corrected, and the injurer is the one who has undertaken to assure correction in the first instance. But because the injurer does not necessarily end up actually shouldering the burden of correction, these situations are at some remove from a conception of corrective justice as the face-to-face correction of a moral imbalance between individuals. For this reason, there is a difference of opinion among the commentators as to the importance of corrective justice in modern tort law settings, where defendants typically are either large corporations or individuals who are covered by liability insurance.

B. *Civil Recourse*

Whereas corrective justice focuses on what and why the defendant is obligated to pay the plaintiff, another group of rights-oriented scholars have focused on what the plaintiff is entitled to receive. These scholars argue that tort liability is better understood not as ensuring that injustice is corrected, but as providing victims with recourse for civil wrongs. Under this view the payment of damages for tortiously-caused harm should not be seen as being, or even aspiring to be, fully compensatory or fully correcting a wrong. Instead, the imposition of liability is a complex social practice that vindicates victims' need for recognition that they have been wronged, in a manner that is proportional to the seriousness of the wrong and the seriousness of their injury. What both the corrective justice and civil recourse views of the function of tort law have in common, despite their differences, is that they both understand tort law as being mainly concerned with the moral or civil rights arising out of the relationship between the plaintiff and the defendant, rather than with affecting the behavior of future actors or with achieving the other sorts of instrumental goals that are described below.

C. *Optimal Deterrence*

The imposition of tort liability not only corrects wrongs or provides civil recourse for wrongs that have already occurred; it also helps to prevent future tortious actions, by threatening potential wrongdoers with liability if they cause actionable harm. That is, tort law is not only backward looking, but may also be forward looking. It is not only about the relationship between injurer and victim, but also about reducing the undesirable consequences of risky activity. Not all risky activity is worth deterring, however, or we would be required to take endless safety precautions at unlimited cost. Rather, the function of tort liability in this respect is to promote *optimal* deterrence—that is, to deter *excessively* risky activity so that only those losses worth avoiding are avoided.

Two points about this notion are worth emphasizing, for they are sometimes difficult to appreciate. First, it follows from the principle of optimal deterrence that deterring certain losses is not worth what it would take to deter them. That is, imposing liability for harm caused by an activity that poses some risk but that is not excessively risky would require foregoing some of the benefit of that activity. Virtually every activity poses some risk, and therefore sometimes results in loss—safely driven automobiles sometimes collide, knives sometimes cut fingers, and so forth. Up to a point tort law threatens liability for risky activity, but beyond that point it does not, and the law tolerates the losses that result. Put harshly, some losses—and this includes some personal injuries—are not worth avoiding. Otherwise we would not require proof of negligence in a whole series of cases, but would instead always impose liability regardless of negligence. From the optimal deterrence standpoint, the negligence requirement implies that some losses are worth avoiding (those caused by negligence) but that some (those caused without negligence) are not.

Second, nothing in the principle of optimal deterrence dictates what values should be taken into account in determining which losses are and which losses are not worth deterring. Some supporters of the principle of optimal deterrence promote it as an economic concept that compares the monetary costs of risking losses with the monetary costs of preventing losses. And some opponents of the principle object to it for precisely that reason, since it seems to them to ignore important human values. But the economic approach to optimal deterrence is merely one among a number of possible conceptions. One might reasonably take the position that the economic conception of deterrence is unacceptable and that the pain and suffering that results from personal injury should not be reduced to a monetary value in comparing it to what must be done to reduce the risk that injury will occur. But that is not the same as saying that no effort should be made to compare the social benefits gained by reducing the risk of injury with the social costs, economic and otherwise, that must be incurred in order to reduce this risk. Making such a qualitative rather than an economic or quantitative comparison may be difficult, but being willing to make it is consistent with accepting the principle of optimal deterrence, even while rejecting an economic conception of that principle.

D. *Loss Distribution*

Defendants who are held liable in tort actions often do not shoulder the burden of compensation themselves. Sometimes defendants are covered by liability insurance and the insurer literally pays the plaintiff on behalf of the policyholder/defendant. On other occasions even an uninsured defendant may be able to include its prospective liabilities in the price of the products it sells; or the defendant may have shareholders whose investments decline in value as a result of the payment of a liability by the company whose shares they own. In each of these situations the cost of the loss suffered by the plaintiff is not simply transferred to the defendant, but is distributed through the defendant to a larger number of individuals. Promoting the broad distribution of losses is therefore often considered one of the functions of tort liability.

Whether loss distribution in itself is a good thing, and even if it is, whether imposing tort liability is a good way to achieve loss distribution, are both disputed questions. Suppose you suffer a $500 loss, and the law pays you for that loss by charging $1 to each of 500 people. Unless the sum of the value that each of these individuals attaches to the $1 they pay is less than the value you attach to the $500 you have lost, economically speaking nothing has been gained by the transfer. There is still a total loss of $500. On the other hand, when people purchase insurance they are confirming the notion that losing a small sum for certain (the premium they pay) is a lesser loss than the low probability of suffering a larger loss later. This is much like saying that 500 losses of $1 suffered by 500 people do in fact entail less loss than a single loss of $500 suffered by one person. Tort law has long reflected the similar intuition that, other things being equal, having a large number of people bear a small loss is better than having a single person bear a large one. Thus there has been an inclination to develop rules of law that permit the imposition of tort liability on businesses and institutions that can distribute their liabilities through the purchase of insurance or by raising the price of their products or services.

This rationale has some power, but it also has a weakness. The loss distribution rationale for the imposition of tort liability contains no stopping point. Like the compensation justification for imposing liability discussed next, loss distribution cannot explain why tort liability often is *not* imposed on parties who might, in fact, be good loss distributors. Moreover, imposing tort liability through a lawsuit is a cumbersome and expensive mechanism for achieving loss distribution. Simpler and more broadly applicable insurance systems (e.g., health insurance, disability insurance, social security) can broadly distribute losses at lesser cost if that is desired. Nonetheless, despite the objections that can be leveled at loss distribution as a rationale for the imposition of tort liability, there can be no denying that loss distribution has been and is likely to continue to be one of the effects of the imposition of tort liability.

E. *Compensation*

It is sometimes said that a function of tort law is to promote the compensation of those who have suffered injury. For most analysts of tort law, this is only true in a very limited sense. There is no doubt that anytime tort liability is imposed, a plaintiff is awarded compensation. There is also no doubt that, other things being equal, most of us feel enough natural sympathy for the victims of injury (especially physical, as opposed to solely economic, injury) to view the event giving rise to the injury as an appropriate occasion for considering whether (and how) society might assist the victim of the injury. And it is probably true that up to a point we are all better off—because we feel more secure and are therefore willing to take socially productive risks that we would not otherwise take—knowing that if we suffer certain kinds of injury, then compensation for that injury may be forthcoming. If by a "function" of tort law we mean a beneficial effect of the imposition of tort liability, then it is accurate enough to say that providing compensation to victims is a function of tort law.

But if by the term "function" we mean a "goal" of tort law, the notion that providing compensation is a function of tort law is debatable. The desirability of providing compensation to a particular class of injury victims rarely explains the lines that are drawn to distinguish those who are and those who are not entitled to prevail in a tort claim. Rather, time after time, some other factor or factors explain the occasion for the imposition of tort liability, or tort law's refusal to impose liability. As Holmes put it with characteristically ruthless clarity over a century ago,

> The general principle of our law is that loss from accident must lie where it falls, and this principle is not affected by the fact that a human being is the instrument of misfortune. * * * The undertaking to redistribute losses simply on the ground that they resulted from the defendant's act would not only be open to [other] objections, but * * * to the still graver one of offending the sense of justice.[7]

Since the time Holmes wrote, the scope of liability in tort has expanded substantially, but the principle he expressed still stands. Liability is not imposed in order to provide compensation to victims. Rather, victims are provided compensation in order to serve the other goals of tort law, such as corrective justice and deterrence. If it were otherwise then the basis of liability would be the

7. Oliver Wendell Holmes, Jr., THE COMMON LAW 76–78 (M.Howe ed. 1963).

suffering of misfortune, not the commission of a tort by another. Since in order to justify the imposition of liability, we require something in addition to the bare fact that the plaintiff suffered an injury caused by another party, describing "compensation" as one of the functions of tort liability cannot tell us why or when tort liability will or will not be imposed. At best, the desirability of providing compensation will be a factor that, when linked with others, makes it more likely that there will be tort liability for a particular category of conduct. And even on that view, providing compensation *under certain circumstances* rather than in general is what is really going on when tort liability is imposed. For that reason, these "other circumstances"—whatever they turn out to be—are likely to reflect more clearly the actual functions, or goals of tort liability, than the goal of compensating victims. Compensation is a good thing when the prerequisites to the imposition of liability are satisfied, but victims go uncompensated when these prerequisites are not satisfied.

F. *Redress of Social Grievances*

Even in situations in which the foregoing rationales for the imposition of tort liability will not be served or are shown to be inapt, people sometimes have the sense that tort liability should be imposed anyway. Of course, one view is that such people are wrong and that tort liability should never be imposed if it would not effectively serve one of the functions described above. But another view is that, even apart from these functions, the right to sue in tort promotes the redress of social grievances, especially against large, impersonal institutions. In this sense tort law is a populist mechanism that permits ordinary people to put authority on trial. Surely the lawsuits brought in the past involving the Dalkon Shield, asbestos-related lung disease, and breast-implants exhibit some of this quality. Future suits may do so as well. Standing alone, this justification for the imposition of tort liability may not be strong; but when allied with one or more of the other functions of tort liability, the possibility that imposing liability on an impersonal institution will help to redress social grievances may well help to explain why some close cases are decided the way they are.

G. *A Mixed System?*

A last possibility is that tort law does not perform only a single function or serve only a single goal, but a set of different functions whose importance is likely to vary with the situation. Tort law might thus perform a "mixed" set of functions. In some cases concern for corrective justice or civil recourse might dominate, but in others deterrence or concern for loss distribution might be the key. Or in many instances the imposition of liability might be justified on both rights-based and instrumental grounds, because it simultaneously rights a wrong and deters future wrongdoing, for example. It may even be that, for a doctrine to persist and be stable, it must serve more than one function or satisfy both rights-based and instrumental concerns. For those who seek perfect coherence in a body of law, this may be an unsatisfying state of affairs. But tort law is a human institution; there is not necessarily any reason to suppose or even to demand that it be perfectly coherent.

2

INTENTIONAL PHYSICAL AND EMOTIONAL HARM

It is common to begin studying tort law by considering the intentional torts of battery and assault. Although only a small percentage of tort litigation involves these torts, the concepts at their core as well as the interests they protect are both important and easy to identify. They are therefore good conceptual building blocks. Everyone understands the difference between an injury inflicted on purpose and a mere accident. Cases involving a deliberate punch in the nose typically are therefore fairly simple. As might be expected, however, more difficult issues often arise in some intentional tort cases. In addition, two other torts that are close relatives of the torts of battery and assault—false imprisonment and intentional infliction of emotional distress—pose interesting and challenging issues. After considering these four personal injury torts, we turn to a brief discussion of torts involving intentional harm to property and their defenses, including a more extended discussion of the conditional privilege of necessity. Other torts that are sometimes described as "intentional," such as defamation, invasion of privacy, and fraud, are covered in Chapters 13 and 14.

I. The Personal Injury Torts

A. *Battery*

Battery involves actual physical contact, whereas assault is the threat of contact. Technically, a battery is a harmful or offensive contact with another, resulting from an intention to cause that contact, or from an intention to put another in apprehension that a harmful or offensive contact is imminent. Unpacking this definition reveals each of its features.

1. The Physical Contact Requirement

There must be some physical contact with the plaintiff, or at least something that is in contact with the plaintiff. Ordinarily this is direct physical contact between the plaintiff and the defendant. But the contact may be by some object set in motion by the defendant, such as a weapon, or by some force such as electricity. In fact, the force need not literally be set in motion by the defendant, as long as the contact results from the defendant's intention. For example, in *Garratt v. Dailey*,[1] the defendant a pulled chair out from under the plaintiff as she was about to sit down. The plaintiff was injured when she fell to the ground. Literally speaking it was the plaintiff who, by attempting to sit down, set in motion the force that caused her injury. But the harmful contact with the ground was intended (or at least expected) by the defendant, and that was sufficient to satisfy this element of the tort. That was as it should be, since what is at stake in battery is the plaintiff's interest in protection of his or her bodily well-being and dignity from intentional invasion, not merely in avoiding specific methods of invading that interest.

2. Harmful or Offensive Contact

The contact at issue in battery need not cause actual physical injury to the plaintiff; an offensive but not harmful contact is sufficient. What is "offensive" is likely to be context-dependent. Certainly it would be a jury question, at the least, whether an unwanted kiss was offensive even if planted politely on the cheek. And many courts probably would grant a motion for a directed verdict for the plaintiff on this issue if the circumstances spoke of sexual harassment rather than romantic excess. Similarly, in most circumstances a pat on the back is both harmless and inoffensive. But a pat on the back of a female employee by a male supervisor whose romantic advances the employee has rejected in the past is likely to be offensive in context. Any contact that intentionally interferes with a reasonable sense of personal dignity is offensive. Of course, a certain amount of touching and jostling is to be expected in a crowded world, but an "invasion" of bodily autonomy—a touching without consent—may be offensive even if it is not physically harmful.[2] The tort protects not only physical security, but also personal autonomy and dignity.

1. 46 Wash.2d 197, 279 P.2d 1091 (1955).

2. Probably the outer reaches of this concept are reflected in *Fisher v. Carrousel Motor Hotel, Inc.*, 424 S.W.2d 627 (Tex. 1967), in which the defendant grabbed a plate from an individual in a buffet line, stating, "a Negro could not be served in the club." The plaintiff sued for battery. Although the defendant's action in that case was offensive, one might wonder whether it was the contact that took place when the defendant grabbed the plate that was offensive, or the defendant's motive in taking the plate. To put it another way, perhaps it was not the plaintiff's *bodily* autonomy that was invaded in that case as much as his integrity as a human being. That might be another tort, such as intentional infliction of emotional distress, even if it were not a battery.

Sometimes everything depends on whether the touching in question is or is not ordinarily to be expected under the circumstances. For example, in *Vosburg v. Putney*,[3] the defendant (age eleven) reached his foot across the aisle of a classroom and either touched or kicked the plaintiff's leg. The defendant did not intend to harm the plaintiff, but the contact aggravated an earlier injury. The court held that the plaintiff could maintain an action for battery under these circumstances, emphasizing that the defendant's behavior was a violation of the order and decorum of the classroom. The court even called the behavior "unlawful," by which it apparently meant "inappropriate" under the circumstances and therefore not impliedly consented to by the plaintiff. In reaching this conclusion, the court distinguished what might be expected in a classroom—order and decorum without physical contact—from what might be expected on a school playground, and therefore what is impliedly consented to in other such settings, including a certain amount of non-malicious but intentional physical contact.

3. Intent

There can be no battery without the requisite intent on the part of the defendant. But that intent is not necessarily an intent to harm. The defendant must intend the contact against which the law protects the plaintiff, but need not have a malicious intent or even any understanding that what he is doing is wrongful. Thus, in *Vosburg*, the circumstances in which the parties found themselves (a classroom) gave the plaintiff the right not to be touched by the defendant. That the defendant intended the touching was sufficient, even though the defendant did not necessarily intend the touching to be harmful or offensive. The defendant must either desire to bring about such contact, or act with substantial certainty (i.e., expect) that the contact will result from his actions. In *Vosburg*, for instance, it was substantially certain that the touching would occur. And in *Garrett v. Dailey*, there was evidence that the defendant knew that the plaintiff would make contact with the ground when he pulled the chair away as she was sitting down. It is not sufficient, however, for the defendant to know that his action merely *risks* harmful or offensive contact if there is no intent to cause such contact. There must be more than a mere awareness of risk; awareness of near-certainty is required.

The result of this two-fold approach to intent is that, if the defendant acts with an intent to cause a harmful or offensive contact, it does not matter that the probability of harm or offense is low; liability is imposed if what was intended occurs. On the other

---

3. 50 N.W. 403 (1891).

hand, if the defendant does not intend contact there must be a near certainty that it will occur. Intent to harm is sufficient, but not necessary. This makes pretty good, straightforward sense. Acting with the intent to cause harm or offense is so objectionable that even when the probability of harm or offense is low the intent standard is satisfied. But when one does not desire harm or offense to occur, his conduct is merely risky until he knows that harm or offense is substantially certain to result from it. Such low-risk action might constitute some other tort, such as negligence, but it is not battery, even when the unintended harm occurs.

The intent standard is subjective. The question is whether this defendant had the requisite state of mind, not what people similarly situated would have intended under the same circumstances. But it is important to distinguish the subjective nature of the intent standard in battery from the objective evidence that might be employed to prove that the standard was or was not breached. Truly "direct" evidence of a defendant's state of mind usually is not available, unless the defendant actually has voiced his intention to cause harm. So the plaintiff's proof often is "external" to the mind of the defendant and therefore is only "circumstantial" evidence of intent. That is, the jury is permitted to infer that the defendant did or did not intend the harm at issue from the surrounding circumstances. The jury must determine the likely internal, subjective state of mind of the defendant based on the objective, or at least external, facts. What facts were staring the defendant in the face? What is his explanation for the action he took? What was the history of relations between plaintiff and defendant? Answers to these and similar questions are the typical basis for the jury's decision about the defendant's subjective state of mind.

Why is there liability not only when the defendant desired to cause harm, but also when he knew that harm was substantially certain to occur? Surely part of the answer is obvious: ordinarily, acting in the face of knowledge that one's act is substantially certain to cause harm is only slightly less morally objectionable than acting with the desire to cause harm. In addition, however, the difficulty of proving the defendant's state of mind directly also helps to explain the substantial-certainty basis for battery liability. A defendant who acted with substantial certainty that harm would result from his act will very often have desired this harm to occur. It is the rare, though not unheard of case in which a defendant knows that he is very likely to cause harm but does not desire that harm to occur. Why else act if one knows that what he is doing will very likely harm someone? Only when the defendant had some other end in view, and the harm that would almost certainly occur as a result was a mere side effect of achieving that end, will the defendant have acted with substantial certainty yet not intended the harm (e.g., shooting at a target with a crowd of people standing near it). For this reason, often it will be valid to infer intent to cause harm from evidence that the defendant knew that harm was substantially certain to occur. However, what the defendant *knew* often can be more reliably proved than what the defendant *intended*. So the awareness-of-substantial-certainty basis for battery liability is in this sense not merely an independent basis for liability, but also a surrogate for proof of the intent to bring about harm.

The intent standard is double-barrelled in another way as well. The standard is satisfied when the defendant intends to cause an offensive contact but a harmful contact results, as well as when he intends to cause a harmful contact but an offensive contact results. A number of justifications can be offered for this approach. One justification is that the underlying wrong is the intention to invade another person's bodily integrity, and that both harmful and offensive contacts are simply different consequences of this same underlying wrong. A second justification is that each form of contact is sufficiently likely to result from an intent to cause the other that an act intended to cause one form of contact should be regarded as intended also to cause the other. Still another justification (though only for one-half of the approach) is that all intentionally harmful contact is also offensive; intention to cause harm therefore is necessarily intention to cause offense. And a final justification is that it is sometimes difficult for the plaintiff to prove which form of contact the defendant intended, even though the plaintiff can prove that the defendant definitely intended one or the other. If the defendant brings a dog to the home of a person whom he knows has a phobia about being bitten and the dog jumps on that person, it should not matter whether the defendant intended a harmful contact or "merely" an offensive one. The consequence of requiring proof of the kind of contact the defendant intended would be that sometimes the defendant would avoid liability for tortious contact, because of the difficulty of determining which form of tortious contact he intended. It would be odd, for example, if the defendant who intended harmful contact could avoid liability for an offensive contact on the ground that he had intended something possibly worse than what actually occurred.

4. Transferred Intent

A fourth feature of the definition of a battery also relates to the intent standard. Although the defendant must intend a harmful or offensive contact with another person, the individual who actually suffers the contact need not be the person whom the defendant intended to harm or offend. This rule is known as the doctrine of *transferred intent*. The core explanation for this doctrine is that the defendant's conduct is so blameworthy that it would be inappropriate to allow him to escape liability on the ground that he did not harm or offend the particular person he intended to harm or offend. But practical problems of proof also play a role in supporting the doctrine. The doctrine does not simply apply to the clear case in which the defendant's intentions were directed at A, but B was injured. Rather, sometimes a plaintiff will easily be able to prove that the defendant intended harm to someone, or acted with knowledge that harm to someone was substantially certain to occur, but the plaintiff will be unable to prove precisely to whom. Suppose, for example, that a defendant surreptitiously disposes of hazardous waste in a community's water supply. If the defendant must intend harm to a particular individual or particular group of individuals, then there will be no liability for battery under these circumstances. The doctrine of transferred intent solves this problem, by making the identity of the particular target of the defendant's intentions irrelevant.

B. *Assault*

An assault occurs when the defendant, intending either to cause a battery, or to threaten one, puts the plaintiff in fear of an imminent harmful or offensive contact (i.e., of suffering a battery). In contrast to battery, the interest protected in assault is the plaintiff's mental peace, rather than her physical well-being and bodily autonomy. The operative word in the definition of assault is "apprehension" of imminent harmful or offensive contact. Although typically the plaintiff "fears" imminent conduct, fear is not required. Rather, only "anticipation" of such contact is required, for even anticipation of a battery without fear of it substantially disturbs one's mental peace.

The elements of assault are virtually identical to those of battery, except that there is no requirement of actual contact with the plaintiff's person. In fact, virtually every battery is also an assault, since normally the plaintiff is first put in apprehension of imminent physical contact, and then suffers the contact. The converse, of course, is not true. Sometimes an assault is only an assault, either because it was intended only as an assault, or because it was an attempted battery that missed.

29

Aside from the issues that also arise in battery (such as the meaning of intent and offensiveness), there are two key issues in assault. The first issue is how close to consummation a threat of contact must be in order to constitute an assault. The answer, not entirely helpful standing alone, is that the harm threatened must be "imminent." The cases make clear, however, that imminent means a number of things. The threat must be *immediate* in terms of time: a statement by the defendant that he is going home to get his rifle and will return to kill the plaintiff is not an assault. The threat also must be *close* in terms of space: a threat made over the telephone is not an assault. And the threat must be *actual* rather than potential. The defendant's statement that "If I were a violent man I would tear your eyes out" is not an assault.

These requirements make sense on several grounds. The idea behind assault is to protect the mental peace that is breached when one is about to suffer a battery. Talk is cheap; until the plaintiff faces immediate action by the defendant his concern is about a battery that might take place in the future, not a battery that is about to take place now. In addition, until a battery is in fact imminent, the defendant's intention and therefore the amount of blame that should be ascribed to him for contemplating invading the plaintiff's person is uncertain. Imminence strengthens the inference of the defendant's intent. Finally, the courts could have their hands full with all manner of claims if there were liability not only for the mental suffering caused by the imminent threat of battery, but for concern over potential future battery as well.

A second issue that arises distinctively in assault involves the extra-sensitive plaintiff. Some people are of course more sensitive than others. Ordinarily there is no liability for the making of threats that would not satisfy the demands of the tort of assault if made to a typical person, even if the extra-sensitive plaintiff did actually regard a battery as imminent. Imposing liability for conduct that the defendant could not reasonably have understood to be tortious would deter conduct that would not ordinarily be tortious. The rationale for this limitation on liability for assault, however, also suggests its own exception. Once the defendant knows of the plaintiff's extra-sensitivity, the reason for declining to impose liability for threats of battery that fall just short of imminent disappears. Because in this situation the defendant knows the effect his threat will have on the plaintiff, he has the requisite intent to put the plaintiff in apprehension of imminent harm, even if the ordinary person would not feel such apprehension.

C. *False Imprisonment and Intentional Infliction of Emotional Distress*

These two torts, the first established for centuries and the second of more recent vintage, are worth discussion not only in their own right, but also because of what they illustrate about the nature of legal rules more generally. These torts reveal that at times the desirability of expanding the degree of protection afforded by the law of torts is in tension with the need for easily administrable rules governing the scope of liability. A choice must often be made about the mix of predictability of outcome and flexibility of application that should be combined in a particular rule.

1. False Imprisonment

Battery and assault do not protect against all intentional interferences with physical well-being and autonomy, because they require either physical contact or apprehension of it. Early on it was recognized that one particular form of interference that does not involve contact or apprehension is nonetheless sufficiently objectionable to be made actionable in tort. The essence of this tort of "false" (in the sense of "unjustified") imprisonment is the restriction of the plaintiff's freedom of movement, not harmful or offensive contact. To be actionable, a confinement must be total—forcing the plaintiff to take the long way around in order to reach a desired destination is not sufficient to constitute imprisonment. But giving him no way out of where he is, even no way out of a large space, constitutes the necessary confinement. Keeping an individual in a closed room, physically barring his only way out, or detaining an individual in a retail store by threat of force each may constitute false imprisonment.

Note the interests that the tort of false imprisonment does and does not protect. The tort is narrowly tailored to meet a particular need—the failure of the torts of assault and battery to remedy a different, discrete form of interference with bodily autonomy. The cause of action is specifically and exclusively for false imprisonment, not a general claim for intentional interference with bodily autonomy. In fashioning the cause of action to deal with this one problem alone, the courts have been able over time to develop rather specific rules about what does and does not satisfy the elements of the tort. Thus, *total confinement* rather than partial confinement is required; generally the plaintiff must have *conscious awareness* of the confinement; and the restraint on the plaintiff's freedom must be *intentional*, but physical force is not necessary if there is a threat of force. Although these requirements are not self-applying and leave some room for judgment, often they enable the courts to determine as a matter of law whether a valid claim exists. The result is a substantial amount of predictability that can help potential litigants sort out by themselves the cases that should and should not be brought or defended. Instead of operating under a rather general cause of action which is likely to send most questions to the jury, potential litigants can understand in advance the limits of what is actionable, and make decisions about whether to institute a claim and whether to defend against or settle it.

This predictability is achieved, however, by limiting the discretion of the trial courts and juries to determine, on a case-by-case basis, which intentional interferences with bodily autonomy should be actionable. That decision has already been made at a "high level of generality": assaults, batteries, and false imprisonments. Any other form of intentional interference with bodily autonomy that does not fall within one of these categories is unlikely to be actionable, no matter how unsavory the defendant's conduct or how deserving the plaintiff. Denying liability to the occasional sympathetic plaintiff who has clearly been wronged, but by conduct that is not quite assault, battery, or false imprisonment, is just the cost of having rules, whose very purpose is to draw lines between situations that are and are not actionable. Sometimes a case simply falls a hair short of being within one of the actionable categories.

This bright-line approach becomes less and less tolerable, however, as the number of instances in which there is need for more flexibility increases. Then the predictability tail seems to be wagging the justice dog. This is a generic problem in the formulation of legal rules. For this reason, the pattern of development that occurred next is also common.

2. Intentional Infliction of Emotional Distress

A common pattern of legal development was taken by what has now become the tort of intentional infliction of emotional distress. The courts began to be presented with a cluster of cases that fell outside the existing three categories of actionable intentional interference with bodily autonomy, but that had certain common features. Although in these cases there was no physical contact, no threat of contact, and no confinement, in each case the defendant had acted in a manner that was intended to interfere severely with the plaintiff's peace of mind. At first the defendants were innkeepers or common carriers, who it was said were under a "contractual" obligation not to engage in such conduct. But eventually the contractual prerequisite disappeared, and defendants of all sorts were subjected to liability for what later came to be recognized as the tort of intentional infliction of emotional distress.

It is no surprise that even before the tort had a name, the cases in which the courts first felt compelled to permit the imposition of liability involved extremely outrageous conduct by the defendant. For example, malicious practical jokes, such as a false story that the plaintiff's husband had been grievously injured, were typical of the cases in which the courts felt justified in imposing liability. In such cases the defendant had not merely intended to distress the plaintiff, but also had gone beyond the reasonable bounds of decency in doing so. The courts were understandably concerned, however, that they might be opening a Pandora's box in authorizing a general cause of action for intentional infliction of emotional distress. Such a cause of action could have created a potentially unlimited expansion of litigation over the kind of unmannerly conduct that, while distressing, is only too common and therefore to be expected by almost anyone who has social or commercial relations with other people. An unbounded tort of intentional infliction of emotional distress would also have risked fraudulent claims by those who had merely been insulted or aggravated rather than truly and deeply distressed.

The result was that the *extreme outrageousness* of the defendant's conduct and the *severity of the plaintiff's distress* that were characteristic of the early cases became elements of the tort itself. These requirements help to satisfy the two concerns that would otherwise be troubling about the tort. Because only extraordinary instances of misbehavior satisfy this requirement, there is no chance that liability will be radically expanded; and because this kind of misbehavior is more likely than ordinary rudeness to cause severe emotional distress, the requirements of extreme outrageousness and severe distress tend to reduce the risk of fraudulent claims. The cause of action has been held to apply in a variety of circumstances, including the malicious practical jokes that gave rise to it, but also harassment by debt collectors and child sexual abuse by clergy. A few courts have even relaxed the requirement that the plaintiff be present when the infliction occurs, thereby permitting the parents of children who were the subject of such abuse to maintain actions for intentional infliction along with their children. But the U.S. Supreme Court has held that there are constitutional limits, based on the First Amendment right to freedom of expression, on the scope of the cause of action in suits by public officials and public figures.[4]

4. *See, e.g., Hustler Magazine v. Falwell*, 485 U.S. 46, 108 S.Ct. 876, 99 L.Ed.2d 41 (1988).

For the most part, however, the requirements of extreme outrageousness and severity of distress have limited the instances in which liability is imposed. The result has been that cases involving spousal abuse and workplace sexual harassment, which might otherwise have been expected to be areas of significant increases in liability—because of seemingly greater social sensitivity to these abuses and greater awareness of them—have not been a proving ground for expansion of the tort.[5]

3. Some Observations about the Nature of these Legal Rules

The development of the tort of intentional infliction of emotional distress can tell us something more generally about the nature of legal rules. The very concept of a rule implies a division—a line—between the situations in which liability is imposed and those in which it is not. When rules govern, some fact situations fall squarely within the confines of a tort, such as battery, assault, or false imprisonment, and some situations fall outside those confines. When a situation falls far outside those confines, typically there is no reason for concern. But when a sympathetic fact situation falls just outside the confines of an established cause of action, the courts sometimes are inclined to create an exception to the rule that will make that fact situation actionable.

There is nothing necessarily right or wrong about this tendency. The prior rule may have been too limited, and the combination of that rule plus the exception—in effect a new, broader rule—may be just right. But a rule is not a rule if it does not have limits. If any situation that falls just outside the confines of the rule may nonetheless be made the subject of a new exception, then the rule is infinitely malleable and infinitely expandable, and in effect is no rule at all. That is not what happened in the development of the tort of intentional infliction of emotional distress. Rather, a few cases that were not quite battery, not quite assault, and not quite false imprisonment were held to be actionable, and then a new rule governing a new tort emerged, based on the common characteristics of that narrow class of cases and subject to its own limits.

Things might have developed otherwise. Instead of fashioning a new but carefully circumscribed rule to fit the new, actionable fact situations, the courts might have decided that in actuality a whole series of hard-to-specify wrongs ought to be actionable, including but not limited to battery, assault, false imprisonment, and inten-

5. See Martha Chamallas & Jennifer B. Wriggins, THE MEASURE OF RECOVERY: RACE, GENDER, AND TORT LAW 64–87 (2010).

tional infliction of emotional distress. The courts might then have dispensed with the use of *rules* to determine which such wrongs were actionable, and instead could have employed what have been called *standards*—less specific principles that could loosely guide decisions about what was actionable but that would have been too indefinite to decide particular cases. For example, the standard might have reflected the putative tort of "wrongful and intentional interference with personal autonomy or dignity," but left the courts and juries in particular cases to decide which such intentional interferences would be actionable. Eventually more specific guidelines, very much resembling rules, might have emerged; or perhaps it simply would have been left to juries to decide what was actionable, on a case-by-case basis. Things never developed that way, however, and the intentional injury torts remain governed largely by rules and not standards.

In practice, the distinction between rules and standards is sometimes less firm than I have described it. No rule is perfectly specific and no standard is entirely indefinite. The distinction between the two kinds of legal "norms" is a matter of degree. The closer a legal norm comes to the rule side of the spectrum, the more predictable the application of the norm to any particular fact situation is likely to be. The cost of such predictability, however, is the relative incapacity of the norm to accommodate situations that do not qualify according to the norm's strict limits. Conversely, the closer a norm comes to the standard side of the spectrum, the less predictable its application will be, but the more discretion decision-makers will have to distinguish between situations that are and are not actionable. At one extreme lie rules with highly predictable applications and very little flexibility. At the other extreme lie standards that afford enormous discretion and whose application is very difficult to predict. In between lie most of the actual rules of tort law.

II. Defenses

Even after the plaintiff in a tort case proves a *prima facie* case—i.e., submits evidence supporting each element of his or her case—the defendant may avoid liability by making out a defense to liability. In connection with the four personal injury intentional torts, most of these defenses fall into the category of "privileges"—that is, actions taken under circumstances that justify or excuse what would otherwise be tortious. Although there are a number of defenses, the main ones are consent (which technically is not a privilege) and the privileges of self-defense and defense of others.

Another privilege—"necessity"—is discussed later in this Chapter, in connection with intentional injury to property.

A. *Consent*

If the plaintiff has consented to conduct by the defendant that would otherwise be tortious, an essential element of the plaintiff's case is missing, because the defendant's conduct is not wrongful. As the Latin phrase *volenti non fit injuria* indicates, "he who consents is not injured." For example, an intentional touching by the defendant to which the plaintiff consented is not a wrong at all. Ordinarily the plaintiff can make out a *prima facie* case without making reference to consent. Procedurally, therefore, consent is a defense in the sense that the defendant is the party who typically raises the issue and bears the burden of proving it. Naturally there are often questions of fact regarding the existence of consent. Some questions are purely factual—what did the defendant say, what did the plaintiff reply? Other questions are interpretive, since consent may be not only express but also apparent or implied—what physical contacts does a person playing touch-football or someone taken unconscious to an emergency room impliedly consent to? And in other situations nominal consent has been given, but is not legally effective because there was fraud, duress, certain forms of mistake, or the legal incapacity of the plaintiff to give consent.

Even when consent has been given, the defense does not apply when the scope of the consent is exceeded. For example, in *Mohr v. Williams*,[6] the plaintiff consented to have the defendant surgeon perform an operation on her right ear. While the plaintiff was under anesthesia, the defendant examined both ears, and decided that the condition of the plaintiff's right ear was less serious than expected and that the left ear required surgery. He therefore operated on the left ear. The plaintiff sued for battery. On appeal, the court held that plaintiff's consent to an operation, and indeed an operation on her right ear, did not constitute consent to an operation on her left ear. The defendant had therefore exceeded the scope of the plaintiff's consent and was liable for a battery.

One of the most vexing problems regarding consent involves inter-subjectivity. Consent must be communicated, but communication sometimes misfires. An uncommunicated consent, if there could be such a thing, probably is a defense. But what about the situation in which the plaintiff has not consented but the defendant incorrectly, yet honestly, believes that the plaintiff did consent?

6. 95 Minn. 261, 104 N.W. 12 (1905).

Often cases involving sexual conduct or misconduct such as alleged "date rape" raise such issues. These issues are highly charged, but they cannot be avoided in a discussion of consent simply because they are controversial.

The traditional rule holds that the defendant cannot escape liability merely by honestly believing that there was consent, but must have "reasonably relied" on a manifestation of consent by the plaintiff. For example, suppose that the defendant John suggests, after a certain amount of physical intimacy with the plaintiff Jean, that they engage in sexual intercourse. The plaintiff then says, "Oh John, I love you but I don't know if I want to," after which she simply freezes up and says nothing more. They then have sexual intercourse. The plaintiff sues for battery, and the defendant alleges consent.

Under the traditional approach it probably would be a question of fact whether this constituted sufficient manifestation of consent on which the defendant could reasonably rely. But even determining whether the defendant has submitted enough evidence to make the defense of consent a jury question is highly situation-dependent. Whether the defendant could reasonably have understood the words "I love you but I don't know if I want to" as consent depends very much on how the plaintiff and defendant had communicated in the past, and on how they had interpreted facially ambiguous statements about their intentions, such as "I don't know." If the plaintiff and defendant had little or no history of communication that could help to resolve the issue, then whether the defendant could reasonably have understood the plaintiff to be consenting might depend on prevailing cultural norms regarding consent to sexual contact. And if the plaintiff and the defendant came from settings in which these norms differed, then the traditional approach might well permit a jury to find that the defendant reasonably believed that there was consent, even though the plaintiff was, in effect, communicating one message ("I do not consent") and the defendant was hearing another ("I do not object"). The very formulation of the consent defense in these reasonable-reliance terms means that sometimes there is no liability even when the plaintiff did not in fact intend to consent, as long as some people would reasonably have understood her to have consented. The traditional approach might therefore be regarded as being somewhat pro-defendant, which in most sexual offense cases will translate into "pro-male."

On the other hand, it would be possible for the law to take the position that unless there has been an express, affirmative consent by the plaintiff, the defendant can never have reasonably relied.

Then the message "I do not object"—even assuming that "I just don't know" could reasonably be understood to mean "I do not object"—normally would not count as affirmative consent: not objecting is not the same as consenting. This approach would emphasize the plaintiff's state of mind rather than the defendant's. The question would not be whether the defendant reasonably relied, but whether the plaintiff actually consented. However, although the ultimate issue under this formulation of the defense would be the plaintiff's state of mind, often the only evidence of this state of mind aside from the plaintiff's own subsequent assertions would be her words and actions at the time. As a consequence, for practical purposes the issue in such cases often still would be whether, objectively speaking, those words and actions actually constituted consent.

There is room for some variation under this alternative approach. On the one hand, the approach could be formulated so as to be nearly identical to the traditional approach—directing the jury to determine whether the plaintiff consented by asking how a reasonable person would have understood the plaintiff's words and actions. On the other hand, the defense could be formulated so as to be noticeably less pro-defendant than the traditional approach, by instructing the jury that the consent defense must be rejected unless there was an actual, affirmative indication of consent by the plaintiff. Under this formulation the consent defense is less likely to prevail even when some people would have believed that there was consent.

It is worth remembering, however, that except in the unusual case in which the court could rule that there was no consent as a matter of law, the legal differences between these formulations will be reflected mainly in the language in which instructions are given to the jury. Under any of these formulations, whether there was consent is very likely to raise a jury question, since even under the alternative to the traditional approach the defendant will contend that the plaintiff's words or gestures should be interpreted as an express affirmative consent. The outcome of claims involving unwanted sexual behavior will therefore still depend more on the values and experiences of the members of the jury than on the subtleties of the particular instructions read to them by the trial judge. Jurors who believe that a woman who does not say "yes" in one way or another to a male sexual overture has not consented to it are less likely to find consent under these circumstances than jurors who believe that a woman who does not affirmatively object to male sexual pressures impliedly consents to them.

B. *Self–Defense and Defense of Others*

The defenses of self-defense and the defense of others are known as "privileges;" that is, they afford the defendant the privilege of causing what would otherwise be tortious harm to the plaintiff, in order to prevent himself or others from suffering such harm. To be entitled to engage in self-defense or the defense of another, the defendant must reasonably believe that the use of physical force is necessary to prevent or repel an impending attack or imprisonment. Thus, when there would actually have been no attack, the defendant can avoid liability for a mistaken belief that an attack was about to occur, or was occurring, only if that mistake was reasonable. What constitutes a reasonable belief that an attack is likely to occur can be highly situation-sensitive. A person who feigns a threat against someone whom he knows to be unusually nervous because of a recent mugging risks a privileged effort at self-defense by the person threatened, even though self-defense might not be privileged under otherwise similar circumstances.

Although the use of reasonable force in defense of oneself or others is privileged, if the defendant exceeds the scope of the privilege he is liable for injury caused by the use of unreasonable means or excessive force. Commonly the defendant has been required to make a split-second decision about the need for defense and the amount of force to use, however, and as a consequence the jury is likely to afford considerable leeway when the defendant or the person he was protecting was actually at risk of serious harm by the plaintiff. The only important limitation on the jury's discretion in this regard is the "equivalence" rule: if there is a threat of death or serious bodily harm, then the defendant is privileged to defend himself or another with an equivalent amount of force; but if the threat is of lesser harm, then lesser force must be used in defense or the privilege is lost. Sometimes it is also said that if there is a means of escape or retreat, the use of force in defense is not privileged, except in one's home. Probably it is more accurate, however, to say that on some occasions discretion is the better part of valor, and that the jury's decision whether the defendant used a reasonable amount of force in defense may take into account both whether there was an avenue of escape or retreat, and whether it would have been reasonable under all the circumstances to have chosen escape or retreat rather than defense.

A number of the issues relating to defense of self and others are similar to those that arise in connection with the consent defense. In each situation the plaintiff communicates something to the defendant (an alleged threat or an alleged consent, respectively) that the defendant later claims authorizes or justifies the taking of an action that would otherwise be tortious. In each case it is possible that the defendant has misunderstood that communication, mistakenly believing that there is a threat of an immediate attack or that there has been consent. In each case the law is that a subjectively honest but unreasonable mistake is no defense, but that an objectively reasonable and honest mistake does excuse what would otherwise be tortious. If the typical, reasonable person would have believed she was under attack or that the other party had consented to be touched, then the law permits a defense despite the mistake, but otherwise not. Finally, even when inflicting harm that would otherwise be tortious is authorized, the law places limits on the amount of force that may be used, depending on the scope of the consent or the severity of the threatened attack.

III.   The Property Torts

There are three torts concerned with intentional injury to property: trespass to land, trespass to personal property, and conversion.

A.   *The Nature of the Torts*

The two forms of trespass are just what they appear to be: wrongs in which the defendant breaches the boundary of or touches the plaintiff's real or personal property, or otherwise physically interferes with the plaintiff's right of possession, which includes the right to exclude others from occupying or using that property. The defendant need not have intended to trespass, but only to have intended to be present on or interfere with the possession of property that turns out to be owned by the plaintiff. Trespass is actionable without proof of actual damage, although in modern times it would be highly unusual to bring a trespass action only as a matter of principle. In contrast to trespass, in which the defendant himself interferes with the plaintiff's right of possession, the defendant in conversion typically has undertaken the unauthorized transfer of the plaintiff's personal property to a third party's possession. The essence of all three of these torts is interference with the plaintiff's right to possess and control his or her property. The situations to which the torts apply run all the way from traditional trespass to land to damage to, and sometimes even interference with, a computer or network by spam or spyware.

Although the concern with bodily autonomy that characterizes the personal injury torts is not present here, it would be a mistake

40

to suppose that the property torts are concerned only with monetary loss resulting from damage to property. On the contrary, while few such tort actions would be brought unless there were monetary damage, often more is at stake than money alone. Property ownership is not merely an economic but also a personal right. The way people live their lives may be influenced, sometimes even protected by, their property. Think of people who live on rural tracts of land to obtain privacy and solitude, or derive great pleasure from unique paintings or sculpture. Interference with the rights of possession and ownership of such property, especially intentional interference, is likely to engender indignation or outrage. This is true even of inanimate property, but is even more true of household pets, which the law also treats as property. The person whose property is trespassed upon or whose pet is intentionally harmed typically feels personally invaded. Sometimes there is no way to completely separate these intangible losses from the more easily measured monetary losses that may be the result of trespass or conversion. At one level the law proceeds as if these intangible losses are irrelevant; but there can be little doubt that in some cases both courts and juries take these losses into consideration.

B. *Defenses: Especially The Privilege of "Necessity"*

A series of related privileges may serve as defenses to actions for trespass and, occasionally, conversion. These include public or private necessity, defense of property, recapture of chattels, recapture of land, and action in pursuance of legal process. Necessity is by far the most important privilege for our purposes, however, since this defense raises issues that can help us make a conceptual transition from the intentional torts to those involving negligence and strict liability.

In a sense, all the privileges that serve as defenses to liability for intentional harm to persons or property are based on necessity, broadly conceived. But the technical term necessity is reserved for those cases in which the defendant has acted reasonably in damaging or destroying the plaintiff's property in order to avoid harm to himself or his property, but the risk of harm to the plaintiff has not been created by the plaintiff. In contrast, when such privileges as self-defense, defense of others, or defense of property are invoked, the risk of harm has been created by the plaintiff.

Two forms of necessity must be distinguished. Cases of *public necessity* arise when there is a risk to the property of a sufficiently large number of people to make the risk "public" and that risk can be reduced or eliminated by damaging or destroying the property of the plaintiff. For example, the plaintiff's house may be torn down in order to prevent the spread of a fire to the remainder of a town. In cases of public necessity the privilege is "absolute;" that is, the privilege of necessity is a complete defense to liability. The defendant has the right to make use of the plaintiff's property without incurring liability for damage that results. And because the defendant possesses an absolute privilege, the plaintiff does not have the right to prevent him from using the plaintiff's property. We will return briefly to public necessity at the end of this Chapter.

In contrast, cases of *private necessity* arise when there is a risk to one party or his property only, and this party can reduce or eliminate that risk by damaging or destroying someone else's property. In such cases the privilege of necessity is said to be "qualified" or "conditional." Because the privilege is only qualified rather than absolute, the defendant is liable to the plaintiff for the damage done to the latter's property. That is, the privilege is conditioned on the privileged party's later compensating the other party for using the latter's property.

1. *Ploof* and *Vincent*: The Basics

These principles are illustrated by two celebrated cases. In *Ploof v. Putnam*,[7] the plaintiffs were sailing on Lake Champlain when a sudden storm forced them to tie up at the defendant's dock. The defendant then had his servant untie the ship, as a result of which the boat and its contents were destroyed and the plaintiffs were injured. The court held that the privilege of necessity had entitled the plaintiffs to tie up at the defendant's dock. Because doing so therefore did not constitute a trespass, the defendant did not have the right to exclude them from the dock. Some might say that having the plaintiffs untied in effect "trespassed" on the plaintiff's "property." That is, private necessity afforded the plaintiffs what amounted to a limited property interest in the defendant's dock (the right to tie up for the duration of the storm), with which the defendant had interfered. The defendant therefore was liable to the plaintiffs for the harm that ensued when they were untied.

Two years later, in *Vincent v. Lake Erie Transportation Co.*,[8] the defendant's ship had been unloading at the plaintiff's dock when a storm arose. By the time the unloading was completed it would have been dangerous to venture out into the storm, so the ship remained moored to the dock. As the mooring lines parted or

7. 81 Vt. 471, 71 A. 188 (1908).
8. 109 Minn. 456, 124 N.W. 221 (1910).

chafed they were replaced. The plaintiff sued for the damage that resulted from the buffeting of the ship against the dock during the storm. The defendant argued that because it would have been negligent, perhaps even foolhardy, to untie the ship from the dock because of the risk to life and the ship, it should not be liable for the damage to the dock. But the court disagreed, holding that the defendant had a conditional privilege only. Although the defendant had done nothing wrong, it had saved the ship at the expense of the dock and was liable for the damage that resulted.

2. The Property Rights Explanation

The notion that because the defendant in *Vincent* used the plaintiff's property it should bear liability may seem appealing on the surface, but is it persuasive? After all, the defendant behaved responsibly, and the plaintiff should have felt a moral obligation to make the dock available during the storm. A world in which people do not expect compensation for helping others would be attractive. On the other hand, to say that the defendant did nothing wrong and that the plaintiff had a moral obligation to provide assistance is simply another way of saying that the defendant had the privilege of staying moored to the dock and that the plaintiff therefore had no right to exclude the defendant in an emergency. As the court put it, "the ordinary rules regulating property rights were suspended by forces beyond human control * * * ". However, the whole point of the conditional privilege, it can be argued, is that when such property rights are suspended and the defendant is privileged to use the plaintiff's property, the defendant is obligated to pay for any damage that results.

But why? It may seem self-evident that if I use someone else's property, I should pay for doing so. If that were the principle underlying *Vincent*, however, then the defendant should be liable only for the rental value of the dock for the period in question, since this was what he was entitled to use without needing permission. This was not a case, that is, in which a starving man has a privilege to enter a cabin in the woods and open canned goods for food, as long as he pays for the food. The defendant in *Vincent* did not choose to consume or to damage the dock, but only to risk damaging it.

The explanation for the law's refusal to credit this distinction between intending harm and merely risking it could be that the risk in *Vincent* was sufficiently high that it was so nearly tantamount to intentionally damaging the dock as to bring it within the confines of the rule governing conditional privilege. After all, we choose to risk damaging other people's property all the time, yet are usually held liable for damage that actually occurs only if it was negligent to take the risk. For example, I create a risk of non-negligently damaging nearby property when I drive to work, since I may have a tire blowout that causes my car to run off the road and damage a neighbor's house. But the risk is very low. I am therefore liable for such damage only if I have been negligent. In contrast, in *Vincent* the risk must have been high, or the case would in fact more closely resemble my driving to work. Moreover, the fact that as the mooring ropes parted or chafed the defendant replaced them highlights both the element of choice made by the defendant and the apparently high probability of harming the dock. In fact, some commentators understand the court's reference to the re-mooring as a holding that the defendant knew that it was harming the dock.

But the question why liability is imposed remains. A perfectly respectable answer is simply that, as between two innocent parties, the one whom nature put at risk should bear the cost of saving himself or his property, rather than the owner of the property that does the saving. For many people that is a sufficiently persuasive answer to end the inquiry.

The trouble with this answer is that if both parties are innocent—i.e., neither was negligent—then the conditional privilege rule looks more like a way to break the moral tie between the parties than a method of achieving corrective justice. It will not do to argue that the shipowner made a choice to risk the dock, but that the dockowner made no such choice. After all, the dockowner chose to have a dock where ships might tie up when storms arose. Until we know what legal rule governs the rights of ship and dock owners, we cannot make assertions about what they did and did not "choose" to risk. This is an important point, for it reflects the fact that legal rules not only honor expectations of safety; sometimes expectations of safety are derived from legal rules about when there is liability. In such situations the decision about what legal rule to have is in essence a decision about what expectations to create.

For example, if the governing rule were that the dockowner cannot recover from the shipowner unless the shipowner was negligent in staying moored to the dock, then the dockowner could be said to have "chosen" to risk being non-negligently damaged by ships moored to the dock during storms. We cannot deduce the scope of the dockowner's tort rights from the applicable property rights, because what we are determining is the scope of the "property" rights a tort liability rule should or should not give the dockowner. One of these rights, though only one, involves the dockowner's possible right of recovery for damage resulting from ships moored during storms. The dockowner's right in this regard might be the broad one afforded by *Vincent*, or it might be a narrower one that would make the shipowner liable for damage only when it was caused by the shipowner's negligence.

Thus, the scope of the dockowner's property rights does not determine the appropriate tort liability rule; rather, the appropriate tort liability rule determines the scope of the dockowner's property rights. To put it another way, the dockowner's property rights do not come to us already established and independent of the tort liability issue. On the contrary, what is at issue is the scope of those rights. One way to understand this is to imagine how things would change if the shipowner were not liable in the *Vincent* situation. Then the risk to dockowners would rise, and the risk to shipowners would fall. Presumably docks would be worth slightly less than they would otherwise be (since owning a dock would entail one less "right") and ships would be worth slightly more than they would otherwise be (since owning a ship would entail one more "right").

When the issue is understood in this light, the question is whether there is some moral or other basis for favoring dockowners over shipowners, or vice versa. We might say that when we talk in ordinary language about property "ownership," we include in that notion the right not to have the safety of our property consciously and deliberately risked by others. As Blackstone said long ago, "There is nothing which so generally strikes the imagination and engages the affections of mankind, as the right of property or that sole and despotic dominion which one man claims and exercises over the external things of the world, in total exclusion of the right of any other individual in the universe."[9] If pressed we might acknowledge the limitation on property rights that was recognized in *Ploof v. Putnam*, but only on the condition that if our property were damaged when another person used it in an emergency, that person must be required to compensate us for the damage. It might follow that unless there were some good reason for departing from this instinctive conception of property rights, the law should reflect that conception, in order not to upset people's expectations and undermine confidence in the firmness of property rights.

In my view, however, this explanation—though many people find it congenial—is just short of being circular, since the explanation rests on a pretty vague and probably not universally shared notion of what it means in this very particular context to "own" the dock. Nonetheless, for those who still think that the proper explanation of *Vincent* is that the shipowner really did "take"

---

9. 2William Blackstone, Commentaries on the Laws of England 2 (Univ. of Chi. ed. 1976).

something from the dockowner, the property rights explanation does work.

3. The Deterrence/Resource Allocation Explanation

The question then becomes whether there could be a good reason for departing from the ordinary conception of what it means to "own" property and denying the dockowner a right to recover even if the shipowner was not negligent. Up to this point we have been talking only about compensation for damage to the dock that has already occurred, without reference to the possibility of avoiding such damage. We have been talking about doing justice between the parties, but not about the incentive effects on others that may be produced by whatever rule is adopted. Perhaps a concern for reducing future losses, for example, a concern for deterrence, can supply a justification for departing from the ordinary conception of what it means to own property.

a. Who Should be Liable?

Suppose that dockowners were much better situated than shipowners to determine the best way to prevent damage to their docks when ships stayed tied to them during storms. This is a plausible supposition, since dockowners are likely to know more about docks than shipowners. If dockowners can nonetheless recover from shipowners for non-negligently caused damage to docks during storms, then dockowners will have less incentive to take measures to reduce the risk of damage to their docks, since they will have to pay for those measures themselves, whereas shipowners will have to pay if the measures are not taken and damage occurs. Denying dockowners the right to recover from shipowners for damage done to docks during storms might therefore tend to increase dockowners' incentive to take additional precautions that would protect their docks.

But this is only half the story. Sometimes it would make economic sense for the ship to stay moored at the dock, but at other times the total risk to both the dock and the ship might be reduced by untying and venturing out into the storm. Denying dockowners the right to recover from shipowners in such situations will increase the tendency of shipowners to risk damaging docks, because shipowners will not have to pay for damage to docks. Shipowners will tend not to venture out into a storm, risking damage to the ship, if they can stay moored at the dock without having to pay for non-negligent damage to the dock. In contrast, under the rule in *Vincent* the shipowner always has an incentive to compare the risk to the dock if the ship stays moored, against the risk to the ship if the ship does not stay moored, because under *Vincent* the shipowner must pay for whatever damage occurs: he is liable to the dockowner for damage, and as the owner of the ship he must bear the cost of any damage that occurs if the ship ventures out into the storm. Conversely, and importantly, the rule encourages the dockowner to "permit" the shipowner to stay tied up, and not to behave like the dockowner in *Ploof v. Putnam.*

This analysis illustrates the general principle that threatening a party with liability gives this party an incentive to compare the cost of liability with the cost of alternatives that may avoid liability. Sometimes the threat of liability induces more careful behavior; but if, all things considered, it is cheaper to bear liability than to avoid it, then the threat of liability gives the party that is threatened an incentive to make that choice. One way to view the issue in *Vincent*, therefore, is not to ask which party should be liable for the damage to the dock, but rather, which party is in the better position to compare the risk to the dock with the risk to the ship.[10] I suspect that this is a close question, since while dockowners are likely to know a lot about their docks and at least something about ships and storms, shipowners are likely to know a lot about their ships and about storms, and at least something about docks. In other situations, however, it may be that one party knows a whole lot more about both sides of the comparison than the other party. Then, on this theory, the party with both the most relevant knowledge and the capacity to act on it should be liable. This may or may not be the party who seems to have "used" the property of another; it may instead be the party whose property was "used."

b. When It Matters Who Is Liable: The Coase Theorem

Since it is probably a close question which party is in a better position to make the decision in cases like *Vincent*, we are likely to get pretty good decisions whether or not the shipowner is liable for non-negligent damage to the dock, as long as the party who is liable has the right to choose between the two alternatives of staying moored or venturing out. The privilege of necessity gives the shipowner the right to make this choice, but charges him with the cost of doing so. This approach also assures the dockowner that he will be compensated for all the damage to the dock that results. The converse of this approach would deny the shipowner the privilege of

---

10. In one of the most important books on tort law written in the twentieth century, THE COSTS OF ACCIDENTS (1970), Guido Calabresi terms this party the "cheapest cost avoider."

tying up at the dock, but would have to make the dockowner liable for damage to the ship if he had the right to deny use of the dock during a storm. The *Vincent* approach thus makes sense if shipowners know more about ships and docks than dockowners know about docks and ships.

If we are not sure who knows more, or if the answer varies depending on the kind of ship and kind of dock, then giving shipowners and dockowners freedom to bargain in advance about what will happen during storms may help to solve the problem. For example, if there were no legal privilege of necessity, shipowners might be willing to pay dockowners for the contractual privilege of staying tied to docks during storms, but dockowners might grant them this privilege only in return for higher mooring fees that would compensate the dockowner in advance for damage that might be done. Shipowners might look at these higher costs and decide that they could more cheaply bear liability for damage to docks by installing cushioning devices such as tires on the dock-sides of their ships, and offer to bear liability in return for lower docking fees. The point is that, when the parties themselves can identify the most cost-effective approach and can inexpensively set aside the otherwise-applicable tort liability rule, then the cost of the courts' adopting the "wrong" rule, so to speak, is simply the cost of setting the rule aside in advance by contract. The parties themselves will contractually arrive at the best rule for them if they can. This was one of the insights flowing from the famous theorem developed by Nobel Laureate Ronald Coase, that in the absence of "transactions costs" the rule of liability does not matter.[11]

When the parties have no pre-existing relationship the costs of bargaining are in effect prohibitive, however, and the teaching of the Coase theorem is that whether liability is imposed can make a big difference. The plaintiffs in *Ploof* could not contract in advance with every dockowner on Lake Champlain about the right to tie up in the event of a sudden storm. And because I cannot go around bargaining with everyone who drives on the same roads as I do about how to order our liability relationship if our vehicles collide, it is important that tort law adopt a rule governing automobile collisions that creates the correct incentives for reasonably safe driving. That rule, whatever it is, must be the "right" rule, because practically speaking contracting around the rule would not be feasible.

Interestingly, all this leads us back to public necessity. If at least one of the fundamental purposes of imposing liability is to

---

11. Ronald H. Coase, *The Problem of Social Cost*, 3 J.L. & Econ. 1 (1960).

give those who risk doing injury or damage the incentive to make the correct comparison between taking such risks and avoiding them, then why is there an absolute privilege in cases of public necessity? Why isn't the party who destroys the plaintiff's property entitled to do so, but also liable to the plaintiff for the damages that result? For example, it would seem that when a house in the path of a fire is torn down to save the remainder of a town, the owner should be able to recover for his loss. Otherwise those who tear down the house will be like a shipowner who never has to pay for damage to the dock, tearing down houses whenever there is even a slight risk to the remainder of the town, even if there were other, more prudent courses of action.

A partial explanation for the seemingly anomalous rule that there is no liability in such a situation—i.e., that there is an absolute rather than only a conditional privilege—is that in the vast majority of public necessity cases, the plaintiff's property would have been destroyed anyway by the oncoming fire or other force that threatened the public's property. When this is true, the plaintiff really has not lost anything, and the decision to destroy the plaintiff's property was in fact correct. But a more satisfying explanation, I think, is that when the public necessity rule emerged, there would have been no feasible way to hold the appropriate parties liable. Because towns and municipalities did not exist as legal entities until relatively recently, there was no way for the plaintiff to hold a "town" liable. And because the individual or individuals who actually tore down the plaintiff's house were acting not only for themselves but also for others and for the public good, it would have been inappropriate to hold them liable as individuals. Yet it would have been difficult if not impossible to identify and recover from the large number of people whose property had benefited enough from destruction of the plaintiff's property to warrant imposing liability on them. By the time municipalities gained a legal existence that would have rendered them an appropriate target of liability, the public necessity rule had already crystallized.

* * *

This discussion of necessity may seem to have wandered far from the defenses that may be raised in suits for intentional injury to property. But the discussion illustrates the way in which any effort to reject superficial answers and to delve further into the reasons that tort liability is or is not imposed almost inevitably leads to considerations of principle and policy at a deeper level. The questions raised in considering the defense of necessity run throughout the law of torts: In fashioning the rules governing tort liability and the defenses to it, how much stress should be placed on the goal of doing justice between the parties and how much on promoting optimal deterrence? When should liability be imposed even in the absence of a wrong committed by the defendant? These questions return, again and again, whether intentional torts, negligence, or strict liability are involved.

3

THE NEGLIGENCE STANDARD

Even if the defendant did not intend to physically injure the plaintiff or to invade another interest of the plaintiff that the law of torts protects, liability may be imposed for injury or damage caused by the defendant's negligence. Most tort cases are negligence cases. The vast majority involve comparatively minor or modest injuries and are settled on a fairly routine, almost bureaucratized basis. A few involve serious injuries or pose complex or unusual legal issues. A higher percentage of these cases, but still only a minority, go to trial. But although most negligence cases are settled, they are settled in the shadow of the law of negligence and in anticipation of what would happen at trial.

Negligence is easily defined: it is the failure to exercise reasonable care to avoid injury or damage to another person or property. Ordinarily one is under an obligation—that is, has a duty—to exercise reasonable care to avoid causing foreseeable physical injury to other people or their property. This is a duty not to be negligent. Failure to do so constitutes a breach of duty, thus comprising the first two of the four elements of any tort (duty, breach of duty, damages, and causation). In most negligence cases involving bodily injury or property damage the question of "duty" therefore stays in the background, though it is logically present in every case. But there are important situations in which the law holds that there is no duty to exercise reasonable care to avoid causing foreseeable physical harm. And there are many situations in which there is no duty to exercise reasonable care to avoid causing foreseeable non-physical injury, such as economic or emotional loss. This Chapter addresses the set of cases in which the "duty" question stays in the background and the issue is whether the defendant was negligent. The law governing the situations in which the nature and scope of the duty question are actively in play is addressed later, under the rubric of "proximate cause" (Chapter Six) and "affirmative and limited duty" (Chapter Eleven).

The law of negligence tends to afford more protection against bodily injury and property damage than pure economic or pure emotional loss for a number of reasons, not the least of which is that personal health and physical well-being are essential to the pursuit of most of other goods. The quandary is why property also receives this protection. A plausible answer, I think, is that because many of the same actions that risk causing bodily injury simultaneously risk causing property damage, imposing liability for negligently-caused property damage also tends to reduce the risk that negligence will cause bodily injury. But there are also reasons of history—rights of property were once considered more important than many people think they are today. And measuring property losses is easier than measuring some other kinds of losses (e.g., fear) for which there is sometimes less protection.

What is "reasonable care" depends on the circumstances. Negligence cases are therefore heavily fact-driven and usually are decided by a jury. Nonetheless, a number of important rules of law regarding negligence have developed over time. These rules affect the admissibility of evidence, rulings on motions for summary judgment, rulings on motions for directed verdicts and judgments notwithstanding the verdict (in the federal system these are termed motions for judgment as a matter of law), and the wording of jury instructions, among other things. At the core of all of these rules is the meaning of the concept of negligence.

This Chapter examines the meaning and application of the concept of negligence, first looking briefly at the history of negligence law, and then scrutinizing the modern negligence standard by exploring a number of subjects within it: the reasonable person standard; Judge Learned Hand's negligence "calculus;" the role played by evidence of compliance or non-compliance with custom; professional negligence, or malpractice; violation of statutes; and finally, *per se* rules and the role of judge and jury in negligence cases.

I. A Page of History

When Oliver Wendell Holmes, Jr. said that "a page of history is worth a volume of logic," he meant that understanding how a rule of law developed over time may provide a more satisfactory explanation for its current character than exclusively logical analysis of the rule. For us as well as for Holmes, a bit about the history of negligence law can help to place the modern law of negligence in a more comprehensible context.

A. *The Scope of Liability in Trespass*

Tort law emerged out of criminal law, and was therefore originally concerned principally with violent breaches of the peace.

The early tort "forms of action" were for what amounted to battery or trespass to land. To bring a tort action one needed a *writ*. The principal writs for battery and trespass to land were called "trespass *vi et armis*" (trespass by force of arms) and "trespass *quare clausum fregit*" (trespass by breaching the plaintiff's boundary). The allegations of the plaintiff's complaint had to conform to the requirements of the applicable writ or the action could not be brought. For example, trespass required that the injury to the plaintiff be direct and forceful.

If the plaintiff's claim fell perfectly within the contours of trespass he had a very strong chance of recovery. This was because, early on, the defendant was liable virtually without regard to whether he was to blame for the plaintiff's injury, as long as he had caused it. Thus, in *The Thorns Case*,[1] the defendant was sued for trespassing on the plaintiff's land in order to retrieve the branches of a hedge of thorns that had fallen while the defendant was cutting the hedge. The court held that the defendant was liable simply by virtue of having trespassed. There was some language in the case, however, leaving open the possibility that if the defendant had proved that he had done all in his power to keep the thorns off the plaintiff's land, the result might have been otherwise. But in the absence of such a showing, trespass was what we would today call a strict liability tort.

Over time the courts made increasing reference to the possibility that a defendant could avoid liability in trespass by proving that he was, as they sometimes put it, "utterly without fault," or that the injury to the plaintiff was an "inevitable accident." But for both substantive and procedural reasons, the defense apparently was very narrow. For example, in perhaps the most noteworthy case on the issue, *Weaver v. Ward*,[2] the parties were both English soldiers. The plaintiff's complaint alleged that in the course of a military training exercise the defendant shot the plaintiff. This bare allegation made out a *prima facie* case of trespass *vi et armis*. The defendant could then avoid liability only by pleading and proving that he was utterly without fault. What the defendant actually pleaded in *Weaver* was that the shooting was accidental. From the modern point of view this plea seems to come pretty close to alleging that the defendant was "utterly without fault."

The court in *Weaver* held, however, that the facts pleaded by the defendant did not show him to be utterly without fault. To avoid liability, the court said, it would have been necessary for the

1. Y.B. Mich. 6 Ed. 4 f.7, pl. 18 (1466).
2. 80 Eng.Rep. 284 (K.B.1616).

defendant to plead and prove that the plaintiff had run across the line of fire while the defendant was shooting, or otherwise to have shown that the accident had been "inevitable, and that the defendant had committed no negligence to give occasion to the hurt." Given this language, the best interpretation of *Weaver* is that there was liability in trespass for direct and forceful injury except when the defendant could not be said in any way to have been responsible for what happened. Merely having exercised what today we would regard as reasonable care was not enough to show that the defendant was "utterly without fault" and therefore not enough to avoid liability. In addition, *Weaver* makes it clear that, as a matter of procedure, the defendant in trespass had the burden of proving that he was utterly without fault. The plaintiff could recover for direct and forceful injury unless the defendant succeeded in proving that the circumstances fell within the substantively narrow defense of being "utterly without fault."

Indeed, the meaning of "utterly without fault" was apparently so narrow that there are few recorded cases over a period of centuries in which the defense prevailed. There may have been unreported cases—trials that did not result in appeals, for example—in which the defense prevailed. And there was often a procedural explanation for the defendant's loss that makes it difficult to pinpoint the substantive scope of the defense "utterly without fault." Over time two distinct defenses emerged. One was a "general" defense that was raised by a general plea or denial. This plea denied the facts alleged, or at least the critical allegation that the defendant's act caused the plaintiff's harm. The other was a "special" defense or plea that admitted that the cause of the plaintiff's harm was the defendant's act, but further alleged that although he had caused the harm he was otherwise was utterly without fault. In some cases the defendant seemed to lose because he had entered a general plea when he should have pleaded specially, and vice versa.

Consequently, it may be that some defendants even in the recorded cases would in fact have prevailed on the defense that they were "utterly without fault" had they employed the proper plea in raising their defenses. That is, there may well have been more scope for escaping liability because of the absence of fault than the recorded cases suggest. But even if this were true, it is fair to say that there was precious little room for avoiding liability on this basis, although there seemed to be more and more room as the beginning of the nineteenth century approached.

B. *The Rise of Trespass on the Case and the Transition to a Negligence Standard*

Plaintiffs had their problems too. For a while (centuries, perhaps) there was no liability for bodily injury that did not fall within the contours of trespass—i.e., that was not direct and forceful. Eventually, however, a new form of action emerged, under which liability sometimes was imposed when the harm was indirect, or consequential, as long as the defendant was negligent in risking the harm. But the plaintiff shouldered the burden of proof on the negligence issue. Since the writ system was in full force when this form of action emerged, it first became actionable as "trespass in a similar case," then as "trespass on the case," and finally (more or less for short) as "case." The question that was often raised after this alternative approach to liability became established was whether the plaintiff should have sued in trespass or in case, since the requirements of these two alternatives varied. Trespass would lie (that is, was the appropriate form of action) when the harm alleged was direct; the defendant could escape liability for trespass only in narrow circumstances, by proving that he was utterly without fault. On the other hand, case would lie when the harm was indirect or consequential, and in case the defendant was only liable for negligence. Trespass was obviously a more favorable form of action for the plaintiff, because liability was imposed virtually without regard to whether the defendant was at fault, and even the utter absence of fault was an affirmative defense to be proved by the defendant, whereas in case there was liability only if the defendant was negligent, and the plaintiff had the burden of proving it. But if the plaintiff sued in trespass (for direct harm) when he should have sued in case (for indirect harm), he lost.

This was precisely the issue in the memorable case of *Scott v. Shepherd*.[3] There the defendant threw a lighted squib (a firecracker or torch of some sort) into a marketplace, and it was tossed like a hot potato from person to person until it injured the plaintiff, who sued in trespass. The defendant argued that because the harm was not direct, the plaintiff should have sued in case. The court held that the harm was direct and that trespass therefore would lie, but in so holding revealed how arbitrary the distinction between trespass and case actually was. A plaintiff "lucky" enough to be able to sue in trespass usually recovered very easily; but a plaintiff forced to sue in case had a harder time, since he had to prove negligence.

---

3. 96 Eng.Rep. 525 (K.B.1772).

Similarly, a defendant unfortunate enough to have caused direct injury and to be sued in trespass was almost certainly going to be liable, whereas a defendant who was sued in case could avoid liability if he had exercised what came to be understood as reasonable care. And these differences depended on something that increasingly seemed morally and practically irrelevant: whether the harm had occurred in a direct or indirect manner.[4]

Although it took more time than one might expect to sweep away this distinction between trespass and case, eventually it did happen. On this side of the Atlantic the leading decision was *Brown v. Kendall*,[5] the dogfight case. The plaintiff and defendant owned dogs that were fighting, and in attempting to break up the fight with a stick, the defendant accidentally struck the plaintiff in the eye. The plaintiff sued in trespass, alleging that the defendant was liable for a direct and forceful injury. The opinion for the highest court of Massachusetts was written by Chief Judge Lemuel Shaw, who happened to be the father-in-law of Herman Melville and may well have served as the model for Captain Vere in Melville's novel, BILLY BUDD.

Shaw's opinion in *Brown v. Kendall* inaugurated a new era in American tort law. The plaintiff claimed that because his action properly was brought in trespass, he needed only to prove direct, forcible injury, and that the defendant could only escape liability by showing that he had exercised extraordinary care (presumably, something like being "utterly without fault"). Shaw rejected this contention outright. He said that the statements in the cases to the effect that trespass will lie in cases of direct injury all had been made in reference to the question whether trespass and not case will lie, *assuming that some action would lie*. But neither trespass nor case will lie, he said, unless the defendant had intended to injure the plaintiff or had negligently injured him. And Shaw went on to say that the plaintiff has the burden of proving either intent to injure or negligence, whether the action is brought in trespass or in case. Finally, Shaw indicated that while there may be instances in which the reasonable thing to do would be to exercise extraordinary care, the standard by which the defendant is to be judged is always one of "ordinary" or reasonable care. If the defendant has exercised ordinary care then he is not liable, whether the action is brought in trespass or in case.

4. *See* Charles O. Gregory, *Trespass to Negligence to Absolute Liability*, 37 VA. L.REV. 359 (1951).

5. 60 Mass. (6 Cush.) 292 (1850).

As legal history, probably this was inaccurate, to say the least. The case law over the centuries certainly strongly implied that, for practical purposes, liability in trespass was imposed even when the defendant was not negligent. So *Brown v. Kendall* arguably did not merely redescribe existing law, but changed it substantially. No longer was there any question whether a plaintiff could recover for a direct injury even if the defendant had acted carefully: there was no such recovery. No longer did the defendant bear the burden of proving that he had met the requisite standard of care: the plaintiff now had the burden of proving breach of that standard. And the cause of action for negligently-caused harm now had the potential to become a general standard rather than being a series of particular duties. In short, there was no longer any substantive difference between trespass and case; that difference was merely procedural, affecting the kind of writ the plaintiff had to obtain, but not what the plaintiff had to prove in order to succeed. There could be no recovery in the absence of negligence or conduct even more blameworthy, such as acting with intent to cause harm.

Very quickly this approach became nearly universal. *Brown v. Kendall* is only the most famous of the mid-nineteenth century decisions out of which the new negligence regime emerged. But although there is no doubt about the fact of this development, there is controversy among legal scholars about the way in which the new regime meshed with nineteenth century social and economic attitudes. Certainly the idea that there could be no liability unless the defendant had done something wrong was consistent with the rugged individualism and industrial expansionism of the age. Some scholars have gone further, however, asserting that the new negligence regime was designed to provide a subsidy to infant industry, by removing the threat of strict liability that might have hindered industrial development. In the view of these scholars, the development of contributory negligence (i.e., negligence by the plaintiff) as a complete defense to a negligence action further subsidized potential defendants by further narrowing the scope of liability. Other scholars have examined the facts of large samples of negligence cases during that era, however, and concluded that the "subsidy thesis" is too simplistic, since the move to negligence aided all kinds of defendants. *Brown v. Kendall*, after all, did not involve an industrial or commercial defendant, but two individuals. Moreover, although trespass may until that time have been a strict liability action, both trespass and case had limited applicability in earlier centuries. In a sense there was a background of no liability with a few exceptions to it.[6] But over time the occasions in which liability

---

6. *See* Robert L. Rabin, *The Historical Development of the Fault Principle: A Reinterpretation*, 15 GA. L. REV. 925 (1981).

might be imposed had slowly expanded, especially as the number of accidents that could cause bodily injury increased. Although *Brown* and cases like it did narrow the basis of liability, certainly the cumulative effect of all these developments was that the incidence of liability increased between the seventeenth and the nineteenth centuries.

In any event, the term "subsidy" is in a sense pejorative. Defendants as a group may have been better off after *Brown v. Kendall* than before, and plaintiffs worse off. But if that case adopted the correct, or fairest, or preferable rule, then it did not create a subsidy. It put matters right, for under the prior rule (on this view of it) there had been a "subsidy" to plaintiffs. On the other hand, if the correct, or fairest, or preferable rule had been what amounted to strict liability, then the move to negligence was indeed a subsidy, in the sense of creating an artificial advantage for defendants. In short, rule changes may produce changes in entitlements, with the advantages to plaintiffs or to defendants that come with the change. But whether a change is a subsidy or its opposite—the elimination of a subsidy—depends on what one considers the "correct" rule to begin with.

Regardless of the way one views the issues posed by the subsidy thesis, it is indisputable that by the late nineteenth century, negligence was the dominant standard. Even today, while the areas in which strict liability is imposed have slowly expanded somewhat, negligence remains the dominant basis for imposing liability in cases of non-intentional bodily injury or property damage. The question today, then, is what it means to be negligent.

II. The Reasonable Person Standard

Negligence is the failure to exercise the care that would have been exercised by the reasonably prudent person under the circumstances. Reasonable care is sometimes referred to as due care, or ordinary care, which might be thought, incorrectly, to mean only average care, no matter how risky average care is. Strictly speaking, reasonable care is not necessarily average care. The question is not what average people actually do, but what they ought to do.

Standing alone the definition of negligence as "reasonable care" is useful only as loose guidance for the jury. It is not a concrete rule, but a general standard that asks for a normative or evaluative judgment, not a finding of pure empirical fact. In many negligence cases, therefore, enormous reliance is placed on the jury to resolve the negligence issue, which is often referred to as "mixed question of fact and law." The core of the question is, "should the defendant have behaved more carefully?" Karl Llewellyn once drew an analogy between legal rules and the game of golf. Rules, he said, are like chipping from off the green. They can get the ball onto the green, but you still have to putt to get the ball in the hole—i.e., apply the rule to the facts. What Llewellyn said of concrete rules is even more true of general standards. In negligence cases the jury does the putting.

A general negligence standard can work well in many negligence cases. When jurors are familiar with the activity that gave rise to the plaintiff's injury, then they can easily apply the conscience of the community in evaluating the defendant's conduct. The kind of activities juries are likely to know about will vary with the time and place. For example, in *Vaughan v. Menlove*,[7] the defendant was sued for damage to the plaintiff's cottages resulting from a fire that started in one of the defendant's hay stacks. The question was whether the defendant had behaved negligently in placing a hay stack so near to the plaintiff's cottages, in light of the dry condition of the hay. I doubt that many of today's readers would feel competent to make that judgment without some assistance from expert witnesses. But in rural England in 1837, jurors probably would know how the community would expect the defendant to behave. The issue was one on which the jurors were likely to have had experience and a confident opinion.

The equivalent today would be an ordinary intersection accident between automobiles. Virtually everyone drives, and virtually everyone would feel capable of judging whether the defendant drove reasonably under the circumstances. In contrast, in cases involving complex or technical activities with which most of us are not automatically familiar—the provision of medical care or the design of products, for example—the task is more difficult and the jury must be educated by the parties before it can be expected to render an informed verdict. As we shall see, the law has ways of helping this process of education along, but even with this help the result must sometimes fall short of the ideal of the well-informed decision-maker invoking settled community norms.

The idealized picture of the jury as the informed conscience of the community in negligence cases sometimes is unrealistic in another way as well. In some cases there may be well-developed and fairly uniform standards regarding the proper way to engage in a particular activity. Farmers may know and agree on the proper way to build hay stacks, and drivers may know and agree on the proper

7. 132 Eng.Rep. 490 (C.P.1837).

way to change lanes on a four-lane divided highway. But often, perhaps even usually, there are no pre-existing, sufficiently concrete and uniform norms that jurors can invoke in order to decide whether the defendant was negligent. The facts of actual cases are so varied that general norms do not definitively resolve them. For example, in a highway accident case the jury's sense of the proper way to change lanes might depend on how much traffic there was on the highway; how fast the vehicles were traveling; and how much space between vehicles the drivers on that highway ordinarily maintain. To the extent that this is true, there is no precise rule that the jury can use to resolve the negligence issue. Rather, in effect the jury must create a rule for the particular case at hand based on the general "reasonableness" standard and then apply that rule to evaluate the defendant's behavior.

In situations such as this when no concrete, self-applying rule applies across the board, different juries may well resolve the negligence issue differently in cases involving the same or highly similar facts. Nothing in negligence law requires that like cases be decided alike by different juries. Rather, when there is no applicable rule that makes the reasonableness standard more concrete, instead of having negligence rules that resolve disputes on their own, we have only a "process" for resolving negligence cases by submitting them to the jury.[8] Nonetheless it is possible to tease out of the general concept of negligence a number of ways in which conduct might fall short of the reasonableness standard. Some are simply ideas that lawyers, commentators, and juries may or may not find attractive. Others have crystalized into actual rules.

In the former category are two notions. First, negligence is not necessarily one single thing, one single form of falling short of a standard, but several. Conduct might be unreasonable because it is careless, in the sense of being inadvertently inattentive to safety. For example, I might take my eyes off the road while driving because I daydream. Conduct might instead be unreasonable because it is foolish. That is, a party may be aware of the risk his or her conduct posed for others, but consciously make a poor judgment about what to do. Or a party might be foolishly ignorant of a risk. One or the other of these kinds of foolishness might have been present in *Vaughan v. Menlove*. Finally, conduct might selfish, the product of weighing one's own interests too heavily and the interests of others not heavily enough. The defendant in *Vaughan* said that he would "chance it" because he had insurance. This might be an example of selfishness. Negligence law has no rule that subdi-

---

8. For further discussion of this issue, *see* Kenneth S. Abraham, *The Trouble with Negligence*, 54 VAND. L. REV. 1187 (2001).

vides conduct in these ways, but thinking about negligence as *carelessness*, *foolishness*, or *selfishness* may still be helpful.[9]

A second way in which conduct may fall short of reasonableness involves the rate of compliance with the standard. Juries are not required, but clearly are permitted, to find that parties must behave reasonably all the time. For example, if reasonable care requires driving no more than 30 miles per hour on a particular road, the jury is entitled to find the defendant negligent for driving at 40 miles per hour, even if the defendant proves that he has driven on that road his entire life and never before exceeded the speed limit. The option of the jury to apply a *perfect compliance requirement* helps avoid trying the defendant's character ("is he generally reasonable?") and avoids inquiry into conduct that occurred on occasions other than the one in question.[10]

These two ways of thinking about negligence (as well as any number of others) are optional. Fortunately, however, over time the law has put a bit of meat on the bones of the reasonableness standard by creating some more or less concrete rules that are mandatory, and direct the jury as to the proper way to make its negligence/no negligence decision. The most important such rules are the objective standard, the special rules governing children and the infirm, and the foreseeability requirement.

A. *The Objective Standard*

Perhaps the most important specification of the general negligence standard is that it is objective, not subjective. With the few exceptions described below, reasonable care "under the circumstances" does not include the incapacities or limitations of the person whose behavior is under evaluation. That the defendant did his best or acted in good faith is no defense. Rather, the question is how the reasonably prudent person would have acted under the circumstances, not whether the defendant meant well or was in good faith. Indeed, evidence of the defendant's benevolent state of mind ordinarily is not even admissible, because under the objective standard this evidence is irrelevant.

It may seem somewhat anomalous to hold that a defendant was negligent even if she could not have done any better. In morality, "ought" presupposes "can." How can the defendant be at "fault" if she did her best? One answer is that, if the defendant is still at

---

9. I am grateful to Professor Vincent Blasi for suggesting this subdivision.

10. Mark F. Grady, *Res Ipsa Loquitur and Compliance Error*, 142 U. PENN. L. REV. 887, 908 (1994).

"fault" when she did her best, then legal fault obviously differs from moral fault. Perhaps some of what we call "negligence," and liability imposed under that rubric, has more in common with strict liability—liability without fault—than it has with moral blameworthiness. It may be, that is, that there is a pocket of strict liability within negligence.

The question, then, is why negligence law takes this approach and adopts an objective standard. There are a number of arguments in favor of this standard. One set of arguments relates to the cost and ease of adjudication and to the feasibility of fact-finding. A subjective standard would be infinitely variable, depending on the particular strengths, weaknesses, and experiences of the individual in question. Applying such a standard would require much more complicated and difficult fact-finding than applying an objective standard. To apply a subjective standard the jury would have to determine how careful the defendant was capable of being, and whether she employed all her abilities. But to apply an objective reasonableness standard the jury need only compare the actual conduct of the defendant with that standard. The great advantage of an objective standard is that it asks the members of the jury to judge the defendant based on their own knowledge and experience in the world. They need not engage in psychology or attempt to look into the defendant's mind. They need only decide how the reasonable person would have behaved, and measure the defendant's behavior against that standard. In addition, a subjective standard would encourage fraud and deception. If the negligence determination depended on the characteristics of the defendant, then the defendant would have an incentive to mislead the jury about those characteristics, understating her strengths and overstating her weaknesses. An objective standard does not create this problem because those strengths and weaknesses do not count.

A second set of arguments relates to incentives and deterrence. Because the defendant's strengths and weaknesses do not count, the objective standard has greater potential for encouraging the defendant to exercise all the care and skill that she can. Admittedly, the defendant can only do as well as she is capable of doing; but under a subjective standard she may not even do that, relying on the vagaries of the fact-finding process for protection. In contrast, the objective standard is unforgiving; the threat of liability under an objective standard may therefore push potential defendants to do their best, especially if the reasonable person standard is set (as juries typically set it) at a level that is well within the reach of most people. And when a defendant recognizes that he is incapable of complying with the objective standard, he may reduce the level of his involvement in the activity in question in order to avoid exposure to liability. If I am a very poor driver, I may tend to let others drive or to take public transportation. The threat of liability under the objective standard may thereby affect not only safety levels, but activity levels as well. An objective standard also gives the public assurance that those to whose actions they are exposed will either act with a predictable level of care or be liable for the consequences of failing to do so. Members of the public can therefore more accurately gauge the level of self-protective care that they need to employ than would be possible if the amount of care that could be expected from others varied with the characteristics of each individual.

A third set of arguments concerns the fairness of the objective standard. Although the objective standard burdens some individuals more than others, it treats everyone equally. If a subjective standard were applied, some individuals would need to plead what could amount to an excuse for not behaving as carefully as everyone else does. They would have to stigmatize themselves in court in order to avoid liability. The objective standard declines to stigmatize the disabled in this way, though at the cost of their incurring more liability than others. This liability, however, they can usually cover with insurance. In addition, everyone benefits from the degree of safety that the objective standard helps to encourage. If a subjective standard applied, then those whom this standard exonerated from liability would obtain the benefit of extra safety from others, without providing others this extra safety in return. Applying the objective standard to those who cannot comply with it provides others with the substitute benefit of the right to recover for their losses.

These arguments for the objective standard have considerable weight, but they are not indisputable. For example, it would be far from unthinkable for jurors to inquire into the state of mind of the defendant in deciding whether she was negligent. Juries must do exactly that in cases involving battery and assault; they could do so in negligence cases as well, assessing the credibility of the defendant in order to minimize perjury. It is also true that a benefit of the objective standard is that it may create an incentive for defendants to exercise all the care they can; but this incentive cannot be created unless the fact that the standard is objective is communicated to and understood by the below-average individuals who are most likely to be affected by the standard but least likely to appreciate its significance for them. And although the objective standard may make some people's behavior more predictably safe, in light of the variable application of even the objective standard from jury to jury, the size of this effect is debatable. Finally, although the objective standard treats everyone equally, it is not clear that treating differently-situated individuals equally in this situation is more consistent with fairness than treating them differently.

Despite the strength of some of these counterarguments, the law has long adhered in conventional cases to the objective standard. There are situations, however, in which the standard is relaxed and at least some subjectivity is permitted to find its way into the negligence decision. The main cases involve children and the infirm.

B. *Children and the Infirm*

Notwithstanding the objective standard, the law has always made certain accommodations for children and the infirm. The scope of these accommodations sheds some additional light on the overall purpose of the objective standard.

1. Children

Children below about the age of five cannot be negligent at all, presumably because they cannot be expected to exercise care. Until about the mid-twentieth century the rule governing children above that age was that they were expected to exercise the degree of care that would be reasonable in a child of similar age, intelligence, and experience. This is what might be called a semi-objective standard, in that the reasonableness of the child's behavior was measured against the capacities of similar children in that age group. But a child of unusual intelligence or experience might be expected to exercise more care than would usually be expected of other children of his age.

This rule was a concession to the reality that there is a limit to the degree of care that can be expected of children. The incentive-creating effects of an objective standard on adults whose capacities are below average are highly unlikely to influence children. Those who come into contact with children understand this and can exercise additional self-protective care when necessary. Moreover, until the middle of the twentieth century there was little point to suing children in tort, since parents were not and are not liable for the torts of their children (though they may be liable in their own right for negligent supervision) and children ordinarily have no substantial assets of their own. In any event, the younger the child who has caused an injury to another person, the greater the likelihood that the victim will in fact have an independent claim against the child's parents or caretaker for negligent supervision.

The semi-objective children's reasonableness standard has now been qualified in many jurisdictions, however, by the proviso that when children engage in *dangerous adult activities*, they are held to an adult standard of care. The point made in the cases that have established this proviso is that potential victims of children who drive motor vehicles, fly airplanes, or operate motor boats, for example, have no way to anticipate which driver or pilot is a child. There is therefore no realistic way to exercise the additional self-protective care that is required when one encounters children engaged in children's activities. Furthermore, there is no particular social benefit to be gained by immunizing children against liability for harm caused by engaging in adult activities; unless a child is capable of complying with an adult standard of care he or she should not be driving, flying, or operating a motor boat. Finally, with the post-World War II rise of auto and homeowner's liability insurance, children are much more likely than in the past to be independently insured under their parents' liability insurance policies and thereby able to satisfy judgments rendered against them in cases involving adult activities. Where insurance has gone, tort law has tended to follow.

2. Infirm Adults

Pinpointing the standard that applies to physically and mentally infirm adults is more complicated. Typically, physical infirmities are taken into account in judging the reasonableness of behavior, but mental infirmities are not. The traditional common law rule was that even insane people are liable for their torts. What might account for this difference? Indeed, why would there be a departure from the objective standard at all where physical infirmities are concerned? The answers tell us something about both the objective standard and the exceptions to it.

The main difference between physical and mental infirmities is that the former are typically visible, measurable, and verifiable. By contrast—especially in the nineteenth century when these rules developed—mental infirmities are invisible, hard to measure, and incompletely verifiable. The whole focus of the objective standard, in fact, is the classic example of this problem. The defendant in *Vaughan v. Menlove* (the haystack case) and others like him, for instance, may assert that he just doesn't have the judgment or intelligence to be as careful about avoiding risk to others that the average or reasonable person has. The objective standard rejects this assertion, not because it is necessarily false, but because it is not necessarily true and because it is difficult to know when it is true and when it is not. One might respond that even if minor mental deficiencies are difficult to verify or measure, those who have serious mental illness can now be easily and reliably identified and diagnosed. Perhaps, but even now psychiatric diagnosis is a dicey enterprise. Moreover, people who suffer delusions often have periods of lucidity. During such periods it may be negligent not to take action to prevent oneself from causing harm while delusional. This was the basis of the court's decision, for example, in *Breunig v. American Family Ins. Co.*,[11] in which the defendant thought that she and her car could fly "because Batman does it." This was in effect an application of the more general "emergency" doctrine, which holds that when a danger arises without warning, this circumstance may be taken into account in assessing the reasonableness of the behavior of the party faced with the danger. When there was warning of the danger, however, then the fact that there was opportunity for deliberation rather than merely instinctive reaction must be considered. Finally, often people who are psychotic or delusional may nonetheless be capable of being careful. Just because I think that I am Napoleon doesn't mean that I don't know that I should stop at a red light. In any event, such people commonly have guardians who have an interest in preserving their assets and therefore an incentive to monitor and control their behavior. This incentive would be diminished if the mentally ill were not liable for negligence.

In contrast, physical infirmities pose measurement and verifiability problems to a much lesser degree and are therefore subject to a semi-objective standard. A blind person cannot read a sign that says "Warning: Highly Flammable Vapors. Do Not Smoke." If his smoking starts a fire, the jury will be instructed in a suit by the owner the property damaged by fire that it may (probably must) take into account the defendant's blindness in determining whether he behaved reasonably or negligently under the circumstances. However, although usually a semi-objective standard is more lenient than an objective standard, there are times when the existence of the defendant's infirmity can cut the other way. The jury is permitted to take the defendant's physical infirmity into account in deciding whether his physical limitation should have led him to take precautions different from or additional to those expected of a reasonable person without the physical infirmity in question. Most obviously, a blind person should not drive a motor vehicle; a person in a wheelchair should be more hesitant about "jaywalking" than others.

11. 45 Wis.2d 536, 173 N.W.2d 619 (1970).

It is worth noting, however, that over time our social attitudes toward physical and mental infirmities have evolved in favor of greater and greater involvement of people with those infirmities in everyday activities. At the very least, evidence of what people with the same disability as the defendant's are capable of doing would be admissible in his defense. And given evolving attitudes, in making the negligence decision at least some juries would be likely to reflect the evolution of our attitudes in this regard. What once would have been considered the taking of an imprudent risk by a disabled person might not be today.

C. *The Foreseeability Requirement*

The logic of reasonable care depends on the connection between knowledge and behavior. A defendant is not negligent unless he knew or reasonably should have known that his actions posed a risk of harm. Even then, the defendant is not negligent unless a reasonable person under the circumstances would have taken precautions that the defendant did not take in order to avoid that risk. It would be nonsensical to say that someone was negligent for failing to reduce or eliminate a risk about which he did not and could not know. Consequently, a person cannot be negligent for failing to take precautions against an unforeseeable risk of harm.

The term foreseeability can be unnecessarily confusing. In this context, the term refers to the known or knowable possibility that there exists a risk that will result in harm. So understood, foreseeability and unforeseeability are not binary concepts, but involve degrees of probability and improbability, although some risks are completely unforeseeable. That is, they are so improbable that a reasonable person need not anticipate them at all.

For example, in one of the early cases on this issue, *Blyth v. Birmingham Waterworks*,[12] a record freeze apparently caused leakage from one of the defendant's underground water mains, damaging the plaintiff's house. The trial court left it to the jury to decide whether the defendant was negligent (presumably either in the design of the system, or in failing to inspect it, or both), and the jury found for the plaintiff. However, on appeal the court held, in effect, that a directed verdict should have been granted for the defendant, reasoning that it was not unreasonable to fail to take precautions against a frost that "penetrated to a greater depth than any which ordinarily occurs south of the polar regions." For practical purposes the court seems to have concluded that the risk that

12. 156 Eng.Rep. 1047 (Ex.1856).

materialized in harm to the plaintiff simply was not foreseeable. That is, in the court's view the risk was so improbable that as a matter of law a reasonable person need not take it into account in determining what precautions to take.

Today, *Blyth* would almost certainly pose a question of fact for the jury. Few risks are so unforeseeable as to warrant granting a directed verdict to the defendant on that ground alone. That is especially true of weather. Nothing is so foreseeable as more severe weather than is normally likely to occur. That is what is meant by 100 year floods and even 1000 year floods. But a 1000 year flood may not be sufficiently probable to permit a jury to find that it is reasonably foreseeable. It is foreseeable that such things will happen, though on a very infrequent basis. Depending on the context, therefore, it might be said as a matter of law that a 1000 year flood is not "foreseeable." But even if the improbability of the risk that caused harm is not, in itself, a basis for exonerating the defendant, this factor may figure in the overall negligence calculation. To put it another way, rarely does a defendant escape liability purely because a risk was utterly unforeseeable. Yet how likely or unlikely it was that a particular risk would materialize in harm is very relevant. We turn next, therefore, to what has been called the negligence "calculus," in which the probability of harm plays an important part.

III. The Negligence "Calculus"

Despite the different clarifications of the reasonable person standard that tort law has developed, the notion is still very general. A different angle of analysis that has emerged to help clarify what it means to be negligent has come to be called the negligence "calculus." The negligence calculus affords a way of thinking about the circumstances under which a reasonable person would risk harm or would instead take steps to reduce that risk. A major contribution of the calculus is that it unpacks the general notion of reasonable behavior into three components: the probability that a particular act or omission will cause harm; the magnitude of that harm if it occurs; and the value of the interest that must be foregone or sacrificed in order to reduce the risk of harm.

A. *The Learned Hand Formulation*

The negligence calculus received its most famous expression in an opinion by Judge Learned Hand in *United States v. Carroll*

Towing Co.[13] In that case the question was whether it was negligent not to have personnel at all times on a barge under tow. Hand put the issue this way:

> the [barge] owner's duty, as in other similar situations, to provide against resulting injuries is a function of three variables: (1) The probability that she will break away; (2) the gravity of the resulting injury, if she does; (3) the burden of adequate precautions. Possibly it serves to bring this notion into relief to state it in algebraic terms: if the probability be called P; the injury, L; and the burden, B; liability depends upon whether B is less than L multiplied by P: i.e., whether B is less than PL.

Although Hand's use of even simple algebra might be overly technical for some people, the intuition behind the negligence calculus is straightforward. To determine whether taking a particular risky action is or is not reasonable, it is useful to compare the expected accident costs that will be incurred from taking a particular action with the costs of avoiding these costs. To do this comparison, these three factors can be taken into account. The first two factors—the probability of harm and the magnitude of harm if it occurs—measure expected accident costs. The third factor—the interest that must be sacrificed in order to reduce the risk of harm—measures accident avoidance costs, or the "cost" of reducing or avoiding the risk of harm. When the first two factors are more weighty than the last, then the cost of risking harm is greater than the cost of avoiding or reducing it. According to the negligence calculus, taking the risky action is unreasonable in this situation because expected accident costs outweigh accident avoidance costs. Conversely, if accident avoidance costs—the interest that must be sacrificed to reduce or avoid a risk (the cost of safety precautions, and whatever benefits are sacrificed by exercising more care)—is more weighty than expected accident costs, then it is not unreasonable to take the risk. This comparison between the cost of risking accidents and the cost of avoiding them is sometimes referred to as cost-benefit or risk-benefit analysis.

The substance of the negligence calculus has been embodied in Section 3 of the Restatement (Third) of Torts: Liability for Physical and Emotional Harm,[14] and in many statements by appellate courts.

---

13. 159 F.2d 169 (2d Cir.1947).

14. "A person acts negligently if the person does not exercise reasonable care under all the circumstances. Primary factors to consider in ascertaining whether the person's conduct lacks reasonable care are the foreseeable likelihood that the person's conduct will result in harm, the foreseeable severity of any harm that may ensue, and the burden of precautions to eliminate or reduce the risk of harm."

The calculus can also be used in a number of ways at the trial level, though its litigation usefulness should not be overestimated. Juries could be instructed that they are permitted to take the factors comprising the negligence calculus into account in deciding whether the defendant (or plaintiff) was negligent. But such instructions are rare and even when given probably should leave the jury the option of ignoring them. Certainly the calculus can also help a court to determine whether certain evidence (directed at one or more of the factors comprising the calculus) is relevant. And the intuition behind the negligence calculus, or reference to the specific factors articulated by the calculus, may help a court to rule on motions for summary judgment or for directed verdicts.

For example, in *Eckert v. Long Island R.R.*,[15] the plaintiff's decedent had saved a small child from near-certain death by sweeping the child off the tracks of a negligently-operated train. In the course of the rescue, however, the rescuer was killed. At the trial of an action by the rescuer's estate against the defendant railroad, the defendant moved for a "nonsuit"—in effect, a directed verdict—on the ground (among other things) that it was negligent as a matter of law for the rescuer to have risked his life as he did and that such "contributory" negligence by the plaintiff barred recovery. The court rejected this contention, stating that "[t]he law has so high a regard for human life that it will not impute negligence to an effort to preserve it, unless made under such circumstances as to constitute rashness in the judgment of prudent persons." But in a passage making it clear that something like the negligence calculus was at the heart of its reasoning, the court went on to indicate that if the rescuer had attempted merely to protect property from harm, the result would have been different.

If all this seems like ordinary common sense, in a sense it is. In these circumstances the negligence calculus is merely a way of identifying the factors that may lead to common-sense conclusions about which risks are worth taking and which are not, depending on what is at stake: the probability of harm (the risk of death or serious injury to the rescuer); the magnitude of harm if it occurs (death or serious injury); and the interest that must be sacrificed to avoid the harm (the chance that the child will be hit by the train). In other, more complex cases, reference to the factors that comprise the negligence calculus may also help to guide a judge's or a jury's thinking: How many people's safety did the defendant's action risk? How likely was it that harm would occur? What would have been involved in developing safety measures that would have reduced the

15.   43 N.Y. 502 (1871).

risk of harm? How much could different possible safety measures have reduced the risk? When counsel for the parties direct some of the evidence in the case to these factors, they will assist the judge or jury in making sense out of the negligence question: whether one or both of the parties' conduct was reasonable or unreasonable under all the circumstances. This does not necessarily even have to take place under the rubric of the negligence calculus. Rather, the calculus is a clarification of why it makes sense to do what, in all probability, we would intuitively do anyway—think about the factors that might make a risk too dangerous to take.

In another sense, however, the negligence calculus is subject to criticism. First, the negligence calculus takes a unitary concept (reasonably prudent conduct) based on a simple prototype (the reasonably prudent person) and turns it into something that is both complicated and sometimes unrealistic, inappropriate, or both. A norm such as reasonableness is not always a decision calculus, but a settled way of behaving, or at least of evaluating behavior. Certainly we would say this about the behavior in *Eckert*. If we were simply balancing lives, the plaintiff's decedent in *Eckert* might have been negligent in attempting a rescue. In any event, reasonable driving, reasonable shoveling of snow from a sidewalk, even reasonable use of signs to warn of danger are notions that most people do not break down into their components. Indeed if (as I suggested earlier) we think of one aspect of negligence as carelessness, the negligence calculus would not have much to tell us about whether allegedly careless behavior is negligent. It is theoretically possible to identify the costs of paying greater attention to one's behavior, but that is not the way ordinary people think about inadvertence, and most ordinary people probably would not find it insightful or helpful to evaluate inadvertence in that way. Thus, although the negligence calculus may map well onto the considerations that are relevant to the evaluation of considered decisions, it does not address momentary lapses very well at all.

Second, even when applied to considered decisions, the negligence calculus omits something that some people may consider important: whether a party engaged in impartial deliberation about a possible course of action. Some people—and therefore some jurors—might permissibly consider the fact that the defendant tried in good faith to reach the right decision to be relevant to the question whether the defendant behaved reasonably. That is, the defendant may have made the wrong decision from the standpoint of the negligence calculus, but made the decision unselfishly. On one view such a decision should be judged by the objective standard, and if a reasonable person would have made the decision correctly, the defendant was negligent. Of course, it does not follow that defendants will always be better off engaging in impartial consideration of the negligence calculus. The famous Pinto case, in which a jury held the Ford Motor Company liable for $125 million in punitive damages, illustrates the point.[16] Ford designed the Pinto after engaging in a number of cost-benefit calculations that involved estimating the value of a human life. Most observers believe that the jury was outraged by the callousness of engaging in such a calculation. But that is exactly what the negligence calculus advises. It is possible, however, that the jury was outraged by the low value it thought Ford had placed on a human life and not by the fact that Ford did the calculation at all.

B. *Is the Calculus a Moral or an Economic Theory of Negligence?*

One view of the negligence calculus is that it adopts a certain moral perspective on selfishness. The calculus requires that the interests of others, represented by expected accident costs (the probability and gravity of the injury that may result from an act) be given equal weight when being compared with one's own interests (the burden of precautions, or accident avoidance cost). At the core of this requirement is the norm of equal concern and respect for others that is the hallmark of at least certain conceptions of morality. On this view, the calculus provides a method of striking an appropriate balance between the liberty of injurers and the security of victims.

On the other hand, some academics working in the "law and economics" mode have pressed the concept of the negligence calculus in a very different direction, suggesting that Hand was articulating what amounts to an economic theory of negligence. Most notably, Judge (then Professor) Richard Posner argued in a famous article that the factors in the calculus are essentially economic.[17] Posner said that multiplying the probability of loss times the amount of loss that will be suffered if it occurs yields a measure of the economic benefit to be derived from avoiding the loss. Similarly, the cost of preventing the loss may be the cost of installing safety equipment or the benefit foregone by curtailing or eliminating the activity. If the cost of preventing the loss is greater than the benefit to be gained by avoiding it, said Posner, then society would be better off, in economic terms, to have the accident that results in

16. *Grimshaw v. Ford Motor Co.*, 119 Cal.App.3d 757, 174 Cal.Rptr. 348 (1981).

17. *See* Richard A. Posner, *A Theory of Negligence*, 1 J. Legal Stud. 29 (1972).

the loss than to avoid it. In such a situation a defendant should not be considered negligent for failing to take precautions that would have been more costly than the result they would have avoided. Conversely, if the cost of a loss is greater than the cost of preventing it, society benefits from avoiding the loss and a defendant who fails to avoid it should be considered negligent.

Proponents of this economic theory of negligence often see it not only as the appropriate method of determining whether a party has been negligent, but also as a tool for deterring future accidents. For those who believe that tort law should be concerned with doing justice between the parties to an accident and not with affecting the behavior of others in the future, the economic theory of negligence is objectionable not only on the ground that it is concerned with costs and benefits rather than with rights and justice. The theory is also objectionable when it is employed to support an approach to tort liability that is concerned at least as much with deterring future misconduct as it is with remedying past wrongs. The economic theory of negligence is therefore implicated in the ongoing debate about whether tort law should be remedial, regulatory, or both.

In addition, many who encounter the economic theory of negligence find it repulsive because it seems to reduce the entire accident problem, whether from a remedial or a regulatory standpoint, to a question of money. Presumably the reasonably prudent person takes action to avoid those accidents that are "worth" avoiding, and does not take action to avoid accidents that are not "worth" avoiding. The whole question is what we should then take into account in deciding which accidents these are. That was Learned Hand's point in *Carroll Towing*. However, the implication of this point—that sometimes we will tolerate risking injury rather than requiring that it be avoided—is not entirely comfortable, and it is a fact about which many people are ambivalent.

Especially when this point is rephrased as a choice between injury and money, many people are unwilling to go along, for a number of reasons. These concerns, and possible responses, are as follows. First, it is not clear that economic efficiency—understood as maximizing resources and minimizing the waste of resources—is necessarily a goal to be preferred over others. True enough. But although the economic theory of negligence may err in its exclusive focus on efficiency, it would be foolhardy to say that the law should simply ignore the impact that its rules have on the allocation of resources. Virtually everyone would agree that negligence law shouldn't encourage people to "waste" money on safety precautions. If that is true, then the issue is when we would consider money wasted, not whether being efficient about the way the law encourages people to spend money on safety is desirable. Whether safety precautions are cost-effective might be something to take into account—even if it were not the only thing.

Second, to be operational the economic theory of negligence requires that we place a dollar value on human safety in order to decide how much it is worth paying to avoid injury. It seems wrong to value human safety only in this way. But whether we like it or not, in tort law we are forced to place a monetary value on human safety and physical well-being. For a jury to determine how much compensation to award an injured plaintiff it must engage in monetary valuation of precisely this kind. If a jury must do this in order to make an award after it has decided that the defendant was negligent, then it does not seem at all outrageous to imagine that such a valuation would be made as part of the process of determining whether the defendant was negligent to begin with.

Finally, the notion that the factors that would figure in the negligence calculus in many cases—human safety, convenience, the value of jobs foregone, and so forth—can all be reduced to a single currency of exchange and balanced against each other seems unrealistic. Admittedly, it is unrealistic to suppose that all the factors that could properly be taken into account under the negligence calculus could very often be reduced to a monetary value and then be accurately compared. Learned Hand himself recognized this point early on, when he noted that his calculus required a choice between "incommensurables"—things that cannot be compared.[18] More than that, however, the factors that make up the negligence calculus are likely in most cases to be difficult even to quantify, let alone to compare with each other. Statistics about the probability of particular kinds of injury in particular situations generally are not available, and when such statistics are available their relevance is debatable and their implications are complex. For example, the probability of harm depends on the severity of the injury with which one is concerned. Typically minor injury is a more probable consequence of any risk than major injury. The cost of safety precautions is likely to be easier to pinpoint on occasion, but not always. As a consequence, the precise comparison of quantitative values that seems to make the economic theory of negligence unpalatable—the economic cost of avoiding injury as against the economic benefit of doing so—will rarely be possible. Instead, as Hand envisioned, more or less loose efforts at quantification ordi-

18. *Conway v. O'Brien*, 111 F.2d 611, 612 (2d Cir.1940).

narily can do no more than center attention on the factors that might be determinative in a given case.

Even staunch opponents of the economic theory of negligence, however, would do well to remember one additional point. Whether or not tort law adopts an economic theory of negligence, the parties that find themselves frequently involved as defendants in negligence suits—most notably sizeable corporate enterprises—are likely to behave in accordance with the theory. Even if the law were to employ a thoroughly non-economic approach to negligence, such defendants still would attempt in advance to compare the monetary cost of risking liability for particular categories of injury against the cost of taking safety precautions to reduce that risk. Such enterprises would attempt to avoid the accidents "worth" it to them to avoid, but would prefer to incur liability for the accidents not "worth" avoiding, because by taking this approach their liability costs would be lower than their avoidance costs. They might not always do this entirely in accordance with the negligence calculus, however.[19] For example, instead of taking optimal precautions, they might act in a way that merely reduced their probability of losing future suits, or decreased the amount of damages they could expect to pay, perhaps by ensuring that they preserved the best evidence supporting them or subjected low-income rather than high-income people to risk.

Still, whether we like it or not, for those who are concerned with deterrence, the economic theory of negligence is likely to be relevant to tort law's calculations about the best way to affect the behavior of those whose actions risk causing accidents. In this sense the theory is highly practical, for it predicts how defendants who are economically motivated will behave in response to the threat of liability for negligence, however that concept is defined.

C. *A Boiled–Down Calculus: The Untaken Precaution*

It is sometimes said that the plaintiff is under no obligation to prove the particular safety measure that the defendant should have employed; rather, the plaintiff need only prove that in acting as he did, the defendant did not behave with reasonable care. This may be true, but in most cases the plaintiff goes further, and actually attempts to prove that there was a particular precaution that the defendant should have taken, and that, more probably than not, if this precaution had been taken the plaintiff would not have been

---

19. *See* Margo Schlanger, *Second Best Damage Action Deterrence*, 55 DePaul L. Rev. 517 (2006).

harmed.[20] Often the nature of the untaken precaution is obvious. If a defendant allegedly was inattentive and collided with the plaintiff at an intersection controlled by a traffic signal, the untaken precaution is the defendant's failure stop at the red light. Defendants who have been momentarily inattentive should have been paying attention. This is where the possibility of requiring perfect compliance with the reasonableness standard, referred to earlier, is implicated. Although in theory the negligence standard could take the high cost of achieving consistently reasonable conduct into account, that does not necessarily occur. The law permits a jury to find that a driver who takes his eyes off the road one time out of a hundred was negligent for doing so, and most juries probably would find negligence in this situation. In such cases, the implication is that the reasonable person never fails to behave reasonably.

In many cases, however, the best way to show that the defendant did not exercise reasonable care is to prove some less obvious precaution or safety measure that was available, inexpensive, and potentially effective. Disputes over the viability of an untaken precaution are often at the core of negligence cases involving activities with which jurors are not ordinarily familiar. Such disputes often presuppose something like the negligence calculus, even when it is not made explicit. The plaintiff points to a precaution and proves—sometimes through expert testimony, sometimes not— that it would have been easy enough for the defendant to have taken the precaution, especially in light of the risk of severe injury that the precaution would have reduced or avoided. Then the defendant attempts to show that the precaution could not easily have been employed, either because it would in fact be expensive, or would interfere with the easy or safe conduct of the activity. The dispute is formally about whether the reasonably prudent person would have taken the precaution, but that dispute is informed by evidence and argument about the factors that comprise the negligence calculus. But of course the evidence may not be quantitative in the way that the economic theory of negligence envisions.

IV. Custom

The rule governing "custom" is well-developed and reasonably clear. Evidence of non-compliance with custom may be used offensively (as a "sword") to show negligence, and evidence of compliance with custom may be used defensively (as a "shield") to show reasonable care. This evidence is relevant and admissible, but it is

---

20. *See* Mark F. Grady, *Untaken Precautions*, 18 J. LEGAL STUD. 139 (1989).

not dispositive. That is, even in the face of uncontradicted evidence of a party's compliance or non-compliance with custom, the jury may find that the party's action was or was not negligent.

Whether a particular practice is sufficiently widespread to constitute a "custom" may itself be in question. A practice need not be universal to constitute a custom, although it must be more than just one of a number of different practices. At the very least it must be something done by most of those whose behavior is relevant to the issue. If the practice in question does qualify as a custom, then the party on whose behalf the evidence of compliance or non-compliance was admitted is entitled to an instruction expressly permitting the jury to consider the fact that there was compliance or non-compliance with that custom. But even if a practice does not qualify as a custom, evidence of non-compliance with a practice in which some others engage may be admitted and considered by the jury anyway. The plaintiff is certainly entitled to point to an untaken precaution that he or she contends the reasonable person would take. Evidence that some others take the precaution helps to prove that it is reasonable to take it, even if it is not so widespread as to be customary. Even if the evidence is not admissible on the general question of negligence, it may be relevant to such questions as the feasibility of taking the precaution or the foreseeability of the risk that the precaution addresses. Thus, failing to prove that a practice with which a party did not comply is a custom ordinarily will not prevent the party from proving some of what he wishes— that the other party failed to take a precaution that some others take, although it probably will preclude showing how many others take the precaution.[21]

Why do we have a special rule about custom, when the effect of the rule is simply to make custom evidence admissible? After all, ordinarily we simply rely on the general rules of evidence, in particular the rule that relevant evidence is admissible unless there is a specific reason for rendering the evidence inadmissible, to determine whether evidence that purports to prove or disprove negligence, is admissible. Most tort law rules typically do not simply confirm or provide for the admissibility of evidence. They actually have some sort of binding effect. There are both historical and substantive reasons for having a separate custom rule.

A. *The History Behind the Custom Rule*

21. Kenneth S. Abraham, *Custom, Noncustomary Practice, and Negligence*, 109 Colum. L. Rev. 1784 (2009).

The historical explanation for having a separate, merely evidentiary rule about custom begins with the recognition that there was a time when the now-dominant custom rule had two competitors. Each of these rules addressed the significance of compliance with custom. One competitor was the rule that compliance with custom is conclusive on the issue of negligence. The leading case on the subject held that business custom was the "unbending test of negligence."[22] Under this rule, proof of compliance with custom provided a safe harbor and resulted in a holding that the defendant was free from negligence as a matter of law. The other competing custom rule was that compliance with custom was irrelevant and therefore that evidence of compliance was not even admissible.

The custom rule as we now know it competed with the safe-harbor and irrelevance rules. The rule was reflected in a series of 19th century cases and was then enshrined in the canonical opinion by Judge Hand in *The T.J. Hooper*.[23] In that case, the defendant was an operator of tug boats towing barges that were lost in a storm along with their cargo. The negligence alleged was the failure to supply the tugs with radios which would have warned them of the approaching storm. Although many tug boat captains carried their own radios, the court concluded that it was not the custom of tug owners to supply radios. Nonetheless, the court upheld a finding of negligence on the part of the tug owner for failing to supply radios: "Indeed in most cases reasonable prudence is in fact common prudence; but strictly it is never its measure; a whole calling may have unduly lagged in the adoption of new and available devices * * * [T]here are precautions so imperative that even their universal disregard will not excuse their omission." The court ruled that the failure to have radios was negligent as a matter of law, but in most cases whether a whole calling is negligent would be a jury question.

Thus, although the now-dominant custom rule is in a sense a weak rule because it is merely evidentiary, its historical force is stronger than appears on its face. Each of the rules that competed with the custom rule that eventually gained dominance was a strong rule. The safe-harbor rule was a *per se* no-liability rule. And the irrelevance rule precluded the jury from even considering custom. The modern, seemingly weak rule that merely makes evidence of compliance with or departure from custom admissible

22. Titus v. Bradford, Bordell & Kinuza Railroad Co., 136 Pa. 618, 20 A. 517, 518 (1890).

23. 60 F.2d 737 (2d Cir. 1932).

but not conclusive is actually a strong rejection of both of the two rules that once competed with it.

B. *The Rationales for the Rule*

Turning to the merits of the modern custom rule, we can identify a number of arguments in its favor. First, custom may have direct normative force. That is, based on experience and the authority that comes with a widespread way of doing things, custom may be probative of what constitutes reasonable care, because what is generally done often tends to be what ought to be done. The jury is therefore permitted, but not required, to get a reasonable care "ought" from a customary "is." Moreover, holding somebody liable for behaving like everyone else does (in the case of compliance with custom) will often seem unfair. Like expert opinion, however, evidence of custom is likely to be more persuasive when it is explained and justified on the merits, rather than merely asserted based on authority or general experience. The alternative to reliance on custom as authority or experience, therefore, is reliance on custom as confirmation of the proper cost-benefit determination. Persuading a jury that a particular custom has probative weight will therefore often require addressing the merits of the custom. That is, the proponent of custom evidence will attempt to show that the custom has been justifiably adopted, because the risks it poses are outweighed by its benefits. Similarly, in order to refute the normative force of custom evidence, the opponent of that evidence will attempt to show that the custom is too risky—that it does not satisfy a cost-benefit comparison.

Second, admitting evidence of compliance with custom cautions the jury that if it finds that an actor was negligent despite compliance with custom, the jury is in effect finding that an entire industry, and not a single actor, is behaving unreasonably. On the other hand, evidence of an actor's departure from custom assures the jury that in finding the conduct in question negligent it is not finding that the conduct of an entire industry is unreasonable. Of course, a party may be able to explain why he departed from the custom of his industry: complying with custom may have been dangerous under the circumstances, or he may reasonably (and perhaps correctly) believe that his precautions are superior to customary precautions. Third, evidence of compliance with custom is some evidence of the lack of an opportunity to learn of other precautions that might have been taken. And evidence of departure from custom demonstrates a party's opportunity to learn of a feasible precaution that might have been taken.

Fourth, in certain instances custom serves a coordinating function. Potential victims sometimes are aware of the customary practices of potential injurers. On this basis potential victims can make judgments about the necessary levels of self-protective care they should take themselves. Non-compliance with custom may thus tend to show negligence if the plaintiff can also show that the defendant knew or should have known that potential victims were relying on the defendant's taking customary precautions. Similarly, proof of compliance with custom may show that the defendant took the precautions that potential victims generally anticipate, and therefore may tend to show that the defendant's behavior was reasonable.

It could certainly be argued that, on average, departure from custom is more probative than evidence of compliance. An entire industry may well be negligent, but it would be rare indeed for an entire industry to exercise more care than is reasonable. Self-interested actors tend not to invest more in safety than they expect the law requires. There is therefore a potential argument for privileging evidence of departure from custom over evidence of compliance with custom. Some actors who depart from custom, however, do so not by exercising less care than is customary, but by exercising a different form of care than is customary. Evidence of sub-conformity is likely to be more probative than evidence of non-conformity, because a non-conforming practice may well be just as safe as the custom, whereas a sub-conforming practice is by definition less safe than the custom. But applying this distinction between sub-conformity to custom and non-conformity with custom would be necessary to invoke a rule that privileged evidence of departure from custom, and it would be administratively costly to do that. That may be a reason why we don't require that the two be distinguished.

Finally, the legal system also has an interest in promoting reliable and accurate decisions about whether conduct is or is not negligent. A trial with no evidence about how others engage in the same activity as the defendant would be curiously devoid of information that would be considered to relevant to decision making in almost any other context. Almost the first thing that most people deciding how to do something consider is how other people do it. As negligence cases move from simple to complex activities, from the familiar to the unfamiliar, juries need increasing assistance in understanding the nature of the activities under scrutiny and in forming judgments about the way in which to evaluate the degree of care that it is reasonable to employ in conducting these activities. Many jurors in the nineteenth century were capable of making such judgments about farming accidents almost without assistance, just as modern jurors are readily capable of determining whether the defendant in a run-of-the-mill automobile collision drove reasonably. But modern jurors are likely to know a lot less, for example, about the shipping industry, or about the various advantages and disadvantages of shatterproof glass. Evidence of industry custom— as well as of non-compliance with custom—can help to educate jurors about these activities and thereby to put them in a position to make more informed decisions.

V. Malpractice

In contrast to the rules that apply in ordinary negligence cases, different rules govern the conduct of professionals, including physicians, attorneys, and accountants. Most of the "action" in this field today involves medical malpractice, although in the future the continuing growth of the American service economy may spawn suits in a variety of fields. Medical malpractice litigation has grown exponentially in the last several decades. In 1960 across the nation, physicians and hospitals paid under $100 million for insurance against liability for medical malpractice—a rough measure of the direct cost of medical malpractice litigation. In contrast, over fifty years later, physicians and hospitals are paying more than $10 billion annually for such insurance—an increase of about 10,000 percent. A variety of factors have contributed to this enormous expansion in the cost of medical malpractice liability: legal changes permitting more suits; increases in the cost of health care, which is of course a component of the damages awarded for medical malpractice; the greater willingness of some people to bring suit against physicians, some of whom are merely specialists with whom the plaintiff has no longstanding relationship; the increased specialization and consequently greater ability of plaintiffs' attorneys; and, ironically, medical advances themselves, which create greater opportunities for medical "error" than in the past.

A. *The Special Standard of Care for Professionals*

In ordinary negligence litigation, the failure to comply with custom is not automatically negligent, and complying with custom is not automatically reasonable care. In contrast, in cases involving professionals, the majority rule is that compliance with custom insulates the defendant from liability, and failure to comply with professional custom is malpractice. A minority of jurisdictions seem to follow a general reasonableness standard, which makes evidence of compliance or non-compliance with professional custom admissible but not dispositive. In medical malpractice, the standards of the medical profession are the relevant "custom." Thus, the plaintiff's proof that the defendant committed malpractice consists of evidence that the defendant violated a standard of the profession. Conversely, the defendant's case on the issue consists of evidence that the defendant complied with the standards of the profession. Indeed, in many jurisdictions a "two schools of thought" or "respectable minority" rule obtains, under which non-compliance with a standard rejected by much of the profession is not malpractice, as long as the defendant complied with a school of thought or practice followed by a respectable minority of practitioners.

What justifies so radical a departure from the treatment of custom in ordinary negligence cases? The answer must lie in necessity. As a general matter the activity that is the subject of scrutiny in professional liability cases is considerably more complex, and the jury is substantially less familiar with it, than the activities that are the subject of ordinary negligence cases. In a medical malpractice case, for example, to ask the jury to go beyond professional standards to determine whether it was reasonable for the defendant to follow a particular medical course of treatment would in effect ask for the jury's medical judgment—something that no member of the jury is likely to be capable of giving without relying heavily on evidence of the relevant professional standard.

For the reader who thinks that this approach lets physicians and other professionals off too easily, remember that the dispositive effect of custom in medical malpractice cases cuts both ways: although compliance with custom automatically insulates the physician from liability, deviation from custom is malpractice. One might even argue that, to the extent that the justification for this overall approach is the jury's inability reliably to adjudicate cases involving complex, technical, and scientific issues, the problem is not that malpractice law departs from the normal treatment of custom, but that the law ought to find a way to apply the approach to custom taken in professional liability cases to complex cases involving non-professional liability as well. After all, the jury is just as likely to be at sea in making judgments about what constitutes reasonable care in other technically complex and unfamiliar cases as it is in medical malpractice cases. Yet largely for reasons of history and continuing solicitude for professionals—one group of whom are appellate judges who are former practicing lawyers—the special rule governing professional liability has not spread to other areas.

Another reason for the application of the special standard to professionals alone is that in practice the standard may not operate so differently from ordinary cases. Like most legal issues, many difficult medical issues cannot be resolved by reference to a definitive, black-letter professional standard; medical judgment is required. Expert testimony therefore does not usually point to a precise professional standard that governs the problem that the defendant faced. Rather, experts for each side tend to testify about what they would have done in the defendant's place, and what they believe good medical practice required. Often this kind of testimony could be interpreted to be about medical custom and to trigger the insulation from liability afforded by the "respectable minority" rule referred to earlier. But a number of courts interpret such testimony as being in conflict about what the prevailing medical standard actually is, and leave that question to the jury. In addition, of course, many malpractice cases turn heavily on disputed facts and must therefore go the jury regardless of the prevailing standard of care. Given the maze of facts and issues presented to it, the jury may well give the court's instruction on the respectable minority rule less consideration than might otherwise be expected. This may help to explain how it is possible that malpractice costs have risen 10,000 percent during a fifty-year period in which compliance with custom purportedly has provided physicians with immunity from malpractice liability.

B. *The Demise of the "Locality" Rule*

The demise of the locality rule is another factor that has contributed to the escalating cost of medical malpractice liability. That rule operated in the following way. Proof of the relevant medical standards almost always is provided in the form of expert testimony by physicians practicing in the defendant's specialty. Without such testimony the plaintiff could not survive the defendant's motion for a directed verdict or judgment as a matter of law, since the jury is rarely familiar on its own with the relevant standards. For many years this testimony had to come from a physician competent to testify as to the medical standard prevailing in the defendant's own community. Often courts held that only a physician actually practicing in that very community could provide such testimony. This "strict locality" rule made it extremely difficult for a potential plaintiff to secure an expert both competent and willing to testify. In any locale where physicians knew each other well and worked together, personal colleagues often were reluctant to testify against each other. The result came to be called the "conspiracy of silence," since it often appeared to plaintiffs and their attorneys that physicians "conspired" not to testify against their colleagues. When plaintiffs could not secure an expert witness whose testimony would be admissible pursuant to the strict locality rule and such a witness was a prerequisite to making out a *prima facie* case, there was no point in going to trial, and sometimes no point even in making a claim.

The strict locality rule may have made sense when medical standards varied significantly from community to community, especially when the limited resources available in small communities influenced or dictated the kind of treatment that could be provided. As the degree of variation declined and medical standards became increasingly uniform and national, however, the justification for the strict locality rule diminished. At that point the rule served mainly to place an artificial obstacle in the way of plaintiffs' search for experts willing to testify on their behalf. A rule that had once been grounded in the substantive differences between localities became a technical requirement without much substance to support it.

It is no surprise, therefore, that the rule broke down in a variety of ways and then eventually disintegrated. For example, some courts held that although the standard to be applied in assessing the defendant's conduct still was that of the locality in which she practiced, physicians from other localities who had familiarized themselves with the standards of the defendant's locality were competent to testify about those standards. Other courts went further, holding that the strict locality rule was too restrictive, and that the appropriate test to measure the defendant's conduct was the standard of practice prevailing in the same locality or localities "similar" to the locality where the defendant practiced. With the increasing nationalization of medical standards, this approach is tantamount to the adoption of a national standard but with a soft restriction on those who can testify to the standard, perhaps with some leeway for taking into account any limitation on resources available in smaller communities. Finally, many courts (including some of those that first took only one of the intermediate steps just described) have gone all the way in rejecting any form of locality rule, holding instead that national standards govern and that any expert familiar with such standards can testify about them.

The result has been a much more freewheeling litigation environment, in which some physicians have become professional witnesses, spending most or even all of their time as experts in litigation rather than practicing medicine. A number of states have enacted rules limiting potential witnesses to those who still practice medicine, or have other, advanced medical qualifications such as board certification. In some states things have thus come full circle from the old days of the conspiracy of silence, and concern is frequently voiced about excessive numbers of frivolous malpractice suits. Although available data do not support the claim that more than a small proportion of malpractice suits are completely groundless, other criticisms of the system can be made. For example, only a fraction of those who are injured by medical malpractice actually sue and obtain recoveries. Conversely, some of those who do obtain recoveries appear, from a careful retrospective examination of their records, not to have been the victims of malpractice. Apparently the system is not terribly good at compensating deserving claimants, and has mixed success at denying compensation to claimants whose claims do not warrant it. In short, there is a considerable mismatch between those who deserve compensation under the rules governing malpractice and those who receive compensation.

C. *The Duty to Disclose and Informed Consent*

Over time there has developed a cause of action distinct from ordinary medical malpractice, based on the physician's duty to disclose relevant treatment-related information and the failure to obtain the patient's informed consent to treatment. The interest protected by this cause of action is the patient's right to determine whether to take the risks associated with any given form of medical treatment. A totally unconsented to treatment would of course constitute battery. In contrast, actions for informed consent sound in negligence or malpractice, for they involve the claim that although the patient consented to treatment, consent was not sufficiently informed because of the physician's failure to provide the patient with the requisite information about the risks and benefits associated with the treatment.

1. **Disclosure and Informed Consent Standards**

Most medical treatments involve some risk. The treatment itself may not succeed; pain, inconvenience, or disturbance of normal bodily functions may accompany treatment; and some treatments or procedures may risk serious, permanent side effects such as incontinence or paralysis. The doctrine of informed consent requires the physician to inform the patient of these risks, so that the patient may decide whether to take the risks of submitting to treatment, to seek alternative treatment, or to select no treatment at all. Because for most people the decision whether to risk the possible side effects of medical treatment depends on what is to be gained from the treatment, the physician must also inform the patient of the benefits of the treatment, including the probability that it will or will not be successful. Note that to prevail on a claim sounding in informed consent the plaintiff need not show that the treatment that was provided was malpractice. Rather, the plaintiff may prevail even when the treatment was provided in accordance with all relevant medical standards, *if* the treatment resulted in bodily injury and *if* the plaintiff would have decided not to consent to even properly provided treatment if he or she had been adequately informed.

In recognizing the need to protect patients' interests, however, we must take care not to adopt too unrealistic a view of the process by which informed consent is obtained. There is a difference between an "informed" decision by the patient and an "independent" decision by the patient. The doctrine of informed consent attempts to secure the former, not the latter. Sometimes the opinions in cases involving the doctrine speak as if the two were the same, and that the physician's disclosure of information transmits to the patient everything needed for the patient to make a treatment decision. This ultra-rationalistic model of patient decision-making is unrealistic. Many patients who find that they have serious medical problems become psychologically dependent on others, including their physicians. This condition of dependency, along with genuine ambivalence about what treatment to pursue, is not compatible with the ultra-rationalistic model of patient decision. The doctrine of informed consent quite properly requires that patients be informed of the risks and benefits of proposed treatments. But patients in a condition of dependency and vulnerability are unlikely simply to take the information and make entirely independent decisions about treatment. They will want to talk at length with their family and their physicians to obtain the opinion of these other people about the right course of treatment to follow. It may be that the most salutary function of the doctrine of informed consent, therefore, is not simply to inform the patient, but to help the patient's physician, family, and friends to open an informed dialogue with the patient about the course of treatment that will best reflect and protect the patient's values and concerns.

There are two different standards for determining whether the requirements of the doctrine of informed consent have been satisfied. The *reasonable-patient* standard requires the physician to disclose information about the risks and benefits of treatment that a reasonable patient in what the physician knows to be the patient's situation would wish to know.[24] This standard does not ask the physician to be a mind-reader; if the patient has unusual

24. *See Canterbury v. Spence*, 464 F.2d 772 (D.C.Cir.1972).

interests or concerns of which the physician is unaware, then disclosure of information that a reasonable patient would not desire but that this patient would in fact have desired is not required. If I am a model for male earrings and therefore cannot risk scarring to my ear under circumstances that would not trouble the ordinary patient, then my physician is not liable for failing to disclose the risk of scarring if she has no reason to be aware of my idiosyncratic situation. On the other hand, once the physician knows of the patient's unusual interests or concerns, then the disclosure necessary to satisfy those interests or concerns is required.

The reasonable-patient standard employs what amounts to an ordinary negligence test to determine whether proper disclosure has been made and informed consent has been obtained. Evidence of medical standards regarding information disclosure may be relevant in actions brought under this standard, but is not dispositive: under the reasonable-patient standard, the failure to obtain informed consent is not actionable as malpractice, but as negligence. Consequently, expert testimony still is ordinarily required in order to establish what the risks and benefits of the treatment in question were; but there need be no expert testimony regarding the defendant's violation of the standard of care because the jury, having heard this expert testimony, is then in a position to determine what a reasonable patient would have wanted to know under the circumstances.

In contrast, under the *reasonable-physician* standard the failure to obtain the patient's informed consent is actionable only as malpractice. The plaintiff-patient must therefore meet the requirements of a malpractice action by proving that the defendant-physician failed to comply with the standards of the profession regarding disclosure of information to patients in the plaintiff's position. Expert testimony is required not only as to the relevant risks and benefits, but also as to the applicable medical standard regarding disclosure of these risks and benefits.

On their face these two standards represent very different philosophies. The reasonable-patient standard appears to put the patient in complete control, rejecting medical determination of the information to be disclosed. The reasonable-physician standard seems to place the medical profession in control, permitting the profession to determine what information the patient needs to know. In practice, however, most contemporary physicians, simply out of concern for their patients, tend to disclose the information that they think their patients want, regardless of the jurisdiction in which they practice. Consequently, the medical standard for disclosure and patient desires for information are likely to converge, notwithstanding the logical possibility that under the reasonable-physician standard the profession as a whole could decide to disclose only a little information, without fear of liability. In fact, the courts probably would not be comfortable with the reasonable-physician standard if that were to occur. The major differences between the two approaches, therefore, lie in the requirement that there be expert testimony as to the applicable standard of disclosure under the reasonable-physician standard, and in the possibility that liability will be imposed less often under that standard where the respectable-minority rule applies.

2. Causation in Informed Consent Cases

Even after the plaintiff has proved the failure of the defendant to make proper information disclosure, proof of a causal connection between that failure and the plaintiff's injury is required. The matter of causation is the subject of another Chapter, but a brief exploration here helps to tell us a bit more about informed consent. To prove causation, the plaintiff must show that "but for" the defendant's failure to disclose the requisite information, the plaintiff would not have suffered the harm resulting from the treatment provided. Ordinarily this means that the plaintiff must show that he would have declined the treatment that caused his injury if he had been given the requisite information about the risks posed by the treatment. Some courts also require the plaintiff to show that the treatment he would have selected (including no treatment) would have caused less injury.

Proving causation in an informed consent case often is difficult, because many people—perhaps most—take the advice of their physician even after he or she has disclosed the information required by the doctrine of informed consent. People are likely to decide to follow a physician's advice except in two situations: when there are two plausible courses of treatment and the physician recommends one but believes the other also to be reasonable; and when the patient is sufficiently idiosyncratic that the physician's sense of what risks are worth taking and the individual's sense of this are very different. Of course, the plaintiff would not even be suing if she did not contend that, had the requisite information been disclosed, she would have chosen a different course of treatment. Consequently, the plaintiff's own conclusory testimony on this score may not be worth very much as proof for the jury.

Many courts have therefore adopted what amounts to an objective standard governing the causation issue. There are two views of what this standard entails. Under what might be called the fully-objective standard, the test is what an objectively reasonable person without the plaintiff's idiosyncrasies and particular preferences would have done if she had been appropriately informed. This approach makes it unnecessary for the jury to sift through the plaintiff's contentions about what her idiosyncracies actually were. But of course the price for avoiding this complexity is that sometimes the plaintiff will be unable to recover, even though she would in fact have declined the treatment—i.e., even though the defendant's failure to obtain informed consent was in fact the cause of the plaintiff's harm.

In contrast, under what might be called the semi-objective view, the test is whether a reasonable person in the plaintiff's position would have declined treatment if the requisite information on risks and benefits had been disclosed. The plaintiff is permitted to testify, and her idiosyncracies and preferences are relevant, but her testimony is simply one piece of evidence for the jury about what she would have done had her informed consent been properly sought. With the benefit of hindsight the plaintiff may now believe that she would have declined treatment; but the question for the jury is what a reasonable person in the plaintiff's position would have done. In this regard the plaintiff's testimony can be either almost useless or extraordinarily helpful. If the plaintiff merely asserts that she would have disregarded her physician's advice, but without providing a persuasive explanation for this contention, the jury may regard the testimony as merely self-serving. But if the plaintiff identifies a previously documented or manifested idiosyncracy or value that would have caused her to disregard her physician's advice, such testimony can be very persuasive. The plaintiff may have an unusual concern about scarring, or prefer a shorter life expectancy without the rigors of chemotherapy. As the court in *Scott v. Bradford* put it, "the causation question must be resolved by examining the credibility of the plaintiff's testimony."[25] If these sorts of idiosyncracies or values asserted by the plaintiff can be corroborated through evidence about plaintiff's past behavior or even serious conversations with others in the past reflecting these values or idiosyncracies, then the plaintiff's testimony will be all the more credible. For example, suppose that the plaintiff's close friend testifies that they had engaged in many conversations over the years about the pride the plaintiff took in her left profile. Under these circumstances the plaintiff's testimony that she would have rejected surgery on her left cheek if she had been informed of the risk of scarring would have greater credibility than it would otherwise.

---

25.   606 P.2d 554 (Okl. 1979).

These considerations suggest that there are really two different interests that may be protected by the doctrine of informed consent. First, by using a semi-objective test for causation, the doctrine can protect the interest of patients who do not share the values of their physicians or of most patients, and who would therefore act differently from the ordinary patient if adequately informed of the risks and benefits of proposed treatment. Second, even if the test for causation is fully objective, the doctrine can encourage the dissemination of information to the great mass of "ordinary" patients who will take their physicians' advice with or without the information, but whose autonomous right to make informed decisions is promoted by encouraging physicians to make fuller disclosure of the risks and benefits of treatment.

D. *Medical Malpractice Reform*

The rising cost of malpractice insurance and the concern of physicians about the threat of liability have led some states, over a period of decades, to enact statutory reforms of medical malpractice law. The statutes address a variety of doctrines and practices, some of which are discussed generally in subsequent Chapters. Major reforms affect the qualifications of expert witnesses, limit the application of the doctrine *res ipsa loquitur* (Chapter Four), place monetary ceilings on the amount that may be awarded as damages for pain and suffering (Chapter Ten), reform the collateral source rule (Chapter Ten), require the submission of cases to pre-trial screening panels that make non-binding decisions, specify the percentage of a recovery that attorneys for plaintiffs may charge, and restrict the application of joint-and-several liability (Chapter Five).

Aside from the adoption of monetary ceilings on damages in malpractice cases, empirical studies suggest that the reforms have a modest or no effect on the cost of insurance or on the amounts awarded in malpractice cases. Nonetheless, medical malpractice reform periodically finds a place in debate about tort reform that is out of proportion to its direct economic importance, which is about two percent of the cost of health care in the United States. One reason is that medical malpractice liability has an indirect economic impact. Physicians sometimes engage in "defensive medicine"—the ordering of laboratory or other tests which they would not order were it not for the threat of liability. The cost of defensive medicine is unclear, though it may be a multiple of the amount spent on medical malpractice insurance itself—$40 billion a year, as compared to $10 billion a year for malpractice insurance. Of course, some defensive medicine is "positive," reflecting expenditures that are desirable and that the threat of liability encourages. Other defensive medicine is "negative," reflecting unnecessary and undesirable testing that physicians think makes legal, but not medical, sense to order.

Another explanation for the prominence of medical malpractice reform proposals is that physicians occupy a critical place in the health care structure. Thus, when obstetricians decide not to deliver babies any more because of the high cost of malpractice insurance, their decision gets considerable attention, for obvious reasons.

Finally, medical societies and other physicians' organizations are able to exercise political influence that individual practitioners could not exercise. As a consequence of these and other factors, it seems likely that medical malpractice law will continue to occupy a place on the reform "agenda," and that more fundamental reforms (of the sort discussed in Chapter Twelve) that do not alter tort liability, but create a substitute for it, will be considered and perhaps even adopted in the future.

VI. Violation of Statutes

We live in an age of statutes. For this reason, many acts alleged to be negligent also violate statutes. Federal statutes are sometimes held to preempt (i.e., preclude) the imposition of state tort liability, either expressly or by strong implication. Most preemption cases involve products liability, a subject addressed in Chapter Nine, where preemption is also discussed.

Conversely, from time to time statutes create civil liability for their violation, again expressly or by implication. Most statutes say nothing, however, expressly or impliedly, about the role their violation is to play in tort actions. The standard approach in this situation holds that the unexcused violation of a statute designed to promote safety is negligence "per se"—that is, negligence as a matter of law. A minority of states hold that violation of a statute is not negligent per se, but evidence of violation is admissible and relevant. And all states hold that evidence of compliance with a statute is admissible, although such evidence usually does not have much weight, because statutes only prescribe minimum standards. Reasonable care may require more than mere compliance with a statutory requirement.

The majority, negligence per se rule was enunciated by Judge Cardozo in the famous case of *Martin v. Herzog.*[26] If the legislature actually provided in each statute it enacted that there shall be an

---

26. 126 N.E. 814 (1920).

action in tort for injuries caused by violation of the statute, then the reason for this standard approach would be easy to see. But as noted above, most statutes do not contain such provisions. Occasionally statutes provide for such causes of action, but more often they provide only for criminal penalties in the event of violation. One might even speculate—though probably inaccurately—that since the legislature knows how to include a cause of action for statutory violation in the laws it enacts, the absence of such provision should be taken as an expression of legislative intent that there be no such cause of action. Consequently, legislative intent is not a satisfactory explanation of the rule that violation of a statute is negligence per se.

It is more accurate to understand the negligence per se rule as a common law creation, based on the notion that the reasonable person does not violate statutes. The result is that in the ordinary case, the jury is not permitted to decide whether the violation of a statute was or was not negligent: the unexcused violation of a statute is negligence. In some jurisdictions the rule also applies to the violation of administrative regulations and municipal ordinances, though often such violations are only considered evidence of negligence. In any event, since sometimes the violation of a statute can be "excused," technically there is only a presumption that violation of a statute is negligence per se. Under this formulation, in the absence of a competent excuse the jury is required in the majority of states to find that violation of a statute is negligent. In the minority that do not apply the negligence per se rule, virtually all putative excuses are admissible and subject to consideration by the jury.

A. *Legally Cognizable Excuses*

Under the negligence per se rule a great deal may then turn on when a party may be "excused" for the violation of a statute. The conventional categories of excuse are somewhat opaque: necessity, incapacity, and emergency. The cases themselves, however, shed some light on their meaning. Children are excused if they are incapable of complying with a statute; reasonable efforts at compliance by adults, even when there is a violation, are sometimes sufficient; if an individual does not have a reasonable opportunity to know of factual circumstances that make a statute applicable, he may be excused; and if noncompliance is safer, then the excuse of emergency may be available. For example, in *Tedla v. Ellman*,[27] the

---

27.   19 N.E.2d 987 (1939).

plaintiff was struck by the defendant's vehicle while she was walking with her back to the traffic on her side of a road instead of walking with her face to the traffic on the other side of the road, as a statute required. The plaintiff argued that she was not negligent, because on that day the traffic was much heavier on the side of the highway where the statute seemed to require her to walk, and that it would therefore have been much more dangerous for her to comply with the statute than to violate it. In an opinion not distinguished for its clarity, the court agreed, seeming at least in part to suggest that a statute (such as the one in question) that codifies a common law rule rather than reversing it should be read to contain an implied exception for cases in which compliance with the statute would involve a greater risk of harm than violation. But it may also be sensible to think of *Tedla* as involving the excuse of necessity.

The significance of these categories is not simply that they are limited, but also that they provide the courts with a means of ruling out some putative excuses as a matter of law. In negligence per se states, merely because the defendant contends that his statutory violation was excused does not mean that the excuse issue goes to the jury. If the defendant testified that he was speeding because he was driving his son to school and they were late, the court would almost certainly rule that the defendant's putative excuse is not legally cognizable. In the absence of any factual dispute as to violation, therefore, the defendant would be negligent per se.

B. *The Defense of Limited Statutory Purpose*

A second defense permits the defendant to show that the plaintiff was not in the class of persons, or did not suffer the type of harm, intended to be protected by the statute that the defendant violated. For example, in *Di Caprio v. New York Central Railway Co.*,[28] the defendant violated a statute requiring that fences be erected to keep livestock off its tracks. There was no recovery when the plaintiff's young son was killed after wandering onto the tracks, because protection against this risk was not the object of the statute.

Despite the theoretical availability of this defense in cases involving violation of statute, the defense rarely prevails in practice. Statutes usually do not carry their purposes on their face. Rather, their purpose is a matter of judgment and of judicial

---

28.   131 N.E. 746 (1921).

construction. Unless the plaintiff could not by any stretch of the imagination have been an intended beneficiary of the statute's protection, modern courts are likely to hold that at least a "secondary" purpose of the statute was to protect individuals in the plaintiff's situation. There are a number of cases in which defendants have violated statutes apparently designed mainly for the protection of persons other than the plaintiff, yet the courts hold that those in the plaintiffs' situation do fall within the class of those protected. For example, "dram shop" statutes in many states prohibit the sale of alcoholic beverages to those who appear to be inebriated. In a number of cases the individual who has been served in violation of the statute is shortly thereafter involved in an auto accident in which a third party is injured. The plaintiff third party then sues both the driver and the server, and the server's defense is that the statutory protection does not extend to the plaintiff. Many courts reject this defense, construing the statutory purpose broadly.[29] Similarly, statutes or municipal ordinances sometimes prohibit leaving vehicles parked with keys in the ignition. When a thief steals a vehicle parked with a key in the ignition and his negligent driving injures the plaintiff, the courts typically hold that the purpose of these enactments is not only to protect the vehicle's owner, but also to protect those who might be injured by the negligent driving of the thief. The defense of limited statutory purpose therefore does not protect the owner or custodian of the vehicle in a suit by a third party injured by the thief's negligent driving.[30]

There are two ways of predicting how the courts will rule on this scope-of-statutory-purpose issue. The first is to see whether there is legislative history or a preamble to the statute in question, indicating its purpose or purposes. If there is any reference at all to those in the plaintiff's situation, then the courts are highly likely to find that the plaintiff is an intended beneficiary, or that the plaintiff suffered the type of harm contemplated by the statute. The absence of such reference, however, is not determinative: the courts may still find one or both to be the case.

The second predictor is more complicated. If violation of the statute does not at all increase the risk of harm to those in the plaintiff's situation, then the courts are very unlikely to hold that the plaintiff is an intended beneficiary. It would not be sensible to say that a statute is intended to protect a particular class of persons if violation of the statute does not increase the risk to those in the

29. *See, e.g., Vesely v. Sager*, 486 P.2d 151 (1971).
30. See, e.g., *Ross v. Hartman*, 139 F.2d 14 (D.C.Cir.1943).

class. For instance, suppose that I borrow your car and the car is damaged by lightning while I am exceeding the speed limit. I am negligent per se; and if I had not been speeding, the car probably would not have been damaged by the lightning, because it would have been at a different place when lightning struck. Violating the statute, however, did not increase the risk of lightning damage; therefore you are not in the class of intended beneficiaries, at least as to this risk. In contrast, if violating a statute does increase the risk of harm to those in the plaintiff's situation—such as the plaintiffs in the dram-shop and key-in-the-ignition cases—then the courts may well hold that the plaintiff falls within the class of the statute's intended beneficiaries. The greater the increase of risk to those in the plaintiff's situation resulting from a violation of the statute, the greater the probability that the court will hold that the statute protects the plaintiff. All this sometimes takes place under the rubric of "proximate cause" (a subject that we take up in Chapter Six) rather than negligence per se, but the analysis is essentially the same.

VII. Negligence and No Negligence as a Matter of Law: The Roles of Judge and Jury

Thus far we have been exploring the ways that the law pours meaning into the concept of negligence, largely in order to assist the jury in making the negligence determination. This exploration has assumed that the jury ordinarily makes that determination. But that is not always the case. First, there is a class of cases in which the defendant is not liable for negligence. An example involves a landowner's limited duty to trespassers. A landowner is not liable to a trespasser for injury caused by the failure of the landowner to exercise reasonable care, but only for injury caused by wanton and wilful misconduct. Duty and no-duty questions such as this are typically decided by the court as a matter of law. These no-duty cases are the subject of Chapter Eleven, which addresses affirmative and limited duty.

Second, even when the defendant has a duty to exercise reasonable care to persons in the plaintiff's position, there are cases in which, as a matter of law, the defendant did, or did not, breach that duty. For example, as we have already seen, in the case of the violation of statutes that decision is kept from the jury and made by the court as a matter of law. But there is also a general rule about whether an issue is or is not a jury question. Issues are submitted for decision by the jury if "reasonable people could disagree" about the resolution of the issue. And issues are decided by the court as a matter of law if "reasonable people could not disagree." This rule applies both to pure questions of fact (i.e., entirely empirical issues) and to mixed questions of fact and law, such as whether a party was negligent—that is, whether the party breached its duty to exercise reasonable care.

The decision whether a particular issue poses a jury question is made at trial through rulings on motions for a directed verdict and, in more complicated situations, through jury instructions. For example, if there is uncontradicted evidence that I drove blindfolded down Main Street and collided with the plaintiff's vehicle, then whether I was negligent will not be a jury question. Rather, at the close of the evidence the court would grant the plaintiff's motion for a directed verdict on the issue of my negligence. Reasonable people could not disagree that I was negligent. But if the factual question whether I drove blindfolded is in dispute, then the court could not simply grant a directed verdict on the issue. Instead, the jury will be instructed that, if it finds that I drove blindfolded, then it *must* find that I was negligent, because driving blindfolded is negligent as a matter of law.

This is, in effect, lawmaking by the courts about what constitutes negligence. In granting a motion for a directed verdict on the negligence issue, a court is not ruling that a jury *would not* find for the defendant, but that the jury *should not* and therefore *may not* so find, because it would be unreasonable to do so. There is of course an element of judgment involved in the granting of directed verdicts on mixed questions of fact and law. The judgments of different trial courts on such questions involving the same or similar sets of facts are therefore harmonized through the appellate process. Whether a directed verdict should have been granted is a question of law that can be reviewed and decided on appeal. Over time, this process of review can give the trial courts guidance regarding the kinds of questions that should and should not be submitted to juries. If the rationale for ruling that particular behavior was or was not negligent as a matter of law is broadly applicable (e.g., that it is negligent to drive blindfolded, or to violate statutes), then the decision in effect creates a rule of law about that conduct. On the other hand, if the rationale for the decision is applicable only to the unique set of facts presented in the case, then it is more in the nature of a ruling that there was negligence (i.e., breach) as a matter of law in this case than it is a rule with any generality.

There is also considerable significance in a decision to deny a motion for a directed verdict, that is, to decline to rule that conduct was or was not negligent as a matter of law. In holding that reasonable people could disagree about the negligence issue in a particular case, a court is necessarily implying that a decision for either the plaintiff or for the defendant would be acceptable. Since the only precedent set by such a holding is that the facts of the case pose a jury question, it follows further that if the same situation arose again, it would be acceptable for a different jury to decide the issue differently. This is hardly a prescription for deciding like cases alike, notwithstanding that such treatment is a core principle in our system. The only equal treatment that like negligence cases receive in this respect is that they are submitted to the jury for decision.

Over a century ago, writing in THE COMMON LAW, Holmes argued that this state of affairs was unacceptable:

> But supposing a state of facts often repeated in practice, is it to be imagined that the court is to go on leaving the standard to the jury forever? Is it not manifest, on the contrary, that if the jury is, on the whole, as fair a tribunal as it is represented to be, the lesson which can be got from that source will be learned? Either the court will find that the fair teaching of experience is that the conduct complained of usually is or is not blameworthy, and therefore, unless explained, is or is not a ground of liability; or it will find the jury oscillating to and fro, and will see the necessity of making up its mind for itself.

Nearly four decades later, as a Justice of the U.S. Supreme Court, Holmes put his idea into practice in *Baltimore and Ohio R.R. v. Goodman*.[31] Goodman was killed when the truck he was driving was struck by the defendant railroad's train at a grade crossing. The railroad's defense was that Goodman was negligent as a matter of law and that since contributory (i.e., the plaintiff's) negligence was then a complete defense, the case could not go to the jury. The trial court denied the railroad's motion for a directed verdict in its favor, and submitted the issue (plus others) to the jury, which found for the plaintiff. The U.S. Supreme Court reversed, holding that "nothing is suggested by the evidence to relieve Goodman of responsibility for his own death" and that, if necessary, someone in Goodman's situation "must stop and get out of his vehicle, although obviously he will not often be required to do more than to stop and look." Thus, the Supreme Court held that a directed verdict should have been granted for the defendant because the plaintiff was negligent as a matter of law. It is probably not entirely a coincidence that the rule in *Goodman* meant that the U.S. Supreme Court, in that pre-*Erie* era in which appeals of tort suits involving diversity of

---

31. 275 U.S. 66, 48 S.Ct. 24, 72 L.Ed. 167 (1927).

citizenship came to the Court, would be presented with fewer such suits.

Seven years later, however, Holmes' ideal of a set of rules about what counts as breach of the duty to exercise reasonable care that could be applied without the need for jury decisions and their accompanying variability was dealt what has turned out to be a fatal blow. In *Pokora v. Wabash Railway Co.*,[32] the U.S. Supreme Court was faced with a similar though not identical fact situation. The trial court directed a verdict for the defendant on the authority of *Goodman*. In an opinion by Justice Cardozo the Supreme Court reversed, noting that

> Standards of prudent conduct are declared at times by the courts, but they are taken over from the facts of life. To get out of a vehicle and reconnoitre is an uncommon precaution, as everyday experience informs us. * * * In default of the guide of customary conduct, what is suitable for the traveler caught in a mesh where the ordinary safeguards fail him is for the judgment of a jury.[33]

In effect, the Court said that the plaintiff in *Goodman* may have been contributorily negligent as a matter of law given the particular facts of his case, but that it does not follow that everyone who has not stopped, looked, listened and (if necessary) gotten out of his car at a railroad crossing is contributorily negligent. That depends on the circumstances.

The move from *Goodman* to *Pokora* reflects the treatment that Holmes' view has received generally. There has not been a tendency over time for rules of law to develop regarding the kind of behavior that is and is not negligent. Rather, if anything, the courts' inclination has been to leave juries with even greater discretion and to grant fewer directed verdicts.

This entire issue involves the distinction between *rules* and *standards* that was referred to in Chapter One. Rules are comparatively concrete, comparatively self-applying norms. Standards are more general norms that require comparatively more judgment and discretion for application. Each has its particular characteristics. Rules facilitate predictability of outcome and therefore are likely to produce more settlements. Rules more easily treat like cases alike. Rules have a greater capacity to avoid the dangers inherent in the exercise of discretion, including prejudice. And in negligence cases, rules may circumvent the conundrum of when inadvertence is

---

32. 292 U.S. 98, 54 S.Ct. 580, 78 L.Ed. 1149 (1934).

33. 292 U.S. at 104–06, 54 S.Ct. at 582.

negligent and when it is not. This is because a rule that a particular form of conduct is or is not negligent as a matter of law makes the reason the conduct occurred immaterial. Whether violation of a safety statute was inadvertent or deliberate, it is negligent *per se* unless excused.

In contrast to rules, standards permit greater flexibility. They leave more room for nuanced distinctions between fact situations. And they are more conducive to doing justice, all things considered. Of course, these are pure types. In fact there is a continuum running from pure rules at a high level of generality on one end, to pure under-all-the-circumstances standards on the other. In the time since Holmes wrote and recommended the greater use of directed verdicts, with the implication that there should be a greater use of rules, the tendency has been to reject his recommendation.

There are two reasons why things have developed this way. First, fact situations that are sufficiently similar to warrant the development of rules of law governing them have not recurred. Instead, the courts have usually concluded—as did Justice Cardozo in *Pokora*—that reasonable people could consider the factual variations between cases such as *Goodman* and *Pokora* to be sufficiently important to permit juries to decide them differently. Just as not every railroad grade-crossing accident is the same, so not every lane-changing automobile accident and not every slip-and-fall case is the same. Second, it is both politically less dangerous and less elitist for elected judges (and most state judges, who hear most tort cases, must stand for re-election) to leave close decisions about norms of behavior to juries rather than deciding these issues themselves. In the long run such decisions probably have greater preceived legitimacy and help to reduce the influence of politics on the outcome of tort claims.

However, the kinds of cases in which the position Holmes took is most satisfactory are precisely those that are constantly recurring because they arise out of precisely the same facts. For example, in *Andrews v. United Airlines, Inc.*,[34] the court ruled that whether the defendant had breached its duty to maintain safe overhead bins on its airplanes was a question for the jury. Since bins are identical on all of the same model of aircraft, this is likely to be a recurring question. Similarly, the modern, mass tort or class action cases in which the same product or behavior is alleged to have injured large numbers of people raise recurring questions. If these kinds of cases are tried individually, then the question of the defendant's negli-

---

34. 24 F.3d 39 (9th Cir. 1994).

gence must be submitted to different juries dozens or hundreds of times, and the same action or product design can be judged negligent or not negligent by many different juries. If, for example, a defendant failed to warn purchasers and other users of the dangers of exposure to asbestos in 1963, many commentators would argue that at some point that behavior should be judged either negligent or not once-and-for-all, rather than permitting dozens of juries to "oscillate to and fro" on the issue, as Holmes put it. The courts have tried to find ways to give a definitive answer, but through only partially effective modern procedural devices such as collateral estoppel and class actions, rather than through the rules of law that Holmes envisioned.

4

PROOF OF NEGLIGENCE

Ordinarily there is nothing distinctive about proving negligence. The plaintiff introduces direct evidence of the defendant's behavior and contends that the defendant failed to take a precaution that it would have been reasonable to take. This may be real physical evidence (e.g., a misassembled tool), demonstrative evidence (e.g., a video of the accident), or eyewitness testimony. Sometimes, however, direct evidence of what the defendant did or did not do is unavailable. In such cases negligence is not proved directly, but by circumstantial evidence. This Chapter is about how negligence is proved in cases such as this, and about a doctrine that is sometimes used in aid of proving negligence—*res ipsa loquitur*, or literally "the thing speaks for itself." In order to understand proof of negligence by circumstantial evidence, as well as *res ipsa*, it is necessary first to understand the allocation of the burden of proof in negligence and other tort cases generally.

I. The Burden of Proof

A. *Burdens in the Ordinary Case*

The plaintiff in a tort suit bears the burden of proof on each element of his case. That burden is composed of two parts: the *burden of production* and the *burden of persuasion*. The burden of production is sometimes termed the burden of "going forward with the evidence." After all the plaintiff's evidence is introduced, that evidence must be capable of supporting an inference by the jury that the defendant breached the applicable standard of care, that the plaintiff suffered injury or loss, and that the defendant's breach caused this injury or loss. In negligence cases, of course, the plaintiff must prove breach by showing that the defendant was negligent. This means that based on the evidence an inference of negligence must be permissible, not that such an inference is required. Satisfying the burden of production is sometimes referred to as making out a *prima facie* case.

The decision whether the plaintiff has satisfied the burden of production is made by the court, which makes this decision by ruling on the "legal sufficiency" of the evidence. If the evidence is legally sufficient on all elements—if "reasonable people could disagree" as to each element—then a motion for a directed verdict by the defendant at the close of the plaintiff's case is denied. If the evidence is legally insufficient on one or more elements, then the defendant's motion for a directed verdict is granted. In contrast to the legal sufficiency question, the jury actually determines the "weight" of the evidence. Merely because the evidence is legally sufficient to permit an inference of negligence does not mean that the jury is required to draw that inference. When an inference of negligence is merely permissible then an inference of no negligence also is permissible.

Once the burden of production is met and the evidence goes to the jury, the plaintiff bears the burden of persuasion. The jury is instructed that the plaintiff has satisfied this burden only if it is persuaded by a preponderance of the evidence that the defendant breached the applicable standard of care, that the plaintiff suffered injury or loss, and that the defendant's breach caused this injury or loss. If, for example, the jury finds that it is only as probable as not that the defendant was breached the applicable standard of care (that the evidence as to this element is "in equipoise"), then the plaintiff has not satisfied the burden of persuasion. The jury must be persuaded that the defendant "more probably than not" breached the applicable standard of care, or the plaintiff has not satisfied her burden of persuading the jury by a preponderance of the evidence.

It is sometimes observed that this approach ignores the mathematical theorem that the probability that each of a series of independent propositions is true is the product of their separate probabilities. Thus, if the probability that 1) the defendant was negligent, 2) the plaintiff suffered an injury, and 3) the defendant's negligence caused the plaintiff's injury were each 75 percent, then the probability that the defendant was negligent and caused an injury to the plaintiff would be roughly 42 percent ($.75 \times .75 \times .75 = .421875$) and—speaking mathematically alone—the plaintiff would have failed to satisfy his burden of proof.

There are several possible explanations, however, for the law's declining to apply this product-of-the-probabilities theorem to the burden of persuasion. First, even the simple mathematics of the theorem may be too complicated for many jurors. Second, in most jurisdictions the decision of the jury must be unanimous or comprise a super-majority (for example, 10 out of 12). The requirement of unanimity or near unanimity helps to ensure a high degree of confidence by the jury in its findings that offsets the product-of-the-probabilities theorem. Third, if the theorem were applied, then the defendant would have an incentive to generate a series of factual issues for jury determination, in order to benefit from the impact of the theorem. According to the theorem, if there were 10 separate factual propositions at issue, the likelihood that all were true would be substantially below 50 percent even if the independent probability that each individual proposition was true were over 90 percent. Finally, in the typical case, in which both sides submit evidence as to each disputed issue, the practical issue for the jury is which side's contentions have a greater probability of being true. That is, once the party bearing the burden of production has satisfied that burden, the jury's task is to assess the comparative persuasiveness of the parties' positions, not to calculate probabilities. For all these reasons, the product-of-the probabilities theorem does not figure in the burden of persuasion.

The next issue is how the plaintiff actually proves negligence. Because negligence is the failure to exercise reasonable care, typically negligence is proved by showing 1) what the defendant did; and 2) that what the defendant did or failed to do did not constitute reasonable care. In addition, it is virtually always in the interest of the plaintiff also to show 3) what would have constituted reasonable care, though it is sometimes said that such proof is not required. In nearly every case, therefore, the plaintiff attempts to prove some untaken precaution that he or she contends would have constituted reasonable care on the part of the defendant and that would have avoided the injury at issue.

B. Circumstantial Evidence of Negligence

A difficulty arises, however, if the plaintiff does not have specific evidence of what the defendant did or did not do, or of all the potentially relevant facts associated with the cause of the plaintiff's injury. Then there is only circumstantial evidence that the defendant was negligent, if there is evidence at all. Sometimes proof of the circumstances is sufficient to permit an inference of negligence, but sometimes it is not. For example, suppose that you are walking in the fruit and vegetable aisle of the local supermarket when you suddenly slip and fall. Immediately after the fall you see a fresh yellow banana peel stuck to your foot. In your negligence suit against the supermarket you prove only these facts, plus the scope of your injuries.

You have a problem. A jury would be permitted to infer that you had fallen because of the presence of the banana peel on the aisle. And a jury would be permitted to find that the defendant was required to use reasonable care to assure that there were no banana peels in its aisles. But, based on these facts alone, should a jury be permitted to find that the defendant had failed to exercise reasonable care?

I think not. In this case the plaintiff has not introduced evidence of what the defendant did or failed to do that was negligent.[1] The defendant might be expected to conduct periodic, perhaps even frequent inspection of its aisles to remove dangerous material from them. But the evidence is not sufficient to permit any inference that such inspections were not conducted. For all anyone knows the banana peel had only been in the aisle a few seconds before the plaintiff slipped on it. Reasonable people could not find that the defendant should be constantly inspecting that very aisle. A simple Learned Hand calculus confirms this—people would not want to pay a price for fruit and vegetables that included the cost of constant guarding of the aisles where they are shelved. Note that this is not a conclusion that the defendant was *not* negligent; it is only a conclusion that a jury would not be warranted in drawing any inference, one way or the other, about whether the defendant was negligent.

All of this follows from the fact that the plaintiff bears the burden of production: the jury could not conclude based on the evidence that, more probably than not, the defendant did not conduct a reasonably frequent and competent inspection. Therefore, after the plaintiff has rested his case, the defendant would move for a directed verdict on that ground, and the court would—or should—grant that motion, without requiring the defendant to introduce any evidence at all. At first glance this may seem unfair, since we do not at this point know whether or not the defendant was negligent; we simply do not have enough evidence one way or the other to decide. But the very idea behind the burden of production is that the plaintiff must introduce evidence from which the jury could conclude that the defendant was negligent; the defendant need not prove that it was not negligent.

Now let us change the hypothetical a bit. Suppose that all the facts are the same except that the banana peel on which the plaintiff slipped was turning brown. Can the plaintiff now survive the defendant's motion for a directed verdict? This is a much closer question. It is a matter of common knowledge, not really needing any proof, that banana peels tend to darken after they have been removed from bananas for a period of time. Consequently, the plaintiff has now introduced some evidence—though admittedly not very much—from which it could be inferred that the peel had been

---

1. *See Goddard v. Boston & Maine Railway Co.*, 60 N.E. 486 (1901).

on the floor for more than just a moment when the plaintiff slipped on it. And based on the permissible (though not required) inference that the peel had been on the aisle for more than just a moment, it might be permissible for a jury to conclude that a reasonably frequent and competent inspection of the aisle would have discovered the peel and caused it to be removed during the period when the peel was on the floor.

Nonetheless, some courts still would grant the defendant's motion for a directed verdict, because the evidence of the banana peel's condition provides only a very slight basis for inferring that it had been in the aisle long enough to have been discovered by a reasonable inspection.[2] There are other alternatives, and the evidence gives the jury only a slight basis for choosing among them: the peel might have been removed from a brown, ripe banana and dropped on the floor just a moment before the plaintiff slipped on it; or someone might have carried the peel into the store and dropped it on the floor just a moment before the plaintiff encountered it. Based on ordinary experience these seem to me to be less probable alternatives, however, and if I were the trial judge I probably would deny the defendant's motion for a directed verdict. But the point here is that, because the evidence now supports a finding that the peel had been lying in the aisle for some time, the facts of this revised hypothetical come much closer than do the facts of the first hypothetical to permitting an inference that the defendant did not conduct a reasonable inspection. Of course, the evidence merely creates a *permissible* inference that the defendant was negligent. The jury is still free to find that the defendant was not negligent, except in those rare cases in which reasonable people could not disagree.

Notice that this analysis proceeded without any need for the use of the Latin phrase *res ipsa loquitur*, or reference to anything speaking "for itself." The question was simply whether there was enough evidence to support an inference that the defendant had not conducted an adequate inspection of the aisle in its supermarket. In the first hypothetical the answer clearly was that there was not enough evidence and that the plaintiff therefore did not meet the burden of production. In the second hypothetical the question was closer. The great mistake that students of this subject often make is to jump too quickly to the use of the Latin phrase *res ipsa loquitur* in situations such as these, instead of engaging in hard-headed analysis. *Res ipsa loquitur* is not a substitute for evidence. Rather,

---

2. *See, e.g., Joye v. Great Atlantic and Pacific Tea Company*, 405 F.2d 464 (4th Cir.1968).

as we will see, it is a doctrine about what counts as legally sufficient circumstantial evidence of negligence.

Unfortunately, there can be no general principle to use in determining when there is enough circumstantial evidence to warrant saying that a particular type of accident does or does not ordinarily happen because of negligence. For example, in *McDougald v. Perry*,[3] a 130 pound spare tire came out of its cradle underneath the defendant's trailer and collided with the windshield of the plaintiff's vehicle. The question was whether the jury could infer negligence in this situation. The court held that the case should go to the jury, stating that in the usual circumstantial case the inference of negligence is drawn on the basis of "past experience" that is "common to the community." Obviously, however, the court could not have been referring to a common community experience with this particular kind of accident. Rather, the experience in question is the common, intuitive understanding of laypeople about how the physical world usually works when things are done right. A good deal of judicial judgment is required to make this assessment, and in close cases a defendant may well wonder how the court knows the teaching of experience on the issue in question.

Sometimes the possible causes of an accident are sufficiently technical that there is no common past experience that can resolve the issue. In such situations many jurisdictions permit expert testimony to supply the crucial factual predicate that the kind of accident that occurred does ordinarily happen because of negligence. Medical malpractice cases, in which neither courts nor jurors have a common "past experience" on which to base the necessary judgments, are a prime example.

In light of all this, one might plausibly wonder when, if ever, there is any need for a special doctrine regarding proof of negligence. Thus far, all we have seen is that in the absence of direct evidence of negligence, sometimes circumstantial evidence is sufficient to permit an inference of negligence, and that sometimes circumstantial evidence is not sufficient to permit such an inference. The question, then, is whether (and if so, when) there is any need for a separate "doctrine" in these kinds of cases.

II. *Res Ipsa Loquitur*

In fact there is a class of cases in which a particular form of circumstantial evidence of negligence is introduced, and the doc-

---

3.   716 So.2d 783 (Fla.1998).

trine *res ipsa loquitur* is invoked. To the extent that the doctrine does identify a particular class of cases, they involve circumstantial evidence that the defendant was probably negligent in some way, without supporting an inference of the particular way in which the defendant was negligent. Thus, if a defendant's car left a 300 foot skid mark on a street with a 25 mile per hour speed limit, the skid mark is circumstantial evidence that the defendant was exceeding the speed limit. Strictly speaking, this is not a *res ipsa* case, because there is evidence (though circumstantial) of what the defendant's negligence consisted of. On the other hand, if the defendant's vehicle struck the plaintiff on a sidewalk, there is circumstantial evidence that the defendant was negligent in some way, but not of the particular way in which the defendant was negligent. He may have been inattentive; may have swerved to avoid an animal but have been unable to control his vehicle because he was speeding; or his vehicle may have malfunctioned because he had failed to have it properly maintained and inspected. Further, the cause of harm in such instances usually is not, but in this case nonetheless may have been, someone else's negligence (e.g., the manufacturer of the car) or someone else's non-negligent conduct (a freak breakdown of the steering linkage not caused by any defect in design or fabrication of the car). Because defendants who collide with people on sidewalks ordinarily do so because of negligence of some sort on their part, there is sufficient circumstantial evidence of negligence to permit the plaintiff's case to go to the jury. *Res ipsa loquitur* is the doctrine confirming that circumstantial evidence of this particular sort will support a jury verdict that the defendant was negligent in some undetermined way.

Res ipsa loquitur has long been so firmly established in tort doctrine that black-letter prerequisites to its application have been developed. It is always a condition of invoking the doctrine that the event causing the plaintiff's injury must be one that

(1) ordinarily occurs because of negligence by someone in the defendant's position.

The traditional approach also adopts the following requirements:

(2) the instrumentality causing the injury must be within the exclusive control of the defendant; and

(3) the injury must not be due to any voluntary action or contribution by the plaintiff.

Note that, taken together, these are bright-line prerequisites to a finding that, all things considered, the defendant was negligent. Requirement (2) is especially rigid, and over time caused the courts to balk. In contrast, the modern formulation takes a less bright-line and less restrictive view, simply requiring that causes other than the defendant's negligence (the defendant's non-negligent conduct, the negligent conduct of someone else, and the non-negligent conduct of someone else or some thing) be sufficiently eliminated by the evidence. That is, the evidence must support an inference that the cause of the plaintiff's harm was the defendant's negligence rather than all other possible causes. In effect, this approach applies requirement (1) but not requirements (2) and (3).

Both sets of requirements are ways of stating what it takes to establish a circumstantial case of negligence on the part of the defendant, though of course the modern approach is considerably more flexible than the traditional one. Note also that, in most jurisdictions, the application of *res ipsa* means only that there is a permissible inference of negligence. The jury is still free to find for the defendant, even if the defendant introduces no evidence that it was not negligent. In a few jurisdictions, however, the application of *res ipsa* creates a presumption of negligence that actually has weight.

A. *Applications*

When the requirements of *res ipsa* are met, in most jurisdictions the effect is that the jury is permitted, though not required, to find that the defendant was negligent. This means at the least that the plaintiff survives the defendant's motion for a directed verdict at the close of the plaintiff's case. Ordinarily it also means that the case will go to the jury, although occasionally the evidence thereafter presented by the defendant shows as a matter of law that the defendant was not negligent and the defendant is granted a directed verdict at the close of his case. For example, suppose that the plaintiff shows that he was a passenger on the defendant's train when it derailed. Such accidents ordinarily do not happen in the absence of negligence. Therefore the plaintiff has made out a *prima facie* case on negligence. But then the defendant proves by undisputed evidence that moments before the train derailed the track had been sabotaged, without any warning or reason to expect sabotage. Probably the defendant would then be granted a directed verdict.[4] But in the absence of such a definitive, undisputed defense, the plaintiff's *res ipsa* case goes to the jury.

In most jurisdictions the jury is given an instruction that states the applicable requirements of *res ipsa*, though without naming the

---

4. *See Kanter v. St. Louis, Springfield, & Peoria R.R.*, 218 Ill.App. 565 (1920).

doctrine. States applying the traditional rule instruct the jury as to requirements (1), (2), and (3) noted in the preceding section. States applying a more modern approach apply only requirement (1), simply instructing the jury that it is entitled to decide that the defendant was negligent based on the circumstantial evidence introduced, if accidents such as the one in question ordinarily happen because of the negligence of those in defendant's position, rather than due to other causes.

The application of *res ipsa* is illustrated by *Byrne v. Boadle*,[5] one of the earliest cases to employ *res ipsa loquitur* expressly. The plaintiff there was struck by a barrel of flour that fell out of a window of the defendant's warehouse. The plaintiff introduced no evidence of the manner in which the barrel came to fall or that the defendant's employees were responsible. The court held that the plaintiff had nonetheless made out a *prima facie* case, because there are some cases in which the mere fact of the accident having occurred is evidence of negligence. In these cases "the thing speaks for itself," and what it speaks of is negligence.

It is worth recognizing that, from one point of view, *res ipsa loquitur* does not actually do any work in situations such as this, other than naming a subclass of cases in which there is sufficient circumstantial evidence of negligence. That is, on the facts of *Byrne v. Boadle* the plaintiff has made out a *prima facie* case on the two issues that often figure in cases in which *res ipsa* is invoked: identification of the defendant as the party physically in control of what occurred, and negligence of some sort by the defendant or its employees. First, on those facts it would be permissible to infer that the defendant's employees were responsible for the barrel's falling. After all, the barrel fell from the defendant's warehouse. It is of course possible that someone other than the defendant's employees was responsible (a customer supervising the lowering of the barrel out the warehouse window, for example), but in the absence of any other evidence on the issue, proof that the barrel fell from the defendant's warehouse satisfies the plaintiff's burden of production by identifying the defendant as the party who is probably responsible for the negligence in the case, if any. Second, based on this evidence it would be permissible for the jury to find that barrels ordinarily fall out of warehouse windows because of negligence, and therefore that the defendant was negligent in having failed in some way or other to take reasonable precautions to prevent the barrel from falling.

5.   159 Eng.Rep. 299 (Ex.1863).

On this point of view, the case is simply one in which the evidence on both issues satisfies the plaintiff's burden of production. What distinguishes the case from an ordinary negligence suit is that, because there is no direct evidence of what the defendant's employees were or were not doing at the time the barrel fell, and no circumstantial evidence of any particular untaken precaution, the plaintiff cannot point to a specific act of negligence that caused the barrel to fall. Many cases in which *res ipsa loquitur* is invoked share this characteristic. They are simply cases in which there is only circumstantial evidence on the issues of identification and negligence, but that evidence is sufficient to satisfy the plaintiff's burden of production. In such cases *res ipsa* is merely a label for this class of cases. That is, the doctrine does not create any inference that is not already permissible anyway on the basis of evidentiary probabilities alone.

There is a point a view that understands *res ipsa* always to do work, that is, to make a difference, when it is applicable. The implication of this point of view, however, is that if were not for the doctrine, the cases to which it applies would not go to the jury. Under the traditional approach I can understand this point of view. Under this approach there must be evidence satisfying requirements (1), (2), and (3) for application of *res ipsa*, and if there is not such evidence, then the case does not go to the jury, even when there is circumstantial evidence of the defendant's negligence. Under the modern approach, however, only requirement (1) must be satisfied, and requirement (1) seems merely to state that if there is circumstantial evidence of the defendant's negligence, the case can go to the jury. Surely this is just a statement of the ordinary rule governing circumstantial evidence, not a basis for getting to the jury that is added by *res ipsa*.

In any event, whichever requirement or requirements are applied, an instrumentalist way to understand res ipsa, is to think of the decision that the plaintiff has met his burden of production as a way of minimizing the degree of error that would otherwise result. Suppose that in cases like *Byrne v. Boadle* the plaintiff were held not to have satisfied his burden of production, and that the defendant's motion for a directed verdict were granted at the close of the plaintiff's case. If it is in fact true that barrels do not ordinarily fall out of warehouse windows in the absence of negligence by the warehouser, then the probability is at least 51 percent that the defendant has been negligent when a barrel does fall. If the defendant's motion for a directed verdict is nonetheless granted in such cases when there is no direct evidence of negligence, then the defendant wins 100 percent of the time. The rate of error is therefore at least 51 percent, since ordinarily a barrel does not fall in the absence of negligence. On the other hand, if the plaintiff is held to have satisfied his burden of production, then even if there is no other evidence at all and even if the jury finds for the plaintiff 100 percent of the time, the error rate is 49 percent or less, because the defendant is in fact negligent at least 51 percent of the time. Thus, submitting the case to the jury produces a lower rate of error than granting the defendant's motion for a directed verdict.

B. *"Smoking Out" the Evidence from the Defendant*

All of this, of course, assumes that the defendant will not produce any evidence. If the defendant's motion for a directed verdict is denied, however, then unless the defendant presents some evidence in an effort to show affirmatively that he was not negligent, the case will go to the jury with only the plaintiff's evidence, and the jury will probably draw the inference it is permitted but not required to draw—that the defendant was in fact negligent. Note, however, that in states where *res ipsa* permits an inference but does not create a presumption of negligence, a jury is not required to find for the plaintiff even when the defendant has not introduced any evidence tending to show that it was not negligent. Nonetheless, denying the defendant's motion for a directed verdict on the ground that the plaintiff has satisfied his burden of production creates a strong incentive for the defendant to put on some kind of case. In *Byrne v. Boadle* this might have consisted of testimony (for example) by the defendant's employees indicating how careful they were being when the barrel fell, or indicating that the pulley holding the rope being used to lower the barrel unexpectedly broke.

Because invoking *res ipsa loquitur* results in the denial of defendant's motion for a directed verdict at the close of the plaintiff's evidence, it is sometimes said that the great advantage in cases where *res ipsa* is invoked is that the defendant is then forced to present evidence—forced, that is, to defend himself rather than hide behind the difficulty the plaintiff faces in adducing direct evidence about the accident. Indeed, older decisions sometimes said that cases in which the defendant had superior access to evidence on the negligence issue were particularly appropriate for use of *res ipsa*.

On this view, *res ipsa* is not merely a label, but actually performs the function of "smoking out" evidence in the possession of the defendant. If this were often true and the ordinary rules of evidence would have dictated that the defendant's motion for a directed verdict at the close of the plaintiff's case be granted, *res ipsa* would do real work: the doctrine would create an artificial inference of negligence, in order to give the defendant the incentive to explain what actually happened. The inference would be "artificial" because, if the ordinary rules governing drawing an inference of negligence from circumstantial evidence would on their own have required that the defendant's motion for a directed verdict be denied, then there would be no need for *res ipsa*. Ironically, then, in this situation *res ipsa* actually would more than merely label what would have happened anyway, because it would be invoked in precisely in those cases in which the thing does not speak for itself!

How often *res ipsa* is in fact needed in order to perform this function, however, is open to question. In the days before modern discovery, it may well have been true that the only way to force the defendant to produce direct evidence about the accident was to wait until trial and then to deny his motion for a directed verdict at the close of the plaintiff's case. Indeed, the court in *Byrne v. Boadle* seemed to think that the plaintiff could not have made out his *prima facie* case by calling witnesses from the defendant's warehouse to prove that they were negligent. Perhaps this was because the court believed that the witnesses would not tell the truth, but it may also have been because in the absence of discovery the plaintiff would not have known in advance what they would have said. But with the aid of modern discovery procedure, today's plaintiff could depose under oath everyone who was involved in handling the barrel and everyone responsible for safety at the warehouse. Whatever the defendant's employees know about the accident, the plaintiff can force them to disclose during discovery. Any evidence generated in this manner that is favorable to the plaintiff can then be adduced as part of the plaintiff's *prima facie* case. Thus, it may be that *res ipsa* came into being partly in order to help smoke-out evidence that was not otherwise available to the plaintiff. But it may equally be true today that because of modern discovery the doctrine is no longer needed to perform this function.

C. *The* Ybarra *Problem*

A situation in which *res ipsa* still might perform the function of smoking-out evidence involves multiple defendants. Suppose that two or more parties have control over a possible cause or causes of harm, but the plaintiff cannot prove which party's negligence caused the harm. For example, a landlord and its commercial tenant might both have control of rooftop tiles, or a group of physicians and nurses might have control of a patient while he is unconscious. If, through discovery, the plaintiff would otherwise be unable to obtain evidence of which party's negligence caused harm, the threat of liability might cause the party who has that information to disclose it.

Should *res ipsa* apply in these situations, even though it cannot be said, regarding any individual defendant, that the harm in question ordinarily happens because of the negligence of someone in that defendant's position? In both the hypotheticals I have just posed, the defendants are in a sense connected to each other. They may not be conducting a joint enterprise, but they neither are they strangers. This means, first, that they are more likely to have information about the quality of each other's conduct than strangers. If a flower pot falls out of the window of a building containing fifty apartments, there is little reason to believe that some occupants will have observed the quality of care exercised by the others. But landlords and tenants, physicians and nurses, are more likely to have observed each others' conduct. Second, the fact that the defendants are connected to each other also means that there is greater justification for imposing on them a duty either to observe each others' conduct or, in the absence of observation, to bear responsibility for it. The physicians and nurses in a large hospital may not literally know each other, but they are engaged in a common effort within the four walls of the hospital. The possibility that they may end up being liable for each other's conduct often seems more acceptable than it would be if they were not connected in any way.

The result is that in situations of shared control, whether simultaneous or serial, and especially in medical situations where the plaintiff/patient was injured while he was unconscious, the courts have sometimes been willing to apply *res ipsa loquitur* to multiple defendants. Perhaps the most celebrated case in which this occurred was *Ybarra v. Spangard*.[6] In that case the plaintiff, a patient who underwent surgery in a hospital, awoke with an injured neck after an appendectomy. He sued several different health care providers who had treated him, one of whom more probably than not committed malpractice while he was unconscious. No single defendant was more probably than not negligent. But absent the application of *res ipsa* none of the defendants would have had an interest in telling what they knew. None of the defendants had any financial incentive to reveal what, if anything, he or she knew about the injury because each would automatically be granted a directed verdict at the close of the plaintiff's case. The

---

6.   25 Cal.2d 486, 154 P.2d 687 (1944).

party who had actually caused the plaintiff's injury obviously had no incentive to do anything but stay silent, and none of the other defendants who may or may not have witnessed the act of negligence of another had any incentive to do anything but stay silent either. Without evidence regarding which defendant was responsible for the injury, the plaintiff could not have survived the defendants' motions for a directed verdict at the close of his case, because each individual defendant was less likely than not to have been negligent. The Supreme Court of California held, however, that *res ipsa* applied. This meant that there was an incentive for any defendant who did have relevant evidence to testify about what he or she knew. But on remand each of the defendants testified that nothing untoward had occurred in handling the patient. The trier of fact then found them all liable.

Invoking *res ipsa* in *Ybarra* created the possibility of smoking-out evidence from one of the defendants who had witnessed another's malpractice, or from the particular defendant who had actually committed the malpractice in question, who might have preferred to admit his wrongdoing rather than see his or her colleagues held liable for something they did not do. But in order for *res ipsa* actually to be able to smoke-out the evidence, two factors must exist in situations such as *Ybarra*: 1) One or more of the defendants must actually have knowledge about the cause of the plaintiff's injury that would be useful as evidence. This will not necessarily be the case, since sometimes no defendant will have any evidence of negligence to provide. One of the defendants may simply have mishandled the patient's neck without anyone, including that defendant, knowing it. 2) Any defendant who does have evidence that would be useful to the plaintiff must be willing to lie under oath in a deposition but willing to tell the truth under oath at trial. Otherwise *res ipsa* is not needed, since the defendant would reveal his evidence in a deposition and that evidence could then be used as part of the plaintiff's case in chief at trial even if *res ipsa* were not available to get the plaintiff past a motion for a directed verdict. I suppose that sometimes both factors will exist, but how often is not at all clear. Just as often, I suspect, either no defendant will have any useful evidence, or the party who does have it will not be willing to reveal it at all, preferring to have his or her malpractice insurer pay his or her fraction of the judgment instead of "ratting" on a colleague. The price that must be paid in order to use *res ipsa* to smoke-out evidence when it is in fact capable of being smoked-out, therefore, is to permit the jury to impose liability on all the defendants, even when none has any evidence and even when all but one of them, in all probability, were not negligent.

This analysis reveals that the strength of the argument for *res ipsa* as a means of generating otherwise unavailable evidence in multiple-defendant cases, depends in part on two empirical questions that are not really answerable at a general level: in cases in which there is no direct evidence of negligence and the circumstantial evidence alone is legally insufficient, how often there is any evidence to be smoked out, and how often would *res ipsa* smoke it out? If there were good reason to believe that often there is evidence to be smoked out and that *res ipsa* often could do the smoking, then that would justify the doctrine's separate existence. In light of the limited number of situations in which *res ipsa* is likely to be useful in this way, however, then what is its function in multiple defendant situations? I think that for those who support applying the doctrine in these situations, the risk of error that would result from invoking *res ipsa* even when the thing does not speak for itself is worth tolerating because, in their view, strict liability is preferable to negligence as a basis for liability. On this view, invoking *res ipsa* when the thing does not speak for itself and no evidence is smoked out simply permits the jury to impose strict liability through a verdict of negligence. *Res ipsa* under these circumstances is a way of obtaining under-the-table strict liability. Invoking the doctrine properly holds liable a set of defendants who are connected to each other in a way that justifies holding them responsible for the harm each other causes.

The trouble with this view is that it is unclear how to limit this notion. Does it apply only in hospitals? Only when the plaintiff was unconscious when he was harmed? Or does it apply whenever a set of defendants, one or more of whom may have negligently caused harm, are connected to each other in a way that justifies making them legally responsible for either producing evidence or bearing responsibility for each other? What is it about the category of cases in which there is no direct evidence of taken or untaken precautions—that is, the category of cases in which *res ipsa* is potentially of value to the plaintiff—that warrants making these particular cases special candidates for strict liability? Why set things up so that the jury can most easily impose strict liability in the very cases in which there is the least evidence of negligence? For possible answers we will have to await the discussion of strict liability in Chapter Eight.

5

CAUSE–IN–FACT

In any tort suit the plaintiff must prove not only that the defendant was negligent or otherwise breached the applicable standard of care, but also that the defendant's act or omission caused the injury or damage for which the plaintiff claims compensation. This means proving that, in the absence of the tortious conduct of the defendant, the plaintiff would not have been injured. Notice that this seemingly simple, single issue actually may involve one or more components: 1) what caused the harm, 2) who caused the harm, 3) whether negligence caused the harm, and 4) what part of the harm was caused by what or whom.[1]

In many cases this is an utterly straightforward matter to prove. If the defendant fails to stop his vehicle at a red light and collides with the plaintiff's vehicle proceeding with the green light, there is no question that the defendant's negligence caused the plaintiff's harm. But in other cases the issue is more difficult. In such cases understanding the purposes served by the causation requirement becomes more important, because these purposes help to inform application of the requirement to the facts at hand. And often in these problematic cases the complexity of the very idea of causation becomes evident.

I. The "But For" Test

The simplest and most widely accepted test for cause-in-fact is the "but-for," or *sine qua non* test. This test requires a determination whether, "but for" the defendant's negligence (or breach of another applicable standard of care), the plaintiff would have suffered injury or damage. If the answer is "no," then cause-in-fact is proved. But if the answer is "yes," then ordinarily the test is not satisfied and the defendant is not liable, because the plaintiff would have been injured even if the defendant had not been negligent. For example, suppose that a person falls off a boat that negligently carries no life buoys to throw to those in the water. That person sinks immediately below the surface and drowns.[2] Although the

1. Dan B. Dobbs, THE LAW OF TORTS 405–07 (2000).

2. For a case whose facts are highly similar to this hypothetical, see *New York Central R.R. v. Grimstad*, 264 F. 334 (2d Cir.1920).

defendant was negligent, that negligence was not a but-for cause of the drowning. Even if there had been a buoy to throw, there would have been no way for the buoy to reach the person drowning, because he sank beneath the surface immediately. On the other hand, if the decedent had bobbed onto the surface several times before drowning, it might be a jury question whether a properly placed buoy could have been thrown to him and would have saved him. But some courts would require testimony about the likely placement of each omitted buoy, and the throwing ability of those who were on board at the time, before permitting the causation issue to go to the jury.

Note that there are many causes in fact—but-for causes—of any event. Being a cause-in-fact is not the same as what, in common parlance, would be called the "responsible" or the main cause of an occurrence. In an automobile collision case, if the defendant's parents had not met, if the defendant had not travelled to work on the day of the collision, if the defendant had not gone to college, bought a car, or run the red light, he would not have collided with the plaintiff. The key is whether one of these many but-for causes was negligent. If so, then the act or omission of the party responsible for this negligence is "a" cause-in-fact. A but-for cause, however, is not necessarily what we would call "the" cause of the plaintiff's harm. Being a negligent but-for cause makes a defendant eligible for liability, so to speak, but the defendant is not liable unless his negligence was also a "proximate cause"—a concept examined in the next Chapter. To put it another way, if the defendant's negligence was not a cause-in-fact of the plaintiff's harm then ordinarily there can be no liability, because the defendant's negligence was not even "a" cause of the plaintiff's harm. To be a negligent cause-in-fact is a necessary, but not a sufficient, condition of liability.

Unlike pure empirical questions of fact, and unlike mixed questions of fact and law, the causation question is not factual, but "counterfactual." It does not require a finding of what actually happened, but of what would have happened if the defendant had not been negligent. We cannot actually rewind a hypothetical recording of the accident, remove the defendant's negligence, and see what happened. Instead, the jury must rely on its own experience and knowledge of the world to make its decision about what would have happened. The but-for test asks the jury to engage in retrospective prophecy. And it asks the court, in ruling on whether the evidence of causation is legally sufficient to go to the jury, to determine whether an inference of what would have happened if the defendant had not been negligent is permissible.

Because of the counterfactual nature of causal proof, all we can do is ask the jury to make a judgment, based on the evidence and its own experience, about what would have happened if the defendant had not been negligent. The counterfactual nature of causal proof therefore requires the assumption that the jury has knowledge of it own, or testimony from experts, about the way the world typically works in the accident situation under scrutiny. This means that jurors' own conscious or unconscious biases about what is normal, including what they think of the capacities of different groups of people—young and old, men and women, etc., may affect jury decisions.[3] The more strictly we require that there be a concrete experiential basis for making that judgment before submitting the case to the jury, the more often we will say that the plaintiff has not made out a *prima facie* case on the causation issue. In this sense, cause-in-fact is a bit like *res ipsa loquitur*. In *res ipsa* a case goes to the jury only if an inference of negligence *in this situation* is permissible because of what in general happens *in situations like this*. Similarly, in cause-in-fact disputes a court must decide whether an inference about what would have happened *in this situation* if the defendant had not been negligent is permissible, because of what ordinarily happens *in situations like this* when the defendant has not been negligent.

There is no rule about precisely how much narrative detail a court will require before ruling that the plaintiff's burden of production on the causation issue has been satisfied. The courts have a tendency, other things being equal, to prefer evidence about the particular case at hand over generalizations about situations. To return to the earlier drowning hypothetical, jurors know generally that people who fall into bodies of water manage to stay on the surface for a while, and that people trying to rescue those who fall into the water often react aggressively to such emergencies. For some courts that would be enough evidence that the negligent absence of a buoy was a but-for cause of the decedent's drowning. For other courts, however, there would not be enough evidence about causation in "this" particular case without proof of where a buoy would have been placed and the ability of those on the boat to throw it. Apparently the courts want to have a comfort level that there is evidence about the very situation being litigated rather than merely about situations generally resembling this one. Partly this stance is a product of the way most people think about causation, and partly it is a legacy of distrust of statistics and

3. Martha Chamallas & Jennifer B. Wriggins, THE MEASURE OF INJURY 128–29 (2010).

generalizations from a time when these were less reliable than they often are now.

Instead of the but-for test, some courts occasionally ask whether the defendant's negligence was a "substantial factor" in bringing about the plaintiff's injury or damage. The "but-for" test requires a finding that, more probably than not, the defendant's negligence was a prerequisite to what happened, whereas the "substantial factor" test could be understood merely to require a finding that the defendant's negligence was influential in some way. That is not a helpful way of thinking about the problem. It may be that, for reasons of policy, there should be exceptions to the but-for test in certain classes of cases. But substituting the substantial factor test is a vague way to achieve that end. Therefore, except in cases (described later) where multiple separate acts of negligence each would have been a sufficient but-for cause of the plaintiff's harm, the substantial factor test is misleading and unhelpful. As a general alternative to the but-for test, the substantial factor test is therefore rejected by most courts.

A.   *"Self–Proving" Causation: Fall–Downs, Dart–Outs, and* Zuchowitz

There is a set of cases in which the courts hold that the plaintiff has introduced sufficient evidence of causation if the negligence of the defendant substantially increased the chance that the plaintiff would be injured. But negligent conduct always increases the chance that someone or something will be harmed; that is one of the defining and necessary features of negligent conduct. Conduct that does not increase the risk of harm is not negligent. All negligence cases involve an increased risk of harm, but not necessarily a substantial increase and not necessarily of a single form of harm. For example, conduct that only slightly risks harm may still be negligent if it risks great harm. And conduct that moderately increases the risk of a number of different forms of harm to different categories of plaintiffs may be negligent. So the notion that, in cases where negligence *substantially* increases the risk of harm to the plaintiff, there is sufficient evidence of causation, seems to suggest that, in this set of cases, evidence of negligence is evidence of causation, because the main thing that makes the conduct negligent is that it substantially increases the probability of causing the particular kind of harm that occurred. Causation in such cases is, in this sense, "self-proving."

One such set of cases involves plaintiffs who slip and fall, often on negligently maintained stairs. Another involves plaintiffs who

suddently dart out into a street and are run down by a speeding
vehicle. In these cases the plaintiff might have fallen if the stairs
had been properly maintained, or been struck by the vehicle even if
it had not been speeding. For example, in a case cited in many
casebooks, *Reynolds v. Texas & Pacific Ry. Co.,*[4] the plaintiff
weighed 250 pounds and was warned to hurry up to catch a train.
Hastening down unlighted steps, she fell and was injured. In the
plaintiff's suit alleging negligence on the part of the railroad in
hurrying her down an unlighted stairway, the defendant railroad
contended that she might just as easily have fallen in broad
daylight while moving at a regular pace. But the court held that if
the plaintiff proves that the negligence of the defendant "greatly
multiplied" the chances of the accident, the plaintiff has made out a
jury question on the causation issue.

Is there enough "self-proving" causation in *Reynolds* to permit
the case to go to the jury? The court thought so.The jury knows
that more often than not people don't fall down stairs, even if they
are overweight. It is true that factors other than the defendant's
negligence may well have caused Mrs. Reynolds to fall. But in her
case two negligent factors—the fact that the stairs were not lighted
and that she was told to hurry—were arguably the result of the
defendant's negligence. Since there was no evidence that Mrs.
Reynolds frequently fell on lighted stairs when she was not hurrying, what the defendant did or did not do is a sufficiently plausible
explanation for what caused her to fall. In the absence of evidence
of other probable causes, the defendant's negligence is the probable
cause (or at least so the jury is permitted to find). Thus, sometimes
the most effective way to prove that the defendant's negligence
caused the plaintiff's harm is to eliminate a series of other possible
causes. That leaves the defendant's negligence as a cause.

This process of proving that negligence caused harm by eliminating non-negligent causes is used not only in simple fall-down
and dart-out cases, but also when expert testimony regarding
causation is required. For example, in *Zuchowicz v. United States,*[5]
the suit was for injuries and death that were allegedly caused by an
overdose of a prescription drug. The question was whether there
was sufficient evidence of causation to support the verdict in
plaintiff's favor. The first question was whether even an appropriate dose could have caused the harm in question, but the second
question was whether the negligent overdose caused the harm. In
an opinion by Judge Guido Calabresi, one of the great torts scholars

4. 37 La. Ann. 694 (1885).
5. 140 F.3d 381 (2d Cir.1998).

of the twentieth century, the court found the testimony of the plaintiff's experts sufficient to support the verdict on these issues, largely on the ground that the experts had ruled out a series of other possible causes, which as a result made the plaintiff's contention more likely. Calabresi also noted that "it is often true that the higher the dosage [of any prescription drug] the greater is the likelihood of ... negative side effects." Notice that this kind of reasoning comes close to invoking "self-proving" causation.

It is worth noting, however, that in *Zuchowitcz* there appears to have been little data about any of the causes of the very rare disease the plaintiff contracted, and no direct evidence that the excess dosage of the drug the plaintiff took greatly increased the chance of harm, rather than slightly or modestly increased the chance of great harm—in that case, death. There was only the supposition, just quoted, that it is "often" true that the higher the dosage of prescription drugs, the greater the likelihood of harm. It is not at all clear, therefore, whether there would have been a sufficient independent basis for invoking "self-proving" causation in *Zuchowicz*. It may well be that proof of negligence alone was not sufficient to prove causation, and that the plaintiff's burden of production was satisfied only because there was also testimony from the plaintiff's experts that ruled out other possible causes.

B. *Expert Testimony:* Daubert

Once causation questions start to turn on expert testimony such as this, the rules governing the admissibility of such testimony come into play. In recent years there have been several important cases decided by the U.S. Supreme Court on this issue. Although these decisions formally govern only litigation in federal courts under the Federal Rules of Evidence, many state courts have very similar rules of evidence and look to interpretations of the Federal Rules for guidance. And although these cases involve expert testimony regarding causation (and thus are discussed here), they pertain to expert testimony generally. The most significant decision is *Daubert v. Merrell Dow Pharmaceuticals*,[6] in which the Court specified the standards that the trial courts should employ to exercise their "gatekeeping role" in ruling on the admissibility of scientific expert testimony. The Court directed the trial courts to make a preliminary assessment of the reliability and applicability of the testimony as a condition of its admissibility, taking into account not only general acceptance of the theory underlying the testimony,

---

6.   509 U.S. 579, 113 S.Ct. 2786, 125 L.Ed.2d 469 (1993).

but also whether the theory has been tested, peer reviewed, and published, and in the case of a scientific technique, the known or potential rate of error. In subsequent cases the Court has held that the trial courts should exercise analogous gatekeeping authority in cases involving non-scientific expert testimony, and that rulings by trial courts on the admissibility of expert testimony should be reversed only for abuse of discretion.[7]

It is not easy, however, to pinpoint the distinction between an assessment of the *reliability* of expert testimony and an assessment of the *persuasiveness* of that testimony. Yet that is precisely what *Daubert* and its progeny require, allocating the former to the trial court and the latter to the jury. Sometimes the line between the two functions is very fine indeed. In any event, there is no doubt that these U.S. Supreme Court decisions have given rise to a much more extended and detailed process for determining whether and when expert testimony is admissible. Because the decisions of trial courts on this issue can be reversed only for abuse of discretion, however, it is unclear how much impact there has actually been on the frequency at which expert testimony is or is not admitted into evidence.

II. Multiple Causes, Indeterminate Causes, and Exceptions to the Conventional Test

The but-for test usually works in straightforward fashion in cases involving only one defendant. On the other hand, when multiple possible causes are involved, the causation requirement is sometimes held to be satisfied even when the defendant's negligence is not a but-for cause of the plaintiff's harm. The exceptions to the conventional test are a mixed bag that do not all fall into a single category. To understand these exceptions, it is helpful first to step back from the two conventional tests for causation to look at the theories underlying the causation requirement.

A. *Theories Underlying the Causation Requirement*

Why is causation, however defined, always an element of a cause of action in tort? At first glance the answer may seem utterly obvious: if the defendant did not injure the plaintiff then there is no causation, no one injured, no damages, and no plaintiff to bring

---

7. *See, e.g., Kumho Tire Co. v. Carmichael*, 526 U.S. 137, 119 S.Ct. 1167, 143 L.Ed.2d 238 (1999) (non-scientific testimony) and *General Electric Co. v. Joiner*, 522 U.S. 136, 118 S.Ct. 512, 139 L.Ed.2d 508 (1997) (abuse of discretion standard applied on appeal).

suit. But of course that answer is only half-right whenever the question matters. In any case in which causation is disputed, there *is* a plaintiff with an injury and damages or there would have been no suit to begin with. So the question is, if there is an injured plaintiff and a negligent defendant, why must there be a causal connection between what the defendant did and what happened to the plaintiff? This question could just as appropriately have been asked at the outset of this Chapter in setting out the but-for test. But it turns out that it is in cases where exceptions to the but-for case are created or considered that theories underlying the causation requirement often bear the most weight.

1. Justice between the Parties

One justification for requiring that there be a causal connection between what the defendant did and what happened to the plaintiff is concern for doing justice between the parties. If the defendant did not cause the plaintiff's loss, then it seems obvious that the defendant has not wronged the plaintiff. There is no injustice to be corrected and no basis for giving the plaintiff civil recourse against the defendant.

But is this conclusion always as obvious as it seems? Consider any of the causation cases that we have discussed or that you have studied thus far. In each of these cases the defendant was negligent—that is, unreasonably risked harming the plaintiff. If the plaintiff has proved that the defendant was negligent in risking harm to the plaintiff, then in one sense the defendant has wronged her. If I exceed the speed limit on Main Street I am no less negligent toward those whose harm I risked if I am able to stop the car without having caused harm than if I injure someone as a result of speeding. And the person I almost harm would be understandably indignant at my misbehavior—she would think I had committed a wrong, and consider herself much more involved and implicated than someone watching from a position of safety. My "wrong" consists of risking the harm that may result from what I have done. That is, we tend to judge whether an act is blameworthy by asking what the defendant knew or should have known at the time of the act—by the act's potential consequences—and not exclusively by the consequences that actually materialize.

Many commentators would reject this analysis. They see the causation requirement in tort law as evidence that there is no wrong without a relation between the plaintiff and defendant that consists of the defendant harming the plaintiff. But that is only an accurate description of the structure of tort law if tort law insists on causation as a matter of principle, rather than for practical reasons. Ultimately I think that is the case, but let us push the analysis based on risks-as-wrongs a bit further anyway and see where it leads.

Suppose we were to think of the wrong of the negligent defendant, whether or not it actually caused harm, as consisting of taking the risk of harming. What kind of damages should then be awarded? It would seem that the measure of damages payable to someone I do injure should not be that plaintiff's actual loss, but a sum equal to the probability that he would suffer harm, multiplied by the amount of harm that could be expected if harm did result. This, after all, is the "amount" of the risk that I took, and taking that risk was the wrong I committed. If I were held liable for that amount to everyone I risked harming on each occasion I did so, whether or not they were injured, then over time I would pay out the same sum in damages (though in smaller amounts to more people) as I would if I were only liable to those whom I injured.

Under such a system people would be compensated for the "wrong" I committed in risking harm to them. Why don't we do it that way? One of the reasons we do not have such a system, of course, is that the people whose harm is risked but who are not injured have no immediate need for the money, and those who are injured do. That problem could only be solved if risk-based damages were always awarded, and uninjured plaintiffs who received compensation saved it for the time they were injured. For practical purposes that would be an impossible system to operate, since everyone whose harm was risked could sue, and in every such suit the precise degree of risk posed by the defendant's acts toward each possible victim would be at issue. Under this theory, therefore, we require proof of causation for practical reasons rather than reasons of deep principle.

What are we to make of this analysis? On the one hand, it misses something important. We have much more indignation at a defendant who harms a plaintiff than at a defendant who merely risks harming the plaintiff. Treating them the same seems inappropriate, and requiring proof of causation makes perfect sense. On the other hand, ignoring the fact that the underlying wrong is risking harm doesn't seem entirely sensible either, as a matter of principle. Defendants who don't injure anyone are simply lucky, but are just as blameworthy as those who do.[8]

Perhaps these are just irreconcilable points of view. For those who still think that causation should be a moral prerequisite to

---

8. For disagreement, see John C.P. Goldberg & Benjamin C. Zipursky, *Tort Law and Moral Luck*, 92 CORNELL L. REV. 1123 (2007).

liability, the analysis is not persuasive. But even for those who think that the risks-as-wrongs analysis makes sense, or that the two views each say something important, in most cases the issue will be beside the point, because usually it is not practical to dispense with the causation requirement. As we will see, however, in occasional cases it is practical to dispense with the conventional causation requirement, and the issue must be confronted.

2. Causation and Deterrence

An instrumental view of the causation requirement sees it from the standpoint of deterrence rather than justice between the parties. The whole point of imposing tort liability in order to deter unreasonable behavior is to give potential injurers the incentive to compare the amount of liability that they *anticipate* they will incur from taking a particular risk with the cost of reducing that risk by taking safety precautions. But the amount of liability they will incur from any given risky act is utterly variable, because the amount of damages suffered by any given victim is almost random. Insurance companies and repeat-player defendants may be able to predict with a fair amount of reliability how frequently they will be held liable, but the severity of the injury that any given victim is likely to suffer is in fact much harder to predict. Designing a truck without extra strength in its doors risks greater injury in side-collisions, but a collision under a particular set of circumstances may cause no harm, a sprained ankle, or death. The best that potential injurers (or their insurers) threatened with liability can do is to anticipate that, if a risk they take materializes in harm, they will incur liability equal to the average amount of damages that a potential victim will suffer.

From a deterrence standpoint, therefore, requiring proof of causation is not a moral imperative, but simply a way of communicating to the defendant in advance the scope of the liability it will face. If we had another way of threatening potential defendants with liability for the cost of the risks they take without requiring proof of causation, and charging defendants with this amount of liability—for example, by imposing liability for average damages rather than those actually caused in any given case—then this alternative approach could serve the aim of deterrence just as well, if not better. Usually there is no reliable and accurate way of threatening liability so as to achieve optimal deterrence without requiring proof of causation. So the but-for test is used. On the rare occasions when alternatives to the conventional test for causation are available, however, the law sometimes carves out exceptions to the conventional test, discussed next.

B. *Injury Caused by Multiple Sufficient Causes*

The first set of problems involves cases in which two forces converge on the plaintiff, and either one alone would have been sufficient to cause all of the plaintiff's harm. In cases of "overdetermined causation" of this sort,[9] sometimes the forces converge simultaneously, sometimes sequentially. Sometimes only one of these causes is negligent, sometimes both are negligent. To assure that the differences between these situations is clear, I will use the classic illustration of two fires reaching the plaintiff's house, either one of which is sufficient to destroy the house. But of course the point of the illustrations is that the fires represent forces set in motion by different parties and that these might be defendants causing injury not involving fires, but products, toxic substances, drivers, trains, or other forces.

1. Two Simultaneous Causes: Both Negligent

Suppose that two independently and negligently-set fires are burning toward the plaintiff's house. Either alone would be sufficient to destroy the house, but they both reach the house at the same time, destroying it together. In a suit against those who set the fires, the plaintiff cannot satisfy the but-for test: but-for either defendant's negligence, the house would have been destroyed anyway. Nonetheless, the courts universally hold that neither defendant can escape liability on this ground. Both are held to have caused the plaintiff's loss.

One way to explain this result is to say that, although neither defendant was a but-for cause of the plaintiff's harm, each was a substantial factor. I think that a more fruitful and candid way of explaining this result, however, is to understand that both the but-for and substantial-factor tests are not definitions of the concept of causation, but merely useful proxies for the concept. Here the tests don't really capture what we mean in ordinary language by "cause." Picture each fire reaching a different portion of the house at the same time and starting to burn the walls. Everyone would say that each fire was an actual physical cause of the harm. It would be absurd to say that neither was a cause of the harm, when in fact both were, and doubly absurd to deny the plaintiff recovery because his house happened to be destroyed by two defendants rather than one. Moreover, here the choice is between over-imposition of liability (since the harm will occur anyway even when one of

---

9. *See* Jane Stapleton, *Legal Cause: Cause-in-Fact and the Scope of Liability for Consequences*, 54 VAND. L. REV. 941 (2001).

the defendants is careful), and under-imposition of imposition of liability. The law chooses the former, threatening "too much" liability rather than too little.

2. Two Simultaneous Causes: One Negligent, One Not

Next suppose the same facts, except that only one of the two fires is negligently set. Again, the but-for test is not satisfied, though here too one might say that the substantial-factor test is satisfied. Whether the negligent party should be liable even though the but-for test is not satisfied is a close question. Clearly the negligent party's fire was a physical cause of some of the damage; it would be peculiar to say that it was not. On the other hand, the house would have been destroyed even absent that party's negligence, and if that party is held liable it will be liable for the entire amount of the loss, since the other party's fire was not negligently set. Imposing liability on the negligent party will give such parties the incentive to take precautions against harms that will occasionally occur anyway because of a simultaneous non-negligent cause. And here the plaintiff has much less basis for objecting to denying his recovery here than where both fires are negligent, because here his house would have been destroyed regardless of what the negligent party did. Many courts do not hold the negligent defendant liable in this situation, but some courts do. And as discussion of the following hypothetical demonstrates, it is essential to the courts that do impose liability in such cases that the negligent fire arrive no later than the non-negligent fire.

3. Sequential Causes: Pre-emptive Causation

Next, suppose that two fires arrive sequentially. The first totally destroys the plaintiff's house, very shortly after which the second arrives. Again, neither fire can be said to be a but-for cause of the harm, but the first fire was the actual physical cause of the harm: it was what might be called the "pre-emptive" cause. Probably this is enough to explain why the party responsible for the first fire is liable if the fire was negligently set, and why the party responsible for the second fire is not responsible, even if that fire was negligently set. Sometimes one party is negligent but lucky enough not to cause harm, either because no one is harmed, or (as here) because some other earlier force has already caused harm that one's own negligence would have caused, but for that force. The first fire was not a but-for cause, but physically did the damage. The second fire risked harm, but simply was not a cause of the harm, no matter how one defines that concept. The party responsible for the first fire, and only that party, can be held liable, assuming he was negligent.

Although these rules are firmly established, they are not entirely consistent with analogous rules. For example, suppose I am on my way to the airport to catch a plane and you negligently run into me and break my leg. As a result, I miss my plane. That plane crashes, killing everyone aboard. You are still liable to me for my broken leg. On the other hand, if I have terminal cancer and you negligently break my leg, the damages you owe me will take into account the fact that I have only a few months to live. In the first hypothetical the damages you owe me are not affected by the fact that I would have lived only a few hours if you had not struck me, whereas in the second hypothetical the damages you owe me are affected by my life expectancy. It is true that the former hypothetical is treated under the law of causation, whereas the latter is treated under the law of damages. And in the former hypothetical my life expectancy was determined by outside forces (the plane crash) that had not yet materialized, whereas in the latter hypothetical my life expectancy was determined by internal forces (my cancer) that had already materialized. But it is not clear why these distinctions should make a difference. In the former case an act of negligence entirely pre-empts a later probable cause, whereas in the latter case an act of negligence only partially pre-empts a later probable cause. The treatment of the two cases thus does not seem entirely consistent, though the differential treatment seems compelled by the applicable rules.

C. Joint and Several Liability

When, for whatever reason, two or more defendants are liable to the plaintiff for the same harm, the law typically treats them under the doctrine of "joint and several liability." This is a confusing phrase that more nearly means "entire liability." In situations like the first fire hypothetical discussed above, for example, the parties responsible for each negligently set fire would have been held jointly and severally liable to the plaintiff. This means that each is liable to the plaintiff as if he were the sole wrongdoer, responsible for the entirety of the plaintiff's damages. The plaintiff is therefore entitled to recover the full amount of his damages from either defendant. However, the plaintiff cannot ever recover more than the amount of his damages; if he has recovered the entire amount from one defendant, he can recover nothing in addition from the other defendant. And if he has recovered some from one defendant, then he can recover only the remainder from the other defendant.

At common law that was the end of the matter. When one defendant paid the plaintiff in full the second defendant who paid nothing to the plaintiff got a windfall, and when each defendant paid only a portion that was the way things stayed. This obviously unfair result has long since been remedied in every state by statutes that create rights of *contribution* among jointly and severally liable tortfeasors in such situations. A right of contribution is essentially a right to be reimbursed by another defendant for a share of the amount paid to the plaintiff. Traditionally such rights operated on a straight fractional-share basis. Thus, if there were two jointly and severally liable defendants, a defendant paying the plaintiff in full was entitled to contribution from the other defendant equal to one-half of the amount paid; if there were three jointly and severally liable defendants, the defendant paying the plaintiff in full was entitled to contribution from each of the other defendants equal to one-third of the amount paid, and so on. That is still the approach taken in some states.

Since the net effect of rights of contribution is to allocate a share of responsibility to each co-defendant, one might then ask why this complicated method of allocating responsibility among multiple defendants is followed. Why not simply hold each defendant liable to the plaintiff for its share in the first instance? The answer is that one or more of the defendants may be insolvent or otherwise impossible to collect from. Imposing joint and several liability places the risk of any defendant's insolvency on the other defendant or defendants rather than on the plaintiff. As between an innocent plaintiff and a group of negligent or otherwise-liable defendants, it is preferable for the defendants to bear the risk that one of their number cannot pay its share.

But in recent years contributory negligence has been replaced by comparative negligence in most states, as we will see in Chapter Seven. Now, the plaintiff is not always innocent. A negligent plaintiff is not barred from recovery; his recovery is reduced in proportion to the amount of negligence attributable to him. So many states now assess contribution shares of co-defendants in proportion to the amount of negligence attributable to each co-defendant, rather than on a straight fractional basis. And several dozen states have enacted statutes modifying their rules governing joint and several liability itself. Some impose such liability, for example, only on a defendant whose negligence consists of more than 50 percent of the negligence attributable to all the defendants.

Joint and several liability is imposed in three main situations. First, the defendants may be *joint tortfeasors*. If you and I together engage in a joint enterprise (e.g., a business partnership) and one of us is negligent, then we are jointly and severally liable for harm that results. Second, *independent tortfeasors* are jointly and severally liable for a *single, theoretically indivisible harm*. For example, suppose that one defendant speeds through an intersection and another fails to stop at a red light. The two vehicles collide and one runs onto the sidewalk, injuring a pedestrian. Under the but-for test for causation each defendant is a cause-in-fact of the pedestrian's injuries, because neither alone would have been sufficient to cause the injury. But because there is no way, even theoretically, to pinpoint the extent of either defendant's causal responsibility for the pedestrian's harm, each is jointly and severally liable for that harm.

Finally, independent tortfeasors are jointly and severally liable for a *single, theoretically divisible but practically indivisible harm*. At early common law the plaintiff could not recover because he could not prove the amount of harm each defendant caused, but the modern rule is that each defendant is entitled to prove how much harm it caused. If this proof is successful, liability is apportioned based on the amount of harm caused by each defendant. But otherwise all defendants are held jointly and severally liable for all the plaintiff's harm. For example, in *Maddux v. Donaldson*,[10] one defendant's negligence caused a collision with the plaintiff's vehicle, and then a second defendant's negligence caused a second collision. In theory each defendant caused a certain portion of the plaintiff's harm, but for practical purposes the harm was indivisible—because the evidence did not support an inference as to the amount of injury caused by each defendant.

D. *Indeterminate Causes*

A cluster of cases that is especially troublesome under the conventional rules governing proof of causation is comprised of those in which a plaintiff is clearly injured by tortious conduct but cannot prove which of several possible defendants was more probably than not the actual cause of his or her injury, or a defendant has clearly injured some but not all plaintiffs, and they cannot prove which of them the defendant injured. These problems have generated a number of classic cases, and several different approaches that constitute exceptions to the conventional test for causation.

10.   362 Mich. 425, 108 N.W.2d 33 (1961).

1. Alternative Liability: *Summers v. Tice*

In *Summers*[11] two different hunters negligently shot in the direction of the plaintiff, a third hunter. One shot struck the eye of the plaintiff, who sued both hunters. Each defendant was *as probably as not* the but-for cause of injury to the plaintiff, but not more probably than not the cause. The court held that under these circumstances the burden shifted to each of the defendants to disprove that he had caused the harm. But in practice *Summers* is ordinarily understood to involve more than a mere shift of the burden of proof on the causation issue. It is the classic case of "alternative" liability, imposing liability on negligent defendants, each of whom is equally likely to have harmed the plaintiff.

The rationale for the decision is not easy to find in the *Summers* opinion. The court apparently sought to justify its decision by saying that applying the conventional but-for approach would exonerate the defendants, even though both were negligent and the injury resulted from the negligence of only one of them. This is not a reason for dispensing with the but-for test, however, but just an assertion of the obvious: that applying the but-for test sometimes relieves a negligent defendant of liability. Making that point does not explain or justify departing from it. Interestingly, alternative liability is rare, and the cases in which it is applied often involve only two defendants. This limitation suggests that an explanation for the result in *Summers* and some of the other cases in which the doctrine of alternative liability is applied is that each defendant is so nearly "more probably than not" the cause of the harm that the courts are unwilling to immunize them from liability. Add a third defendant and this dramatically ceases to be true: the per defendant probability drops from 50 percent to 33 and 1/3 percent. There can be little doubt that the courts' comfort level will be much higher in cases involving only two defendants, but this cannot be the entire explanation, because there are decisions applying alternative liability where there are three or more defendants.

I think that another factor involved in cases invoking alternative liability is the connection between or among defendants. Pure strangers are much less likely to be subject to this doctrine than defendants who are in some sense acting in the same "arena." Notice that if the defendants in *Summers* had been involved in an actual joint enterprise of the sort described in the preceding section, then they would have been held joint and severally liable without need for proof of which of them had caused the plaintiff's harm. Perhaps the plaintiff did not contend that they were part of a

---

11. 199 P.2d 1 (Cal. 1948).

joint enterprise out of fear that, if they were, he would have been considered part of the same enterprise, their negligence would have been attributed to him, and he would have been barred from recovery by attributed contributory negligence. But the two defendants were acting in the same "arena"—they were hunting together. Defendants who had been hunting separately would have been less likely to be subject to alternative liability. Indeed, RESTATEMENT (THIRD) OF TORTS § 28, *Comment* j implies that the existence of a "close connection" between or among defendants characterizes many alternative liability cases. So it may be that some sort of nexus or connection among defendants tends to be a necessary condition to the application of the doctrine, especially in cases involving more than two defendants.

2. Industry–Wide Liability: *Hall v. E.I. Du Pont De Nemours & Co., Inc.*

In *Hall*,[12] six manufacturers of blasting caps were sued by thirteen children injured in separate accidents. The court held that if a child could establish that it was more likely than not that any of the six defendants manufactured the particular cap that caused that child's injury, then the burden shifted to each defendant to prove that a cap it manufactured did not cause the injury in question. The theory behind the decision in *Hall* has never been entirely clear, but it seems to rest on two factors: a) the fact that the defendants acted consciously in parallel to produce caps in a fashion that made their manufacturer difficult to identify after they exploded, plus b) the comparatively small number of defendants. The flavor of the opinion suggests that, although the defendants may not have acted together to cause the injuries at issue, the threat of liability in similar situations in the future might encourage industries with a small number of companies to act together either to prevent injury, or at least to take steps that would enable victims to identify the individual company responsible when a product did cause injury.

3. Loss of a Chance to Survive

Herskovits v. Group Health Cooperative[13] and *Matsuyama v. Birnbaum*[14] are the best known of a series of decisions that involve an already-injured or ill plaintiff, whose chances of recovery or survival are reduced by the negligent actions of the defendant. Both involve the failure of a physician to diagnose cancer, from which

12. 345 F.Supp. 353 (E.D.N.Y.1972).
13. 99 Wash.2d 609, 664 P.2d 474 (1983).
14. 452 Mass. 1, 890 N.E.2d 819 (2008).

the patient would have had a better chance of surviving if the physician had not missed the diagnosis. And in both cases, the patient died. But in both cases, the patient's chance of surviving even if he had been properly diagnosed was less than 50 percent. That is, in each case it was not more probable than not that, but for the defendant's negligence, the death would not have occurred. So under the conventional but-for test, there would have been no recovery.

For example, the defendant in *Herskovits* failed to diagnose the plaintiff's cancer until his chances of survival were only 25 percent. There was testimony, however, that even absent the defendant's malpractice (i.e, but for the malpractice), Herskovits' chances of survival would have been only 39 percent and his chances of dying therefore 61 percent. The court nonetheless held that there could be a recovery, though not for all of the damages resulting from Herskovits' death. The majority opinion did not specify how damages were to be calculated, but a concurrence suggested a method that the case has come to stand for: the plaintiff should recover 14 percent of his damages.

One way to describe what happened is to say that the defendant is held liable for the loss of the opportunity to survive. That is how the *Herskovits* and *Matsuyama* courts described it. Superficially this description can be squared with the traditional statement of the plaintiff's burden of proving causation, since in a sense the defendant was more probably than not the but-for cause of this *loss* of or *reduction* in decedent's chances. Indeed, the defendant was 100 percent responsible for this 14 percent reduction in *Herskovits*.

It is important for the courts to understand the claim in this way not only because it aligns with the traditional requirement of proving but-for causation, but because the courts would otherwise be on a slippery slope. Describing the recovery as compensating for loss of a chance avoids awarding damages based on the probability that the defendant caused the harm, which might undermine the but-for requirement more generally. To see why, suppose that, instead of looking at the loss of a chance, we were to look at the probability that the defendant's negligence caused the plaintiff's death. The defendant's negligence in *Herskovits* increased the plaintiff's risk of dying from 61 percent to 75 percent. Consequently, the probability that the defendant's negligence caused the plaintiff's death was 19 percent (14/75), and implies that the plaintiff should recover 19 percent of the value of the patient's life, not 14 percent. This latter description not only would yield a different measure of damages, but also would imply a different explanation for the results in *Herskovits* and *Matsuyama* and a less confining rule. If that were the approach taken, it would seem to be just one example of a more general problem: the defendant who can never be proved more probably than not to have caused any particular individual's injuries, but whose behavior over time is likely to injure 19 percent of the individuals whose harm his actions risk. But of course damages are not awarded in such cases.

Describing recovery as loss of a chance avoids this potential inconsistency, but it does not avoid all inconsistency. There are many cases in which a defendant's negligence causes the plaintiff to lose a chance, but there is no recovery. The pest-control company that negligently fails to find insects in a house that would have had less than a 50 percent chance of avoiding infestation even if they had been discovered is an example. So is the negligent failure of a 911 operator to obtain accurate information from a caller, even when the chance of rescuing the caller would have been less than 50 percent in the absence of negligence. If chance has value, this explanation for the lost-chance cases argues for applying the doctrine to any lost-chance situation.

But this is not done. There is liability for loss of a chance only in medical cases. One possible explanation is that, in contrast to other negligent defendants, health care providers undertake to maximize a patient's chances of survival, and that their failure to do so should be actionable. Ordinary actors who negligently risk causing harm have not undertaken such a duty, but certainly the pest-control company and 911 service have undertaken duties to make people or their property safer. It can also be argued that, if physicians in situations such as *Herskovits* and *Matsuyama* were not liable, they would have insufficient legally created incentives to exercise care in treating patients with probably-fatal conditions. But physicians have non-legal incentives to do so; presumably they became physicians in part because they wanted to help cure such patients. And in any event, this is a deterrence-based argument that apparently is not weighty enough to persuade the courts to apply the rule to all lost-chance cases, so it is not clear why such an argument would be more persuasive in the medical context.

The explanation that is more persuasive to me is that there is scientifically valid data about survival rates in many medical cases—especially those involving cancer such as *Herskovits* and *Matsuyama*—but there is much less often valid data in other situations. Limiting loss of a chance cases to medical situations avoids litigating on a case-by-case basis whether the loss of a chance doctrine should apply across the board, and avoids litigating the validity of data in other types of cases.

Whether or not these various possible distinctions are persuasive, somehow the lost-chance cases appear on the surface to be sufficiently different from the general problem of risking harm that the courts are satisfied that this class of cases can stand on its own. Moreover, because it is rare in any kind of case to have reliable quantitative data on the precise probability that the defendant's action caused the plaintiff harm, the issue usually can simply be sidestepped on this ground.

4. Market–Share Liability

The defendants in the seminal market-share liability case, *Sindell v. Abbott Laboratories*,[15] were manufacturers of the drug DES. The class of plaintiffs consisted of women whose mothers had taken the drug while they were pregnant. The plaintiffs/daughters alleged that they suffered injury as a result of exposure to DES *in utero*. The problem was that no individual plaintiff could identify which manufacturer or manufacturers had made the DES that her mother had taken. The court circumvented this problem by holding that the plaintiffs need not prove individual causation. Rather, each plaintiff could recover from each defendant a portion of her damages equal to the defendant's share of the market for DES.

The theory behind *Sindell* is that, once it is clear that each defendant's DES injured some of the plaintiffs, the defendants should not escape liability merely because the plaintiffs cannot show which defendant injured which plaintiff. Because the DES made by the defendants was chemically identical, market share was a very accurate surrogate for the amount of harm each defendant caused. Consequently, imposing liability on defendants in proportion to market share forces each defendant to pay compensation for the amount of injury it caused, although not necessarily to those particular persons harmed by any given manufacturer's DES. In terms of deterrence this approach is optimal in theory, because each defendant pays what it should. Corrective justice is less well served by market-share liability, however, because there is no matching up of each plaintiff with the defendant whose DES injured her. Under market-share liability the wrong done to each plaintiff is corrected, but it is not necessarily corrected by the party who wronged that plaintiff.

Although market-share liability might seem at first glance to be a solution to the general problem of proving causation in toxic exposure cases, a number of practical considerations have limited this approach to DES cases and a very few other claims. First, in

---

15. 607 P.2d 924 (1980).

the DES cases the plaintiffs alleged that their disease—vaginal adenocarcinoma—could be caused *only* by exposure to DES *in utero*. This was in effect a "signature disease": if the plaintiff had that disease, then it was caused by DES. But there are very few signature diseases—diseases that have only one cause. Market-share liability will work in cases of signature disease, because 100 percent of the market caused 100 percent of the disease. But when there are also other causes of the disease suffered by the plaintiffs, market-share is not an accurate surrogate for the total amount of the disease caused by any given defendant, because some people have a disease that was not caused by any of the defendants. For this reason, market share liability has overwhelmingly been rejected in cases involving such other substances as asbestos, lead-based paint, and other drugs.

Second, the same toxic substances produced by different defendants are not always chemically identical. For example, in *Skipworth v. Lead Industries Association*,[16] the court refused to apply market-share liability to manufacturers of lead pigment that was in the past used in house paint, in part because different pigments had different chemical formulations. Because these pigments therefore resulted in different levels of bioavailability to the plaintiffs, different manufacturers did not necessarily cause harm in proportion to their market shares.

Third, even when the substances produced by different defendants are chemically identical and plaintiffs do suffer from a signature disease, the relevant market-share data is not always available, especially when the relevant time period for determining market share—as in the case of DES—is twenty or more years before suit. And in any event, it is not clear which is the relevant market: national, state, or local. This choice would not only affect the relative shares of each defendant, but conceivably who was liable in the first instance: would a particular defendant be permitted to show, for example, that it did not market its product in the state where the plaintiff lived when she was exposed to the risk of harm, or would that be considered irrelevant?

Finally, usually it is not feasible to sue all possible defendants. Some have gone out of business, others may not be subject to the jurisdiction of the court where suit is brought. The result is that less than 100 percent of the relevant market is before the court. What is the scope of the liability to be shouldered by the defendants who are before the court in such a situation? A *relative-market-share* approach (which seemed to have been taken by *Sindell* itself,

---

16. 547 Pa. 224, 690 A.2d 169 (1997).

and only later set aside)[17] is to require that a substantial share of the market be joined as defendants in the suit, and then to hold those defendants liable (in proportion to their market shares) for 100 percent of the plaintiff's damages. Thus, if defendants who held 80 percent of the relevant market were joined in the suit, a defendant who had held 20 percent of the market would pay 25 percent (20/80) of the plaintiff's damages. This approach has the obvious disadvantage of imposing "excessive" liability on the defendants who are liable, much as does joint and several liability when some defendants are judgment-proof. The alternative, *absolute-market-share* approach, is to hold defendants liable only for their actual market share. One disadvantage of this approach is that the plaintiff is incompletely compensated for his or her losses. Another is that a multiplicity of suits may result unless there is a requirement that a substantial share of the market be joined in any suit, even though liability will be based on absolute rather than relative market shares.

These concerns reflect more than merely practical problems to be solved. Each concern suggests how market-share liability in practice may fail to achieve the theory behind this form of liability: there are so few signature diseases that market-share liability may be useful only occasionally; the limitations of market-share information may render accurate imposition of liability difficult; the same product made by different manufacturers is not always fungible; and in most cases there will either be over-imposition of liability or under-compensation of the plaintiff. This combination of difficulties has prompted only about a third of the courts to apply market-share liability to DES cases, and for many courts to reject market-share liability outright. A few courts have applied the concept to other products, such as lead pigment in paint and the gasoline additive MTBE.

5. Toxic Harms and Statistical Proof of Causation

Consider now the class of non-market-share cases in which an identified defendant has caused injury, but it is not possible to prove which individuals the defendant has injured. For example, suppose that exposure to a substance made by a single manufacturer causes some, but not all of a particular type of cancer—say, 60 percent. With respect to any given plaintiff suffering that form of cancer, the defendant is more probably than not the but-for cause of the plaintiff's harm. For some courts this would be enough proof of causation. For most courts, however, this form of statistical or epidemiological evidence might be admissible but would be insuffi-

---

17. *See Brown v. Superior Court (Abbott Laboratories)*, 751 P.2d 470 (1988).

cient, standing alone, to prove causation, because no plaintiff is able to prove anything about causation in his or her particular situation, but only about similarly situated plaintiffs in general.

Why is "naked" statistical evidence of this sort not sufficient proof for most courts? After all, statistical evidence is simply quantitative proof of probability, and probability is really all that anyone ever proves about causation. For example, suppose that a plaintiff introduces evidence sufficient to support a jury inference that, but for the defendant's having exceeded the speed limit, he would have been able to control his vehicle and would not have struck the plaintiff's vehicle. The plaintiff really has done nothing more than prove facts from which a jury could conclude that in more than half of the instances in which the two drivers act as the defendant and plaintiff did act, the defendant's negligence will cause the plaintiff injury. That evidence at its core is neither different from nor superior to statistics. If anything, when there is actual statistical data on the causation issue, the plaintiff's evidence is entitled to more weight than in the collision case, because statistical data actually quantifies the probability of causation based on something more than casual experience. In the ordinary case such as the collision accident there is no such data, but only general experience on which to base a conclusion. The unwillingness of some courts to rely on statistical or epidemiological proof may therefore reflect their misconception of what goes on in the ordinary case.

On the other hand, many courts probably understand full well what they are doing when they hold that proof based on naked statistical evidence alone is insufficient. They may be reluctant to encourage litigants to gather supposedly objective data about the probability of causation that will tend to be reflected in a battle of experts whose data often will conflict. Or they may be content to live with the all-or-nothing rule that imposes liability on the defendant for 100 percent of the plaintiff's damages when the defendant is more likely than not the cause of the plaintiff's harm, as long as this "discrepancy" between certainty and probability is not too obvious. Statistics bring the discrepancy right out into the open. Moreover, the aims of deterrence are perfectly well served in ordinary cases by threatening the same defendants with liability for 100 percent of the plaintiff's damages in some cases and no liability in others, even when in each case there is only a probability of causation, higher than 50 percent when there is liability and lower than 50 percent when there is not. Finally, permitting the parties to rely exclusively on statistics might discourage the discovery of particularized, non-statistical evidence.

In the long run pretty much the right amount of liability probably is threatened and imposed by this all-or-nothing approach in ordinary cases. Potential defendants who risk injuring others typically cannot know in advance whether they will be advantaged or disadvantaged by the all-or-nothing approach to liability. Consequently, the threat of full liability when they have more probably than not caused the plaintiff's harm, and no liability when they have less probably than not caused such harm, is just as likely to create optimal incentives as a more complicated approach that would award proportional damages, and without the higher transaction costs that would inevitably be associated with a more complicated approach.

What is true in the ordinary case, however, often is not true in the extraordinary case. Suppose, for example, that in the cancer hypothetical the substance manufactured by the defendant causes only 30 percent of all the cancers of a particular type. In that scenario the defendant is less probably than not a but-for cause of any given plaintiff's harm. The manufacturer therefore knows in advance that under the conventional approach to causation it will *never* be held liable for any of the harm that its product causes. The conventional approach therefore cannot create its normal incentive effect in this situation, because the defendant does not face the prospect of "too much" liability in some cases and "too little" in others. Instead there is always too little liability (i.e., none) threatened. The theoretically ideal alternative to denying liability in such cases would be to charge the defendant with liability proportional to every plaintiff's damages. Thus, if the defendant were proved to have caused 30 percent of the cancers in question, it would be liable for 30 percent of each plaintiff's damages. A number of commentators have proposed various versions of this approach.[18]

Yet this approach has not been adopted, for at least two reasons. First, there are few cases in which there is reliable quantitative data to support taking such an approach. Until there are a sufficient number of such cases, making such a radical change seems unwarranted. Second, if it were possible to identify the cases in which the defendant is systematically underdeterred because of its advance knowledge that it will never be a more-probable-than-not cause, then imposing proportional liability in these cases alone could make sense. But in the absence of the capacity to identify these cases, the logic of such "proportional liability" would be difficult to contain. If we were to adopt proportional liability in order to prevent underdeterrence in cases in which the defendant is

---

18. *See, e.g.,* David Rosenberg, *The Causal Connection in Mass Exposure Cases: A "Public Law" Vision of the Tort System,* 97 HARV. L.REV. 849 (1984).

definitely a cause of some harm but less probably than not the cause of any particular plaintiff's harm, then why not be consistent and also adopt proportional liability when the defendant is more probably than not, but only more *probably* than not, the cause of a plaintiff's harm? If proportional liability is designed to remedy underdeterrence, then why not also use it to remedy overdeterrence? The answer, of course, is that adopting this approach would require so radical a shift in the way causation is determined and damages are calculated that no one even imagines that we would do this across-the-board. For both reasons, I think, there has been no real move to adopt proportional liability in cases involving the indeterminate plaintiff.

6

THE SCOPE OF LIABILITY: PROXIMATE CAUSE

A defendant is not necessarily liable for all the harm that his or her breach of the applicable standard of care has caused. This Chapter concerns the scope of such liability. Even after it is determined that the defendant is under a duty to exercise reasonable care, and even after the plaintiff has proved the other elements of his case (breach of duty, damages, and cause in fact), liability is not imposed unless the defendant's actions also were what is often called a "proximate cause" of the plaintiff's injury. Thus, after the other prerequisites to liability are satisfied, the doctrine of proximate cause operates as a limitation on the scope of the defendant's liability. Remember, however, that in connection with negligence suits we are still assuming the existence of a duty to exercise to exercise reasonable care, an assumption that is relaxed when we discuss duty in Chapter Eleven.

The proximate cause requirement also applies in strict liability cases, which are discussed in Chapter Eight. For purposes of analysis here, we will speak about proximate cause in negligence cases. The strict liability analog to the proximate cause questions discussed in this Chapter is to ask whether the plaintiff suffered a harm, the risk of which is one of the bases for imposing strict liability for engaging in the activity in question.

The rules governing the scope of the defendant's liability have long generated unnecessary confusion. In most cases the issue is simple and straightforward. Difficulties arise because the cases in which the issue is contestable tend to involve complex, unusual, or even bizarre sets of facts. In addition, no single formulation of the rules governing the scope of the defendant's liability or the concept of proximate cause can fully describe how these rules or the concept is applied, because they are sometimes used as a "fudge-factor" that permits judges and juries to decide whether liability should be imposed even after the other prerequisites to liability have already been satisfied. Nonetheless, the fundamentals of the law governing the scope of a defendant's liability can be easily understood, especially if one takes care to distinguish the cases in which application of the law is unremarkable from the rare, celebrated cases that

141

have made proximate cause seem so perplexing. The following Sections therefore deal first with the basics; then with the exceptional cases that tend to pose difficulties; and finally step back from the details of the rules to try to understand what they are really designed to do.

I. The Basics

Most cases posing the issue of proximate cause can be resolved by the foreseeability test or by a closely related elaboration, the harm-within-the-risk test. The key to both these tests is to understand that proximate cause actually has as much to do with breach of the standard of care, or the negligence issue, as with causation.

A. *Foreseeability*

In ordinary cases—whether they involve negligence or strict liability—the touchstone of proximate cause is foreseeability. The defendant's negligence is a proximate cause of the plaintiff's harm if causing that harm was a foreseeable result of acting as the defendant did. In ordinary cases there is no question at all that if the defendant was in fact negligent and this negligence was a cause in fact of the plaintiff's harm, then the proximate cause requirement also is satisfied. For example, suppose that the defendant fails to stop at a red light and collides with the plaintiff's vehicle. The defendant is negligent, the plaintiff suffered damage, and the defendant's negligence caused that damage. But is the defendant's negligence a "proximate" cause of the plaintiff's harm? Of course it is. It was highly foreseeable that someone passing through the intersection would be harmed if the defendant did not stop at the red light. Indeed, the risk that this kind of harm would result from running the red light is the principal basis for concluding that the defendant was negligent. It is negligent to run a red light precisely because it is foreseeable that running a red light will cause an intersection collision. This is so indisputable that there is no proximate cause issue to be decided as a question of fact in such a case. If the defendant was negligent and this negligence was a cause in fact of the plaintiff's injury, then as a matter of law the negligence of the defendant also was a proximate cause of the plaintiff's harm. At least in jurisdictions where jury instructions distinguish clearly between cause in fact and proximate cause, the jury will not even be instructed as to proximate cause; the only question is whether the defendant was negligent.

What does this have to do with causation? Not much. Use of the term "proximate cause" in this setting is unfortunate and misleading, which is why I have been describing proximate cause as a "scope of liability" issue. The determination that is made under the rubric of proximate cause has more to do with negligence than with causation. The first phase of the negligence issue is whether the defendant was negligent at all—unreasonably risked harming someone or some thing. That issue is decided under the rubric of negligence. The second phase of the negligence issue is whether the harm to the particular plaintiff or class of those in his position was a foreseeable result of the defendant's negligence. That issue is decided under the rubric of proximate cause. The first inquiry asks a general, all-risks-considered question about whether the defendant was negligent. The second inquiry asks a particular question about the nature of the relation between the defendant's negligence and what actually happened to this plaintiff.

B. *The Harm–Within–The–Risk Test*

The foreseeability test for proximate cause is sometimes clarified and sharpened by the harm-within-the-risk test. The run-of-the-mill negligence case almost always automatically satisfies the proximate cause requirement if the defendant was negligent. Conversely, there are occasional freak cases in which everyone would agree that, as a matter of law, the defendant's negligence was not a proximate cause of the plaintiff's injury, because injury to the plaintiff was not a harm-within-the-risk that made the defendant's action negligent.

For example, suppose that the defendant negligently parks his car next to a fire hydrant. The principal risk posed by this act is that blocked access to the hydrant will result in the destruction of property or injury to people by fire, because firefighters cannot gain easy access to the hydrant. Suppose now that the plaintiff, driving by the hydrant where the defendant parked, skids on the road and collides with the defendant's parked vehicle. The plaintiff proves that, but for the defendant's negligence in being parked where he was, the plaintiff would have been able to bring his vehicle safely to a stop in the few extra feet of road space that would have been available. Thus, the plaintiff has proved that the defendant was negligent, that the plaintiff suffered injury, and that but for the defendant's negligence, the plaintiff would not have been injured. But that is not enough. What about proximate cause?

The question can be answered by applying the harm-within-the-risk test. Is the risk of the injury the plaintiff suffered one of the risks that makes the defendant negligent for blocking access to the fire hydrant? Almost certainly not. This answer can be given so confidently because the act of parking by the hydrant instead of a dozen feet further down the street simply does not increase the risk of the harm that materialized. A motorist passing by that spot is no more likely to skid into a car parked negligently than into a car parked a legal distance away from the hydrant. Negligence is conduct that unreasonably increases the risk of harm, whereas the act of negligence in this case did not at all increase the risk of what happened. In this sense what happened was not foreseeable. That is, the defendant's negligence did not foreseeably increase the risk that the same general type of harm that the plaintiff actually suffered would occur. Note this use of the term "foreseeable." Of course what happened was "foreseeable" in the sense of being "imaginable." But what happened was not foreseeable in the sense that it is not one of the same set of risks we would want the defendant to take into account in deciding whether to park by the hydrant, because parking by the hydrant did not increase the risk that the plaintiff would be harmed in that manner.

A number of well-known cases fall into this category. For example, in *Berry v. The Borough of Sugar Notch*,[1] the question was whether the negligence of operating a trolley above the speed limit was a proximate cause of harm that resulted when a tree fell on the speeding trolley as it passed by. Speeding did not at all increase this risk. Rather, it was simply a coincidence that the trolley was where it was when the tree fell, even though the trolley would not have been at that precise point had it not been speeding. Therefore, as a matter of law, the negligence at issue was not a proximate cause of the damage that occurred. Similarly, in *Gorris v. Scott*,[2] sheep were washed overboard from a ship as a result of negligent violation of a regulation requiring that they be kept in pens. But the regulation was promulgated under a statute designed to protect the sheep from contagious disease, not to keep them from being washed overboard. In both *Berry* and *Gorris*, the harm in question was not even arguably within the risk that had rendered the action causing the harm negligent. Therefore, in both cases, the courts held that the necessary element of proximate cause was absent. In other words, the scope of the defendant's liability for negligence did not extend to these harms.

Thus far we have examined the ordinary cases in which there is proximate cause as a matter of law, and the easy cases at the

1. 191 Pa. 345, 43 A. 240 (1899).
2. LR 9 Ex. 125 (1874).

opposite extreme in which, as a matter of law, there is no proxi-mate cause. In between lie cases that are a bit more difficult. Many of these are difficult largely because the harm-within-the-risk test does not easily resolve them. These are cases in which the risk that the plaintiff would suffer the harm that actually materialized was not the *principal* risk that rendered the defendant's action negli-gent, but that risk was nonetheless a foreseeable (one might say "secondary") and relevant risk. For example, suppose that the defendant violates a statute requiring railroads to fence their rights of way and as a result injures a two-year old who has wandered onto the tracks. The legislative history of the statute reflects concern for injury to livestock from unfenced rights of way. None-theless, many courts would hold that a secondary purpose of such a statute is to reduce the risk of injury to people as well as livestock.[3] These courts would send the proximate cause issue to the jury.

Similar issues arise even when a statute is not involved. Then the question is whether, although the risk that materialized in harm was not the principal risk that made the defendant's action negligent, that risk was sufficiently significant to be a factor in the negligence determination. This is simply another way of posing the question, "Was the defendant's negligence a proximate cause of the plaintiff's harm?" For example, in *Wagner v. International Railway Co.*,[4] the defendant had been negligent in failing to close the door to one of its cars, thereby permitting the plaintiff's cousin to be thrown out as the car rounded a curve. The plaintiff was injured while attempting, with others, to rescue his cousin. Clearly the principal negligence of the defendant was in risking harm to someone who might fall out through the unclosed door. The ques-tion was whether the defendant's negligence was also a proximate cause of the plaintiff/rescuer's harm. Writing for the court, Judge Cardozo held that it was error to instruct the jury that the defendant's negligence was not a proximate cause of the plaintiff's harm unless he had been asked to assist in the rescue. Cardozo explained this result with the famous phrase, "danger invites rescue." In effect the court held that one of the risks that makes it negligent to risk harm to another (when it is in fact negligent to do so) is the risk that a different individual will be injured while attempting to rescue him from the consequences of the defendant's actions. That others will attempt to rescue someone whose safety the defendant's actions put at risk is foreseeable; therefore harm to the rescuer is within the cluster of risks that makes the defendant's

---

3. For a case that nonetheless denies recovery on similar facts, *see Di Caprio v. New York Central Railway*, 231 N.Y. 94, 131 N.E. 746 (1921).

4. 232 N.Y. 176, 133 N.E. 437 (1921).

actions negligent—or so the jury may find. And many jurisdictions now hold that, as a matter of law, negligently-caused danger invites rescue.

The foreseeability and harm-within-the-risk tests, then, are a fairly straightforward way of attempting to understand the basic scope of a defendant's liability for negligence and thereby to understand the doctrine of proximate cause. One cannot stop there, however, for two reasons. First, when the tests are satisfied, there is usually liability for physical harm. But even when the tests are not satisfied, occasionally there is liability nonetheless. Second, the cases that pose difficult scope of liability, or proximate cause issues, come in enough varieties that further examination of the subject is necessary to gain a complete appreciation of the way it is handled.

II. Advanced Issues

Most of the issues that are not directly and immediately resolved by the foreseeability and harm-within-the risk tests fall into one of three categories: (1) cases in which the harm the plaintiff suffers is remote in time or space from the negligent conduct of the defendant; (2) cases of intervention and enablement, in which one party negligently enables or increases the risk that another party will be engage in tortious conduct; and (3) cases involving the issue of what must be foreseeable or, to put it another way, when liability may be imposed even when some aspect of what occurred was unforeseeable.

A. Remoteness in Time or Space, and Directness

One of the literal meanings of "proximate" is "close." It is no surprise, therefore, that as the proximate cause requirement developed, the courts sometimes said that there was no liability if the defendant's negligence was only a "remote" cause of harm. Usually the courts meant that the harm the plaintiff suffered was at some remove, in time, space, or both, from the defendant's negligence. For example, suppose the defendant negligently moors a boat to a dock, the boat floats down the river, bumps into and thereby sets another boat adrift, and three days later that second boat damages a draw bridge. The issue is whether the defendant's negligence was a proximate cause of damage to the plaintiff's bridge.

Historically, many courts would have analyzed this issue by asking whether the harm to the bridge was too remote in time and space from the defendant's negligence for that negligence to constitute a proximate cause. Some courts asked what amounts to the same question using a "directness" test. Under this test, the defendant's negligence constituted a proximate cause if that negligence caused harm to the plaintiff "directly." Of course, in order for harm to be caused directly, the defendant's negligence must almost always be close in time and space to the occurrence of harm. Courts sometimes talked (and sometimes still talk) about a "chain" of causation, using the number of links in the chain as a metaphor for proximity and/or directness.

Both remoteness and directness, however, have tended to fade away as tests for analyzing the proximate cause issue. Certainly very few courts now use the directness test. Instead, both remoteness and directness have been subsumed as considerations that are relevant, among others, under the foreseeability and harm-within-the-risk tests. Other things being equal, the closer the defendant's negligence is in time and space to the harm suffered by the plaintiff, and the more direct that connection, the more foreseeable the harm was to the defendant, and the stronger the arguments for the proposition that the risk of this very sort of occurrence is a harm within the risk that made the defendant negligent. Thus, to return to the above hypothetical, the question for most contemporary courts, in deciding whether to submit the proximate cause issue to the jury, would not be whether the harm the boat caused to the draw bridge was remote, or indirect, but how foreseeable a result of the defendant's negligence a jury could find the harm to the draw bridge to have been. The closeness of the bridge in time and space to the defendant's negligence, and how directly harm occurred, would be relevant considerations, but they would not be determinative.

Thus, remoteness and directness are no longer accepted as independent tests for proximate cause because there are occasions on which harm is both remote and indirect, but still highly foreseeable. For example, a defendant can foresee that fireworks it negligently manufactures in New York and ships across the country in January may cause harm in California on July 4th. Harm from fireworks that then occurs to a plaintiff in California on that day is remote in time and space, and indirect, but it is foreseeable nonetheless. The defendant's negligence in such a case is, or at the least may be found by a jury to be, a proximate cause of that harm.

B. *Intervention and Enablement*

A problem that requires some elaboration of the foreseeability and harm-within-the risk tests involves what are sometimes called intervening or superseding causes. In such cases the subsequent acts of independent third-parties or forces are the immediate cause of harm, but the original negligence of the defendant is also a cause in fact of that harm. Then the question is whether the "first actor" is or is not relieved of liability because of the subsequent acts of the "second actor" or because of the operation of a subsequent force.

The early courts considering questions like this followed the "last wrongdoer" rule, under which only the second actor's negligence was a proximate cause of the harm to the plaintiff. One rationale for the rule appears to have been the mechanical and arbitrary assumption of the early common law that there could be only one proximate cause of a harm in this context. Another part of the rationale for the rule, however, was that the first actor should not be responsible for the negligence of the second actor. Although the last wrongdoer rule disappeared long ago, some residue of this second rationale still lingers in analysis of intervention and enablement cases. The issue is just how responsible the first actor should be for the harm caused by the intentional wrongdoing, negligence, or non-negligent conduct of the second actor. Unsurprisingly, this varies with the situation, though it tends to depend on how foreseeable the second actor's conduct was to the first actor.

Sometimes this question is first addressed by the courts under the rubric of whether the first actor owed any duty to the plaintiff, and (sometimes confusingly) this duty question sometimes also turns at least in part on the foreseeability of the plaintiff. First let us identify this duty question, so that we can distinguish it from the intervention and enablement issues addressed in this Section under proximate cause. Then, having identified this duty question and distinguished it from the proximate cause question, we can set aside the duty question until Chapter Eleven.

Suppose the defendant bartender serves a visibly intoxicated patron who then leaves the bar by car and negligently injures the plaintiff.[5] Or the defendant service station negligently leaves keys in the ignition of a car parked on its lot for servicing, and a thief who takes the car collides with the plaintiff.[6] The question in the first instance in each of these cases is whether the defendant owes a duty to the plaintiff. The courts consider a number of factors in deciding this question, including how foreseeable to the defendant injury to parties in the plaintiff's position is, which party is in the better position to insure against the risk of harm to the plaintiff, and the degree of moral blame that can be ascribed to the first

---

5. *See, e.g., Vesely v. Sager,* 5 Cal.3d 153, 95 Cal.Rptr. 623, 486 P.2d 151 (1971).

6. *See, e.g., Ross v. Hartman,* 139 F.2d 14 (D.C.Cir.1943).

actor. If the duty question is answered in the negative, the cases is over, because the defendant owed no duty to the plaintiff. For example, most courts hold that a social host has no duty to third parties to refrain from serving a guest too much alcohol. On the other hand, assuming that the duty question is answered in the affirmative, and the plaintiff proves the other elements of his case (breach of duty, damages, and cause in fact) then the proximate cause issue arises. Most courts hold, for example, that a bartender in a commercial bar does owe a duty to third parties not to serve a patron too much alcohol.

Turning now to the proximate cause issue, these typically are cases in which the first actor has "enabled" the commission of a subsequent tort.[7] Under the fairly straightforward proximate cause analysis set out above, whether the first actor's negligence is a proximate cause of injury caused by subsequent wrongdoing turns on the foreseeability of the subsequent wrongdoing or subsequent causal force. Standard terminology describes these situations as involving only an "intervening" cause when the foreseeability of injury to the plaintiff is one of the risks that is taken into account in deciding whether the defendant's actions were negligent. In this situation the defendant's negligence is a proximate cause of the plaintiff's injury, or at least the issue is submitted to the jury. The intervening act does not break the "chain" of causation leading from the defendant's act to the plaintiff's injury, because the intervention is foreseeable. Some fact situations involving subsequent intervention are sufficiently recurring to be the subject of rules. A driver whose negligence injures the plaintiff is a proximate cause of injuries caused by the malpractice of a physician who treats the plaintiff; a party who negligently loans a car to a driver who is known to be reckless is a proximate cause of injuries suffered by the driver's victim. On the other hand, when the degree of foreseeability of the risk of injury to one in the plaintiff's position is debatable, then the question of proximate cause is not the subject of a rule and will go to the jury. And when the risk of injury to the plaintiff is so unforeseeable that it is not a factor to be taken into account at all in deciding whether the defendant's actions were negligent, the subsequent act of a third-party or operation of a new force is described as a "superseding" cause, and as a matter of law the negligence of the defendant is not a proximate cause of the plaintiff's injury. The subsequent act of negligence supersedes the defendant's act, because it breaks the "chain" of causation.

---

7. *See* Robert L. Rabin, *Enabling Torts*, 49 DePaul L. Rev. 435 (1999).

Sometimes a second actor's conduct that is intentionally tortious, and perhaps even criminal, is sufficiently foreseeable to render the first actor's negligence a proximate cause of the harm caused by the second actor. But since negligence is more common than intentionally tortious or criminal actions, there are cases in which subsequent negligence by a second actor is foreseeable, whereas more blameworthy conduct is not. Then the first actor's negligence is held not to be a proximate cause of harm caused immediately by the intentional misconduct of a second actor, or it is a jury question whether there is sufficient proximity. In such situations the courts sometimes say that subsequent intentional misconduct breaks the "chain" of causation leading from the first actor, because that misconduct was intentional rather than merely negligent. Of course, there are cases in which the first actor is negligent precisely because his action risks intentional or negligent misconduct by a second party. A service station that leaves keys in the ignition of a car it is servicing is negligent because of the risk of theft—intentional wrongdoing by a second party. Under these circumstances the chain of causation is not broken. It is worth noting, however, that the "chain" metaphor is just that—an image that merely states a conclusion, and not a way of reasoning to a conclusion. It probably would be better if the courts did not use this metaphor at all, and instead identified and articulated their reasoning.

Sometimes the subsequent act of a second actor which causes injury to the plaintiff is not even negligent. For example, suppose the thief who stole a car with the keys left in the ignition by a servce station is driving carefully when he collides with the plaintiff. Then the case is a lot like *Berry v. Borough of Sugar Notch*.[8] It is true that the negligence of the service station did slightly increase the risk to the plaintiff, since absent the theft there would have been one less car on the road at that moment. This is probably not a sufficient increase of risk to permit the proximate cause issue to go to there jury, however, unless there is evidence that in general thieves drive less carefully than those who are authorized to be driving. On the other hand, sometimes injury at the hands of a subsequent, non-negligent third party is sufficiently foreseeable to make that risk one of the things that makes it negligent for the defendant to act as he did. For instance, if I negligently injure you and your injuries are aggravated by subsequent, non-negligent medical care, there is no question that my negligence is a proximate cause of the aggravation. Such aggravation is sufficiently common to make it foreseeable.

8. *See* note 1, *supra.*

All this is doctrinally straightforward, if a bit complicated. But an important non-doctrinal, practical consideration also helps to explain the increasing tendency of the courts to hold that a jury can find the first actor to have been a proximate cause for enabling the second actor to harm the plaintiff. In all of the cases involving the subsequent act of a negligent second actor, that actor is of course liable to the plaintiff. The issue in the cases is whether first actor, whose negligence placed the plaintiff in a position to be injured by the second actor, also may be held liable. Holding that the first actor's negligence also is a proximate cause of the plaintiff's harm (or that the jury is free to find that it is) thus renders an additional party, the first actor, liable or potentially liable.

The economic significance of this kind of development should be obvious: it adds a another pocket from which recovery may be obtained. And it is no surprise that in many of the cases, the first actor is more likely to be solvent, or insured, or both, and therefore more able actually to pay compensation to the plaintiff, than the second actor whose negligence was the immediate cause of the plaintiff's injury. This does not mean that the courts decide these cases in an *ad hoc* manner depending on how solvent the first actor happens to be. But the evolution of the case law to permit the imposition of liability on the first actor probably has been influenced in a general way by the fact that in many of the cases the party who would otherwise be the sole defendant is unlikely to be able to pay a judgment entered against him.

C. *What Must be Foreseeable: When May Liability Be Imposed for the Unforeseeable?*

Many of the more difficult and celebrated cases raising scope of liability, or proximate cause, issues, can be analyzed by recognizing that there are four general categories of cases in which something unforeseeable has occurred, and the question is whether there is (or the jury could impose) liability despite this unforeseeability. These involve: (1) unforeseeable plaintiffs, (2) unforeseeable extent of harm, (3) unforeseeable types of harm, and (4) unforeseeable manner of harm.[9] It turns out that plaintiff unforeseeability matters a lot. Unforeseeability of the extent of harm that occurs, or the manner in which harm occurs, does not. And cases involving an unforeseeable type of harm tend to be decided in ways that make generalization about their results more difficult.

9. *See* Guido Calabresi, *Concerning Cause and the Law of Torts: An Essay for Harry Kalven, Jr.*, 43 U. CHI. L. REV. 69 (1975).

Do not assume, however, that the categories are always self-defining, or that the courts always use these express categories in their opinions. In many, if not most, instances, it will be fairly easy to tell in which category a case properly belongs. When a court says that harm of any sort to this plaintiff was unforeseeable, then the case involves an unforeseeable plaintiff. And when a minor burn might have been expected, but the burn that occurs is much more severe, then the case involves an unforeseeable extent of harm. But sometimes distinguishing between an unforeseeable extent of harm and an unforeseeable type of harm, or between an unforeseeable type of harm and an unforeseeable manner of harm, is more difficult. The classification decision may then determine the outcome of the case. In effect, the court is deciding what counts as a harm within the risk that makes the defendant negligent, and what does not count as such a risk. Conversely, the courts do not always rely on categorization, but sometimes simply address the significance of the fact that something that happened in the case was unforeseeable. In such instances a categorization of the case is an after the fact attempt by commentators or subsequent courts to account for the outcome—an attempt to explain "what was really going on."

It is also worth noting at the outset that three of the most prominent cases in this genre, *Palsgraf*, *Polemis*, and *Wagon Mound*, corresponding to the first three categories listed above (unforeseeable plaintiff, extent of harm, or type of harm), each involve an assumption of unforeseeability that is an artifact of the way they were litigated. In all three cases the foreseeability of the harm that occurred seems plausible. But the plaintiffs chose not to prove or argue that the harm was foreseeable, either through apparent oversight (as seems to have been the case in *Palsgraf* and *Polemis*) or for strategic reasons (*Wagon Mound*). The cases therefore come down to us as involving complete unforeseeability, and the rules they stand for apply only to cases involving complete unforeseeability, rather than to situations in which it might be a jury question how foreseeable what occurred actually was to the defendant. In short, these classic cases are important, but it is crucial to keep in mind both what they do and what they do not stand for.

1. Unforeseeable Plaintiffs

The most famous of all torts cases, *Palsgraf v. Long Island Railway*,[10] involved an unforeseeable plaintiff. A railroad employee helped a passenger onto a train that was pulling out of a station,

10.   248 N.Y. 339, 162 N.E. 99 (1928).

dislodging a package the passenger was carrying. The package contained fireworks, which fell on the tracks and exploded, causing scales that were piled further down the platform where other passengers stood, to topple onto Mrs. Palsgraf. She sued the railroad for negligence. But the negligence of the railroad's employee—if there was any at all—consisted of his failure to exercise reasonable care toward the passenger and his package. Injury to anyone standing down the platform from this action was so unlikely that it was, for practical purposes, unforeseeable. It has often been observed that the scales might not have been dislodged by the concussion from the explosion, as the plaintiff contended, but by people on the platform running away from the explosion. The risk of injury caused by someone on the platform bumping into the scales (and causing them to fall on someone like Mrs. Palsgraf) probably was reasonably foreseeable, or at least might have posed a jury question even for Judge Cardozo. But the plaintiff apparently failed to make this much more straightforward contention, which might have taken unforeseeability out of the case.

The issue, therefore, was whether the case could even go to the jury under the circumstances that were proved. Injury to someone in Mrs. Palsgraf's position was not even remotely one of the risks that should be taken into account by the railroad in deciding how to conduct itself toward the passenger getting on the train, because injury to such a person was unforeseeable—that is, highly improbable. Writing for the majority, Cardozo held that the case could not go to the jury. There is language in the opinion that can be read as suggesting that the railroad had no duty to Mrs. Palsgraf, but that may well be a misreading of what Cardozo was saying. Cardozo probably believed that the railroad had such a duty—a duty to exercise reasonable care to avoid subjecting people to foreseeable risks of harm. Because Mrs. Palsgraf was on the railroad's platform there is no question that she was owed this duty of reasonable care. Cardozo might therefore be understood to have held that the railroad had not breached its duty to Mrs. Palsgraf, because harm to her was not a foreseeable risk of what the defendant had done. Thus, the railroad was not negligent in relation to her. In dissent, Judge Andrews rejected Cardozo's breach of duty analysis. Employing the language of proximate cause, Andrews argued that factors in addition to foreseeability were relevant, including how remote or close in time and space Mrs. Palsgraf was to the defendant's negligence. For Andrews, foreseeability was a more malleable concept than Cardozo believed, and that in any event the question was not whether the railroad was negligent in relation to Mrs. Palsgraf. Once the railroad was negligent in some way, in Andrews' view the question was whether the defendant's negligence was a proximate cause of the plaintiff's injury, and under these facts that question was properly for the jury.

The opinions thus disagreed on two grounds: whether the issue was breach of duty or proximate cause, and whether the issue (whichever it was) should go to the jury. As to the first ground of disagreement, Cardozo said that before the question of proximate cause could even be reached, the defendant must have breached a duty to exercise reasonable care toward the plaintiff, and in this instance that the breach of duty issue was a question of law for the court. In contrast, Andrews said that the issue did in fact concern proximate cause. With respect to this first disagreement there probably was less difference between the two judges than they thought. Whether the explanation given is that there was no breach of duty to Mrs. Palsgraf, or that the defendant's negligence was not a proximate cause of the plaintiff's injury, the basis for the result the majority reached would be the same: Mrs. Palsgraf was an unforeseeable plaintiff as a matter of law.

The second ground of disagreement between Cardozo and Andrews—whether the breach of duty or proximate cause issue should have gone to the jury under the circumstances of the case— was more significant in the context of the case itself. If Cardozo had concluded that injury to Mrs. Palsgraf was even a remotely foresee- able result of what the defendant did, then he might have conclud- ed that the question whether the defendant had breached a duty to her was for the jury to decide. But Cardozo did not think that reasonable people could disagree about that issue, because he did not think that injury to Mrs. Palsgraf was even remotely foresee- able. On the other hand, because Andrews did think that such injury was remotely foreseeable, and because he thought other factors were relevant (e.g., her closeness to defendant's negligence in time and space) he considered the proximate cause question to be appropriate for the jury.

Now it is true that there is a good deal of language in Andrews' dissent suggesting that what I have identified as the first ground of his disagreement with Cardozo (breach of duty versus proximate cause as the proper way to frame the issue) was important to him. Andrews contended that negligence is not a relative concept in the way that Cardozo analyzed it. In Andrews' view, once a defendant is negligent in some way toward someone, then whether that negligence is a proximate cause of the harm that actually results is "all a question of expediency." But then Andrews recited a series of factors to take into account in making the proximate cause deci- sion, some of which in one way or another relate to foreseeability—

the very factor that Cardozo considered dispositive. So the difference between the Cardozo and Andrews approaches in any case in which injury to the plaintiff is not utterly unforeseeable probably is not as great as it may seem.

On the other hand, if we were to read, or misread, Cardozo's opinion as being about the existence of a duty, rather than about breach of duty, then there is a greater difference between Cardozo and Andrews. Typically we tend to think of duty questions as involving legal questions to be decided by the court, and "causal" issues as involving factual questions to be decided by the jury. But if we read Cardozo's opinion as being about breach of duty, then the Cardozo approach will not in principle lead to fewer cases going to the jury. This first difference between the two approaches is likely to be much less important than the second difference—whether or not the court thinks that reasonable people could disagree about the foreseeability of what actually happened. To put the same point another way, Cardozo could have employed Andrews' proximate cause approach to support keeping the case from the jury, just as Andrews could have employed Cardozo's breach of duty analysis to support sending the case to the jury.

Coming now to the core of the difference between the two, the question is whether it should matter that injury to a plaintiff is or is not wholly unforeseeable, if the defendant was in fact negligent toward a different plaintiff. Why not hold, or permit the jury to hold, the defendant liable for the injuries it caused to the unforeseeable plaintiff? After all, the defendant was already taking an unreasonable risk of harm to some foreseeable plaintiff or plaintiffs, or it could not be said that the defendant was negligent at all. Imposing liability for harm suffered by unforeseeable plaintiffs may deter such risk taking toward foreseeable plaintiffs, and that would be a good thing. In response, it could be argued that imposing liability for harm suffered by the unforeseeable plaintiff is too much like imposing liability without fault. The railroad was not at fault in relation to Mrs. Palsgraf, so imposing liability on it is a bit like imposing strict liability for being negligent to someone else. Potential defendants threatened with this kind of liability will not take the risk of harming unforeseeable plaintiffs into account in any precise way when they decide how much care to take, because they do not know how their conduct risks harm to unforeseeable plaintiffs, and are not at fault for failing to consider the risk their conduct poses to unforeseeable plaintiffs.

On this latter view, only if there are reasons for holding the defendant liable that resemble reasons for imposing strict liability would it make sense to hold the defendant liable under the rubric of "negligence" for harm to unforeseeable plaintiffs. And maybe there are in this situation. Why not think of the railroad as being in a better position than Mrs. Palsgraf to build into its decisions the risk of being held liable to plaintiffs that it cannot foresee, and therefore hold the railroad "strictly" liable to such plaintiffs? One answer is that this may be a step onto a slippery slope that leads to much more strict liability generally. How do we distinguish railroads in this situation from all sorts of other defendants who have injured unforeseeable plaintiffs? This depends on the reasons strict liability is imposed—a subject that we will address in Chapter Eight. For now it is enough to see that imposing liability to unforeseeable plaintiffs may implicate something resembling strict liability.

The courts have never fully reconciled the Cardozo and Andrews points of view. Most courts employ Cardozo's conceptual approach, but they are much more inclined than Cardozo seems to have been to let the foreseeability issue, including the time and space considerations that figure in it, go to the jury. In whatever way the issue of the utterly unforeseeable plaintiff is resolved, however, once some harm *to this plaintiff* is even remotely foreseeable, the analysis changes, as in the following category of cases.

2. Unforeseeable Extent of Harm

In contrast to the cases involving utterly unforeseeable plaintiffs are those in which the virtually universal "thin-skull" rule applies. The thin-skull rule governs the rights of *foreseeable plaintiffs* who suffer an *unforeseeable extent of harm*. Under this rule it is no defense that the plaintiff had an unforeseeable weakness or infirmity that caused his or her injury, or that caused injury of much greater severity than would have been suffered in the absence of this weakness. As the courts say repeatedly, the defendant "takes his victim as he finds him." Thus, whereas under *Palsgraf* the defendant is not liable to a plaintiff who was unforeseeable, under the thin-skull rule unforeseeability is irrelevant. How can this difference between the treatment of unforeseeable plaintiffs and an unforeseeable extent of harm be explained?

Two different kinds of explanations can be given. The first explanation for the thin-skull rule is that rejection of the rule would create so many practical problems that the rule is a necessity. For example, suppose that even a foreseeable plaintiff could not recover compensation for injuries of unforeseeable severity. The plaintiff in every case would then be required to prove that the extent of his injuries was foreseeable. To prove that the severity of his injuries was foreseeable, the plaintiff would have to prove what a "normal" amount of injury under the circumstances would have been. But of course in any population of individuals a substantial percentage of them are not in perfect health; indeed, virtually everyone probably has some weakness or other that might qualify as analogous to a thin skull. People are born with some of these weaknesses, they acquire others, and sometimes they are temporarily injured and have their injuries aggravated by tortious conduct. If the thin-skull rule were not in force, in every case the jury would have to address which of these weaknesses, infirmities, and injuries, physical and mental, are "normal," or at least foreseeable. Expert testimony might be required on the question, and certainly would be admissible even if not required. This could turn every case into a complicated, drawn-out affair, and might produce fewer settlements and more trials. The thin-skull rule avoids these complications entirely.

A second explanation for the thin-skull rule might be that the rule imposes a desirable kind of strict liability. Because individuals vary enormously in the degree to which they are weak or strong, the defendant who can foresee the risk of injury to a particular plaintiff or class of plaintiffs must know that there is a distribution of the probable severity of the injury risked by any given action, from slight injury to severe injury. Even a light touch risks the low probability of causing severe injury. Consequently, any potential defendant can always foresee a thin-skulled plaintiff, at least in the statistical sense. For this reason, the threat of liability for an unforeseeable extent of harm can in fact promote optimal deterrence, because potential defendants can make at least rough calculations about the risk that they will injure a thin-skulled plaintiff. Thus, foreseeable plaintiffs with unforeseeable vulnerability are already "in the sights" of potential defendants, whereas all the other people in the world are unforeseeable plaintiffs and are not meaningfully "in the sights" of potential defendants.

The exceptions to the thin-skull rule tend to confirm this explanation for it. There are whole classes of cases—decided under other doctrines altogether—in which the thin-skull rule conceivably could be applied but is not, precisely because it makes more sense for the plaintiff to bear the risk in question than for the defendant to be held "strictly" liable for it. For example, the defendant does not take a negligent plaintiff as he finds him; rather, the plaintiff is either barred from recovering at all by contributory negligence, or under comparative negligence the award is reduced in proportion to the amount of negligence attributable to the plaintiff (for discussion of these doctrines, see Chapter Seven). Similarly, even a non-negligent plaintiff is obliged to take reasonable steps after injury to mitigate the extent of the losses he suffers. In these cases the defendant does not have to take his victim as he finds him; rather, some weakness of the plaintiff is taken into account in deciding whether and for how much the defendant is liable to the plaintiff.

Of course, one might say that it is not unforeseeable that a plaintiff will be contributorily negligent or fail to mitigate his damages after injury. But that would be all the more reason to apply the rule that the defendant takes his victim as he finds him in these situations. Yet the rule is not applied to these cases. The explanation is that it makes more sense for the negligent plaintiff to bear these costs than for the defendant to do so. As to these cases, the defendant's negligence is not a proximate cause of the losses resulting from the plaintiff's negligence or failure to mitigate. In each case, for substantive reasons that typically are not even discussed under the rubric of proximate cause, tort liability does not follow the thin-skull rule. In short, when it makes substantive sense to hold the defendant liable for an unforeseeable extent of harm, the thin-skull rule applies. But in seemingly analogous cases in which the policies underlying the thin-skull rule would not be well-served by applying it, other tort-law doctrines do not require that the defendant take his victim as he finds him.

3. Unforeseeable Type of Harm

Between the extremes of the utterly unforeseeable plaintiff and the foreseeable plaintiff with an unforeseeably thin skull lie cases involving what might be called an unforeseeable "type" of harm to a foreseeable plaintiff. Cardozo himself envisioned such cases toward the end of his opinion in *Palsgraf*:

> There is room for argument that a distinction is to be drawn according to the diversity of interests invaded by the act, as where conduct negligent in that it threatens an insignificant invasion of an interest in property results in an unforeseeable invasion of an interest of another order, as e.g., one of bodily security.[11]

A number of classic cases and hypotheticals fall into this category. Suppose that the defendant negligently leaves a container of nitroglycerine on a shelf, and the container is accidentally knocked off the shelf. The nitroglycerine does not explode, though it lands on and injures the plaintiff's foot. May the jury find the defendant liable, or is there no proximate cause as a matter of law? Commentators differ, and probably courts would as well.

11.   162 N.E. 99, 101 (N.Y. 1928).

At least one reason for the uncertainty of outcome in cases such as this is that the policies that underlie the distinction between the *Palsgraf* and thin-skull rules do not strongly dictate a general result either way in this kind of case. Some cases involving an unforeseeable type of harm to a foreseeable plaintiff resemble *Palsgraf*, in that the defendant is unlikely to be able to predict the scope of liability it may face for unforeseeable types of harm. But other cases resemble thin-skull claims in that a somewhat calculable range of harms might result from the defendant's negligence, even if some types of harm, realistically, are not even remotely part of what enters the determination of whether the defendant was negligent in the first instance. Moreover, if there were always a difference in the treatment of type of harm and extent of harm cases, or in the treatment of utterly unforeseeable and only remotely foreseeable type of harm, enormous pressure would be placed on the classification decision; yet the distinction between the type and the extent of harm, or between an utterly unforeseeable and a remotely foreseeable type of harm, is not always obvious, to say the least.

Thus, in *In re Polemis & Furness Withy & Co.* (an early twentieth-century British Commonwealth case),[12] a plank fell into the hold of a ship in which petrol was stored and caused an explosion that destroyed the ship. There were findings of fact that the defendant's employees were negligent in causing the plank to fall; that the explosion was caused by a spark resulting from the falling of the plank; but that the spark could not reasonably have been anticipated from the falling of the plank, though some damage to the ship might reasonably have been anticipated. From the modern standpoint it seems at least arguably foreseeable that a plank might strike something in the hold that was metal, and that this could cause metal to metal contact, a spark, and a fire. But the plaintiff either chose not to so contend or failed to persuade the finder of fact. The question was therefore whether the defendant's negligence was a proximate cause of the unforeseeable harm. The defendant proposed a distinction between an unanticipated extent of harm and an unanticipated type of harm, which the court rejected. The court held instead that the defendant's negligence was a proximate cause of even unforeseeable harm, so long as the harm was a "direct" consequence of the defendant's negligence. As we saw earlier, this directness test has largely faded away.

Years later, *Polemis* was overruled in the British Commonwealth by *The Wagon Mound*.[13] In that case the defendant negli-

12. 3 K.B. 560 (1921).

13. *Overseas Tankship (UK) Ltd. v. Mort's Dock & Engineering Co. Ltd.*, [1961] A.C. 388 (P.C.Aust.) (*The Wagon Mound, No. 1*).

gently flushed oil from its ship while in Sydney harbor. The oil eventually caught fire and destroyed the plaintiff's dock. It was foreseeable that the oil would foul the dock, but the plaintiff chose not to prove that it was foreseeable that the oil would ignite and burn the dock. Probably this was a conscious strategy—if the oil's catching fire was foreseeable to the defendant, it was arguably foreseeable to the plaintiff, which would have made the plaintiff contributorily negligent. So the unforeseeability of fire had to be assumed. The court held that the defendant could not be held liable for the fire damage to the dock, precisely because that damage was not foreseeable. The court's rationale seemed not only to overrule *Polemis*, but the thin-skull rule as well, since the basis for the decision was that there is no point in holding a defendant liable for anything unforeseeable, even to a foreseeable plaintiff. Yet that has not been how the case has been read by subsequent courts. Rather, the courts have concluded that the thin-skull rule survives after *The Wagon Mound*. Therefore, the case seems to stand for the proposition that there can be no liability when a foreseeable plaintiff suffers an unforeseeable *type* of harm, even if that harm is a direct consequence of such negligence, but that there is still liability to a foreseeable plaintiff for an unforeseeable *extent* of harm.

Even under this limiting interpretation, *The Wagon Mound* states a rule that is broader than most courts in the United States accept. Faced with cases involving an unforeseeable type of harm to a foreseeable plaintiff, most American courts make the proximate cause determination—or decide whether to permit the jury to make it—on a case-by-case basis. They are likely to take into account a variety of factors, including the directness of the harm, the degree to which it more closely resembles an unforeseeable type of harm than an unforeseeable extent of the same type of harm that was foreseeable, and whether the defendant's negligence caused other damage for which it is already being held liable and therefore not being totally exonerated from liability.[14] In short, as to unforeseeable types of harm to foreseeable plaintiffs, no general rule can be confidently stated other than that many such cases will be permitted to go to the jury on the proximate cause issue.

4. Unforeseeable Manner of Harm

The last category of cases involving something unforeseeable arises when injury to the plaintiff is unquestionably foreseeable, and the type of injury that occurs is foreseeable, but that injury occurs in a peculiar or bizarre manner. For example, in *Marshall*

---

14. For the classic statement of this point of view, *see* Judge Friendly's opinion in *Petition of Kinsman Transit Company*, 338 F.2d 708 (2d Cir.1964).

v. Nugent,[15] the defendant's driving forced a car in which the plaintiff was a passenger to run off the road. The plaintiff was at that point unharmed, but suffered injury after he had walked down the road and was struck by a third vehicle as he was attempting to warn oncoming traffic of the danger ahead. Despite the unusual way in which the plaintiff actually was injured, this did not preclude liability on the part of the defendant. As long as the plaintiff was injured at roughly the same time and in roughly the same place as was foreseeable, through the same general forces as were foreseeable, it is not necessary that the precise manner in which the injury took place have been foreseeable. If that were a requirement the defendant's negligence would rarely be a proximate cause of the plaintiff's harm, since there are an almost infinite number of detailed variations on the manner in which a foreseeable injury may occur. Consequently, the general rule is that, unless in retrospect the manner in which a foreseeable plaintiff suffered a foreseeable type of harm appears to be so extraordinary as to be completely unforeseeable, the fact that the harm occurred in an unforeseeable manner does not bar recovery.

III. Judge, Jury, and the Underlying Purpose of Proximate Cause

To round out our portrait of the scope of liability and proximate cause issue, two points must be added. The first point concerns the significance of the relation between judge and jury in making determinations about the issue. The second, related point requires us to step back from the details of the cases and doctrine in order to reflect about their underlying purpose.

A. *Judge and Jury*

Some of the complexity that appears to plague the law governing proximate cause can be reduced by attending to an important feature of the cases that often goes unrecognized. Many of the cases deal with a problem at the extreme end of the continuum: whether the defendant's negligence *was not a proximate cause* of the plaintiff's harm, *as a matter of law*. Thus, the question in these cases is whether the proximate cause issue can even go to the jury. Such famous cases as *Palsgraf* and *The Wagon Mound* fall into this category (though in the Commonwealth there are no juries, so in *Wagon Mound* the issue was simply whether there was a firm rule

---

15. 222 F.2d 604 (1st Cir.1955).

of law that there is no liability for unforeseeable harm or no firm rule).

It is important to recognize, however, that the second category of proximate cause cases does not involve a situation at the opposite end of the continuum. Rather, these cases hold that the proximate cause issue was properly submitted to the jury, or was improperly kept from the jury. Few cases, that is, concern the situations in which the defendant's negligence *was a proximate cause* of the plaintiff's injury, *as a matter of law*. Aside from the thin-skull rule (which does fall into this category), there are few cases that address this problem, because it is unremarkable. If I run a red light and collide with another vehicle at the intersection controlled by the light, then of course my negligence is a proximate cause of the harm that results, as a matter of law. The very reason I am negligent in running the red light is that doing so risks causing precisely this kind of injury. If I am negligent in this situation, it is not a jury question whether that negligence was a proximate cause of what happened. In finding me negligent the jury necessarily has made that determination already.

The occasional opinions that do involve the second category of cases—which rule that the proximate cause issue is properly one for the jury—sometimes give the inaccurate impression that they are holding that the defendant's negligence was a proximate cause of the plaintiff's harm as a matter of law. In their understandable effort to justify rejection of the defendant's contention that, as a matter of law, its negligence was not a proximate cause of the plaintiff's harm, the courts in these cases sometimes seem to be suggesting the opposite. But of course the courts are not suggesting that the defendant's negligence was a proximate cause of the plaintiff's harm, as a matter of law. These decisions merely hold that, because reasonable people could disagree about whether the defendant's negligence was a proximate cause of the plaintiff's harm, the question was properly one to be left to the jury.

Thus, cases such as *Wagner v. International Railway*[16] and *Marshall v. Nugent*[17] are not the polar opposites of *Palsgraf* and *The Wagon Mound*. On the contrary, these cases occupy a middle point between the extreme cases in which as a matter of law there is no proximate cause and those in which as a matter of law the defendant's negligence is a proximate cause. It turns out that (to paraphrase Cardozo's famous line from *Wagner*) danger does not necessarily invite rescue. Rather, under *Wagner*, reasonable people

16. *See* note 4, *supra*.
17. *See* note 15, *supra*.

could disagree about whether danger invited rescue under those circumstances, and that the question should therefore be submitted to the jury. Similarly, under *Marshall v. Nugent*, it is not true that as a matter of law the injury the plaintiff received by being struck by the defendant's car "was not remote, either in time or place, from the negligent conduct of defendant * * *". Rather (as the court took pains elsewhere in the opinion to note explicitly), it was for the jury to decide whether the injury to the plaintiff was or was not "remote."

The lesson to be learned from this distinction is that occasionally there are decisions holding as a matter of law on no-proximate-cause or no breach of duty grounds that the plaintiff's case may not go to the jury (such as *Palsgraf*) or is governed by a rule applied as a matter of law (such as *The Wagon Mound*). But more often the complex proximate-cause reasoning that one encounters in the opinions is verbal overkill, directed at explaining why the issue is simply one for the jury.

B. *The Underlying Purpose of Proximate Cause*

Proximate cause is a liability-limiting doctrine. The proximate cause requirement takes the universe of claims that are eligible for liability and designates those in which liability should not be imposed. Further, by distinguishing between cases that should and should not go to the jury, the doctrine expresses what lies behind its liability-limiting purpose in two different ways. First, decisions withholding a case from jury decision on proximate-cause grounds tend to do so in rule-based formulations that can never capture everything that enters into the decision that there is no proximate cause, as a matter of law. Indeed, in reading Judge Andrews' dissent in *Palsgraf*, I always get the sense that Andrews objects mainly to Cardozo's unwillingness to acknowledge the relevance of the many factors Andrews believes should be taken into account in making the proximate cause decision. His objection to the majority's decision to keep the case from the jury seems almost secondary. The majority opinion in *Palsgraf* gives helpful, but inevitably incomplete guidance to the courts as to the situations in which a case should not go to the jury.

Second, and in contrast, when a proximate cause issue does go to the jury, the very factors that are so difficult to articulate in a formal judicial opinion are likely nonetheless to be considered by the jury. And it is in the jury room, I think, that the most significant and most frequently overlooked application of proximate cause doctrine actually takes place. In the jury room, the common-sense principle underlying proximate cause—that negligent defendants should not always bear liability to all the people or for all the harm they have caused, because at some point liability must stop—can be put into practice. Judgments about such matters as the degree of remoteness of the defendant's action from the plaintiff's harm, and whether the amount of liability that may be imposed on the defendant fits the tort it committed (something like what would be called "proportionality" in the field of criminal punishment), each of which fine-tune the negligence decision itself, can be made by the jury without the need to quantify or explain the weight given to each factor. The doctrine of proximate cause thus creates the need for a jury instruction that acquaints the jury with its responsibility not merely to make a mechanical decision applying the rules of tort law, but also to use its judgment in deciding whether the defendant was sufficiently blameworthy under all the circumstances to deserve to bear liability. Far from being the theoretical and conceptual construct that the appellate decisions sometimes make it seem to be, in this sense proximate cause is the most practical and realistic of doctrines, for it asks the jury to step back after it has applied the individual pieces of the liability puzzle and look at the whole picture before it makes its final decision.

7

DEFENSES BASED ON PLAINTIFF'S CONDUCT

The defenses based on plaintiff's conduct—contributory and comparative negligence, as well as assumption of risk—form an important part of many tort suits. Each is an "affirmative" defense. That is, the defendant bears the burden of pleading and proving the facts necessary to support one of these defenses. The defendant must prove that the plaintiff's conduct was negligent or consisted of assumption of risk, that such conduct was a cause in fact of the plaintiff's injury, and that such conduct was a proximate cause of this injury. In the typical case involving a defense based on plaintiff's conduct, then, each party tries to prove what amounts to a full tort claim against the other. The difference is that the plaintiff attempts to prove that the defendant breached a duty and caused harm to him, whereas the defendant attempts to prove that the plaintiff breached a duty to and caused harm to himself.

I. Contributory Negligence

Contributory negligence is the failure of the plaintiff to exercise reasonable care to protect himself or his property from the risk of harm or loss. Now that comparative negligence applies in at least some negligence cases in all but a few states, the full defense of contributory negligence is a thing of the past. But the concept of contributory negligence still is the reference point for the modern reforms. Most of the discussion here involves the meaning and application of the concepts of contributory and comparative negligence. But it is important to remember that, just as the plaintiff's *prima facie* case against the defendant has the separate elements of duty, breach, causation, and damages, so the defendant's affirmative defense has analogous elements. Thus, the defendant must prove not only that the plaintiff breached a duty to exercise reasonable care to protect himself from harm, but also that this breach was both a cause in fact and proximate cause of his suffering harm.

Almost as soon as negligence emerged in the early nineteenth century as a distinct tort, the defense of contributory negligence began to develop along with it. In *Butterfield v. Forrester*,[1] for example, the court seemed to think it self-evident that a negligent plaintiff had no right to recover from a negligent defendant. From the inception of the doctrine until the 1970's, in most states of the United States the contributory negligence of the plaintiff was a complete bar to recovery. Even a slightly negligent plaintiff could recover nothing from a negligent defendant, if the plaintiff's negligence was both a cause in fact and a proximate cause of his own injuries. At that point statutes in many jurisdictions and a few judicial decisions quickly replaced this complete bar with comparative negligence, under which the negligence of the plaintiff does not bar recovery but reduces it.

Sometimes the conduct that constitutes contributory negligence also is primary negligence, so to speak. For example, almost every act of negligent driving risks harm to the driver and to others; whether the negligent driver or another party (or both) is injured is often just a matter of luck. Logically one would think that whether the plaintiff was negligent ought to depend not only on the risk he took for his own safety, but also on the risk his conduct posed to others. Undoubtedly some juries take both sets of risks into account, but there is little law on the issue. On the other hand, some acts of contributory negligence are only that—they create an unreasonable risk of harm to oneself but not to anyone else—using a defective chain saw unsafely when no one else is foreseeably in the vicinity, for instance.

At the core of the defense of contributory negligence is the notion that it would be unfair to impose liability on the defendant when the plaintiff has negligently contributed to his own injury. The trouble with this notion is that its opposite is also true. It is unfair to completely relieve the defendant of liability merely because the plaintiff's negligence was also a cause of his own injury. Nor can causal reasoning explain the defense. There is nothing in the facts of the countless cases in which the defense of contributory negligence has been applied to suggest that the plaintiff is the sole cause in fact or sole proximate cause of his own harm. Rather, in these cases the defendant's negligence and the plaintiff's negligence are both causes in fact and both proximate causes of the plaintiff's harm. Finally, deterrence cannot explain the defense either. To whatever small extent the contributory negligence defense deters potential plaintiffs from being negligent, it fails to deter potential defendants at least as much. Potential plaintiffs always have an incentive to be careful in order to avoid injury, whereas some

---

1. 103 Eng.Rep. 926 (K.B.1809).

potential defendants are "absentees" whose negligence only risks harming others. Under contributory negligence potential defendants can anticipate being relieved of liability in some cases even when they are negligent, and this undermines deterrence.

Despite considerable historical scholarship on contributory negligence, it is still not entirely clear why the defense developed in the way it did, as a complete bar to recovery. Part of the explanation may be that when negligence was first recognized as a separate tort, recovery on that basis was regarded as sufficiently unusual that it was thought appropriate to make compensation available only to plaintiffs with completely "clean hands." In addition, there has long been speculation by some commentators—though the matter is disputed—that the defense of contributory negligence was employed by the courts as a device to reign in the power of juries, which nineteenth century judges sometimes distrusted. The defense would only have been a fully effective device for achieving this aim, however, when it was possible to hold as a matter of law that the plaintiff had been contributorily negligent and therefore to grant a directed verdict for the defendant notwithstanding the defendant's own negligence. And that would not have been common. Finally, though today we find comparative negligence to be more compatible with our sense of fairness, the nineteenth century courts may simply have been unable to see this approach as a coherent stopping point between the extremes of no-liability and full-liability when the plaintiff's negligence had contributed to his own injury.

Nevertheless, as time went on the courts recognized and became increasingly concerned about the harsh effect that sometimes resulted from the complete bar to recovery effectuated by the contributory negligence defense. Prior to the adoption of comparative negligence, a number of doctrinal exceptions and practices emerged at least in part in order to ameliorate this harsh effect. These are discussed in the following Sections.

A. *The Safety Statute Exception*

Many courts held (and still hold) that when the defendant's negligence consisted of the breach of a statute designed specifically to protect a class of persons unable to protect themselves against the defendant's negligence, the contributory negligence of a member of the protected class is not a bar to recovery. For example, if the driver of a school bus negligently fails to take measures required by statute when students exit the bus, a student's contributory negligence may not be a defense in an action for injuries resulting from the driver's negligence. The safety measures are

167

mandated precisely because of the risk that students will not exercise reasonable care to protect themselves. Similarly, if a statute requires ladders furnished to certain employees to have safety shoes, the negligence of an employee in using a ladder without safety shoes does not bar a negligence action against the party who was under a statutory duty to furnish the proper ladder.[2] The logic behind this rule is not particularly compelling, since much negligent conduct that is not a statutory violation is considered negligent precisely because those whose harm the conduct risks cannot or may not adequately protect themselves against this risk in the first place. Otherwise the risk taken by the defendant might not be an unreasonable risk to take. The safety statute exception seems primarily to have reflected a reaction to the harsh effect of the contributory negligence bar to recovery in a category of cases that seemed on their surface to be conceptually distinct from those in which the defense is ordinarily available, but which on deeper analysis are difficult to distinguish from ordinary cases.

B. *The Greater–Degree–of–Blame Exception*

Contributory negligence was not (and still often is not) a defense to an intentional tort, because the defendant's conduct is so much more blameworthy than the plaintiff's. The same reasoning applied to situations in which the plaintiff was contributorily negligent but the defendant's conduct was more blameworthy than mere negligence, even if it was not intentional. The defendant's conduct may have constituted gross negligence, recklessness, or wanton and willful misconduct. This greater-degree-of-blame exception to the contributory negligence defense was generally applied in any of these situations—whenever the defendant's conduct consisted at least of gross negligence. Just as interesting for our purposes, however, is the fact that the exception did not apply when the plaintiff's conduct was as blameworthy or more blameworthy than the defendant's conduct. For example, even if the defendant's conduct showed wanton and willful disregard for the safety of others, if the plaintiff showed wanton and willful disregard for his own safety, then the plaintiff was barred from recovery. In effect the same degrees of blame cancelled each other out. Thus, something like a rough comparison of the faults of the parties not only determined when there was an exception to the contributory negligence defense, but also when there was no exception.

C. *Last Clear Chance*

A third example of the courts' effort to ameliorate the harsh effect of contributory negligence was the doctrine of last clear

---

2. *See Koenig v. Patrick Constr. Corp.*, 298 N.Y. 313, 83 N.E.2d 133 (1948).

chance. I have never been certain whether last clear chance constituted deliberate judicial obfuscation in the service of a desired
result, or just plain confusion. Either way, last clear chance was a
striking by-product of the contributory negligence defense. If the
negligent defendant had the last clear chance to avoid harming the
plaintiff, then the plaintiff's contributory negligence was not a bar
to recovery. The defendant's last clear chance trumped the defense
of contributory negligence.

Why would that be so? Being the last in time to have an
opportunity to avoid injuring someone does not render the party
who had the first chance to do so any less a proximate cause of the
injury. The first and second negligent actors may both be proximate
causes of what happens because of their negligence. Nor is there
anything particularly more blameworthy about negligently failing
to avail oneself of the last chance to avoid injuring another person
than in negligently failing to use one's earlier chance to do so. On
the other hand, when a defendant has a chance that is both last
and clear, the failure to take that chance may well be more
blameworthy than ordinary negligence. A clear chance is one that is
open and obvious. If that clear chance to avoid injury also is the last
chance—because at that point the plaintiff cannot extricate himself
from danger—and the defendant knows this, then the inference
that the defendant knew that he or she alone could avoid the injury
is also likely to be permissible. Under these circumstances, one
might say that the defendant was an entire order of magnitude
more blameworthy than he would have been had he simply failed to
exercise reasonable care to avoid causing injury, at the same time
that the plaintiff was also failing to exercise reasonable care. That
is surely what was going on in the case in which the last clear
chance doctrine seemed to originate, *Davies v. Mann*.[3] There the
plaintiff was apparently negligent in tying the forefeet of his
donkey together so that it could not move, and then leaving the
scene. The defendant then drove his wagon right over the donkey.
In cases such as this, last clear chance might be understood as a
another version of the greater-degree-of-blame exception to the
contributory negligence defense.

I find all this plausible as an explanation of how the courts first
came to think that last clear chance was an appropriate exception
to the contributory negligence rule. But for several reasons the
comparison of faults explanation of last clear chance tends to

---

3. 10 M. & W. 546, 152 Eng.Rep. 588 (Exchequer 1842).

contain the seeds of its own demise. Sometimes the doctrine applies even when the defendant who had the last clear chance may not have been more blameworthy than a merely negligent defendant—in fact, he may have been merely careless as well. This is because the case law makes it clear that in order to invoke last clear chance, the plaintiff need not prove that the defendant actually appreciated the position of danger in which he encountered the plaintiff. Rather, last clear chance requires only that the defendant "had reason" to appreciate that danger. Having "reason to know" that one is about to injure the plaintiff is not the same as knowing. The requirements of last clear chance therefore can be met without proof that the defendant was any more than negligent in failing to appreciate the facts staring him in the face, and then failing to exercise the opportunity he would have had to avoid injuring the plaintiff. Sometimes, of course, the defendant will have been more than merely negligent, because he will have actually known of the plaintiff's danger. But sometimes not. So the attractiveness of the crude comparison of faults that helps to explain the different-degree-of-blame exception to contributory negligence can justify only a portion of the situations in which last clear chance may apply. Thus, over time, the courts applied the doctrine not only when the defendant had the last clear chance, but also when the defendant's chance was last but not clear, nonetheless calling this "last clear" chance.

And the converse was also true. The doctrine was often applied when the defendant's chance was clear but not last, but it was still called "last clear" chance. This occurred when the plaintiff could have extricated himself from his position of danger up until the moment of injury through the exercise of reasonable care, but failed to do so. For example, the plaintiff may simply be negligently inattentive and just as capable as the defendant until the very moment of injury of avoiding harm to himself, simply by paying attention and getting out of the way. Something like a crude comparison of faults may help to explain the application of last clear chance to this situation, but not because the defendant's chance was last. The plaintiff could also have avoided injury up until the last moment. However, if in this situation the plaintiff is in a position of obvious peril and the defendant knows this but nonetheless injures him, the inference that the defendant did so intentionally or recklessly is likely to be permissible. This is surely more blameworthy than the plaintiff's merely negligent inattentive-ness. But since both the defendant and the plaintiff could have avoided injury to the plaintiff up until the instant before it oc-curred, the defendant did not have the last chance to avoid the injury. The timing of the defendant's chance, which the very name of the doctrine "last clear chance" proclaims to be decisive, is logically irrelevant to the doctrine's application in this situation.

Admittedly, if one is in fact simply comparing the faults of the parties, it makes sense to relieve the plaintiff of the effect of his contributory negligence when the defendant's chance is clear but not last. The party whose chance to avoid the injury is clear probably is more often more at fault than the party whose chance was last but not clear. If this is so, however, then the distinctiveness of last clear chance as an exception to the contributory negligence defense in cases involving sequential negligence has disappeared. Once sequence is logically irrelevant to the calculus, why purport to make sequential negligence by the parties a prerequisite to engaging in what amounts to the comparison of faults? Why not simply move to comparative negligence generally? The answer, of course, is that eventually that is exactly what happened. Last clear chance was a transitional doctrine that has tended to fade away with the advent of comparative negligence, because it was merely a means of ameliorating the harsh effect of contributory negligence in a set of situations that, as the set expanded, could no longer be satisfactorily distinguished from the mine-run of contributory negligence cases.

D. *The Jury Question/General Verdict Approach*

The last reflection of the way in which contributory negligence eventually fell into disfavor was not a doctrine, but a practice. Whether the plaintiff was negligent was, and is, a quintessential jury question. Further, although the rhetoric courts used in determining whether to submit the question of defendants' and plaintiffs' negligence to the jury was highly similar, in practice the courts sometimes were more inclined to submit the latter issue to the jury than the former. Other things being equal, a defendant's conduct was more likely to be held negligent as a matter of law than a plaintiff's conduct. Since juries themselves are known to favor plaintiffs, other things being equal, the very practice of submitting the contributory negligence issue to the jury itself helped to ameliorate the harsh effect of the contributory negligence defense.

A less obvious but just as important effect of this approach was that it permitted the jury to apply what amounted to under-the-table comparative negligence. Although the jury in every case in which the contributory negligence defense was in force was instructed that such negligence is a complete defense, experienced lawyers virtually all agreed that it was common for juries to disregard this instruction. Instead juries often returned "quotient" verdicts in which they reduced the plaintiff's recovery through a rough comparison of the faults of the parties. Juries could most easily circumvent the complete-bar rule in this way when they were asked only for a general verdict. Typically the evidence regarding such items of loss as future medical expenses and lost wages, if any, and past and future pain and suffering, was sufficiently open-ended that awarding any sum within a very wide range of values was within the jury's discretion. Consequently, the jury could make a smaller award than the maximum that might have been expected without necessarily revealing that it had "split the difference." A smaller award than the maximum permitted by the evidence could just as easily reflect a finding that the plaintiff was not negligent at all, but suffered less damage than the plaintiff contended. The result in such cases was that everyone suspected the jury of having invoked comparative negligence, but no one could be sure when this had actually occurred.

II.   Comparative Negligence

Over the last four decades a revolution of sorts has replaced the contributory negligence defense with a comparative negligence regime. All but four states (Alabama, Maryland, North Carolina, and Virginia) and the District of Columbia have now adopted comparative negligence, 36 by statute and 10 by judicial decision. As I have just noted, under-the-table comparative negligence probably was at work in many jury deliberations for a long time, though unsystematically and without control or instruction by the courts. With the formal adoption of comparative negligence, however, an entire system of rules implementing the basic concept had to be developed. There are now hundreds of reported decisions addressing a variety of issues that arise in connection with the new defense. It is nonetheless a measure of the time it takes for a system of common law adjudication to do the backing and filling necessary to produce a mature body of doctrine that, even after several decades, many issues are still unsettled in many states.[4]

A.   *The Basics*

Although the verbal formulation setting out the comparative negligence defense varies, the core of the defense is the same.

---

4.   An extremely useful resource on these issues is RESTATEMENT (THIRD) OF TORTS: APPORTIONMENT OF LIABILITY, which systematically addresses not only comparative negligence, but other issues related to the apportionment of liability.

Under comparative negligence, the contributory negligence of the plaintiff does not necessarily bar recovery. Instead, the plaintiff's recovery is reduced "in proportion to the amount of negligence attributable to him," to quote the typical operative provision. Normally this occurs by assuming that, by definition, the total amount of negligence contributing to the plaintiff's injury or damage was 100 percent. The jury must divide (or compare) the negligence of the parties and attribute a percentage to each. The plaintiff's recovery is then reduced by his percentage. For example, suppose that the plaintiff's damages are $100,000 and that the jury finds the plaintiff to have been 40 percent negligent. Reducing the plaintiff's recovery by 40 percent yields $60,000. He therefore recovers $60,000, because his recovery is reduced in proportion to the amount of negligence attributable to him.

1. Pure Versus Modified Comparative Negligence

There are two forms of comparative negligence. Under the "pure" form, the plaintiff's negligence is never a complete bar to recovery. Rather, comparative negligence applies regardless of how much more negligent the plaintiff was than the defendant. Thirteen states have adopted this approach, 7 by judicial decision and 6 by statute. In contrast, under the "modified" form of comparative negligence, if the plaintiff is found to be more negligent than the defendant (and under some versions, "as negligent" as the defendant), comparative negligence does not apply and the plaintiff's contributory negligence is a complete bar to recovery. Thirty-three states have adopted this approach, 3 by judicial decision and 30 by statute. Under modified comparative negligence, when the plaintiff is entitled to recover anything he recovers exactly what he would recover under pure comparative negligence. The difference is that the plaintiff can always recover something under pure comparative negligence except when he is 100 percent negligent, which is tantamount to saying that the defendant was not negligent at all and therefore not liable. In contrast, under modified comparative negligence a plaintiff who is more negligent than the defendant (and under some versions, as negligent as the defendant) recovers nothing.

Under modified comparative negligence a small variation in the amount of negligence attributed to the plaintiff can mean the difference between a substantial recovery and none at all. Probably the most common jury attribution of negligence is a finding that each party was 50 percent negligent. In a jurisdiction that applies modified comparative negligence as long as the plaintiff's negligence is "not greater than" the defendant's, the plaintiff recovers one-half of his damages under this scenario. In a jurisdiction that applies comparative negligence only if the plaintiff's negligence is "not as great as" the defendant's, however, the plaintiff will be completely barred from recovery when there is a 50–50 attribution. Juries that understand this possibility can take it into account, making sure that they do not attribute "too much" negligence to the plaintiff and thereby bar him from any recovery at all. In most states with modified comparative negligence, the jury is instructed regarding the way in which comparative negligence operates and can make an "adjustment" in the amount of negligence attributed to the parties to assure some recovery for the plaintiff, if the jury so desires. In a few states, however, the jury is simply asked to bring in a special verdict indicating the total amount of the plaintiff's damages and the amounts of negligence attributable to each party. The court then makes the calculations necessary to determine if the plaintiff is entitled to a recovery and, if so, in what amount. In these latter states the difference between a 50/50 and a 51/49 jury finding can have an enormous impact.

2. The Basis for Comparison

Comparative negligence is just what its name implies—comparative *negligence*, not comparative causation. In any individual case it is possible for a party to be slightly negligent and cause a great deal of harm, just as it is possible to be very negligent and yet cause little harm. Note, however, that in comparing negligence there is an automatic comparison of an aspect of causation, because the foreseeable probability of causing harm is a component of what it means to be negligent. A jury's decision regarding the degree of negligence attributable to a plaintiff or defendant should therefore take into account the probability that the conduct in question will cause harm, even though the amount of causal contribution in this particular case is not relevant. Thus, in a sense it is average potential causal contribution under the circumstances rather than the particular causal contribution in the case at hand that is taken into account.

In any event, it would be difficult to operate a pure comparative causation system. The very notion of a causal comparison apart from the parties' negligence is far from clear. Suppose that the plaintiff drives 60 miles per hour in a 30 mile per hour zone and the defendant drives 90 miles per hour in the same zone. One view of the matter would be that the parties' causal contributions should be measured by the amount of their causal negligence. On this view the defendant's contribution is 66 and 2/3 percent and the plaintiff's 33 and 1/3 percent—60 miles per hour over the speed limit versus the plaintiff's 30 miles per hour over. Another view would be that the amount of each party's causal contribution is a matter separate from their negligence, once it is shown that they are negligent. On this view the defendant's causal contribution is 60 percent (9/15ths of the total amount of speed) and the plaintiff's was 40 percent (6/15ths). Both of these approaches, however, ignore other factors that may have caused the damage that actually resulted from the parties' negligence—for example, the weight of each vehicle.

In theory, comparing negligence alone and not causation side-steps these issues. Of course, instructing the jury that it is to take negligence but not causation into account in making its comparative attribution is not the same as assuring that this is done. Moreover, comparing negligence is not always a simpler task than comparing causation, though it is admittedly a different operation. For instance, it not at all clear in the above example that the defendant was twice as negligent as the plaintiff. The defendant was exceeding the speed limit by twice the amount of the plaintiff's exceedence. But plaintiff was driving at a speed (60 miles per hour) at which he was undoubtedly able to control his vehicle. In contrast, at 90 miles per hour the defendant probably had much less ability to control his vehicle, and much less experience doing so at that speed as well. Perhaps, therefore, the defendant was more than twice as negligent as the plaintiff.

Nor is the comparison always between the same "kinds" of negligence. Suppose that the defendant was speeding and that the plaintiff failed to come to a complete halt at a stop-sign. The jury in this case must compare "apples and oranges," so to speak. At least, however, the comparison is between two different kinds of negligent driving. Sometimes the forms of negligence the jury must compare are even less like each other than this. Sometimes, that is, the jury must compare apples with something that isn't fruit at all. For example, suppose that the plaintiff negligently failed to trim a tree on his property and as a result the defendant, who was negligently speeding, did not see a stop-sign obscured by the tree. Braking at the last minute, the defendant skids and injures the plaintiff. The negligence of the two parties adds up to 100 percent. How much negligence should be attributed to each?

The *law* of comparative negligence has nothing much to say about the problems entailed in making such comparisons. And I am not suggesting that it should. These are simply issues for a jury that is instructed to compare the negligence of each party. The jury must struggle, evaluate, and respond with a comparative attribution of the parties' negligence. But no one should assume that a jury's task under comparative negligence is as simple and straight-forward as comparing two quantities that are already in the same currency of exchange. The jury's task is more complicated than that, and sometimes far more complicated.

3. Assessment

There is considerable debate in the literature about the comparative effectiveness of contributory and comparative negligence in deterring accidents. The overall implication of this literature is that neither approach is likely to be a systematically superior method of deterring accidents. Intuitively this seems obvious: other things being equal, plaintiffs are likely to exercise marginally greater care under contributory negligence and defendants are likely to exercise marginally greater care under comparative negligence. No one can say in general whether the loss of deterrence in the one respect will or will not be more than offset in the other respect. In any event, in practice other things usually are not equal. To take just one of many complicating factors as an example, whether potential victims know that a comparative negligence rule is in force may affect the relative deterrence capacity of comparative and contributory negligence rules. Yet some people will know about the comparative negligence rule and others will not. Consequently, one's assessment of the attractiveness of comparative negligence must depend mainly on considerations other than deterrence.

In addition, I am not aware of any studies of the incidence of jury findings in modified comparative negligence states that the plaintiff was more negligent than the defendant. This is an entire area in which contributory negligence in theory still applies and bars the plaintiff from any recovery. On the other hand, it may be that the percentage of cases in these states in which juries find that the plaintiff was more negligent than the defendant and completely barred from recovery is small.

In any event, in my view the appeal of comparative negligence to the ordinary individual's sense of fairness is sufficiently great to render this factor alone virtually dispositive on the issue. The contributory negligence rule that completely barred recovery from a negligent injurer because the victim also was negligent, without regard to the degree of that negligence, was and is highly objectionable to most people's sense of fairness. Virtually every ordinary person's immediate reaction to the contributory negligence defense is that recovery should not be barred in this situation, but that the amount recovered should be reduced in some proportion that takes the victim's negligence into account. One might quibble about

whether the proper approach should be pure or modified comparative negligence, and about the details of the scheme adopted. But
the day when the contributory negligence defense meshed with the
common sense morality of ordinary people—if it ever did—has long
since passed. The adoption of comparative negligence in all but a
handful of states is a reflection of the now-dominant moral sense
that some recovery should be permitted for negligent victims,
though not as much as for those who were not at all negligent.

B. *Applications*

Legislative enactment or judicial adoption of comparative negligence creates the need for a whole new jurisprudence resolving the
many issues that arise under a comparative negligence regime.
Entire treatises are now devoted to these issues, few of which are
resolved in the statutes or judicial decisions that initiate the new
regime.

1. Multiple Defendants

Suppose that the plaintiff is 40 percent negligent and two
defendants each are 35 and 25 percent negligent, respectively. In a
modified comparative negligence jurisdiction, does the plaintiff recover anything? That depends on the underlying logic of modified
comparative negligence. If this logic is that a plaintiff should be
entitled to recover something unless she is principally responsible
for her own harm, then recovery should be permitted. On the other
hand, if the underlying logic of a modified system is that a defendant should not be held liable unless she is at least as responsible
for the plaintiff's harm as the plaintiff, then there should be no
recovery in this situation. Most courts have found the former
answer preferable. The move from contributory to comparative
negligence tends to be made more because of the unfairness of
contributory negligence to plaintiffs than because of a desire to
plug a loophole in the liability of defendants. A focus on the scope
of the plaintiff's responsibility therefore seems most appropriate in
the handling of multiple defendant cases.

2. Joint and Several Liability

Prior to the adoption of comparative negligence, multiple defendants were jointly and severally liable to the plaintiff. Under
contributory negligence, as between a negligent defendant and an
innocent plaintiff (the only kind of plaintiff who could recover at all
under contributory negligence), joint and several liability properly
places the risk of one defendant's insolvency on the other negligent

defendant or defendants. Under comparative negligence, however, the plaintiff is not entirely innocent, because he too was negligent. If the plaintiff and two defendants are 40, 35, and 25 percent negligent, respectively, should each defendant be liable only for its share of the plaintiff's damages, or should each of the two defendants be jointly and severally liable for 60 percent of the plaintiff's damages?

Three approaches, each of which have been adopted in whole or in part in different states by statute or judicial decision, are possible. The first is to hold the defendants jointly and severally liable for the amount of the judgment (for 60 percent of the plaintiff's losses) even though the plaintiff also was negligent. If the defendants are merely concurrent but not joint tortfeasors, then there is no particular logic to this approach, because the defendants are no more responsible for each others' negligence than the plaintiff; this approach is simply a carryover of the prior rule. On the other hand, if the defendants are joint tortfeasors or otherwise acted in concert, the approach has some appeal.

Second, at the other extreme is an approach that in effect revokes joint and several liability and holds each defendant liable only for its own proportional share of the reduced judgment. Thus, the first defendant in the hypothetical would pay 35/60ths of the judgment. If the second defendant, whose proper share is 25/60ths were unable to pay, then the plaintiff would be left without recourse as to that share. This approach presupposes that, in effect, not only are the defendants injurers of the plaintiff, but that the plaintiff is an injurer of the plaintiff. Under this logic, each party is liable to the plaintiff in proportion to the amount of its negligence, and no party should be liable for more than its share.

The flaw in this logic leads to the third and, in my view, most sensible approach. If each party including the plaintiff is an injurer, then the injurers as a group should pay the injured party, and should bear the risk that one of their number is insolvent. On this view, the solvent defendant and the plaintiff should bear the risk of the other defendant's insolvency, in proportion to the amount of negligence attributable to them. In our example, the plaintiff is 40 percent negligent and the solvent defendant is 35 percent negligent. The insolvent defendant is 25 percent negligent and is unable to pay its share of the defendants' total share of 60 percent of the plaintiff's losses. Under the third approach, the plaintiff's and the solvent defendant's responsibility for the insolvent defendant's share would be apportioned by comparing the amount of negligence attributed to them. The total of their negligence is 75 percent. In addition to its own share, therefore, the solvent defendant would be liable to the plaintiff for 35/75ths of the insolvent defendant's share. The plaintiff would have to bear the remaining 40/75ths of the insolvent defendant's 25 percent share himself.

3. Effect on Other Common Law Doctrines

The typical comparative negligence statute is short and makes little or no reference to the new status, if any, of such common law doctrines as last clear chance, assumption of risk, and the greater-degree-of-blame exception to the contributory negligence defense. The courts must therefore fill in what is omitted from the statutes, by deciding the status of these doctrines under comparative negligence.

As a transitional doctrine designed largely to mitigate the harsh effect of the complete bar of the contributory negligence defense, last clear chance should have no role as a separate doctrine once comparative negligence is adopted. Most courts have so held. Of course, to the extent that failing to avoid injuring the plaintiff renders the defendant more negligent than the plaintiff, the jury is entitled to take into account the defendant's failure to use the last clear chance into the negligence comparison. But the jury also is entitled to take other factors into account. Having failed to take the last clear chance should no longer be dispositive on the question whether and for how much the defendant is liable, though that failure may be relevant. Most courts have so ruled.

It is especially important for last clear chance to be abolished entirely or not at all under a modified comparative negligence regime. Otherwise perverse results may ensue. Suppose that last clear chance were merely abolished when comparative negligence applied, but continued to be in force when the plaintiff was more negligent than the defendant. Then a plaintiff injured by a defendant who failed to take the last clear chance would be better off proving that he was more negligent than the defendant—because last clear chance would eliminate the effect of his contributory negligence and he would be entitled to a full recovery. In contrast, if the plaintiff proved that he was less negligent than the defendant, then (because last clear chance would not apply under comparative negligence) he would obtain only a partial recovery. Conceivably a 51 percent negligent plaintiff could recover in full, whereas a 49 percent negligent defendant would recover only 49 percent of his losses. To avoid this cockeyed kind of result, last clear chance must be entirely preserved or entirely abolished.

Treatment of the greater-degree-of-blame exception under comparative negligence varies. Once the jury is directed to compare the faults of the parties, there is little need to place their actions into categories of blame. Instead, faults can be compared directly. Nonetheless, some courts have interpreted their comparative negligence statutes to apply only to negligence actions and therefore to have no effect on the greater-degree-of-blame exception. In effect, these courts have held that the plaintiff's negligence is no defense at all to an intentional or similar tort, but that neither does comparative negligence abolish the same-degree-of-blame defenses to such torts.

Finally, under contributory negligence the defense of assumption of risk (discussed in the next Section of this Chapter) completely bars the plaintiff from recovery when he knowingly assumes the risk that the defendant will injure him. Usually this defense based on the plaintiff's conduct is available, however, only when the plaintiff's assumption of risk was unreasonable and therefore negligent. The majority of courts have concluded, therefore, that it would make little sense to preserve an independent assumption of risk defense within comparative negligence, since the plaintiff's unreasonable assumption of risk can simply be taken into account in making the comparative negligence attribution.

4. Strict Liability

Contributory negligence is a defense to a strict liability action in some jurisdictions and not in others. The availability of the defense also sometimes varies depending on the type of strict liability action at issue. How should the adoption of comparative negligence affect strict liability actions if the statute itself does not address the issue?

The most straightforward approach is simply to apply comparative negligence wherever contributory negligence previously applied. But it could be argued that contributory negligence ought to continue to be a complete defense to a strict liability claim wherever it was a complete defense prior to the adoption of comparative negligence, because the plaintiff is clearly more negligent than the defendant, who is held liable without fault. A fairly persuasive response to this argument is that when a defendant is held strictly liable it is not found to be free from negligence; rather, the issue is simply irrelevant. It is possible that the defendant was negligent, and therefore possible to compare that negligence with the negligence of the plaintiff, if any. Whether the defendant was negligent and, if so, how negligent, would then become issues at the trial of any strict liability action in which the defendant raised the defense of the plaintiff's negligence.

In some strict liability situations, however, contributory negligence was not a defense. Should comparative negligence be applied in these situations? The strength of the argument opposing introduction of this new defense depends on the reason contributory negligence was not a defense. If the point of denying the defense was that the defendant in the kinds of cases that are subject to strict liability is the best bearer of the risk that the kinds of accidents in question will occur, then that does not change with the enactment of comparative negligence. On the other hand, if contributory negligence was not a defense because it was viewed as excessively harsh, then a comparative negligence defense to strict liability might make sense. For example, it may be that in cases involving strict liability for abnormally dangerous activities comparative negligence should not be a defense for this reason, but that in strict products liability actions comparative negligence should be a defense. These forms of strict liability are discussed in Chapters Eight and Nine, respectively.

A final problem, relevant in both of the contexts just discussed, is how comparative negligence can possibly operate if the defendant was not in fact at fault but is held strictly liable nonetheless. What is the jury to compare with the plaintiff's negligence? One possibility is that the plaintiff's negligence should be compared with the way he should have behaved. If he was half as careful as he should have been, then his damages should be reduced in half. But this has not been the answer given by the courts that have addressed the problem. Their answers have not been entirely coherent, and sometimes they have come close to admitting it. For example, in holding that comparative negligence does apply in strict products liability cases, the Supreme Court of California dismissed the argument that the jury in such cases would be required to compare "apples and oranges," and instead redescribed the jury's function. Comparing the fault of the parties, the Court said, was not what the jury was really being asked to do. Rather, the jury was to engage in an "equitable" apportionment of liability.[5] The Court's ultimate conclusion—and that of many courts addressing the issue—was that regardless of whether it is conceptually coherent to employ comparative negligence in strict products liability cases, it will be done because it is fair to do so.

5. Setoffs

Suppose that in an automobile accident in a pure comparative negligence jurisdiction, both the plaintiff and the defendant/coun-

---

5. *Daly v. General Motors Corp.*, 20 Cal.3d 725, 144 Cal.Rptr. 380, 575 P.2d 1162 (1978).

terclaimant are injured. A judgment is entered in favor of each party, specifying the amount of damages to be awarded to each. If neither were insured there would ordinarily be a setoff of the smaller award against the larger one, and the net amount remaining would be awarded to the party who had the larger judgment. For example, if the award to the plaintiff (in light of the amount of negligence attributed to him) were $100,000 and the award to the defendant/counterclaimant (again, in light of the amount of negligence attributed to him) were $50,000, then the plaintiff would be entitled to recover $50,000 from the defendant/counterclaimant, and the defendant/counterclaimant would be entitled to recover nothing from the plaintiff.

But suppose that both are covered by liability insurance. Should the result be the same? If there is no setoff, then the defendant/counterclaimant's insurer owes the plaintiff $100,000, and the plaintiff's insurer owes the defendant/counterclaimant $50,000. On the other hand, if there is a setoff, then the defendant/counterclaimant's insurer owes the plaintiff $50,000, and the plaintiff's insurer owes nothing: the parties' insurers save $50,000 each. The argument for a setoff is that liability insurance simply pays only what a policyholder/defendant owes the plaintiff, and only after a setoff occurs can the amount that a policyholder actually owes the other party be determined. The response to this argument, which has prevailed whenever the issue has arisen, is that a major function of liability insurance, especially in the auto-accident setting, is not merely to protect injurers against liability, but also to assure victims a recovery from negligent parties who cannot afford to pay judgments themselves. A setoff would further deprive victims of compensation, after they have already been awarded only partial compensation in the first instance because of their negligence. It follows that no setoff should be allowed, and that each party's liability insurer must pay his or her adversary's judgment.

III. Assumption of Risk

The notion of "assumption of risk" is used in four different contexts in tort law, often without the clarity necessary to distinguish these contexts from each other. It might actually be beneficial to abolish the phrase "assumption of risk" entirely and use different terms for each of the four situations in which the phrase is now used. But obviously that is not possible. Consequently, we must live with the multi-faceted concept of assumption of risk, taking care to recognize that the concept has different meanings, and different legal consequences, in different situations.

A. *Express Assumption of Risk*

Sometimes an individual contractually agrees in advance to waive his or her right to bring a tort action against a potential injurer. This often happens, for example, in residential leases containing exculpatory clauses or disclaimers of the landlord's liability to the tenant for negligence, in health club membership contracts, or when a skier buys a lift ticket. Often these waivers are valid when entered knowingly, voluntarily, and with appreciation of their significance. The importance of the service or commodity being sold and the bargaining power of the parties also are relevant. Health care providers' disclaimers of liability for malpractice, for example, are virtually always invalid.[6] This form of assumption of risk, when valid, is simply a contractual surrender in advance of the right to sue. The party surrendering this right is in fact assuming a risk, in the sense that she may be tortiously injured but uncompensated. Note that this form of assumption of risk does not hinge in any way on the nature of the plaintiff's conduct, aside from her express agreement to waive her tort rights.

The remaining three forms of assumption of risk are often said to be "implied," in order to distinguish them from an express agreement waiving the right to sue. Because these other three forms of assumption of risk otherwise are very different from each other, however, they must be considered separately.

B. *No Duty of Care Breached by the Defendant*

Suppose you go to a baseball game and sit behind first base. The third baseman fields a ground ball and throws high to the first baseman. The ball flies into the stands and injures you. In your suit against the owner of the stadium, you allege that it was negligent of the defendant to fail to erect a net behind first base to protect fans from the risk of this kind of injury. This theory of liability will almost certainly be rejected on the ground that as a matter of law it was not negligent for the defendant to have failed to erect a net behind first base. But this is not a defense based on the particular plaintiff's conduct, and indeed not a defense at all. Rather, the defendant will prevail because of the failure of the plaintiff to satisfy his or her burden of showing that the defendant was negligent. That is, the defendant did not breach its duty of care to the plaintiff, because the exercise of reasonable care did not require that a net or other method of protecting the plaintiff be provided.

---

6. The seminal case on the issue is *Tunkl v. Regents of University of California*, 60 Cal.2d 92, 32 Cal.Rptr. 33, 383 P.2d 441 (1963).

Another way of saying the same thing is to say that you "assumed the risk" that you would be injured by a high throw to first base. But this way of putting the point is simply the logical corollary of the holding that the defendant was not negligent. Indeed, except in connection with activities that involve strict liability for the injuries they cause, a victim/plaintiff always and necessarily "assumes" the risk that he will be non-negligently injured. "Assumption of risk" in this sense is simply another way of saying that there is no liability if the defendant did not breach a duty of care to the plaintiff. In an unfortunate turn of phrase this form of assumption of risk is sometimes referred to as "primary" assumption of risk, to distinguish it from what is sometimes called "secondary" assumption of risk (discussed in the next Section). However, there is nothing at all "primary" about this usage or the situation to which it is applied, aside from the fact that it is a way of talking about failure of the plaintiff's *prima facie* case rather than about a defense. But the term "primary," though far from universal, is sometimes employed by the courts to describe this notion.

This does not mean, however, that the name "assumption of risk" is applied to such situations for no reason at all. On the contrary, in cases involving assumption of risk of this sort, often the holding that the defendant was not negligent turns on factors that involve the openness of the risk and the voluntariness of typical or ordinary people's participation in the activity in question, in addition to the reasonableness of the risks posed by the activity in light of its benefits. That is why the phrase assumption of risk is more likely to be applied to attending a baseball game than, say, to walking down the street. How much care is owed the audience at a baseball game depends in part on how much the audience in general, though not any particular member of it, knows, and how much self-protective care the audience in general is capable of taking. Note, however, that in walking down the street I "assume the risk" that I will be injured by non-negligent driving. The logical structure of the law applying to these situations is the same, even if the phrase "assumption of risk" seems to apply more comfortably to the baseball game.

C. *A Subset of Contributory Negligence*

Traditionally, the courts regarded the plaintiff's conscious, negligent assumption of risk as a complete bar to recovery. This is therefore the category as to which, since the adoption of comparative negligence, it is rather important to understand the nature of assumption of risk. If unreasonable assumption of risk is a species of contributory negligence (as most courts now conceive of it), then it is subject to comparative negligence and does not result in a complete bar to recovery by the plaintiff.

There are two general ways in which a plaintiff may unreasonably risk suffering harm to himself. The first involves the plaintiff's careless failure to recognize or appreciate a risk. The second is the plaintiff's conscious taking of an unreasonable risk. Each is contributory negligence. But the second form of contributory negligence is typically called "assumption of risk." Unlike the two forms of assumption of risk discussed above, this form of assumption of risk is in fact a defense, and it is based on the plaintiff's conduct in taking a risk. This defense is sometimes called "secondary" assumption of risk. But of course it is secondary only in the sense that it is a true defense, available as a way for the defendant to avoid liability even if proved negligent.

The problem with use of the term assumption of risk to describe this form of contributory negligence is not that the use is inaccurate, but that it is potentially misleading to juries. Ordinarily only the conscious taking of an *unreasonable* risk—negligent assumption of risk—is a defense. If I am walking carefully down the street and you injure me by driving negligently onto the sidewalk, you do not have a defense that I assumed the risk of injury merely because I knew that some people drive negligently. On the contrary, it was entirely reasonable for me to be walking on the sidewalk, and you are liable. Referring to assumption of risk separately in a jury instruction, however, could give the jury the impression that non-negligent assumption of risk is a defense to a negligence claim. A jury instruction that it is a defense (complete or partial depending on whether contributory or comparative negligence applies) if the plaintiff was contributorily negligent *or* assumed the risk of harm would imply that assumption of risk is something different from contributory negligence. Such an instruction would incorrectly imply (or at least could easily be understood to imply) that non-negligent assumption of risk is a defense, separate and apart from contributory negligence.

Now it is possible to avoid misleading the jury, by employing an instruction indicating that assumption of risk is simply one of the two kinds of contributory negligence that may constitute a defense based on the plaintiff's conduct: unreasonable careless risk taking, and unreasonable conscious risk taking. The trouble with this approach is that we do not really have a technical term for the former category, other than "negligence by the plaintiff." For this reason, the very use of the technical-sounding phrase "assumption of risk" to refer to the latter category still runs the risk that the phrase will stand out in the jury's mind and be perceived as something separate from ordinary contributory negligence. This does not mean that the concept should not be used by lawyers and judges analyzing available defenses—this is in fact the one situation in which the term "assumption of risk" seems appropriate and useful. But the potentially misleading character of the phrase "assumption of risk" when used in conjunction with "contributory negligence" suggests that it may be prudent not to use the phrase "assumption of risk" in jury instructions that also refer to contributory negligence.

D. *Conscious, Reasonable Risk–Taking*

The last situation that is sometimes described as "assumption of risk" involves non-negligent risk-taking. For example, in the *Eckert*[7] case described in Chapter Three, the plaintiff's decedent was killed while rescuing a child from being struck by a train. The court held (among other things) that a jury could find that this was not contributory negligence—i.e., assumption of risk—because the decedent's behavior was not unreasonable under the circumstances.

There is no question that as a matter of fact in this and similar situations the plaintiff took a risk—i.e., knew that he might be injured and went forward despite this risk. But that does not mean that he "assumed the risk" in the legal sense. Although the case law by no means provides a uniform answer, the decided trend, especially in the modern cases, is to side with *Eckert* and to hold that the fact that the plaintiff consciously but non-negligently took a risk is not a defense. After all, why should the plaintiff who does not know of a risk negligently created by the defendant be better off than the plaintiff who is aware of the risk and decides reasonably to take it? In most cases it makes normative sense to treat both plaintiffs in the same way, though perhaps room for exceptions ought to be preserved. There are occasional cases in which one would want to say that the plaintiff's actions, in context, amount to a waiver that very much resembles an express assumption of risk, even in the absence of the plaintiff's use of words to that effect. The so-called fireman's rule, which bars firefighters from recovering for injuries they suffer in fighting negligently set fires, may be based on such an assumption of risk. In other settings such matters as the availability of a choice between alternatives that are offered by the defendant at different prices, together with the plaintiff's clear understanding of the risks posed by the more

---

7. *Eckert v. Long Island R.R.*, 43 N.Y. 502 (1871).

dangerous but cheaper alternative, would be relevant in determining whether there had been an implied waiver in that situation.

In short, there are some situations in which the plaintiff is simply in a better position than the defendant to decide whether to risk being injured by the defendant's negligence, or not to do so. For example, suppose that the plaintiff suffers accidental injury on a country road. He needs medical treatment. Along comes the defendant, driving while visibly intoxicated. The plaintiff decides to ride with the defendant, who then drives negligently and further injures the plaintiff. Even if, in view of this emergency, the plaintiff is not negligent in asking for a ride, it still may make sense to relieve the defendant of liability to the plaintiff for driving while intoxicated. Applying assumption of risk to situations such as these, rare though they may be, is tantamount to holding the plaintiff strictly liable for injury to himself, because the plaintiff should bear the consequences of his decision. This recognition makes it easier to understand how some courts in this situation might say that, although the plaintiff's action was not unreasonable and there was no explicitly verbal waiver on the plaintiff's part, the timing, clarity, and voluntariness of the plaintiff's informed decision to take the risk in question yield the conclusion that the plaintiff may not recover because he had "assumed" the risk of the defendant's negligence, even though the plaintiff was not negligent.

8

STRICT LIABILITY AND NUISANCE

This Chapter concerns liability for what have come to be called "abnormally dangerous" activities, for "nuisance," and "vicarious" liability. The first two forms of liability are conceptually important but are not frequently the subject of lawsuits. However, vicarious liability, which includes the liability of employers for the negligence of their employees, is enormously important in practice. It is the most frequently imposed form of strict liability. All three forms of liability are imposed without regard to the negligence of the defendant and are therefore referred to as "strict" liability. It is important to recognize at the outset that these liabilities are strict, but not absolute. That is, liability is imposed in the absence of negligence by the defendant only when a dangerous activity is "abnormally" so, only when an activity rises to the level of a "nuisance," or (in the case of vicarious liability) only when one party is responsible for the actions of another. The key to understanding strict liability, therefore, is to be able to identify the criteria that must be satisfied to render an actor strictly liable—i.e., liable without regard to negligence. To put it another way, since strict liability is in effect activity-based, whereas negligence liability is act-based, the critical question is what characterizes the activities for which the negligence requirement is dropped. To address this question, we turn first to general theories of strict liability, and then to the three main forms that strict liability takes.

I. Theories of Strict Liability

There is no single authoritative or canonical statement of the theory underlying strict liability in tort. A number of judges and scholars have developed different theories that explain or support strict liability. Note that some of these are descriptive theories; they seek to explain the scope and nature of strict liability as it stands in existing law. Others are normative theories; they are addressed to what the law of strict liability ought to be, not what it is. It is also important to recognize that many of the arguments for strict liability accept the notion that some, perhaps even most, liability for accidental harm should be based on negligence. But they contend that in certain contexts, the negligence requirement does not or should not apply, and that strict liability is or should be imposed. Thus, these are not simply theories about strict liability. They are theories about the boundary between negligence and strict liability and about the circumstances under which each approach is, or should be, applied. Since strict liability applies, when it applies, even when the defendant has not been negligent, the essence of a theory of strict liability is the identification of what advantages are or can be gained by imposing an additional increment of liability. Different theories emphasize different advantages.

A. *Reducing Information and Error Costs*

Determining whether a party has been negligent is often a highly fact-intensive process. Adducing proof of negligence may therefore be economically costly and time-consuming. Showing how carefully the defendant acted on a particular occasion may involve more cost and time than showing that the defendant was involved in a particular activity for which strict liability is imposed. For example, expert testimony is more likely to be required or permitted to prove negligence than to prove the defendant's involvement in such an activity. Similarly, evidence of compliance with or violation of a customary practice is admissible because it is relevant to negligence, but is unlikely to be relevant in a strict liability action. And because unexcused violation of an applicable safety statute constitutes negligence, whether a statute was violated may be at issue in negligence but not in strict liability cases. Imposing strict liability makes all these issues irrelevant. There is no need to gather evidence necessary to determine at trial how the defendant acted, whether the defendant complied with a custom or violated a statute, or was negligent in some other way. And there is no need to occupy a trial with these factual questions. Trials may be shorter or may not even need to occur. Strict liability therefore may reduce litigation costs in the classes of cases in which the cost of making the factual findings necessary to resolve issues that negligence make relevant would otherwise be substantial.[1]

Keep in mind, however, that because strict liability does not require proof of negligence, in general it is likely that there will be more claims when an activity is subject to strict liability than when there is liability only for injuries that result from conducting the activity negligently. Thus, although per case administrative costs are likely to be lower under strict liability than under negligence, the cost of litigating additional cases under strict liability must be

---

1. *See, e.g.*, WILLIAM M. LANDES & RICHARD A. POSNER, THE ECONOMIC STRUCTURE OF TORT LAW 65–66 (1987).

figured in if one is making a total-cost calculation. The net effect of the interaction between per-case and total costs depends in part on the level of generality at which a strict liability standard is established. The per case cost of adjudication under a strict liability standard set at a "high level of generality" is very likely to be lower than the per case cost of adjudication under a standard set at a "low level of generality." For example, whether an activity is "abnormally dangerous" can be determined in accordance with a per se rule that admits of few exceptions and is almost cost-free to apply—a rule such as "all use of explosives is abnormally dangerous and results in strict liability." This is a rule set at a very high level of generality. On the other hand, whether there is strict liability might be made to depend on a series of factors that distinguish some uses of explosives from others—for example, how common the use of explosives is in a particular area and how useful it is in that community. This kind of context-dependent rule that is formulated at a lower level of generality will result in case-by-case adjudication that is likely to be more expensive and complicated than litigation under a rule operating at a high level of generality.

In addition to information costs, because negligence is potentially more fact-intensive, there is a greater risk of error in making the negligence determination than in determining whether the facts necessary to support strict liability have been proved. In strict liability, as we will see below, there may be a need only to determine whether the defendant used explosives, or whether bodies of water are common in the area in which a reservoir burst. These factual determinations tend to be subject to less error. In contrast, in negligence, how carefully the defendant did what it did is at issue. Such questions are probably more subject to error in fact-finding. The key is to identify the cases in which this is most likely to be true. Two hypotheticals can illustrate the problem. Suppose that in a class of cases involving one activity—call them Class A cases—juries impose liability for negligence 40 percent of the time, whereas in fact defendants are negligent 60 percent of the time. The rate of error in these cases is 20 percent under-imposition of liability. But the imposition of strict liability in Class A cases would not reduce the rate of error; strict liability would increase error. Under strict liability defendants would be liable 100 percent of the time, whereas they are in fact negligent only 60 percent of the time. The strict liability rate of error would therefore be 40 percent over-imposition of liability, as compared to 20 percent under-imposition of liability under negligence. Some readers may still want to argue that the former is preferable to the latter (and certain of the notions discussed later in this section may support them), but their argument cannot be based on a reduction in the error rate, since strict liability increases the error rate in Class A cases.

Consider now Class B cases, in which the defendant is negligent 60 percent of the time but juries impose liability only 10 percent of the time. The error rate is 50 percent under-imposition of liability. Under strict liability the error rate would be reduced from 50 percent under-imposition of liability to 40 percent over-imposition of liability. What kinds of cases might these be? The best candidate is the class of cases in which evidence of the defendant's negligence is either not available or very difficult to obtain—perhaps because the kinds of accidents that characterize these cases tend to destroy the relevant evidence—but defendants often are in fact negligent. The courts sometimes find the transportation of highly flammable material that is likely to destroy evidence of negligence when it explodes to fall into this category. This may sound a lot like the kind of analysis that leads to *res ipsa loquitur*, which of course is a negligence doctrine. Recall, however, that one of the functions of that doctrine also is to reduce the error rate, and that some *res ipsa* cases closely resemble strict liability. It should come as no surprise, therefore, that *res ipsa* and strict liability have in common their potential capacity to reduce the error rate of the conventional negligence system.

B. *Influencing Activity Level and Research Decisions*

One's initial inclination is to suppose that imposing strict liability will promote additional safety and therefore additional accident reduction beyond what negligence liability alone can achieve. After all, this line of thinking goes, strict liability threatens potential injurers with liability for a greater range of activities and therefore ought to generate more deterrence. In fact, however, this is unlikely to be true as a general matter. Assuming that negligence liability is accurately imposed (a key assumption), strict liability will not cause any particular activity to be conducted with greater safety than negligence liability. Recall from the discussion in Chapter Three that at least in theory the threat of liability for negligence deters all the accidents worth deterring—those whose costs outweigh the costs of avoiding them—because liability for negligence is imposed when accident costs outweigh avoidance costs, and is not imposed when accident costs do not outweigh avoidance costs.

Strict liability goes farther and imposes liability even in the latter cases, when avoidance costs outweigh accident costs. But imposing liability in these cases will not change the level of safety at which potential defendants engage in the activity in question: in these cases it is cheaper to go on having accidents than to invest in the additional safety necessary to avoid them. Because, in these cases, avoidance costs outweigh accident costs, and potential defendants are threatened with liability only for accident costs, it is cheaper to continue causing these accidents than to avoid them, even though one is strictly liable for their costs.

This conclusion does not depend on accepting the Learned Hand calculus as the basis of negligence liability, or on an economic theory of tort liability. Indeed, the conclusion does not even depend on any particular conception of what it means to be negligent. The conclusion depends only on the assumption that potential defendants will tend to act in their own self interest. Setting litigation costs aside, when defendants are held liable, they pay accident costs only—damages suffered by victims. Potential defendants will only avoid paying accident costs by acting more safely when acting more safely is less expensive than incurring liability. Consequently, holding defendants liable even when they have not been negligent will not cause them to act any more safely than it is already in their interest to act because of the threat of negligence liability.

Other things being equal, however, the more a party engages in an activity, even if it exercises reasonable care, the more injury or damage will result. The threat of liability for negligence thus generates no incentive to determine whether it would be more sensible to engage in less of the activity, because exercising reasonable care will insulate a party from any liability for injury or damage that results from engaging in the activity. In theory, liability in negligence could be imposed for engaging in too much of an activity, albeit with reasonable care.[2] In practice, however, negligence liability is rarely imposed for engaging in an excessive level of activity. A party who drives safely is not held liable in negligence for having driven too many miles during the week in which he is involved in an automobile accident; oil companies are not held liable in negligence for drilling too many wells as long as the wells are not drilled in a negligent manner.

A shift to strict liability would give such parties more reason to consider alternative methods of conducting their activities.[3] As long

2. This could also be done indirectly, by charging for auto liability insurance in proportion to the number of miles a motorist drives. See Jennifer B. Wriggins, *Automobile Injuries as Injuries with Remedies: Driving, Insurance, Torts, and Changing the "Choice Architecture" of Auto Insurance Pricing*, 44 LOYOLA OF LOS ANGELES L. REV. 69 (2010)

3. *See, e.g.*, Steven Shavell, *Strict Liability Versus Negligence*, 9 J. LEGAL STUD. 1 (1980).

as a shipper of goods is liable only for negligence it may be cheaper, all things considered, to ship by truck. Once there is strict liability, however, it may turn out that, in fact, other methods of delivery are cheaper, because they are inherently safer—that is, they involve fewer non-negligently-caused accidents. For this reason, shipping by train or air may prove to be less expensive after, but not before, the shift to strict liability. And of course it may be that a partial rather than a complete substitution of one activity for another is the cost-minimizing approach. Thus, strict liability may produce activity-level effects that negligence liability cannot.

Another way of putting this point is to say that under strict liability potential injurers are threatened with liability for the full cost of their risky activities, whereas under negligence liability they are not forced to fully "internalize" these costs. Under strict liability, therefore, potential injurers have the incentive not only to consider whether to conduct their activities more safely (an incentive they already have under negligence), but also a greater incentive to consider whether to shift to safer activities.

As a consequence, strict liability may create additional research incentives, because under strict liability there is more to be gained by avoiding liability. Under negligence, injurers are not liable for accidents that are not worth avoiding. Consequently, injurers have no incentive to attempt to discover cost-effective methods of avoiding these injuries. In contrast, under strict liability, at any given time there is a class of accidents that produces injuries not worth avoiding. But because injurers are liable for these injuries anyway, discovering a cost-effective method of reducing or eliminating the injuries they cause will redound to their benefit. This research may run from the very formal, such as laboratory investigation of new ingredients or designs, to the very informal, such as simple investigation of alternative methods of transportation of the sort I described earlier. Indeed, the informal end of this continuum reflects the connection between the potential activity-level effects of strict liability and research incentives. In a sense some of the research incentives that strict liability may create are incentives to discover activities or activity levels that may substitute for those that currently generate strict liability, in order to reduce net costs.

Like the other potential benefits of strict liability, this matter of research incentives does not admit of easy generalization. Some parties are more likely than others to be in a position to perform formal research; and some activities are more likely than others to be susceptible to change through cost-effective research. Moreover, research itself entails certain costs but uncertain benefits. The payoff from research cannot be known in advance. Investment in research therefore is not investment in accident reduction, but in potential accident reduction. How much research is worth doing can never be known with certainty. Thus, while it is generally true that imposing strict liability can create greater research incentives than negligence alone, it will not necessarily produce additional research in any given situation.

For the above-stated reasons, the reader might quickly suppose that on this score strict liability is therefore categorically preferable to negligence. For two reasons, however, the choice is often problematic. First, there may be activities for which there are no readily available substitutes. Imposing strict liability for injuries caused by these activities could result in more disadvantages than advantages—more claims, no greater safety, and little or no change in activity level. Second, and more significantly, in a sense there is always strict liability and therefore there are always activity-level effects. In fact, the underlying inquiry really is not whether defendants should be strictly liable or liable only for negligence. Rather, the question is who should bear strict liability: potential injurers or potential victims. To see this, focus on what happens in a system in which there is only liability for negligence. Under such a system there still are non-negligently-caused injuries. Because there is no strict liability for these injuries, those who suffer the injuries have no cause of action against those who caused the injuries. This setup can be accurately understood as "no strict liability for injurers." But it is just as accurate to understand a negligence regime as "strict liability for the victims of non-negligently caused accidents." This kind of strict liability system is implemented not by lawsuits, but by the absence of lawsuits—i.e., by declining to impose strict liability on injurers. The operative effect of this denial of strict liability recovery by victims is that victims bear the cost of their non-negligently-caused injuries—they are "strictly liable" for them, to themselves.

The real question, then, is whether there should be injurer strict liability, or only injurer negligence liability plus victim strict liability. In some cases, depending on a host of factors, including the parties' knowledge of and control over alternatives, superior activity-level effects can be expected from injurer strict liability, but in other cases such effects can be more effectively obtained from injurer negligence liability with victim strict liability.[4] This will occur when the most safety can be obtained by influencing potential victims' activity levels. Consequently, the choice often is not an easy one. From the activity level standpoint this insight helps to

---

4. *See* Guido Calabresi and Jon T. Hirschoff, *Toward A Test for Strict Liability in Torts*, 81 Yale L.J. 1055 (1972).

explain why some activities are subject to strict liability and others are governed by negligence. Strict liability should be imposed when potential injurers' activity levels are likely to have more impact on accident rates than potential victims' activity levels. In addition, there is little or no need for strict liability on the part of either potential injurers or potential victims when the exercise of reasonable care, coupled with the defense of contributory or comparative negligence, is sufficient to eliminate the risk of most accidents. For example, if virtually all automobile accidents are caused by negligence, then imposing liability based on negligence alone will create sufficient incentives for accident reduction, and strict liability will not be necessary.

C. *Promoting Insurance or Broad Distribution of Losses*

A third argument for strict liability rests on loss-distributional rather than cost-reduction or incentive-creating considerations. We saw above that in a sense there is always either injurer strict liability or victim strict "liability" for the costs of non-negligently caused accidents. Strict liability might be imposed because a particular category of injurers, rather than a particular category of victims, is in the best position to insure or otherwise broadly distribute the costs of non-negligently caused accidents.

If a particular category of injurers is likely in general to be better insurers of these costs, then their superiority in this respect is an argument for imposing strict liability on them.[5] For example, blasters may be better situated to purchase liability insurance, or to raise the cost of their services, than potential blasting victims are able to purchase health and disability insurance. On the other hand, if particular categories of victims are likely to be superior insurers of the costs of non-negligently caused accidents, then that is an argument against strict liability. Capacity to insure depends in part on knowledge of the nature and probability of the risks posed by an activity. Since such knowledge is also a factor, along with the capacity to control risk, in an actor's ability to influence whether accidents occur, insuring capacity will sometimes, though not always, be congruent with activity-level considerations.

In general, injurers are more likely than victims to be large institutions that can spread the cost of liability directly in their

---

5. For discussion of the positions of two early proponents of this theory, Fleming James, Jr. and Friedrich Kessler, *see* George L. Priest, *The Invention of Enterprise Liability: A Critical History of the Intellectual Foundations of Modern Tort Law*, 9 J. LEGAL STUD. 461 (1985).

prices or services, or to purchase liability insurance whose cost is included in these prices or services. And in automobile liability, the one major area in which injurers are predominately ordinary individuals, access to liability insurance, with the broad loss distribution that such access entails, is virtually automatic. Even in the domain of loss distribution, however, injurers are not necessarily always superior to victims as loss bearers. For example, consider health care costs resulting from a tortious injury—one of the principal components of damages that bodily injury victims recover from tortfeasors. More than three-quarters of the population is covered by health insurance, and the federal health care reform of 2010, if it survives constitutional challenge, promises that more will be insured in the future. To be sure, such insurance does not always cover every dollar's worth of health care expenses incurred by bodily injury victims. But the insurance provides substantial protection. The cost of the health-care component of the vast majority of bodily injury victims' losses is already spread in broad channels of loss distribution. The choice, therefore, is not between broad loss distribution through injurer strict liability or narrow distribution by declining to adopt such strict liability. Rather, the choice is between two different channels of broad distribution.

D. *Satisfying Rights–Based Norms of Responsibility*

The last group of arguments for strict liability are not instrumental in the manner of the arguments discussed above; they are rights-based. They turn on the existence of some norm of responsibility for harm-causing conduct. One version of this approach is the "benefit" theory that goes back about a century. The notion at the core of this theory is that those who benefit from engaging in an activity should rightly bear the costs associated with the activity. The extra cost that strict liability places on injurers burdens them less than what results when victims must bear losses that are nonnegligently caused. The benefit theory leads its proponents to support strict liability on the ground that the owners, employees, and customers of enterprises benefit from their activities and should pay, at least indirectly, for the injuries that enterprises cause.[6]

A second rights-based argument for strict liability is the "reciprocity" theory, which holds that strict liability should be imposed when an activity poses risks for potential victims that the victims do not also pose for others. When the defendant creates a dispro-

---

6. *See, e.g.,* Gregory C. Keating, *The Theory of Enterprise Liability and Common Law Strict Liability,* 54 VAND. L. REV. 1285 (2001).

portionate, excessive risk of harm relative to the victim's risk-creating activity, strict liability should be imposed. Thus, when two airplanes collide, they should be liable to each other only for negligence. But when an airplane causes injury to those on the ground, it should be strictly liable.[7]

A third theory is libertarian, and holds that liability should be imposed when an injurer acts in a manner that causes the invasion of the liberty of others. This is essentially a causal theory, under which strict liability should be imposed, but only should be imposed, when an actor causes harm through the use of force, by some form of compulsion, or by creating a dangerous condition.[8]

* * *

Having examined the potential advantages of strict liability over negligence at a general level, we are now prepared to look at specific doctrines. But it is important to understand the significance of the foregoing analysis. Our task up to now has been to understand what strict liability has the *potential* to do that negligence cannot. Whether and when strict liability actually attempts to do these things is a separate question that is resolved by the specific doctrines to which we now turn our attention.

II. Traditional Strict Liability

What the law of torts terms "traditional" strict liability involves liability for injuries caused by activities—ordinarily uses of land—that were first termed "ultrahazardous" and that are now termed "abnormally dangerous." This Section traces the development of this form of liability and of the limitations on its scope.

A. *The Rise of Liability for "Ultrahazardous" Activities*

Aside from some pre-existing rules governing liability for escaping animals, the modern development of strict liability begins with the English case of *Rylands v. Fletcher*.[9] The defendant in *Rylands* had a reservoir constructed at a point on his property that

---

7. *See, e.g.*, George P. Fletcher, *Fairness and Utility in Tort Theory*, 85 HARV. L. REV. 537, 543–46 (1972)

8. *See, e.g.*, Richard A. Epstein, *A Theory of Strict Liability*, 2 J. LEGAL STUD. 151 169 (1973)

9. LR 3 H.L. 330 (1868). For an analysis of the case and its modern implications, see Kenneth S. Abraham, Rylands v. Fletcher: *Tort Law's Conscience*, in Robert L. Rabin & Stephen D. Sugarman (ed's.), TORTS STORIES 207 (2003).

he did not know lay above, or at least was contiguous with, a former coal mine. The water in the reservoir escaped through the mine, flooding the plaintiff's property. The plaintiff could not show any negligence for which the defendant was responsible, although conceivably the independent contractors whom the defendant had hired to construct the reservoir were negligent in failing to discover the danger in question. The case went to trial and was then appealed through several layers of appellate courts. Ultimately the House of Lords held that the defendant was strictly liable.

Rylands was decided against the background late nineteenth-century rule that there was liability only upon proof that the defendant was negligent. Consequently, the key question in the case is under what circumstances an exception to this general rule would be made. The court purported to answer the question by holding that there would be strict liability for damage caused by what it called the "non-natural use" of the defendant's land. What exactly the court meant, however, was unclear. At the extreme this might mean that the escape of anything brought onto land that was "not naturally there" (to use the language of Justice Blackburn in one of the intermediate appellate courts in the case) would automatically result in liability for the damage caused by the escape. But such an "exception" to the rule that in general there is liability only for negligence would have threatened to swallow up the negligence rule as it applied to land use, since virtually all damage caused by land use results from activities that are not literally "natural" to the land in this sense. A more nuanced conception would regard any use of a particular piece of land that had to be conducted on that site because of its essential character as "natural." The mining of minerals from a site would then be "natural," because the minerals at a site could only be removed from that site. The construction and maintenance of a dwelling on a site would also be natural, since this is a traditional and therefore "natural" use of land.

American courts thought that the *Rylands* exception should be understood in its extreme version and that it did swallow up the liability-only-for-negligence rule. The courts took the case to be rejecting much of negligence law. More firmly wedded to an unbending negligence requirement in the late nineteenth century than the English courts, many American courts therefore rejected *Rylands*, sometimes vehemently. For example, in *Brown v. Collins*,[10] the defendant was sued for damage caused by the non-negligent escape of his horses. The court held for the defendant,

10. 53 N.H. 442 (1873).

stating that "[e]verything that a man can bring on his land is capable of escaping * * *." The court rejected the plaintiff's claim that the defendant should bear strict liability, stating that it is "impossible that legal principle can throw so serious an obstacle in the way of progress and improvement."

Thus the American courts at first took the opposite extreme, rejecting virtually all strict liability. Over the next half-century on both sides of the Atlantic, however, the courts moved away from their seemingly extreme positions and adopted an increasingly intermediate view of the scope of strict liability. In England the courts clarified the meaning of a "non-natural use," explaining that a "natural" use was one that was ordinary or common to the area in which it took place. And in the United States, although the courts often still rejected *Rylands* by name, they began to create a series of specific and at first limited exceptions to the general rule that there was no liability in the absence of negligence. In the beginning only the most dangerous and unusual activities, such as the use of explosives where this was not to be expected, resulted in strict liability. But as time went on the kinds of cases made subject to the exception expanded to include the operation of oil wells and even the storage of unusual quantities of water. Many American courts also recognized the traditional strict liability of the owners of domesticated livestock for damage to land on which these animals intruded. Interestingly, the decision whether to include an activity in a strict liability category came to be one for the court, not for the jury.

Sometimes the U.S. courts called the doctrine under which strict liability was imposed for damage caused by these and other activities "absolute nuisance." But by the 1920s there were enough decisions following a similar pattern for them to be recognized as involving strict liability for conducting an "ultrahazardous activity."[11] The two factors that determined whether an activity was ultrahazardous were the degree of danger it posed and how common it was in the area. The more dangerous and the less common the activity, the more likely it was to qualify as ultrahazardous.

These factors tend to mesh in a rough and ready way with aspects of the theories of strict liability set out in the preceding Section. Remember that in important respects the choice is not between strict liability and no liability, but between strict liability for injurers and negligence liability for injurers with victims being "strictly liable" to themselves for injuries not caused by another's negligence. The two factors that qualify an activity as ultrahazar-

---

11. RESTATEMENT OF TORTS § 520.

dous identify the situations in which imposing liability on potential injurers will maximize certain of strict liability's advantages. First, the more dangerous an activity is, the more violent it is likely to be, and therefore the more likely it is to destroy evidence that would enable the plaintiff the prove that the defendant conducted the activity negligently. Imposing strict liability in such situations is therefore likely to reduce information and error costs. Second, the more uncommon an activity is in a particular area, the more likely it is that the activity-level and research incentives created by the threat of strict liability will be most effective operating on potential injurers rather than on potential victims.

This latter point is true for several reasons. To the extent that an activity or land use is uncommon, those who are its potential victims are unlikely to know much about it and therefore unlikely to be in a position to do much to protect themselves against the risk the activity poses. In addition, land uses tend to involve capital investments and therefore to be comparatively costly to alter. And potential victims of an uncommon land use tend already to be engaged in common uses when the potential injurer makes the decision whether to engage in an uncommon use. If you are already operating a coal mine on your land you cannot very well pick up and go elsewhere when a reservoir is built nearby. The potential injurer is therefore likely to be in a better position to establish optimal activity-levels at the outset, when the cost of doing so is at its lowest, because this does not involve the sacrifice of already-made investments that would be required of potential victims if strict liability were not imposed.

In contrast, when a particular activity is neither especially dangerous nor uncommon in an area, potential injurers probably are not superior to potential victims in their ability to control the risk of injury through activity-level adjustments or research. In fact, to the extent that the activity in question is characteristic in an area—maintaining mill dams in certain New England counties or oil wells in certain Texas counties, for example—then many potential victims are also potential injurers, because they too engage in the activity. So these kinds of activities are unlikely to be considered ultrahazardous. Certainly a potential victim considering locating in the area is on notice of the common risks to which he is subjecting himself and can look to the behavior of existing land owners for guidance as to the best mix of protections to adopt against these risks. In short, strict liability for engaging in ultrahazardous activities is something like common law zoning, designed to encourage similar land uses in a particular area and to impose the cost of engaging in a dangerous and uncommon use on the party who decides not to comply with the "zoning" implications of the strict liability rule.

B. *The Modern Conception: Strict Liability for "Abnormally Dangerous" Activities*

By the time the Second Restatement of Torts was prepared in the 1960's, there had been a sufficient number of strict liability cases that the factors comprising the test for strict liability appeared to be more nuanced than the two blunt criteria figuring in the test for ultrahazardousness. The new test included three different factors affecting dangerousness (degree of risk, probability of harm, and inability to eliminate the risk by the exercise of reasonable care), two factors affecting commonness (the extent to which the activity is uncommon and its "inappropriateness" to the area), plus a new consideration: the extent to which the value of the activity to the community is outweighed by its dangerousness. To distinguish this new test from the one it replaced, it was termed strict liability for damage caused by "abnormally dangerous" activities.[12] This modern test meshed with the theory of strict liability in roughly the same way as did the earlier test, except that the last factor—value to the community—occasionally functioned as a trump, saving from strict liability the rare activity that warranted protection from this regime even when it was dangerous and unusual.

The new test both reflected the tendency of the courts in the modern period to engage in case-by-case analysis of strict liability claims and encouraged this practice. The advantage of this approach was that it had the capacity to draw fine distinctions between activities in light of the weight of the six factors that comprised the test. But the approach also had disadvantages. The great advantage of the earlier ultrahazardous activity approach was not only that it was simpler, but also that, for precisely this reason, it encouraged the formulation of strict liability rules at a comparatively high level of generality. The fact that the question whether to impose strict liability was typically for the court (as it still is) rather than for the jury underscored the importance of the level-of-generality feature of the strict liability decision. But a test that fine-tunes through reference to a series of factors inevitably pushes decisionmaking to a lower level of generality.

It has turned out, however, that certain of the factors specified in the Second Restatement have been more influential than others.

---

12. *See* RESTATEMENT (SECOND) OF TORTS §§ 519–20.

Whether the dangers posed by an activity can be eliminated through the exercise of reasonable care and whether the activity is a matter of common usage have been most significant. The value of the activity to the community, while sometimes mentioned, has been least influential. Indeed, some courts have ruled expressly that this factor is irrelevant to strict liability in their state.

For example, in *Indiana Harbor Belt R.R. Co. v. American Cyanamid Co.*,[13] the defendant was a manufacturer that had shipped 20,000 gallons of a toxic and flammable chemical in a leased railroad tank car. The plaintiff was a company in the business of switching cars from one railroad line to another. The car leaked while in a railroad yard at which it was to be switched. As a consequence the plaintiff was forced to undertake decontamination and other measures to prevent injury and further property damage, including evacuating nearby homes.

The court declined to impose strict liability on the defendant, focusing heavily on two considerations. The first was the probability that the leak could have been prevented through the exercise of reasonable care in the inspection and maintenance of the tank car in question. The court distinguished cases holding transporters of gasoline strictly liable for explosions, on the ground that explosions typically destroy evidence of negligence, whereas leaks do not. The second consideration was the impossibility, in the court's view, of strict liability's having an activity-level effect in this kind of case, because of the difficulty of routing rail-transported material away from the metropolitan areas that serve as railroad hubs.

The court's reasoning may well be correct on the merits. But note the low level of generality at which this application of the criteria for determining whether an activity was abnormally dangerous took place. The court did not ask whether, in general, the transportation of flammable toxic material is abnormally dangerous. Rather, the questions the court considered were whether there is strict liability when the particular means of escape of such material from the railroad tank car in this case could ordinarily be prevented through reasonable care, and whether the adoption of particular alternative routes of railroad transportation would result from the imposition of strict liability. These are highly fact-sensitive and context-dependent questions. As a consequence, the decision in *Indiana Harbor Belt* provides incomplete guidance, at best, as to the proper result when the next tank-car accident involves an explosion rather than a leak, or a smaller quantity of the same

13.   916 F.2d 1174 (7th Cir.1990).

substance that could have been shipped by truck or air instead of rail.

The most recent restatement, RESTATEMENT OF TORTS (THIRD): LIABILITY FOR PHYSICAL AND EMOTIONAL HARM, makes a partial return to the approach of the First Restatement. Section 20 of the THIRD RESTATEMENT hinges strict liability on three black-letter factors: whether an activity poses a foreseeable and highly significant risk of harm, and whether the activity is a matter of common usage. But the Comments to this Section suggest that, aside from whether the activity has value to the community (which has dropped out entirely), the same factors that were considered by Section 520 of the SECOND RESTATEMENT still should be taken into account in making the strict liability determination.

C. *Scope of Liability and Defenses*

The rules governing the scope of strict liability and defenses to traditional strict liability confirm what this form of liability is all about. There is strict liability only for the kind of harm whose risk makes the activity abnormally dangerous—for risks that are "characteristic" of the activity. This is a complicated way of saying that there is only strict liability if engaging in the relevant activity is not only the cause in fact, but also the proximate cause of the harm the plaintiff suffered. That requirement is not remarkable, except that of course the whole point of proximate cause—to assure that a defendant is held liable only for those consequences of his acts which the law wishes to be actionable—underscores that strict liability is not absolute liability for engaging in a particular activity, but only for those consequences that this form of liability is designed to address.

A striking example of this limitation on the scope of liability is *Madsen v. East Jordan Irrigation Co.*,[14] in which the plaintiff's mother mink ate their young after being frightened by blasting. The defendant was held not to be strictly liable, precisely because the possibility that this would occur is not even one of the secondary risks that enters into the decision to impose strict liability for blasting. One way to understand this point is to say that the risk that mother mink will eat their young is not foreseeable to blasters. On this view, if the mink owner had warned the blaster of the sensitivity of the mink, the result might be different; conversely, if the blaster had already known of the presence and sensitivity of the mink, there might at the least have been a duty to warn the mink

14. 101 Utah 552, 125 P.2d 794 (1942).

owner. But a second way to view the decision is to say that the purposes of strict liability are best served by holding the plaintiff strictly liable for this kind of harm, because the risk is not only more foreseeable to mink owners, but much more controllable by them. With respect to the risk that blasting will frighten nervous animals, mink owners are in a better position than blasters to make the activity-level and research calculations that strict liability induces.

For the same reason, from early on it was established that the defendant is not strictly liable if the harm in question results from an Act of God, or the unforeseeable intervention of a third party, or from the plaintiff's knowing and unreasonable assumption of the risk of harm. For example, the harm at issue may result from a flood of utterly unprecedented magnitude, or vandalism, or the plaintiff's own negligence. In these situations the purpose behind strict liability—creating incentives beyond those flowing from the threat of liability for negligence—is less easily served. The cause of the harm in such cases is only remotely foreseeable. Because the cost saving available to the defendant from adjusting its activity levels in anticipation of liability for that kind of harm is therefore likely to be speculative, the threat of liability would affect the defendant only marginally at most, and not much is to be gained from imposing strict liability.

III. Nuisance

A nuisance is a substantial and unreasonable interference with the right of an owner or occupier of land to the *use and enjoyment* of the land. Nuisance is distinct from trespass, which involves interference with the right of *possession and occupancy* of land. Although there are occasional exceptions, nuisances tend to be pollution of one sort or another—contamination of water or air, excessive noise, or other activities that affect use of another's property. There is a sense, however, in which virtually any use of land affects use of a neighboring parcel. The presence of a perfectly tasteful building three hundred feet from my house may affect my view, my ability to live without any noise at all, the number of birds that fly over my land, and so forth. If every such affect were a nuisance, compatible land ownership could never exist: thus the requirement that a nuisance be both substantial and unreasonable to be actionable.

There is some dispute in the commentary and treatises as to the standard of care that applies in nuisance. In the view of some authorities, the standard of care is said to be intention to interfere with the plaintiff's rights. But it turns out that this means only that the defendant must be aware of the effect that its activities have on the plaintiff and then continue to conduct the activities. A nuisance also may be actionable on the basis of negligence or strict liability. Though it is worth recognizing that in particular jurisdictions certain technicalities may make all the difference, a useful working definition is that a nuisance is an activity resulting in a particular kind of harm—interference with the use or enjoyment of land—and that this interference may be actionable not only on the basis of intent, but also on a negligence or strict liability basis if the other preconditions to liability (fault or abnormal danger, respectively) are met.

There are two kinds of nuisances: public and private. A public nuisance is not a tort, but a species of low-level quasi-criminal offense that affects the general public in common. An activity blocking access to a public highway, for example, might be a public nuisance. Actions to abate a public nuisance usually are brought by governmental authority. In recent years certain states and municipalities have attempted to expand the traditional scope of public nuisance by bringing suit against the manufacturers of handguns and of the lead-pigment that was once used in paint, seeking to hold these parties liable for creating a public nuisance by risking harm to the general public. These suits have met with a bit of success but mostly rejection. The only significant overlap between public nuisance and tort lies in the possibility that, where a public nuisance has been committed, a private party who suffers special injury distinct from the general public may bring a tort action against the party who commits a public nuisance, to recover these special damages.

In contrast, a private nuisance is simply a nuisance that affects particular individuals or entities. Private nuisance actions do sound in tort. What makes private nuisance both interesting and distinctive is what sets it apart from ordinary torts involving intention, negligence, or strict liability. Two things stand out: what makes an activity a nuisance to begin with, and the remedies that are available once an activity is determined to be a nuisance.

A.   *When Is an Activity a Nuisance?*

The textbook definition of a nuisance as a substantial and unreasonable interference with the use or enjoyment of land reflects the notion that land uses tend to affect each other. For this reason, minor "interference" by one landowner with certain uses and enjoyments of other landowners is virtually inevitable. Even on a peaceful suburban street I cannot expect complete quiet or a backyard totally free of the smell of hot dogs being barbecued by my neighbor. Nor can the owner of a business located in an industrial area expect to avoid the smells and fumes of ordinary manufacturing. Up to a point the rule is that modestly incompatible uses must "live and let live." To constitute an actionable nuisance, therefore, an interfering use must be both substantial and unreasonable in the particular context in which it occurs.

Once a particular use is more than modestly incompatible with another use, a judgment-call by the courts is required. The need for such a judgment-call is expressed in the rule that in determining whether an activity is a nuisance, the courts "balance the equities." What counts as a "substantial" interference depends on all the circumstances, including the nature of the neighborhood or area in which the plaintiff and defendant occupy or use their properties. And what counts as an "unreasonable" interference (which does not necessarily not mean an unreasonable activity) depends on the same factors.

Nowhere is the fact that the courts balance the equities more evident than in the "coming-to-the-nuisance" problem. Suppose that a particular use—for instance, a factory that emits particulate matter from a smoke stack—has been operating in an area surrounded by a woods. The plaintiff then erects a home in the woods and contends that the factory's emissions constitute a nuisance. Suppose further that if the plaintiff's home had existed when the factory began operation, the factory's emissions would have constituted a nuisance.

On first consideration one might want to say that the plaintiff has only himself to blame and should not be able to recover. Certainly the plaintiff's awareness of what he was getting into is one of the equities to be considered, but further consideration shows why this cannot always be dispositive. First, a rule that the first party to make an active use of property gets the right to do so without fear of liability in nuisance would encourage a race to make active use of land even if such use was otherwise premature. That would cause an undesirable "development race." Second, the "first" use really is not operation of the factory, but maintenance of the nearby property in an unimproved condition. The plaintiff was not failing to use the property at all when the factory began operation. On the contrary, he was "using" the property as woods. To permit the defendant *automatically* to insulate himself from the law of nuisance by building a factory is in effect to give him a right to restrict the plaintiff's potential use and enjoyment simply by being the first in the area to do something more with his land than enjoy its natural condition. This is true even if the plaintiff buys the property after the factory is in operation, since the party selling to the plaintiff has his rights reduced by a decrease in the market value of the property if the plaintiff cannot sue for nuisance.

Moreover, inevitably there must come a point at which, if the factory is otherwise a nuisance, the factory must yield to its neighbors regardless of whose active use was first. For example, once the entire area surrounding the factory is developed with single family homes, the emission of particulate matter is certain to constitute a substantial and unreasonable interference with the plaintiffs' use and enjoyment of their land. The factory owner is not necessarily behaving unreasonably; but his interference with the plaintiffs' use is nonetheless "unreasonable" in the sense of being a greater interference than they should have to tolerate under the circumstances.

A finding that the factory is a nuisance, however, is only the first step in a two-step process of decision that takes place in nuisance actions. The second step requires determination of the remedy that is available once a particular use is held to constitute a nuisance.

B. *The Remedial Alternatives*

Most tortious activity has long since concluded by the time an action seeking compensation for the losses the activity has caused reaches a courtroom. As a consequence, the only practical remedy is the payment of damages to the plaintiff. In nuisance, however, often this is not the case. It is common for the nuisance to be continuing at the time a suit alleging its existence comes to trial. Therefore, two remedies are available. The defendant may be ordered to pay the plaintiff damages for all past and future losses, but may be permitted to continue the activity that constitutes the nuisance. Or the defendant may be ordered to pay the plaintiff damages for all past losses, and be enjoined (prohibited by a court-issued injunction) from continuing the nuisance thereafter.

Traditionally the law of nuisance has been that the court balances the equities not only at the liability stage in determining whether the defendant has engaged in a nuisance at all, but also at the remedial stage in determining whether to enjoin the defendant from continuing the nuisance or to permit the nuisance to continue and to hold the defendant liable in damages only, for the plaintiff's future losses. In making their remedial decisions the courts take a variety of factors into account, including the parties' respective faults, if any, the hardship to the parties in respect of the continuance or discontinuance of the nuisance, and the value of the activity that constitutes the nuisance to the surrounding community. Thus, in *Boomer v. Atlantic Cement Co., Inc.*,[15] the court declined to enjoin the operation of a cement plant that was important to the economy of the area in which it was located, in part on the ground that the cost of discontinuing the nuisance—in both dollars and loss of employment—was grossly disproportionate to the amount of harm the nuisance was causing. This does not mean, however, that a strict cost-benefit analysis occurs in every case. Many courts routinely grant a request for an injunction unless the equities weigh decidedly in the defendant's favor.

Appreciating the nature of this kind of equity-balancing is probably all that is necessary to understand the rudiments of nuisance remedies. For some time now, however, commentators have been investigating the structure of nuisance remedies by uncovering some of the assumptions that underlie the choice among remedies.[16] The commentators' insights reveal a side of tort liability that often remains hidden, because only already-completed harms figure in most tort actions. The starting point for the analysis is the simple point that the plaintiff may be successful or fail in seeking either of two remedies: damages or an injunction. As a consequence, there are in fact four possible remedial alternatives to be considered when a plaintiff sues for nuisance.

1. No Nuisance: Defendant "Enjoins" Plaintiff

In the first situation the plaintiff is completely unsuccessful in his nuisance suit. The simplest way to understand this situation is to say that the court has held that the defendant has not engaged in a nuisance and has therefore denied the plaintiff any remedy. Although such a ruling means that the defendant's activity is not a substantial and unreasonable interference with the plaintiff's use and enjoyment of his land, it means something else as well. In fact, the defendant's activity almost always does interfere in some way with the plaintiff's use and enjoyment, even if not in a substantial and unreasonable way. Consequently, although the legal effect of the failure of the plaintiff's suit is merely to permit the defendant's activity to continue, the practical significance of this permission is that the defendant's activity limits the scope of the plaintiff's use

15. 26 N.Y.2d 219, 309 N.Y.S.2d 312, 257 N.E.2d 870 (1970).

16. See, e.g., Guido Calabresi & Douglas A. Melamed, *Property Rules, Liability Rules, and Inalienability: One View of the Cathedral*, 85 Harv. L. Rev.1089 (1972); A. Mitchell Polinsky, *Resolving Nuisance Disputes: The Simple Economics of Injunctive and Damage Remedies*, 32 Stan. L. Rev. 1075 (1980).

and enjoyment of his land. In effect, then, when a plaintiff's nuisance suit completely fails, the defendant enjoins the plaintiff— i.e., limits the plaintiff's future use and enjoyment of his land. Thus, suppose that you live near me and play loud rock music on Friday evenings in the spring. If my nuisance suit against you fails, then you have enjoined me by limiting my quiet enjoyment of my land.

This ruling need not end the matter, however. You now have what amounts to a property right to play rock music on Friday evenings. But if my quiet enjoyment of my land is worth more to me than your music is to you, after I lose my suit (or even before if I know I will lose) I may want to try to buy your right to interfere with my enjoyment. A contract under which I pay you to stop playing the music would ordinarily be valid and enforceable. There-fore, a decision that you have not committed a nuisance merely allocates to you the right to decide whether to use that right or to sell it to me. Of course, like the owner of any property right, you are entitled to place whatever value you wish on it, including deciding that you will not sell at any price.

2. Nuisance: Plaintiff Enjoins Defendant

The traditional remedy when the defendant's interference is substantial and unreasonable is for the court to enjoin—i.e., prohib-it—the defendant from continuing the nuisance, and to award the plaintiff damages for past losses resulting from the nuisance. For example, if my neighbor's playing of music is so loud and so continuing that I cannot hear myself talk inside my own house, my nuisance suit may succeed. I will then be entitled to damages for my past losses, and perhaps to an injunction from the court directing the neighbor to cease playing music that can be heard outside his home.

Notice however that, like the "remedy" that results when there is a finding of no nuisance at all, the issuance of an injunction need not end the matter. Rather, a holding that the plaintiff is entitled to enjoin the defendant means that the plaintiff has what amounts to a property right to be free from the nuisance being committed by the defendant. But at least in theory the plaintiff may sell that right to the defendant and thereby permit the defendant to continue his activity, at whatever price the plaintiff wishes to charge and the defendant is willing to pay. If the plaintiff sells, in effect he will have substituted his right to an injunction for the payment in advance of future damages, but damages as meas-ured by the plaintiff rather than by a jury.

It may come as a surprise that an injunction issued by a court could simply be ignored by the parties if they agreed that the right amount of money had been transferred from the defendant to the plaintiff. After all, didn't the court order that the nuisance be abated? The answer is that judgments, whether for money damages or for injunctive relief, are just pieces of paper until the party given rights under the judgment seeks to enforce those rights. A defendant found liable for damages in an ordinary tort case is permitted to leave the courthouse without paying the plaintiff—we no longer have debtors' prisons. Nor do courts telephone the parties six months after a judgment is entered to ensure that the defendant has payed his debt to the plaintiff or complied with an injunctive order. If the defendant pays voluntarily, the court never hears about the matter again. If the defendant does not pay, collecting a judgment requires the plaintiff to come back to court to obtain an order directing that the defendant's property be seized and sold in order to satisfy the judgment. But just as a party in whose favor a judgment for money damages is entered can decide not to collect from the defendant, so a party in whose favor an injunction was issued can decide not to enforce it.

The matter often is not as simple as this, however, for two reasons. First, animosity between the parties and their distaste for cash bargaining over their property rights may preclude negotiation subsequent to judgment. Second, sometimes hundreds of people are affected by the nuisance and may be named as plaintiffs in the nuisance suit. The defendant in such a situation is unlikely to be able to succeed in a buyout of an injunction, because of the practical difficulty of dealing with multiple plaintiffs or because the last plaintiff to sell his right has a very valuable asset—with the result that there are multiple "holdouts" seeking to be the last plaintiff to sell. Therefore, whereas a single-plaintiff injunction may well be bought-off by the defendant, a multiple-plaintiff injunction is likely to be enforced.

This prospect leads to an important insight. In the single-plaintiff situation the law can afford, so to speak, to make a mistake. If a court enjoins a nuisance but the benefit to the defendant of continuing the nuisance is wholly out of proportion to the benefit to the plaintiff of discontinuing the nuisance, it is likely that the plaintiff will have his price and that the plaintiff's right to an injunction will be purchased by the defendant. The parties will "correct" the court's "mistake." In contrast, in the multiple-plaintiff situation the law cannot afford to make a mistake, because the "market" in nuisance rights is unlikely to be able to correct that mistake through the sale of the plaintiffs' right to an injunction back to the defendant. For this reason, in the multiple-plaintiff situation a high degree of confidence that an injunction rather than an award of damages is the proper remedy is even more desirable than in the single-plaintiff situation.

3. Nuisance: Defendant Compensates Plaintiff

In view of the above analysis, the first two remedies—defendant enjoins plaintiff and plaintiff enjoins defendant—will need to reflect a high degree of confidence on the part of the court that the proper solution to any particular conflict between land uses is that one should enjoin the other. The next two remedies involve an award of damages rather than the issuance of an injunction. The significance of the decision to employ one of these remedies is more complicated.

Suppose that plaintiffs sue for an injunction or, in the event that the request for an injunction is denied, an award of future damages resulting from the continuation of the nuisance. For either of two reasons, the court might decline to issue the injunction and award damages instead. On the one hand, having balanced the equities the court might decide that the social and economic costs of discontinuing the nuisance are greater than the cost that will result from permitting it to continue. An award of future damages rather an injunction would therefore be the correct solution to the conflict between land uses reflected by the plaintiffs' suit. This was the solution reached in *Boomer v. Atlantic Cement*, discussed above. On the other hand, the court might be uncertain as to the proper solution. As I noted above, when there is reason to believe that the plaintiffs and the defendant can bargain to a solution, then issuing an injunction still permits them to do this. But if a bargained-for solution is unlikely to result because of the large number of plaintiffs involved, the issuance of an injunction could produce the wrong result. But an award of damages permits the nuisance to continue if it can pay its way—that is, if the benefit to the defendant of continuing the nuisance is greater than the amount of damages awarded—which is of course the harm that the jury predicts will result from continuation of the nuisance. Otherwise the defendant will simply discontinue the nuisance instead of paying future damages. One critical difference, then, between issuing an injunction and awarding damages only, is that the former remedy has the potential to permit the *plaintiffs* to decide whether the nuisance should be continued and, if so, at what price, whereas the latter remedy permits the *defendant* to decide.

4. Nuisance: Plaintiff Compensates Defendant

At first glance this fourth possible remedy seems nonsensical and the result only of a desire for symmetry with the previous one. How could a plaintiff bring suit but end up paying the defendant? In fact, however, the remedy has both a logic of its own and a limited basis in the case law.

The logic of the remedy starts from the premise that the correct solution of the conflict between the plaintiffs' and the defendant's land uses is uncertain. An injunction is therefore not the preferable remedy, at least not where multiple parties are involved and the "wrong" remedy cannot be bought off. But suppose that, after balancing the equities, the court concludes that the plaintiffs should be entitled to cause discontinuance of the nuisance only if doing so is worth it to them. The proper remedy would then be to permit the plaintiffs to compensate the defendant for the cost of discontinuing the nuisance. If the benefit to the plaintiffs of discontinuing the nuisance is greater than the cost of doing so—as measured by the jury—then the plaintiffs will pay. And if that cost is not worth it, they will decline to do so and continue to suffer the nuisance.

It is rarely better to have the plaintiffs rather than the defendant decide whether continuing the nuisance is worth its costs, but occasionally the situation does arise. For example, in *Spur Industries v. Del E. Webb Development Co., Inc.*,[17] the plaintiff was a residential developer who came to the nuisance, a cattle feed-lot. Smells and flies emanating from the lot constituted a nuisance to the owners of the developed properties. But the court concluded that, because the developer had come to the nuisance, it should bear the cost of relocating the feed-lot. In effect, the developer, as plaintiff, was entitled to purchase an injunction by compensating the defendant for discontinuing the nuisance.

5. A Synthesis

In each of the four possible nuisance remedies, either the plaintiff or the defendant is found to have an entitlement to use his or her land in the manner that is contested, and the other party must tolerate that use. The successful party's entitlement may be protected strongly, in the manner of a property right by an injunction, or more weakly, in the manner of a tort right, by the payment of damages only.

Thus, the decision that there is no nuisance protects the defendant with a property right, or "property rule," and he can

17.   108 Ariz. 178, 494 P.2d 700 (1972).

decide to sell or not sell, at his price. Similarly, a decision enjoining the defendant from continuing a nuisance protects the plaintiff with a property rule, and she can decide to sell or not, at her price. In contrast, an award of future damages to the plaintiff protects the plaintiff with a liability right or "liability rule" only. In this situation the value of the plaintiff's entitlement as set by the jury, rather than by the plaintiff, prevails. Finally, an award of future damages to the defendant protects the defendant with a liability rule only. And in this situation the value of the defendant's entitlement as set by the jury, rather than by the defendant, prevails.

In short, when an entitlement is protected strongly, as a property right, the party holding the entitlement cannot be forced to sell it. But when an entitlement is protected weakly, as a liability right, another party can force the holder of the entitlement to "sell" it, and the price of sale is set by the jury rather than by the holder of the entitlement. Typically a tort right can only be protected weakly, by a liability rule, because the conduct interfering with a plaintiff's entitlement has already occurred. There is no choice but to permit a jury to place a "price" on the lost or damaged entitlement through an award of damages. But in nuisance, because the defendant's conduct often is continuing, the choice between the strong protection afforded by a property rule and the weaker protection afforded by a liability rule must be made.

IV. Vicarious Liability

The principal example of vicarious liability—liability for injury caused by the conduct of another party—is the doctrine known as *respondeat superior* ("let the superior answer"). Under this doctrine an employer is liable under some circumstances for the torts committed by an employee.

The vicarious liability of an employer for torts committed by employees should not be confused with the liability an employer has for his own torts. An employer whose employee commits a tort may be liable in his own right for negligence in hiring or supervising the employee. If in my business I hire a truck driver who has a record of drunk driving and on whom one day I detect the smell of bourbon, I (along with my employee) may be held liable for negligence if his driving causes injury. But that is not "vicarious" liability—I am held liable for my own negligence in hiring that employee or letting him drive after I know he has been drinking.

It has long been settled, in addition, that employers are vicariously liable even absent their own negligence, for torts committed by their employees "within the scope of employment." The theory behind this form of liability reflects certain of the theories behind strict liability generally. As between the employer and the victim, the employer probably is in a better position to make the activity level and research decisions that can affect accident levels. Moreover, it will often be difficult to prove that a particular employee was negligent, because identifying the employee in question is not possible even when it is clear whose employee he is. So *respondeat superior* may reduce information and error costs. Finally, note that this form of liability does not substitute the employer's liability for the employee's liability. Rather, the employee continues to be liable, but *respondeat superior* adds the employer as an additional defendant. Given that employees as a group are more likely to be judgment-proof than employers, the insurance or loss-distribution function of strict liability clearly seems to play a role in supporting the doctrine.

Two questions then arise. First, who is an "employee?" Second, when is a tort committed "within the scope of employment?" The requirement that the agent of the defendant be an employee is an effort to distinguish at a fairly high level of generality between those situations in which strict liability is likely to have the desired effects and those in which is not. The principal situation in which the party committing a tort is an agent but not an employee involves independent contractors. If I hire an electrician to do work in my apartment, he contracts with me but is not my employee. I do not and could not control the manner in which he works to any great degree. Indeed, if I told an electrician how to perform his work he would probably tell me to get lost. And of course electricians and other independent contractors work for many parties, not just one. The possibility of control by an individual—other than the electrician's own employer—is therefore minimal. Finally, the electrician's employer is just as likely to have a "deep pocket" and therefore to be in a position to spread the cost of liability as is the party who hires him. All this may not be true in every instance, but it is often enough true to make it worthwhile to draw a bright-line distinction (i.e., a rule at a high level of generality) between employees and independent contractors in applying *respondeat superior*.

The second requirement of *respondeat superior* is that the tort at issue be committed within the scope of employment. The idea behind this requirement is that the effects of strict liability can operate through employers only so far. At some point the employer's capacity to control the conduct of employees, and consequently the strength of the argument for imposing strict liability, both diminish. The phrase that captures this point is the distinction between a "detour" and a "frolic." The employer is liable for torts committed on a "mere" detour by the employee, but not for torts committed while the employee is on a frolic of his own. This is an easy enough point to see in the simplest of cases. If I tell my truck driver to deliver a package across town and instead he drives a thousand miles west, I am not liable for the accidents he causes while on that frolic. But if he goes three blocks out of his way to visit his girlfriend, I am liable for accidents that result while he is on that detour. Obviously, it is not always possible to draw a bright line between mere detours and frolics.

In addition, a number of hard cases arise when the employee clearly is on a frolic, but it happens that the employer actually is in a pretty good position to influence the conduct in question. The classic case on this point is *Ira S. Bushey & Sons, Inc. v. United States*,[18] in which a drunken seaman returning from shore leave opened the valve on a drydock and thereby caused severe damage to the ship then in the dock for service. There is no way to describe this as a "mere" detour. But drunken sailors are not only predictable; at least in the case of employees in the military, such conduct is also somewhat subject to control by the employer. And of course the employer in that case—the U.S. government—had the deepest pocket of all. Strict liability could therefore serve loss distribution purposes as well. So perhaps it is not surprising that the court pushed out the envelope of liability a bit farther than it had been in the past and held that the tort was committed within the scope of employment. The decision in *Bushey* is not typical, but its overall flavor is not wholly extraordinary either. What counts as conduct "within the scope of employment" will depend on how effectively imposing liability on the employer for injuries caused by that conduct will serve the purposes of strict liability.

18.   398 F.2d 167 (2d Cir.1968).

9

PRODUCTS LIABILITY

This Chapter concerns liability for injury and damage caused by defective products. A substantial portion of products liability law employs rules governing negligence and strict liability that closely resemble the standards of care that have been covered in earlier Chapters. This area of the law is nonetheless distinctive for two reasons. First, applying the concepts of negligence and strict liability to products liability has proved more difficult than might be supposed. Second, unlike most of the other areas of tort liability covered in earlier Chapters, the parties in a product liability lawsuit often are in an indirect (or sometimes even direct) contractual relationship with each other. The law of products liability is therefore in a position to take the actual and potential terms of this relationship into account in fashioning the tort law rules that apply to product-related injuries.

Most products today are sold in a chain of distribution that begins with the manufacturer, and sometimes even before, with the maker of component parts that are supplied to the manufacturer. The manufacturer sells to an intermediary such as a wholesaler, distributor, or dealer. There may be more than one such intermediary before the product finally reaches a retailer, who eventually sells it to a purchaser. The product may then injure the purchaser, another user of the product, or a bystander. Early on in the history of products liability there was very little basis for recovery against anyone other than the retailer—the "immediate" seller of the product. The right to recover from a "remote" seller such as a wholesaler or manufacturer who sold to the retailer was largely unknown. The "privity of contract" rule—providing that the plaintiff had to have contracted directly with the defendant in order to sue it—made such recoveries impossible.

The history of products liability, however, is the story of the progressive creation and addition of causes of action for injuries caused by defective products. Each new cause of cause of action has complemented rather than replaced a previous basis for liability. Consequently, in a very real sense any study of the history and development of products liability law is at the same time the study of products liability law as it now stands. That history is comprised of four eras: the era of contract privity; the era of negligence; the era of warranty, in which the courts made the transition from negligence to a modern regime that combines negligence and strict liability features; and the modern era of products liability. The expansion of products liability was most rapid between 1960 and 1985, when the courts implemented a new vision of liability that reflected a more general transformation of accident law during this period. Products liability went from being an obscure field doing individual justice to an active and important field in which the imposition of liability became what amounted to an instrument of regulatory and compensation policy. Although any division of an important field of law into four such simple categories automatically oversimplifies, this categorization is a useful way to clarify and organize one's understanding of the field.

I. The Era of Contract Privity

Prior to the twentieth century there was no general law of products liability, and certainly no tort law of products liability. Rather, what liability there was for injuries caused by products arose within the law of contracts. It was therefore accurate to say that there was no products liability in the absence of privity of contract—i.e., unless the person injured was a party to a contract that was breached. And even if there was privity of contract and the product sold pursuant to the contract caused injury, there might not be liability. That depended on what the contract provided, or was interpreted to provide. And in the nineteenth century era of *caveat emptor*—"let the buyer beware"—the courts were unlikely to be sympathetic to the injured purchaser whose contract provided nothing about his rights in the event that he was injured by the product in question.

The leading case reflecting the privity rule is *Winterbottom v. Wright*,[1] an English decision involving a plaintiff who was injured by a defective stagecoach that had been supplied to his employer. In his suit against the maker of the stagecoach, with whom he had no contract, the plaintiff was denied recovery because of the absence of privity. Some commentators say that the case has been misinterpreted and that *Winterbottom* neither stated nor reflected a general rule that a product maker was immune from tort liability in the absence of privity. Be that as it may, *Winterbottom* certainly came to stand for such a rule.

To the modern mind the privity requirement seems unfair. It does not seem sensible to insulate a negligent manufacturer from

---

1.   10 M. & W. 109, 152 Eng.Rep. 402 (1842).

liability to the very people whom its product is most likely to injure if the product is unsafe, on the ground that there is no contract between the manufacturer and the victim. Nonetheless, it is useful to try to imagine what a liability regime based on the privity limitation could have come to look like over time. The privity limitation may still be rejected as inappropriate in the modern context, but the assumptions that lie behind the limitation may not seem nearly so absurd as the modern view of *Winterbottom* makes them appear to be.

Suppose that even today the purchaser injured by a product had no cause of action in tort against any seller, but was limited to a contract suit against the party who had sold him the product. It is nonetheless plausible to suppose that there would have developed a series of contractual undertakings creating some indirect liability on the part of remote sellers such as manufacturers. For example, immediate sellers of certain products probably would find it in their interest to compete for business by offering to compensate purchasers and members of their families injured by unsafe features of the products sold. Intermediate sellers such as wholesalers probably would then find it in their interest to compete for the business of retailers by offering to reimburse them for some or all of the injury-liability costs that the retailers had undertaken by contract. In turn, manufacturers probably would find it in their interest to compete with each other for the business of wholesalers by offering to reimburse them for the costs of reimbursing retailers. In this way the cost of injuries suffered by product purchasers and their families could ultimately be passed up the chain of distribution. The cost of providing this protection would be shouldered first by manufacturers. But in one way or another this cost could be passed down the chain of distribution, since the price of the product at each stage would include either the cost of compensation or the cost of making the product safer so as to avoid the need for compensation, whichever were less.

It is difficult to say exactly what the scope of these various contractual undertakings would be in the absence of any tort liability. Some products might carry no contractual right to compensation; some might carry a right to full compensation on the model of tort damages regardless of the fault of anyone in the chain of distribution; and others might come with a more limited right to compensation—for example, only in the event that the injury resulted from the manufacturer's negligence and only for medical expenses and lost wages resulting from the injury. The difficulty of predicting the precise contours of a privity-of-contract liability regime is not a weakness, however, but part of the argument in favor of such a regime. The reason it is difficult to predict the particular liability rule or rules that would have developed is that different people probably would want to contract for different packages of product price and safety, and compensation for product-related injuries. Similarly, different products might come with different combinations of these features because of differences between the products. Of course, in an age of mass produced products not everyone could have her own liability contract customized with each purchase. But just as today's purchasers of motor vehicles are offered the choice between regular and extended warranties covering their vehicles, so there might have developed a series of different liability packages available at different prices. If it is plausible to suppose that, even in the absence of tort liability for product injuries, consumer preferences operating in product markets could have caused contract-based product liability to develop with at least some of this diversity, then there is also some plausibility to the argument that the uniform tort-based product liability law that has actually developed is sub-optimal.

That this argument is plausible, however, does not necessarily make it correct. First, totally missing from the analysis is any treatment of product injuries suffered by bystanders. Under modern tort-based product liability law a pedestrian (for example) injured by a bus that goes out of control because of defective brakes has a cause of action against the manufacturer of the bus (and possibly the manufacturer of the brakes). A contract-based liability regime could never have developed in a way that would have adequately protected such bystanders, because by definition a bystander has no contract with any party in the chain of product distribution. Tort law rules would have been required to provide such bystanders with a cause of action that *Winterbottom* denied them. Second, just because a contract-based liability regime of some sort probably would have developed if *Winterbottom* had not eventually been overruled, it does not follow that such a regime would have been more suitable than the tort law regime that now prevails. Various imperfections in the product markets might have generated a sub-optimal body of contract-based product liability law. For example, product safety information is not always available to, or understandable by, consumers. And the cost of transactions that would provide consumers liability and compensation options might limit the range of options that could be made available. In short, markets that afford consumers choice, and legal rules that do not afford choice, both tend to be imperfect. The real question is not which approach could operate with high effectiveness, but which approach or combination of approaches has the potential to be less imperfect than the other.

All this has simply been a mental exercise designed to help us see what might have been. The contract-based approach embodied in *Winterbottom v. Wright* was long ago rejected, and the tort-based approach has been dominant for nearly a century. But even today the differences between the contract and tort-based approaches are not entirely academic. At many points in the law of product liability the preferences of consumers for a particular mix of product price, safety, and compensation for product-related injuries can help to inform the choice among possible tort-based rules of liability. For this reason, although the 19th-century contract privity rule has been long been dead, the idea behind that approach—consumer choice—may still aid in the evaluation of modern tort-based rules governing product liability.

II. The Era of Negligence

As so often happens in the development of the law, almost from the very moment that the contract privity rule became firmly established the courts began to create exceptions to it. Perhaps the most prominent exception was the rule in *Thomas v. Winchester*,[2] which eliminated the privity requirement when the plaintiff's injury was caused by an "imminently" or "inherently" dangerous product. In such cases the plaintiff could sue the manufacturer of the product for negligence, despite the absence of privity. In the beginning the number of products found to be inherently dangerous was small, and included only such obviously hazardous things as poison. But slowly the products in this category expanded to include coffee urns, scaffolds, and bottles of aerated water. For all practical purposes at this point the exceptions had swallowed up the rule.

The demise of the privity requirement was not formally recognized, however, until Judge Cardozo's opinion in *MacPherson v. Buick Motor Co.*[3] in 1916. The defendant there had manufactured an automobile that was sold by a dealer to the plaintiff, who was injured when a wheel made of defective wood collapsed. The plaintiff sued for negligence, and the defendant relied on the privity rule, arguing that the rule of *Thomas v. Winchester* did not apply. The court rejected the defendant's argument, holding in effect that the manufacturer of anything that could foreseeably harm a third party

2. 6 N.Y. 397 (1852).
3. 217 N.Y. 382, 111 N.E. 1050 (1916).

if negligently made was subject to liability under *Thomas*. This holding of course totally eviscerated the limitations contained in the *Thomas* rule and functionally overruled the contract privity requirement. Many other states followed *MacPherson* in the years that followed, although for a while some purported still to require that a product be imminently dangerous in order to avoid the privity rule.

Clearly the decision in *MacPherson* was very significant. But it is important to see both what *MacPherson* did and what it did not do for plaintiffs in product liability actions. By eliminating the privity requirement the case obviously made it possible for plaintiffs to sue manufacturers with whom they had no direct contractual relationship for negligence. This was important not only because immediate sellers sometimes had few assets. In addition, with the rise of pre-packaged, mass-produced goods, often the retail seller was a mere conduit for the transfer of the product. As such, the retailer had not been negligent in any way. In such cases *MacPherson* did not create the right to sue an *additional* defendant; in the typical case *MacPherson* created the right to sue the only party who could possibly be found liable for negligence.

Although this was a necessary step for plaintiffs, it was far from sufficient to make recovery automatic, because the plaintiff still had to prove negligence. As a result of *MacPherson* manufacturers could be held liable to ultimate purchasers or users of their products, but only for negligence. Proving negligence was often far from a simple task. Consider the broken wheel in *MacPherson*, which the defendant had purchased from a maker of component parts. The plaintiff had to show not only that it had been defective, but that it had been defective when it left the manufacturer's possession. The car in *MacPherson*, for example, had been driven on rough country roads for a year, and might have been damaged through heavy use.[4] The plaintiff might be able to adduce the necessary proof of negligence, although that would be difficult if the wheel was destroyed in the accident that injured him. But unless the standard to which manufacturers are held is perfection rather than reasonable care, merely showing that there was something wrong with the wheel does not prove that the manufacturer was negligent in placing it on the vehicle. One way to prove negligence would be to attempt to show that a reasonable manufacturer would inspect component parts such as wheels, and that the defendant's inspection in this case was negligent. That approach could require

4. See James A. Henderson, Jr., MacPherson v. Buick Motor Co.: *Simplifying the Facts While Reshaping the Law*, in Robert L. Rabin & Stephen D. Sugarman (ed's.), Torts Stories 41 (2003).

evidence regarding the defendant's methods of training inspectors, inspection standards, the rate at which defects went undetected given these inspection standards, and so forth. All this might have been available in discovery, but only at a cost. And even then the plaintiff had to hope that what he discovered would help to prove negligence rather than show how careful the defendant had been.

Without such evidence, the defendant could contend, whether the defendant was negligent in failing to discover the defect in the wheel of the plaintiff's automobile is speculative, and it would be improper to submit the case to the jury. In some cases *res ipsa loquitur* could solve this problem for the plaintiff. As products and manufacturing techniques become increasingly complex, however, typically it becomes less appropriate to invoke *res ipsa* because of uncertainty as to whether the type of accident in question does or does not ordinarily happen because of the defendant's negligence. In short, because products are not perfect, sometimes they caused injuries even in the absence of the manufacturer's negligence. And even when the manufacturer was negligent, plaintiffs could not always prove it. Thus, *MacPherson* ushered in a new era in products liability, but created new problems for plaintiffs at the same time that it solved old ones.

III. The Era of Transition and the Rise of Warranty Rules

At about the same time that the cause of action against manufacturers for negligence emerged, several other bases of recovery under certain limited circumstances began developing. Each arises out of the notion of "warranty." A warranty is a promise or guarantee. When a warranty about the safety or quality of a product is breached, that breach may give rise to a cause of action, not only for the contract losses flowing from the breach (e.g., the difference between the value of the product as warranted and the value as it actually was), but also for such consequential losses as bodily injury or property damage. During a period that overlapped with the era of negligence, several causes of action based on breach of warranty were slowly recognized.

A. *Express Warranty*

Warranties may be either express or implied. An express warranty is simply that—a promise or guarantee, for the breach of which liability may ensue. Sometimes the warranty is contractual, sometimes less formal and part of an advertising campaign. By the

1930's some courts began to hold immediate sellers and sometimes even manufacturers liable for breach of express warranties.[5] This development was not unimportant, especially when liability was extended to manufacturers. But proving that claims of product quality amounted to an express warranty was difficult, and this form of liability was never an important basis for the imposition for liability for product injuries. Over a period of decades the real action took place in the field of implied warranties, the forms of which are discussed next.

B. *Liability of the Immediate Seller*

The first form of implied-warranty liability arose out of a provision of the Uniform Sales Act enacted in many states after the turn of the twentieth century. The Act provided that a warranty of "merchantability" was implied in every contract for the sale of goods. To be merchantable the goods had to be of fair average quality. If they were not, the seller was liable for bodily injuries resulting from breach of the warranty regardless of negligence or its absence. But the liability ran only from the immediate seller, and typically only to the purchaser and not to other users or bystanders. And, being a creature of the Sales Acts, the implied warranty of merchantability was implied but not mandatory. That is, it was what contract-law theorists today call a "default" rule: an implied warranty could be disclaimed by contract. Nonetheless, limited though it was, this was the first instance of strict liability for injuries caused by product defects.

If one stops and thinks about it, there is nothing at all extraordinary or even counterfactual about the implied warranty of merchantability, especially if it is disclaimable. In the case of mass produced, homogeneous goods, to a very great extent the warranty of merchantability was implied not only by law but also in fact. The Sales Acts simply reversed the old common law rule of *caveat emptor*—"let the buyer beware"—under circumstances in which the reasonable assumption of a buyer would be that what he was purchasing met minimal standards of quality and safety. The legal implication simply followed the factual assumptions of the parties. And because the warranty was implied wherever there was privity, in the absence of a disclaimer the seller held liable for bodily injuries itself had a claim for indemnification from its wholesaler (with whom it was in privity), which in turn had a claim against the manufacturer. In this way liability ultimately would be shouldered by the manufacturer, with a consequent incentive created for the

---

5. *See, e.g., Baxter v. Ford Motor Co.*, 168 Wash. 456, 12 P.2d 409 (1932).

manufacturer to provide an optimal mix of quality, safety, and price in its products. But the manufacturer was still insulated from the ultimate user by several layers of litigation.

C. *Impure Food: Liability of the Manufacturer*

Shortly after the Uniform Sales Act was promulgated and began to make its way through the state legislatures, a few courts went one step further. They held that the manufacturer of food could be held directly liable to the consumer for bodily injuries resulting from the consumption of impure food, on a theory of breach of implied warranty.

This was perhaps the greatest conceptual leap that was made during the period of transition from negligence to strict liability. As I have just argued, the idea that a contractual sale of a product by an immediate seller to a purchaser contains an implied warranty of merchantability is factually and legally unremarkable, though this approach does reverse the ingrained rule of *caveat emptor*. The theory behind the immediate seller's liability is still largely contractual, both because it is reasonable to suppose that the warranty is implied in fact as well as in law, and because this implied warranty remains disclaimable—i.e., subject to express contractual modification.

In contrast, ordinarily there is no contract of sale between a manufacturer (of food or anything else) and a purchaser. To hold that there is nonetheless an implied warranty—which some called a "jumping" warranty—running from the manufacturer to the purchaser which, if breached, gives rise to liability, is to create something out of very little. It is not necessarily wrong to do this; but what is created has little to do with any contract. The cause of action for breach of the manufacturer's implied warranty therefore much more closely resembles tort than contract. And because the cause of action requires no showing of negligence, the tort it resembles is strict liability. The focus is on the product's quality (its "merchantability"), not on the manufacturer's conduct. Admittedly, certain aspects of the cause of action contained residue of the contractual soil out of which warranty law grew: often a contract statute of limitations and the notice requirements of contract law applied, for example. And this form of implied warranty also remained disclaimable, though the only available place to disclaim it was in the contract between the retailer and the purchaser. But the fact remains that the core of the cause of action was largely indistinguishable from strict liability in tort for injuries caused by an unmerchantable product.

D. *The Fall of the Citadel: Liability of Manufacturers Generally*

The rise of the food manufacturer's liability for breach of implied warranty was important conceptually, but for practical purposes the first half of the twentieth century remained mainly an era of negligence liability. The key player—the manufacturer of durable consumer and commercial goods—was liable only for negligence, and only when the plaintiff could prove negligence. Over time there was a slight erosion of this liability limitation, as some courts began to apply the implied warranty theory to manufacturers of products that were not food but were intended for intimate bodily consumption—such as perfume and hair dye. But the arguments for strict liability were growing. Perhaps the most famous came in a concurrence by Justice Traynor of the Supreme Court of California in *Escola v. Coca Cola Bottling Co. of Fresno*,[6] in which he argued that the manufacturer of consumer goods should be strictly liable in tort for product defects, on three grounds. First, the manufacturer is better situated to determine whether to make the product safer. Second, the manufacturer is better able to insure against the risk of injuries caused by the product. And third, the victim will necessarily have difficulty gaining access to evidence of, and proving, negligence, even when there was negligence. These are, of course, some of the potential benefits of imposing strict liability that were discussed in Chapter Eight.

But the first real fall of the "citadel," as Dean Prosser once called it, occurred when a manufacturer of an ordinary product was held liable for breach of an implied warranty of merchantability. That occurred in 1960 in *Henningsen v. Bloomfield Motors, Inc.*[7] The plaintiff there was the injured wife of the purchaser of a new Plymouth, which mysteriously left the road after its steering failed. The decision was double-barreled. The court first held that an implied warranty of merchantability ran not only from the immediate seller, but also from the manufacturer, even if the product was not food.

The problem for the plaintiff, however, was that her husband's contract of sale contained some fine-print labeled "warranty" that was actually a disclaimer of liability for bodily injury. The court's second move was to invalidate this disclaimer, on grounds that did not make it entirely clear whether some disclaimers—if clearly

6. 24 Cal.2d 453, 150 P.2d 436 (1944).
7. 32 N.J. 358, 161 A.2d 69 (1960).

labeled and pointed out to the purchaser—would be binding. But the opinion soon came to be understood to hold that the manufacturer's implied warranty of merchantability could never be disclaimed in connection with bodily injury, no matter how clear and conspicuous the disclaimer. Once this step was taken, there could no longer be any doubt as to what the cause of action really was. A cause of action for breach of an implied warranty that cannot be disclaimed, running from a manufacturer to a party who suffers injury but is not in privity with the manufacturer, is simply strict liability in tort masquerading under another name. The transition from negligence to strict liability was now virtually complete; it only remained for the courts of other states to follow *Henningsen* and to acknowledge what they were really doing.

IV. The Modern Era: "Strict" Liability for Defective Products

Those acknowledgments followed quickly. The first case to make what had happened absolutely clear was the Supreme Court of California's decision in *Greenman v. Yuba Power Products, Inc.,*[8] in which now Chief Justice Traynor wrote the opinion, holding that there was strict liability in tort caused by a defective product. After that the courts were moved very quickly—so quickly, in fact, that by 1965 the Restatement (Second) of Torts § 402A, only slightly ahead of its time, indicated that the majority rule was that any seller of a product in a "defective condition unreasonably dangerous to the user" was strictly liable in tort for bodily injury or property damage resulting from that defective condition. Soon that was in fact the law in most states. And nominally it remains the law today, although a few states still cling to warranty terminology in holding manufacturers and other sellers strictly liable. The language of the § 402A was a bit confusing. Could a product be defective without being unreasonably dangerous, or unreasonably dangerous without being defective?

Probably not, and the authors of the Third Restatement have read the subsequent case law and chosen to drop the phrase "unreasonably dangerous" from their formulation, employing only the adjective "defective."[9] Some commentators believe that the authors of § 402A were thinking mainly about what we now call "manufacturing" defects—departures of an individual unit from the manufacturer's intended design. Others think that the authors

---

8. 59 Cal.2d 57, 27 Cal.Rptr. 697, 377 P.2d 897 (1963).

9. *See* Restatement (Third) of Torts: Products Liability, § 1.

were also thinking of what we now call "design" defects, which afflict every unit that comes off the assembly line. If the authors were also thinking of design defects, they probably had in mind wholly substandard products—those whose designs would have breached the minimal standard of safety that had been captured by the notion of an implied warranty of merchantability. There certainly is little evidence that the authors of § 402A consciously anticipated the litigation over marginal potential design changes that characterizes much contemporary design defect litigation.

The key to understanding modern products liability is the recognition that, by the 1970s, the courts and commentators had actually developed three categories of defect, and that the starting point for any conceptualization of the field and for any claim of liability is to identify the category of defect at issue. In fact, the Third Restatement does not even use the phrase "strict liability" to describe products liability generally. Rather, the forms of liability for injuries caused by defective products are set out separately, using categories that the case law came to employ in the more than three decades following the adoption of § 402A. These categories—manufacturing defects, design defects, and warning defects—shape virtually all current thinking about products liability.[10]

A. *Manufacturing Defects*

A product contains a manufacturing defect when, as produced, it does not conform to the manufacturer's own design. Sometimes called a "construction" defect, a product with a manufacturing defect is different from others coming off the assembly line. Presumably the wheels on most of the Buicks made by the defendant in *MacPherson* and the steering mechanisms on the most of the Plymouths made by the defendant in *Henningsen* did not contain the defects that made the plaintiffs' particular cars dangerous. A manufacturing defect thus results when something goes wrong in the manufacturing process and a product departs from its intended design.

Strict liability for injuries caused by manufacturing defects circumvents the difficulties of proof posed for plaintiffs after *Mac-Pherson* made it possible to sue the manufacturer for negligence. There is no need for the plaintiff to show that the manufacturer used inadequate materials, failed to conduct a proper inspection, or otherwise took a risk whose potential costs were greater than its potential benefits. On the contrary, once the plaintiff shows that

---

10. *See id.*, § 2.

the product departed from its intended design and that this departure caused the plaintiff's injury, the plaintiff has proven a manufacturing defect. The manufacturer is then liable even if it has exercised reasonable care in every aspect of the manufacturing process.

The arguments in favor of this form of strict liability are the arguments in favor of strict liability generally. First, many manufacturing defects probably are the result of some hard-to-pinpoint negligence. Strict liability may therefore produce more accurate results, from the negligence standpoint, than liability for negligence itself. Second, as between the manufacturer and the victim, the manufacturer is in the superior position to conduct research or otherwise discover cost-effective methods of reducing the risk of harm resulting from manufacturing defects, ordinarily by reducing the incidence of those defects. And in general the manufacturer probably is in a better position to spread the cost of the defects that it is not cost-effective to eliminate.

B. *Design Defects*

In contrast to a manufacturing defect, which occurs in only a (usually small) portion of any particular mass-produced product line, a design defect is one that occurs in an entire product line. For example, a car model with a gas tank in a place that makes it vulnerable to explosions in rear-end collisions is designed to have the gas tank in that position. If the placement of the tank in that position makes the car defective, that is a design defect that afflicts every vehicle coming off the assembly line in the condition it was intended to be.

In the case of alleged manufacturing defects there is a readily available standard against which to measure whether there was a defect in the product that injured the plaintiff—departure of the product from the manufacturer's own design. But in the case of design defects that standard obviously is not appropriate, because it is never breached. Of course, a product design can never be risk-free. Perfectly safe products are impossible and in any event would result in products too expensive for most people to purchase. Consequently, it was never expected that "strict" products liability would mean that every injury caused by a product's design would be compensable. Knives are made to cut; if I cut myself with a perfectly good knife the manufacturer is not liable, because the knife was not defective. The courts have therefore had to develop standards for use in determining whether a product design is defective. In effect there has been a search for a middle ground that defines defect in a manner that extends beyond negligence but lies short of liability merely for injuries caused by a product design. Two such standards occupy the field.

The *risk-utility* test acknowledges that deciding whether a design is defective is very much like deciding whether the design is negligent. This test asks whether the risks posed by the design outweigh its utility, understood essentially as the product's benefits. This is little more than a negligence test that focuses on the product rather than the manufacturer's conduct, either with or without a foreseeability requirement, depending on the approach taken. Over time the courts have tended increasingly to adopt this now-dominant test, recognizing that design defect liability is not really strict liability, or at least is a lot less "strict" than manufacturing defect liability. A product design is not defective unless its risks outweigh its utility, whereas that balance does not matter in manufacturing defect cases. Admittedly, if there is no foreseeability requirement much of the blameworthiness that inheres in a true negligence standard is removed, but most courts require foreseeability, or at least make lack of foreseeability a defense. In any event, except in the case of truly unpredictable harms such as rare long-latency diseases, few products whose risks in retrospect outweigh their utility do so in ways that would have been unforeseeable at the time they were manufactured. So in most design defect cases the plaintiff can prove the foreseeability of these risks if that is required. The crux of the issue in design defect cases is how to compare a product's risks to its utility.

An alternative, but less favored test measures the safety of the design against *consumer expectations*. Under this test, if the design is not as safe as consumers expect it to be, it is defective. Unfortunately, in many cases this test is either unworkable or circular. If the consumer expectations test were empirical, then it would require statistical evidence of consumer expectations to prove design defect. This is not required and would hardly be practical if it were. On the other hand, if the consumer expectations test is not rigorously empirical but is instead to be applied through some form of reasoning by the jury, what is it? The ordinary juror would probably think that what the typical consumer expects from a design is a reasonable amount of safety—i.e., all the safety that it is cost-effective to provide. A motor vehicle is expected to be "crashworthy," i.e., to be reasonably safe in a collision. But no consumer expects that if he does not emerge completely uninjured from a crash, the design of his car is automatically "defective." Only "reasonable" crashworthiness is expected.[11] Yet that looks curiously like a negligence test without any of the rigor of the risk-utility approach. Moreover, some versions of the consumer expectations test sidestep the cause-in-fact requirement by asking the jury to determine whether a reasonable consumer would have expected to be harmed in the manner in which the plaintiff was actually harmed. Under the risk-utility test, in contrast, proof of cause-in-fact is a separate element of the plaintiff's action. In any event, most courts that have adopted the consumer expectations test apply it only to simple product designs, about which consumers could reasonably have expectations of safety. Complex designs are subject to the risk-utility test.

Given the dominance of the risk-utility test, much of the controversy surrounding design defect liability involves the difficulty of applying the risk-utility test in practice. Two problems are especially acute. First, in cases involving technical design choices for complex products such as motor vehicles, the design defect test in effect asks jurors to engage in a task for which they do not have the relevant expertise. As in medical malpractice cases, expert testimony is virtually always necessary to provide the jury with the basis for making a decision. Yet unlike medical malpractice cases, in design defect litigation there is no "respectable minority" rule to guide the jury's task. It is not enough that a respectable minority of designers would conclude that the defendant's design was not defective. On the contrary, if the risks of the design outweigh its utility, the design is defective. In effect, the jury is asked to choose the best design or, as some have put it, the jury is asked to redesign the product.

Second, any complex product is a combination of many design choices regarding safety, cost, attractiveness, and functionality. An entire product design, however, does not cause injury. One feature of the design does that. If I am injured in a collision because of the angle and hardness of my steering wheel, the design of my Ford has not injured me; rather, the design of the steering wheel is responsible. The focus of the product liability action I bring will therefore be whether the design of the steering wheel was defective. The jury's tendency will be to evaluate the risks and benefits of that design in isolation from the other elements of the overall design. Of course the steering wheel could have been made more safely, for a price. So could many other features of the design. But at some point what that requires is a Mercedes, not a Ford. Since I purchased a Ford and not a Mercedes, the real question ought to be how safely a

---

11. *See Volkswagen of America, Inc. v. Young*, 272 Md. 201, 321 A.2d 737 (1974).

Ford must be designed as a whole. But that is the very kind of question that jurors are not terribly well-suited to answer, even with the help of experts. Many courts, as well as the THIRD RESTATEMENT, have addressed this problem by requiring that the plaintiff prove not only that the risks of a particular design outweigh its benefits, but also that there was a *reasonable alternative design* that would have reduced the risks in question.[12] Yet that requirement asks the jury to make a second design decision for which it is also not terribly well-suited—whether the alternative design proposed by the plaintiff is reasonable and feasible. Moreover, when and if there can be liability even when there is no alternative feasible design, a finding of liability is in effect a finding that the product should not be sold at all—a dubious decision to leave to individual juries.

All this is far from ideal. The dilemma posed by these weaknesses in design defect liability, however, is that there is no approach that is obviously superior to the current approach. Stronger safety regulation by government is one such alternative, but that does not seem either likely to happen or likely to be effective. Another alternative is to allow the market to decide how much safety it wants, on the model of the *Winterbottom* approach. Just as there is a market for attractiveness and functionality, there is a market for safety. Some people want more safety than others and are willing to pay for it. But the complexity of product designs and the latency of design dangers make it very difficult for the ordinary consumer to assess the safety of complex product designs in anything but a very general way. This is true even in connection with cars, where shopping based partly on safety considerations is common. If I want the most safety money can buy, I may choose a Mercedes. If I want considerable safety but not the most money can buy, I may choose a Ford or a Chevrolet. Because I can never be fully informed about design safety, however, my choice will not necessarily result in Fords or Chevrolets having an overall level of design safety that is optimal for their purchasers. And in connection with other products—lawn mowers, chain saws, etc.—it is unclear how much information about safety the typical consumer can or does take into account. There is therefore a considerable role to be played by the threat of liability for design defects, especially those defects that are latent rather than obvious.

As a consequence, we face a choice between the imperfections of the regime of tort liability for design defects, the imperfections of governmental safety regulation, and the imperfections of the model

---

12. RESTATEMENT (THIRD) OF TORTS: PRODUCTS LIABILITY, § 2(b).

of consumer sovereignty that *MacPherson* long ago rejected in overruling *Winterbottom*. Tort law's design defect approach now dominates, but not without considerable dissatisfaction on the part of many observers of this field.

C. *Warning Defects*

If it were possible to provide product purchasers with complete information about product risks and utility, there would be less need for the other bases for imposing product liability. Complete risk-utility information could be transmitted and consumers often could be left to make their own choices about the desirable mix of safety, price, attractiveness, and functionality in the products they purchase. But of course that is an impossible ideal, and in any event there are some product designs that remain defective even after the consumer has been fully warned about them. For both reasons, complete consumer choice cannot totally displace mandatory product liability.

Warning law occupies the area in which it is both feasible and normatively desirable to transfer risk-utility information to the purchaser and thereby to put the purchaser in a position to decide for himself whether the risks posed by a product design are worth its utility. When these criteria are satisfied, the product seller generally is relieved of liability for harm caused by the risk about which an adequate warning or instructions were provided. In this setting the theory underlying liability for the failure to warn is that, once an adequate warning has been given, the purchaser rather than the product seller is the superior bearer of the risk of injury.

The duty to warn users of pharmaceuticals about side effects illustrates the point. Suppose that I buy a bottle of aspirin warning me about the risk that a small percentage of the users of aspirin will develop ulcers as result of prolonged use. Since there are aspirin substitutes, I can use the aspirin once or twice and then compare its effectiveness with that of a substitute. I can then make an informed decision whether to risk the side effects of aspirin. On the other hand, if the drug in question has no adequate substitutes, then the provision of a warning at least puts me in a position to decide whether to risk the drug's side effects or, instead, to tolerate the medical condition that causes me to seek treatment. Once I have the necessary information—or if the drug requires a prescription, once a learned intermediary such as my physician has the information and consults with me about it—then I am in at least as good a position as the manufacturer of the drug to decide whether its risks are worth its utility. The THIRD RESTATEMENT and much of the case law refer to this kind of product as involving an "unavoidable risk" and decline to impose liability for the injuries that result after an adequate warning of the risk of these injuries is given.[13]

Two areas of controversy dominate warning law: the adequacy-of-warning issue and the connection between warnings and design defect liability.

1. Adequacy of Warning

If complete risk-utility information could be transmitted in warnings or instructions, it would be easy to determine whether the warning or instructions given were sufficient to insulate the manufacturer or seller from liability. But of course providing complete information is never possible. What is required is an "adequate" warning or instruction, typically of foreseeable risks. Warning liability is therefore not truly "strict" liability, since adequacy determinations inevitably take into account the feasibility and cost of providing a warning, as well as the kind of information that purchasers want and need.

One problem here is that there are diminishing returns from providing additional information. The more risks a warning discloses and the more detailed the instructions for safe use that are given, the less likely the user actually is to digest and heed the warning or to follow the instructions. The term "label clutter" is often used to describe the problem. Since the adequacy issue ordinarily is for the jury, however, it is possible for the jury to find in favor of liability in cases in which fairly low probability risks were not disclosed, or the particular phraseology used in the warning is alleged not to have conveyed the nature of the risk in question with an adequate degree of specificity. In *MacDonald v. Ortho Pharmaceutical Corp.*,[14] for example, the warning on birth control pills manufactured by the defendant referred to the risk of blood clots that could lodge in the brain and could be fatal, but did not use the word "stroke." The plaintiff suffered a stroke, and in the plaintiff's suit the court held that her contention that the warning was inadequate raised a jury question. Given the number of different risks that might be disclosed about any given product, the issue is somewhat analogous to asking a jury in a design defect case to decide whether the risks posed by a particular design feature were worth that feature's utility, without looking at the entire product design. A jury may well conclude that the particular

---

13. *See* RESTATEMENT (THIRD) OF TORTS: PRODUCTS LIABILITY, § 6 Comment d.
14. 394 Mass. 131, 475 N.E.2d 65 (1985).

risk that was not disclosed to the plaintiff is the one additional risk about which there should have been a warning, or a differently phrased warning. That is an unfortunate effect of the current approach. But like design defect liability, there does not seem to be any more suitable alternative approach to dealing with the adequacy-of-warning issue. If there is to be a requirement that an adequate warning be given, at some point we must rely on juries—as well as on courts granting directed verdicts—to decide when a warning was or was not adequate.

A second problem is that the plaintiff must prove causation. In warnings cases this means proving that the plaintiff would not have used the product, or would not have used it in the way he or she did, if an adequate warning had been given. The problem is analogous to proving causation in informed consent cases, as discussed in Chapter Three. It may be difficult for the plaintiff to adduce actual evidence of what he or she would have done in the face of a warning, especially in cases involving highly beneficial drugs. Some courts, often but by no means only in vaccination cases, therefore, have created what amounts to a presumption that the plaintiff (or the plaintiff's parent) would have heeded an adequate warning if it had been given. I am skeptical of the factual basis for this "heeding presumption," both because most people think that taking drugs their physicians prescribe make sense, and because certain vaccinations are required for enrollment in school and participation in organized recreational sports. One of two things is going on. The courts may be concerned that without the heeding presumption, few plaintiffs would be able to prove that they would have read a proper warning and decided not to take the drug, and that manufacturers would therefore usually escape liability. Alternatively, the courts may recognize that in certain settings most people would have taken the drug even if they had read a proper warning, but the courts may in effect be creating insurance protection for the unlucky few people who suffer the side effect in question, even if they would have taken the drug after being adequately warned or not. Whether creating insurance through tort liability is a sensible way to create such insurance is, of course, a separate question.

2. The Warning/Design Defect Connection

The risks posed by some products outweigh their utility when there is no warning or instructions, but are outweighed by their utility when the product does carry an adequate warning or instructions. There is no dispute that in such cases there is a duty to warn, and that if that duty is satisfied there is no liability for a risk that is the subject of an adequate warning or instruction. When a reasonable alternative design can eliminate a product defect, however, then merely warning about these risks does not insulate the defendant from liability.

But what about a product that has no reasonable alternative design and whose risks still might outweigh its benefits after an otherwise adequate warning or instruction is given? Can such a product be found to have a design defect, or does the provision of the warning or instruction insulate the seller from liability? Outside the field of prescription drugs, which are subject to the rule governing "unavoidably unsafe" products permitting a warning alone, the answer is not entirely clear. The "patent danger" rule that once prevailed in many states implied that an adequate warning was always sufficient, since this rule provided that when the defects in a product's design were obvious ("patent" rather than "latent") the manufacturer could not be held liable for injuries that resulted. Because many risks are even more obvious when a product carries an express warning about them than when the risks are merely visible, it would seem that under the patent danger rule there should be no design defect liability once an adequate warning has been given.

But the patent danger rule has been overruled in many jurisdictions.[15] And a few prominent decisions have implied that a jury may find that certain products are too dangerous to be on the market at all, even when their risks are known and understood. For example, in *O'Brien v. Muskin Corp.*,[16] the court held that it was for a jury to decide whether an above-ground swimming pool that was 3 and 1/2 feet deep was defectively designed because of the risk of injury from diving into it, even when the risk was obvious. Yet above-ground swimming pools inherently pose a risk to those who dive into them.

It is therefore difficult to see *O'Brien* as anything other than a rejection of consumer sovereignty even in the face of adequate information, although the case was quickly overruled by statute. If consumers are permitted to choose Buicks lacking rear-seat airbags without General Motors' incurring liability for injuries to passengers that would have been prevented by such devices, then why must the makers of above-ground swimming pools pay for injuries that result because their pools have obviously shallow depths and hard bottoms? Nor is the problem solved by saying that the issue is

---

15. See *Micallef v. Miehle Co.*, 39 N.Y.2d 376, 384 N.Y.S.2d 115, 348 N.E.2d 571 (1976).

16. 94 N.J. 169, 463 A.2d 298 (1983).

one for the jury and that the obviousness of the risk can be taken into account, since the issue is whether there should ever be liability under these circumstances. Rather, in this area involving the intersection between design defect and warnings law, the tension between consumer sovereignty and the protective goals of tort law that has been present at least since *Winterbottom v. Wright* will not go away. As long as we simultaneously trust and distrust the consumer, trust and distrust the market for safety, trust and distrust design defect liability, the law governing liability for injuries caused by obviously dangerous products will be unsettled.

V. Products Liability Defenses

Most of the defenses to products liability actions are the same defenses available in other negligence and strict liability cases. Contributory or comparative negligence is always a defense when the essence of the action is negligence, and in many states is also a defense even when the action is in essence based on strict liability. And assumption of risk is typically available as a defense whether the action is regarded as sounding in negligence or in strict liability, although in comparative negligence jurisdictions usually it is not a complete defense, but is subsumed within comparative negligence.

One defense that is distinctive to products liability, however, is product misuse. Suppose that I use a garden rake to boost myself up to a high window sill outside my house, the rake breaks while I am in midair, and I am injured in the fall. In my suit against the rake manufacturer for designing a rake too weak to bear my weight, the manufacturer has a misuse defense, even assuming that I can prove that the rake was defectively manufactured or designed. This misuse defense has become complicated, however, by the development of an exception for injuries caused by a "foreseeable" misuse. The manufacturer remains liable for these misuses. For instance, if I try to use a kitchen knife as a screwdriver and this use causes the knife to splinter into shards that put out my eye, it may be a jury question whether this is a foreseeable misuse. This exception to the misuse defense can be trumped, however, by the plaintiff's assumption of risk. That is, if the plaintiff knowingly and negligently takes the risk entailed by a foreseeable misuse, the manufacturer is not liable.

Whether all this is described as a matter of available versus unavailable defenses or as proximate versus remote cause does not much matter, as long as what is really at stake remains clear. The question is which party under the circumstances at issue is the best bearer of the risk of injury, the plaintiff or the defendant, and whether that issue should be decided by the court or by juries. Liability for foreseeable misuses is best shouldered by the manufacturer or seller; liability for unforeseeable misuses, and for knowing and negligently encountered foreseeable misuses, is best shouldered by the plaintiff.

VI. Disclaimers, Bystanders, and Consumer Sovereignty

In exploring modern products liability law I have tried to suggest that although it may not be appropriate for consumer sovereignty to be the dominant principle in the field, consumer sovereignty might play a greater role than it does. For example, it is virtually never possible to disclaim liability for injury caused by a defective product—i.e., to contract out of that liability in advance. That possibility died after *Henningsen*, as warranty was displaced by pure liability in tort as the principal basis of liability. The law in this field, however, need not be a slave to conceptualism. Why not permit disclaimers of products liability under circumstances in which the market for safety appears to be functioning properly?

One of the reasons, I think, is judicial and legislative distrust of the market's ability to regulate safely effectively. But of course this would not necessarily preclude permitting disclaimers when the market was working effectively. Some products pose one major, salient, danger. Chain saws, for instance, pose such a risk. Some potential purchasers are adept and experienced in the use of chain saws and are therefore willing to bear the risk of cutting off their fingers in return for a lower price. Others are not. It is certainly possible to imagine a regime in which all the major risks posed by chain saws were disclosed, and purchasers then chose between tort and no-tort options, or between full-compensation and partial-compensation options, for different prices.

The reason such regimes have not developed, however, is that the courts probably do not consider themselves to be in a very good position to decide under what circumstances the market for safety could and could not function with sufficient effectiveness to warrant validating disclaimers of or limitations on tort liability. On this view the near-blanket prohibition on disclaimers in products liability can be seen as a rule fashioned at a very high level of generality. Although the rule is not perfectly accurate in that there are some situations in which disclaimers ought to be permitted, the blanket rule generates considerable savings on transactions costs and yields acceptable accuracy in the majority of cases. The critical question would then be whether there may eventually be enough situations in which permitting disclaimers would be desirable, so that relaxing the blanket prohibition and fashioning an effective method of identifying these situations would make sense.

As we saw from the outset in imagining what a modern regime premised on the *Winterbottom* rule might look like, however, missing from this equation is a factor that makes the whole problem somewhat more complex: the role of bystanders. The argument that consumer sovereignty should play a greater role in determining the scope of products liability is premised on the notion that individual consumers know best for themselves what is the optimal combination of product safety, price, attractiveness and functionality. But by definition a bystander is a party who is not in the chain of product distribution, and therefore has no means of contractually waiving or otherwise limiting her tort rights by agreement with potential defendants in return for a better priced or more attractive product. Even if consumer sovereignty were made dominant and full disclaimers were permitted, it can hardly be imagined that bystanders injured by defective products would be left without a cause of action. Rather, two parallel legal regimes would have to develop—one for those purchasers whose liabilities were governed by a contractual disclaimer or limitation of liability, and another for others, including bystanders. For this reason, manufacturers of products who effectively disclaimed liability to their purchasers would still face liability to bystanders. It may be that this would in fact be the best arrangement—choice for purchasers, automatic tort protection for bystanders. But perhaps the prospect that moving toward greater consumer sovereignty could never entirely substitute contract for tort, but instead would result in the development of two separate products liability regimes, has also served to preclude more serious consideration of this alternative.

Some confirmation of the accuracy of these explanations is afforded by the state of the law governing liability for "commercial" losses resulting from product defects. Such losses occur when a product defect causes no bodily injury or property damage but does cause such economic loss as a decline in the value of the product itself, or lost profits. The courts in such cases generally hold that the plaintiff's claim is governed not by tort but by contract law, including the law of sales.[17] Thus, although the very sale of the product in question may carry an implied warranty of merchantability, under the law of sales the disclaimer of such a warranty is virtually always valid if the disclaimer does not pertain to liability for bodily injury or property damage.

17. See, e.g., *East River Steamship Corp. v. Transamerica Delaval Inc.*, 476 U.S. 858, 106 S.Ct. 2295, 90 L.Ed.2d 865 (1986).

Why are such disclaimers permitted? The answer is that, when only commercial—that is, purely economic—losses are at stake, the factors that discourage the courts from permitting contract law to govern are absent: distrust of the market is much less pronounced, people's safety is not at stake, and there is hardly any threat to bystanders. Moreover, as in the tort arena, the rule governing the issue also is set at a very high level of generality, although the rule is precisely the opposite of the tort law rule. The courts rarely inquire into the circumstances surrounding the disclaimer of liability for pure economic loss. Rather, disclaimers of liability for pure economic losses are virtually always valid. Given this structure, it is no surprise that the one area where the courts have had trouble developing an entirely consistent set of rules is the case in which a physically-dangerous defect has (luckily) resulted in only economic loss.

Because this kind of case falls right on the borderline between contract and tort, the principles of contract and tort law each exercise sufficient gravitational pull to make the problem difficult for the courts to resolve, and the rule governing the issue has remained uncertain.

VII. Federal Preemption

Federal laws regulating product safety or products liability, and state products liability law, may sometimes conflict. For example, a federal law might mandate that a product carry a particular warning, but the plaintiff in a state products liability suit might allege that the warning was inadequate. When federal and state law are in fact in conflict, federal law governs, because Article IV of the United States Constitution, containing the Supremacy Clause, provides that federal law is the "supreme law of the land" by which "the judges in every state shall be bound." In such a situation federal law is said to "preempt" state law. In practice the issue here is whether, through preemption, the federal law creates a ceiling on the degree of safety that state products liability law can require. In the absence of preemption, federal law creates no ceiling, but only a floor or minimum standard, and products liability law can demand more safety than federal law requires.

Preemption, based on a federal statute or regulation, can be either express or implied. Both bases for preemption depend on interpretation of the particular federal statute or regulation whose meaning is at issue. For example, in *Riegel v. Medtronic, Inc.*,[18] the

---

18.   552 U.S. 312, 128 S.Ct. 999, 169 L.Ed.2d 892 (2008).

Supreme Court upheld a ruling that an express preemption clause in the federal Medical Device Amendments to the Food, Drug and Cosmetic Act preempted a state products liability claim against a *medical device* manufacturer. But in *Altria Group, Inc. v. Good*,[19] the Court held that the Federal Cigarette Labeling Act did not expressly preempt cigarette smokers' suit against a *tobacco manufacturer* for misrepresenting that its cigarettes had "lowered tar and nicotine."

When the argument is that there is implied rather than express federal preemption, the result tends to depend on whether permitting state claims would be consistent with the purpose of the applicable federal statutory or regulatory regime, which may be a less determinate, or at least a more contestable question, than whether there is express preemption. For example, in *PLIVA, Inc. v. Mensing*,[20] the Court held that federal drug regulations, as interpreted by the FDA, preempted state laws imposing a duty upon *generic* drug manufacturers to change a drug's label. On the other hand, perhaps the most important case for our purposes because of its application to standard products liability duty-to-warn cases involving *brand name* prescription drugs is *Wyeth v. Levine*.[21] There the Court held that FDA labeling requirements did not preempt a state failure-to-warn claim, rejecting the manufacturer's arguments that it could not have modified its warning once the warning had been approved by the FDA and that a state law duty to provide a stronger warning would interfere with the purposes of federal drug labeling regulation.

In short, whether a state products liability cause of action is preempted is a question of federal statutory or regulatory interpretation, and therefore depends on which federal statute or regulation is being interpreted. Of course, interpretation is not a mechanical process, especially in cases involving claims of implied preemption. The substantive issue at stake in preemption cases is how much national uniformity in product liability standards there should be. Under preemption, federal law creates a uniform ceiling, and gives manufacturers a safe harbor that can be occupied by compliance with the federal standard. Without preemption, manufacturers may be subject to different state liability standards. Judicial attitudes toward the value of nationally uniform standards, federal power, and state products liability law may therefore affect decisions about implied preemption. But statutory context and factual particulars are still the place to start in considering preemption issues.

19. 555 U.S. 70, 129 S.Ct. 538, 172 L.Ed.2d 398 (2008).
20. __ U.S. __, 131 S.Ct. 2567, 180 L.Ed.2d 580 (2011).
21. 555 U.S. 555, 129 S.Ct. 1187, 173 L.Ed.2d 51 (2009).

10

DAMAGES

When lawyers litigate tort cases, their concern is at least as much with the magnitude of the damages that may be awarded as with the imposition of liability itself. Awarding damages in tort cases performs at least three functions: 1) achieving corrective justice or providing civil recourse by compensating the plaintiff for losses resulting from the defendant's tortious act; 2) promoting deterrence by threatening defendants with liability for the costs resulting from their tortious acts; and 3) recognizing the social and individual significance of the plaintiff's loss and confirming the weight of the defendant's responsibility for that loss. Consequently, the law governing damages in tort cases is unavoidably linked with the purposes underlying the imposition of tort liability itself. With that linkage in mind, this Chapter examines the basic rules regarding compensatory damage awards; the "collateral source" rule, which affords the plaintiff the right to recover damages even for benefits that have been paid to the plaintiff from her own sources of insurance; damages in cases involving "wrongful death;" and punitive damages.

I. Compensatory Damages

The general rule is that the successful plaintiff is entitled to be made "whole," by recovering damages to compensate her for the losses proximately resulting from the defendant's tortious act or omission. In a case involving injury to property, those damages are measured by the loss in value of the property or the cost to repair (or replace), whichever is less. In addition, the plaintiff may recover damages for consequential loss, such as diminished profits.

The successful plaintiff in a bodily injury case is entitled to recover damages for 1) the "special," or out-of-pocket, losses proximately resulting from the defendant's tortious action and 2) "general" damages for non-economic losses, often referred to as "pain and suffering," although these include all intangible losses. Out-of-pocket, or tangible monetary losses, in bodily injury cases typically consist mainly of health-care expenses and lost earning or lost earning capacity. In contrast, pain and suffering damages for intangible losses may be awarded to compensate the plaintiff for physical and emotional suffering, disfigurement, loss of life's enjoyments, and other similar losses.

The ordinary rules governing the burden of proving the elements of the plaintiff's claim apply to proof of damages. The plaintiff must prove by a preponderance of the evidence that she has suffered, or will in the future suffer, the losses for which she claims damages. Interestingly, compensatory damage awards for bodily injury are not subject to the federal income tax—probably because only the wage-recovery component of such awards should be taxed even in theory, and determining the portion of an award or settlement that was made for wage loss often would be difficult. Yet juries usually are not instructed that awards are not taxable.

Three significant features of this setup are worth exploring in more detail: 1) the principle of a single recovery; 2) the absence of an independent cause of action for inchoate or future loss; and 3) the function of awards for pain and suffering.

A. *The Principle of a Single Recovery: Compensation for Both Past and Future Loss*

Perhaps the most salient feature of the law governing damages in tort cases is that in the ordinary case the plaintiff gets only a single recovery, providing compensation not only for past but also for future losses, if any. Naturally, this principle of a single recovery has both advantages and disadvantages.

1. Advantages

The great advantage of the principle of a single recovery is that the case does not go on forever. Once there has been a trial and appeals have concluded, there is legal closure. For the plaintiff in a bodily injury case, the benefit of closure is that she can get on with her life, both psychologically and physically. The more injured and hurting the plaintiff appears to be at trial, the more damages the jury is likely to award. Under the principle of a single recovery, once that recovery is obtained, the legal incentive for the plaintiff to stay sick or injured disappears. The defendant derives enormous benefits from closure as well. The defendant gets repose that is very similar to the effect of the running of a statute of limitations. Once a case has concluded and the defendant has paid the plaintiff, the defendant's financial exposure and vulnerability to the plaintiff have ended. Economic planning can proceed without uncertainty about whether there will be further liability to the plaintiff in the future. Finally, for the legal system, the advantage of a single recovery is the avoidance of multiple judicial proceedings and their consequent administrative cost.

2. Disadvantages

There can be no doubt, however, that there are disadvantages to the principle of a single recovery. One is that there is almost certainly less accuracy in estimating future damages than there would be if determinations were made periodically as losses were incurred. Predicting how injured (if at all) the plaintiff will be in the future, and then calculating the amount of medical expenses, lost earnings, and pain and suffering that will continue to result from the plaintiff's injuries is bound to be an exercise in informed estimation at best. If awards were made periodically as losses were incurred, surely greater accuracy could be achieved. A second disadvantage is that the plaintiff must be a good investor or she will not have the award when she needs it in the future. This need for investment of awards for future losses is underscored by the practice of discounting awards to present value.

3. Discounting Awards to Present Value

The principle of a single recovery requires the jury to "discount to present value" awards made for future losses by awarding less than the projected dollar amount of those losses. The reason for this requirement is the "time" value of money that is invested today for future needs. For example, if the plaintiff is injured today and will continue for the next ten years to incur medical expenses and suffer physical pain from that injury, making an accurate award for her future losses requires two steps. First, the jury must determine what medical expenses the plaintiff will incur and how much physical pain she will suffer in each future year, and place a dollar value on those losses. One way to do this is to assume that there will be no inflation in the future. Another approach, which requires even more speculation about what the future will bring, is to estimate what effect future inflation will have on such items of loss as medical expenses and wages, and then to take this inflation into account in predicting the dollar value of the plaintiff's future losses.

Either way, a second step is required. Because the function of an award of damages is to compensate the plaintiff for her losses *and no more*, an award today of the full amount that the plaintiff will lose in the future would constitute overcompensation. If invested today that sum would earn interest or otherwise appreciate in value. By the time the losses for which the damages intended to compensate the plaintiff were actually incurred, the plaintiff would have a sum greater than the amount of those losses. The amount of a future loss must therefore be discounted to present value—i.e., reduced to a sum which, if invested, will equal the amount of the future loss at the time it occurs.

This is a mathematical exercise which can easily be accomplished using "present value" tables. But to use a present-value table one must determine what "discount" rate to use. The discount rate is simply the reverse of an assumption about what rate of interest the plaintiff's damages award will earn while it is invested by the plaintiff. If the amount of the award was arrived at on the supposition that there will be no inflation in the future, then a "pure" rate of interest (one which ignores the possibility of inflation) will be used to determine the appropriate discount rate. But if the award assumed that there would be inflation, then an inflation-adjusted interest rate will have to be used to determine the discount rate.

These seeming technicalities have two important implications. First, unless a jurisdiction has adopted uniform rules regarding the appropriate discount rate to be employed in determining the present value of an award, then any case involving potentially substantial future losses is likely to involve testimony by experts about future inflation and the appropriate discount rate. This has always seemed to me to be an unnecessary as well as an unfortunate exercise, since the result is that different juries will make different findings about how much inflation there will be in the future or what the market rate of interest would be in the future if there were no inflation. Both are highly speculative questions. It would make a lot more sense to have a uniform discount rate, promulgated annually by rule of court or otherwise arrived at.

Second, as I noted in discussing the disadvantages of the principle of a single recovery, for the theory underlying the principle of a single recovery to work in practice, the plaintiff must be at least an average investor. The discounting of damage awards to present value assumes that the portion of a single recovery awarded for future losses will appreciate over time through investment. If that appreciation does not occur as assumed by the discount rate used, then the plaintiff will ultimately find herself without sufficient funds to compensate her for future losses when they are incurred, and a major purpose of the law of tort damages will not be served.

B. *Inchoate and Future Loss*

A corollary of the principle of a single recovery is the rule that there is no independent cause of action for losses that have not yet occurred. Once tangible physical loss has taken place, then compensation for all future losses that will more probably than not result from that loss is also recoverable. But if no physical loss has yet occurred, the fact that the plaintiff will more probably than not suffer physical loss in the future ordinarily is not actionable. The very limited inroad made into this firm limitation has been the occasional award of the costs of medical monitoring when a defendant has tortiously exposed the plaintiff or a group of plaintiffs to the risk of suffering future injury such as cancer. Otherwise, recovery is virtually never permitted today for damages resulting from even a reasonable fear that one will suffer harm in the future. Aside from medical monitoring costs, under the principle of a single recovery, liability for future loss must await the actual occurrence of present physical injury.

C. *Pain and Suffering Awards*

1. The Functions of the Award

Awards for pain and suffering perform a number of functions. First, in the case of serious injuries, few people would think that providing compensation for out-of-pocket loss alone could ever make the plaintiff "whole." Money paid for pain and suffering may not remove that loss, but it does further acknowledge the wrong done to the plaintiff and the fact that the plaintiff has experienced intangible losses.[1] And the very fact that the plaintiff has received an award of money compensating for more than out-of-pocket expenses may provide some "consolation" that is itself a value. Second, even if the plaintiff's pain and suffering cannot ever be fully compensated for with money, the plaintiff may be able to use an award to provide activities or enjoyments that substitute for those lost as a result of the injury in question. For instance, if the plaintiff no longer can play soccer because of paralysis, he might use the money from an award of general damages to purchase a satellite dish that will bring televised soccer from around the world into his home, or the plaintiff might use the award to take up an entirely new hobby.

Third, regardless of whether money can compensate in any way at all for pain and suffering, there can be little question that pain

---

1. *See* Margaret Jane Radin, *Compensation and Commensurability*, 43 DUKE L.J. 56 (1993).

and suffering is one of the consequences with respect to which the law aims to achieve optimal deterrence when it threatens potential defendants with tort liability. That is, even if there were no benefit obtained from paying pain and suffering awards to victims, it would make sense to hold injurers liable for these damages. From the standpoint of optimal deterrence it really does not matter whether the defendant pays these damages to the plaintiff, or to a charitable foundation instead, or the dollar amount of pain and suffering damages the defendant is required to pay is placed in a metal bucket and burned in the courtroom. What matters is that the defendant has to pay the money. The requirement of payment assures that other potential injurers are threatened with liability not only for out-of-pocket loss, but also for pain and suffering. And this threat promotes optimal deterrence by encouraging potential defendants to take into account the cost of the pain and suffering that their activities may cause in deciding what safety precautions are worth taking.

Admittedly, in certain contexts this deterrence argument is less persuasive than in others. For example, whenever potential plaintiffs are in a direct or indirect contractual relationship with potential injurers—in fields such as medical malpractice or products liability—the right to bring a tort action can be understood as insurance for which potential plaintiffs pay in advance through increased medical expenses or product costs. Strong arguments have been made and contested in the literature about whether rational purchasers of medical services and products would want to pay for insurance against pain and suffering. If they would not, some commentators argue, then pain and suffering awards should not be made at all.[2] Other commentators have suggested that it is rational to want to purchase pain and suffering insurance.[3] This issue remains contested. But as long as we have a general law of damages rather than damages rules applying separately to malpractice and products liability—and as long as tort law is conceived as more than a mere "insurance" system—the non-insurance arguments for awarding pain and suffering damages seem highly likely to prevail.

The last argument in favor of awarding pain and suffering damages is practical in the extreme. Attorneys representing plaintiffs in bodily injury cases virtually always work on a contingent-fee basis: if the plaintiff loses, she owes the attorney nothing except

2. *See, e.g.,* Alan Schwartz, *Proposals for Products Liability Reform: A Theoretical Synthesis,* 97 YALE L.J. 353 (1988).

3. *See, e.g.,* Steven P. Croley and Jon D. Hanson, *The Nonpecuniary Costs of Accidents: Pain-and-Suffering Damages in Tort Law,* 108 HARV. L. REV. 1785 (1995).

expenses, and sometimes not even that; but if the plaintiff succeeds, the attorney receives a percentage of the plaintiff's award, sometimes as much as 40 percent. Given the prevalence of this type of contingent-fee arrangement, even a plaintiff fully compensated by a jury for her out-of-pocket expenses would receive less than full compensation after she paid a percentage of this award to her attorney. Among other things, therefore, the award of damages for pain and suffering provides the plaintiff a sum out of which to compensate her attorney. It might be a lot more sensible to treat the plaintiff's counsel fees as another item of compensable out-of-pocket expenses rather than using pain and suffering awards as an under-the-table method of paying counsel fees. But as things now stand, juries almost universally understand how counsel fees really are paid and take this into account in making pain and suffering awards.

2. Limitations on Awards

Notwithstanding these justifications for awarding pain and suffering damages, it does not necessarily follow that awards of such damages should always be unlimited. One major criticism sometimes made of pain and suffering awards is that they can be too high. Another is that, because assessment of the value of pain and suffering is so subjective, valuations vary enormously from jury to jury. Predicting the amount of an award is therefore difficult. Critics argue that the occasional high award and their general unpredictability create uncertainty on the part of potential defendants that results in overdeterrence and in the consequent reluctance of certain enterprises, such as pharmaceutical companies, to develop legally risky product lines at all.

In theory, most of the functions of pain and suffering awards can be well served even when subject to certain kinds of limits on what can be awarded for pain and suffering. The traditional approach to the problem of size and variability in award levels (whether for pain and suffering alone or for all damages awarded by a jury) has been to permit courts to restrict awards through the practice of *remittitur*. Under this practice, when a jury award is in excess of what a reasonable jury could award in light of all the evidence, the trial court affords the plaintiff a choice between a new trial and acceptance of a specified reduction in the award. A similar practice known as *additur* is available when the award is unduly low. But these are *ad hoc* approaches that many courts are in any event reluctant to apply except in the most egregious cases of jury error.

The problem posed for those who would favor a more systematic effort to control pain and suffering awards, however, is to develop standards of limitation that are both fair *and* workable. It is easy enough to satisfy one of these criteria at a time, but very hard to fashion an approach that can satisfy both simultaneously. For example, about half the states have placed absolute dollar ceilings on the amount that may be awarded for pain and suffering—typically in the neighborhood of $250,000. Some of these ceilings apply across the board, whereas others apply only to particular types of cases, such as medical malpractice. Ceilings make the average size of awards much more predictable, since no award can exceed the ceiling. But ceilings accomplish this aim at the cost of possible unfairness to the most seriously injured victims—those whose pain and suffering a jury would value at more than the ceiling if this were permissible. Disproportionately these are young, seriously injured victims, since these victims have life expectancies and injuries that are most likely to involve long-term, severe pain and suffering. Ceilings therefore exact much of the sacrifice necessary to achieve predictability of pain and suffering awards from those who are young and seriously injured. Conversely, anyone whose pain and suffering the jury values at less than the ceiling makes no sacrifice at all and receives compensation for 100 percent of his or her pain and suffering.

The alternative would be to exact some sacrifice from all categories of victim, regardless of how modest their pain and suffering, through a "schedule" of pain and suffering awards.[4] This approach would be more fair than dollar ceilings, but less workable. To make this approach work, it would be necessary to construct a schedule of permissible pain and suffering damages calibrated to the age and severity of injury suffered by each victim: a certain amount for death at a given age, a certain amount for paralysis at a given age, a certain amount for loss of an arm at a given age, and so forth. Then the jury in every case would be required to determine in what category in the schedule the plaintiff's injuries fell. The damages awardable by category might be mandatory, or they could serve merely as guidance for the jury. This approach would be cumbersome, though it might eventually work effectively. Workers compensation awards for specified permanent disabilities work in roughly this way. But certainly the creation of a pain and suffering damages schedule of this sort cannot be accomplished through judicial action. Legislative action would be required. This approach, however, has seemed much less attractive to legislatures than the

---

4. *See* Randall R. Bovbjerg *et al.*, *Valuing Life and Limb in Tort: Scheduling "Pain and Suffering,"* 83 Nw. U. L.Rev. 909 (1989).

enactment of absolute ceilings on pain and suffering recoveries that ignore the problem of equity among victims. Consequently, many states still operate with only *remittitur* and *additur* to control damage awards, while others have absolute ceilings on the sums that can be awarded for pain and suffering.

3. Pain and Suffering for Property Damage?

It is black-letter law that pain and suffering damages are not recoverable in cases involving property damage. Despite the fact that I am emotionally attached to a family heirloom that is damaged by the defendant's negligence, I cannot recover for my resulting emotional suffering. I expect, however, that in the years to come this rule will be tested in a series of especially appealing cases. Some states have enacted statutes authorizing the recovery of limited damages for pain and suffering (e.g., $5000) in specified cases, such as those involving the death of pets as a result of defective pet food. Other states may well consider creating limited exceptions to the general rule in the pet food cases. And one can think of other cases—negligent destruction of wedding photos, for example—in which creating an exception may have its attractions. Consequently, the black-letter limitation on recovery of pain and suffering damages for property damage may well start to give way a bit as time goes on.

II. Collateral Sources and Benefits

The modern economy is replete with insurance, both private and public. Plaintiffs are often insured for all or part of their losses, by health, disability, life, fire, and other forms of insurance. Whether the payment of collateral benefits such as insurance to the plaintiff is taken into account in setting damage awards can make a substantial difference in the amount of an award. The treatment of the benefits paid to plaintiffs by these and similar sources of compensation that are collateral to any tort recovery is therefore of considerable importance in any tort case. The traditional "collateral source," or "collateral benefits," rule provides that evidence of payments made or to be made to the plaintiff in the future by collateral sources such as insurance is not admissible in the plaintiff's tort action against the defendant. The result is that the plaintiff is entitled to prove losses, and to recover damages from the defendant, that have already been paid by the plaintiff's own insurer. The arguments for and against this rule are analyzed below.

A. *The "Rewarding Prudence" Argument for the Rule*

The traditional argument for the collateral source rule is that the plaintiff who has invested in insurance coverage should not be penalized for his prudence in doing so. There is something to this argument, but less than there seems to be at first glance. The plaintiff who has purchased insurance would not be "penalized" if insurance benefits were taken into account in setting damages, any more than a plaintiff who invested in a sprinkler system is "penalized" when his recovery for a negligently-started fire is lower than it would be if the sprinkler system had not prevented some of the damage to his property. Rather, the plaintiff's own action has mitigated the amount of the loss he actually has suffered. After all, the defendant must suffer the disadvantage of injuring an unusually vulnerable plaintiff and must "take his victim as he finds him" when the victim has a thin skull. Why not also permit the defendant an advantage when he injures an economically "strong" victim—i.e., one who has insurance? If there were a need to avoid "penalizing" the plaintiff for his prudence in purchasing insurance, the way to do that would be to reimburse the plaintiff for the insurance premium he had spent unnecessarily, rather than permitting him a recovery for a monetary loss he did not suffer.

Moreover, health, disability, life, and fire insurance cover losses no matter how they are caused, and therefore insure against far more than losses caused by a third-party's tortious act. The plaintiff in a tort action has received the insurance he paid for—broad insurance protection against medical expenses, lost wages, or fire losses, whether tortiously caused or not. Offsetting a damage award by the amount of benefits paid to the plaintiff by any of these sources of insurance would therefore "deprive" him of only a small portion of the insurance he had purchased. Finally, vast amounts of insurance covering potential victims is not purchased voluntarily through individual prudence, but is provided automatically as a fringe benefit of employment or by government entitlement programs such as veteran's benefits or Medicaid. It is much harder to see how the "reward for prudence" argument has any bearing on whether the plaintiff should get the benefit of payments made by this very large category of collateral sources.

B. *The "Preventing Double Recovery" Argument against the Rule*

One of the most common arguments made against the collateral source rule is that it permits the plaintiff to recover twice—once from his insurer and then a second time from the defendant. Such duplication of payment, the argument goes, violates the principle underlying all of damages law—that compensation should as nearly as possible make the plaintiff whole, but that the plaintiff should not obtain a net financial gain as a result of a tort recovery. Like the "reward for prudence" argument in favor of the collateral source rule, this argument against the rule also is less strong than it first appears to be. First, the desirability of promoting deterrence supports the collateral source rule. The expenses incurred as a result of the plaintiff's injury are real costs even if they are incurred, for example, by his health insurer rather than by the plaintiff himself. If the collateral source rule did not permit recovery of these expenses, then defendants would no longer be threatened with liability for them, and deterrence would be sub-optimal. So there is a tension between the desirability of avoiding overcompensation and the desirability of optimally deterring potential injurers. The collateral source rule resolves that tension in favor of optimal deterrence, even if this means occasional overcompensation.

A second reason that the double recovery argument is less strong than it may appear to be involves the contingent-fee system. Since the plaintiff must pay his attorney out of his award, even if the collateral source rule did permit "gross" overcompensation, probably it does not often result in "net" overcompensation after payment of a percentage of the total award to the plaintiff's attorney. This may not be the most sensible way to help to assure the plaintiff a means of paying counsel fees, but because the collateral source rule is already in place, the contingent-fee system that has grown up around it should influence the decision whether to retain the rule.

C. *The Subrogation Solution*

Both the prudence and double recovery arguments regarding the collateral source rule presuppose that the plaintiff keeps whatever "excess" payment results from the rule. Proponents of the rule therefore attempt to justify double recovery and opponents attack double recovery. But in fact the double-recovery issue is largely, though not entirely, a red herring. There is a third alternative that much more accurately describes what actually happens in practice: The plaintiff gets a judgment that includes a double recovery of that portion of his losses that are already insured, but then reimburses his insurance company out of the judgment, for the amount of the benefits paid by the company. Under this approach, which is applied to all forms of insurance except life insurance,[5] both of the purposes of the law of damages are achieved. The plaintiff is fully compensated (setting aside his obligation to pay his own attorney out of his recovery) but not overcompensated, yet the defendant is held liable for the full amount of the costs resulting from his tortious act.

This all takes place through the legal device known as "subrogation." Subrogation occurs under the terms of the insurance contract between the plaintiff and his insurer. Except for life insurance, virtually all insurance policies contain clauses giving the insurer rights of subrogation. The insurer with a right of subrogation steps into the shoes of the plaintiff (is "subrogated to" the plaintiff's rights) to the extent of payment made by the insurer to the plaintiff. Thus, whatever rights the plaintiff has against the defendant the plaintiff's insurer also has, though only to the extent of the insurer's payments to the plaintiff. The plaintiff's insurer therefore has the right to sue the defendant for negligence and to recover the amount of payments the insurer has made to the plaintiff. But this suit is usually unnecessary, since the plaintiff is already suing the defendant. So the insurer's rights of subrogation are translated into a right to be reimbursed (in insurance language, "indemnified") for the amount of its prior payments to the plaintiff out of the plaintiff's tort recovery. And by virtue of the collateral source rule, that tort recovery will be for all the losses incurred as result of the defendant's act, including those paid by the insurer. After reimbursing the insurer, the plaintiff keeps what he lost, the insurer receives what it had paid, and the defendant ends up paying the full amount of the losses he caused.

The fact that subrogation is available in this way certainly adds strength to the case for retaining the collateral source rule. However, subrogation reimbursements paid to plaintiffs' insurance companies do not always occur. One reason is that it may take considerable effort to secure such reimbursement. Insurance benefits typically are paid long before any tort recovery is obtained. For example, a health insurer normally pays hospitals and physicians

---

5. An exception is made for life insurance, which is never subject to subrogation or reimbursement and therefore may be involved in "duplicate" recovery, for reasons analyzed in Kenneth S. Abraham, THE LIABILITY CENTURY: INSURANCE AND TORT LAW FROM THE PROGRESSIVE ERA TO 9/11 207–11 (2008).

treating injuries within months of billing. But the patient may not obtain a tort recovery or settlement until years later. To secure reimbursement out of that subsequent tort recovery, the insurer must first have identified the subset of its many thousands of claim payments that are potentially reimbursable—i.e., those in which the patient's injury may have been caused by tortious action. The insurer must then determine whether the plaintiff later brought suit to recover these losses from a third party. Next the insurer must either file a lien that will result in automatic reimbursement in the few situations where this is permitted, or monitor the course of the plaintiff/insured's tort suit. Finally, the insurer must make known to the parties to the suit its putative right to reimbursement and then seek to vindicate that right before a judgment or settlement is paid, or at least before the plaintiff disburses or sequesters the award. Making this effort is likely to be worthwhile for insurers only in cases involving payment of very substantial health or disability insurance benefits.

A second reason that subrogation reimbursements are less than systematic results from the fact that most tort payments are the product of settlements, not judgments. Almost by definition, settlements are for less than the full amount of the plaintiff's damages. As a consequence, the portion of any settlement that should be paid to an insurer in reimbursement of already-paid benefits is contestable. Paying the insurer the full amount of these prior payments off the top of any settlement would deprive the plaintiff of compensation; yet computing what fraction of prior payments should be reimbursed requires some formula that would specify the portion of the plaintiffs' total losses that the amount paid in settlement constituted. For example, if we knew that the plaintiff's total losses were $100,000 and he settled for $60,000, then the settlement would be for 60 percent of his losses. It would therefore make sense to reimburse the plaintiff's health insurer for 60 percent of its prior benefit payments. But this $100,000 valuation of the plaintiff's total losses is not available when there has been a settlement: litigating the total amount of the plaintiff's losses is precisely what the settlement was designed to avoid. So there is a dilemma about how to divide the settlement. In some states fairly firm rules have emerged to guide the division of settlements in order resolve this dilemma. But in many states the rules are underdeveloped and the entire process is more a matter of lore than law. The result is unsystematic reimbursement of collateral sources. Thus, whereas in theory subrogation reimbursement can prevent double recovery by the plaintiff even while the defendant pays the full amount of the losses it caused, in practice sometimes such reimbursement of past payments occurs and sometimes it does not.

As to future payments of insurance benefits the issue is even more cloudy. Suppose that the plaintiff secures a large judgment under a general verdict for both past and future losses, and then reimburses his health insurer in full for prior payments. But then the plaintiff continues to incur medical expenses resulting from his earlier, tortiously-caused injuries, and these expenses are covered by his health insurance. Presumably part of the judgment has compensated him for these losses. In theory his insurer health insurer should not have to pay these medical expenses or should pay and then be simultaneously reimbursed for them by the insured. But in practice the insurance often does pay, because ordinarily the plaintiff has secured a general verdict that does not indicate what sum has been paid for future medical expenses. The result is a double recovery of these expenses. The special exception is Medicare, which by statute takes the position that it may not pay when a tort judgment or settlement has been for future medical expenses that it would otherwise cover. In short, as to both past and future benefits paid by collateral sources, the collateral source rule achieves only mixed success at simultaneously securing the proper level of compensation for plaintiffs while optimally deterring potential defendants.

As a result of pressure from defendants' interest groups, over the past few decades a number of state legislatures have reexamined the collateral source rule. Finding the rule unsatisfactory, over a dozen have enacted statutes that either partially or completely eliminate the rule. The operation of these statutes varies. Some direct that there be a reduction in the plaintiff's award equal to collateral benefits paid in the past or payable to the plaintiff in the future; others merely make evidence of such payments admissible. Some make exceptions in cases in which the insurer paying prior benefits to the plaintiff has a right of subrogation—thus acknowledging that in some sense the purpose of the statutes is to prevent double recovery only when that is a real threat. But other statutes draw no such distinction and apply more generally.

The great problem that is faced in implementing these statutes arises in cases involving substantial future losses. To be faithful to the purpose behind the statutes, the plaintiff's recovery of damages for future losses should be reduced by the amount of the collateral benefits that more probably than not will be paid to the plaintiff in the future. But determining the amount of such future benefit payments to the plaintiff requires predicting what sources of insurance, public and private, the plaintiff will have in the future, sometimes the distant future. The more serious and long-term the plaintiff's injuries are, the more speculative the entire exercise is likely to be, and the less likely it is that there will be any substantial offset of future losses by the amount of estimated future collateral benefits.

III. Damages in Wrongful Death, Survival and *Consortium* Actions

At common law a plaintiff's cause of action died with him. But in the nineteenth century, statutes enacted in both England and the United States altered this rule. In virtually all states, therefore, the law governing recovery in death cases is in the first instance a creature of statute, though with an overlay of many decades of common law interpretation and elaboration. There are two general classes of statutes, with variations within each. By far the most important are *wrongful death* statutes, which create a new cause of action on the part of those who survive the decedent. In contrast, *survival* statutes preserve the deceased's cause of action. Some states have enacted only a wrongful death statute, some have enacted only a survival statute, and some have enacted both.

A. *Wrongful Death Actions*

Typically a wrongful death statute provides that upon the death of an individual caused by the wrongful act of another, the person or entity "that would have been liable had death not ensued" continues to be liable. Although this phrasing implies that the statute preserves the decedent's cause of action, in fact that is not exactly what happens. Statutory treatment of three issues makes this clear: who are the beneficiaries of a wrongful death action; what damages are recoverable by these beneficiaries; and what defenses to this action are available.

1. Beneficiaries

Wrongful death statutes provide that recovery is for the benefit of designated individuals. Typically these are the "heirs at law" of the decedent—those who would, by the terms of another statute, inherit his estate if he died "intestate," that is, without a Will. These other statutes—known as statutes of "descent and distribution"—direct, for example, that the estate of an intestate go to a surviving spouse, or half to the spouse and half to surviving children, or if there is no surviving spouse in equal shares to surviving children, and so forth. The exact terms of the statutes of descent and distribution vary from state to state. But whatever the terms of these statutes of descent and distribution, under wrongful death statutes the statutorily designated "heirs at law" are the beneficiaries of the wrongful death cause of action, even if the decedent did have a Will leaving his estate to others.

2. The Measure of Damages

A beneficiary's recovery is measured by the losses she suffers as a result of the decedent's death. In the past these were limited to out-of-pocket, economic losses that would have been paid by the decedent in support of the beneficiary, and there were often statutory ceilings on the dollar amount that could be recovered in a wrongful death action. Both these limitations are a thing of the past in most states. Damages for both economic and emotional loss are recoverable, usually in unlimited amounts. Thus, if the beneficiaries are the parents of a deceased ten year old their recovery is likely to be substantial, whereas when the beneficiary is an adult child of an aged parent the recovery will probably be much smaller. Regardless, the principle that what is recovered is measured by the *beneficiary's losses* makes clear that, for all practical purposes, the cause of action is the beneficiary's and not the decedent's.

3. Defenses

Because a cause of action exists only if the deceased would have had one had death not ensued, the defendant can invoke any defense it would have had against the decedent. But most courts also hold that defenses that would be available against the beneficiary in an ordinary action also are available in wrongful death action. Thus, if the decedent was negligent then the beneficiaries' recovery is reduced in accord with the applicable comparative negligence statute. But even if the deceased was not negligent, if a beneficiary was negligent, then the contributory or comparative negligence of the beneficiary is available as a defense to that beneficiary's action. Once again, this setup makes it clear that for most practical purposes, even if not for all, the cause of action is the beneficiary's.

B. *Survival Actions*

All states have enacted statutes that preserve a cause of action for losses suffered by a decedent before he died. Thus, if before he died the decedent incurred medical expenses or experienced pain and suffering as a result of the defendant's tort, by statute damages for these losses are recoverable in an action by his estate, and pass through his estate to those entitled to inherit it. These are one form of "survival" statute.

A number of states have gone further, however, and have provided by statute for a cause of action to recover economic losses that are incurred as a result of the decedent's death. Typically the measure of these losses is the amount that would have been in the decedent's estate had he or she lived a full life expectancy. To make this computation a jury must predict the decedent's gross future earnings, and then subtract all payments and expenditures that he would have made in his lifetime, including support that he would have provided to his family, but also any money he would have spent on himself or non-family members. This cause of action is for the benefit of the decedent's estate and any recovery passes through the estate, to whomever is entitled to inherit. Entirely depending on the decedent's Will if he has one, this may be a surviving spouse, children, or anyone else. In the absence of a Will, this recovery will pass with the rest of his estate to his heirs at law under the applicable statute of descent and distribution.

C.   *Loss of Consortium*

The phrase loss of consortium refers to the deprivation of the benefits of a family relationship because of tortious conduct that causes injury but not death. At common law a husband had a cause of action for loss of consortium against a tortfeasor who injured his wife, for both economic and non-economic loss. Many decades ago this common law discrimination against women was remedied by giving wives the same cause of action for injuries to their husbands. A minority of states has extended the cause of action to parents whose children are injured, and/or to children whose parent or parents are injured.

D.   *The Underdeterrence Problem*

Any state that has enacted only a wrongful death, only a survival statute, or has limited rights of recovery for loss of consortium, has a potential underdeterrence problem, at least in theory, because of the under-compensation that these approaches entail. For example, a wrongful death statute imposes liability only for losses suffered by those who survive and suffer losses resulting from the decedent's death; there is no liability imposed for sums that would have been in the decedent's estate when he died a natural death. Conversely, a survival statute imposes liability only for sums that would have been in the decedent's estate when he died a natural death; there is no liability for losses suffered by those who survive a decedent. Some states, partly for this reason and partly out of solicitude for survivors, have enacted both types of statutes.

Notice, however, that even states that have enacted both types of statutes still face a potential deterrence gap, though a smaller one. Even both statutes together impose liability on the defendant only for the losses of the decedent's heirs at law and for what would have remained in the decedent's estate had he lived a full life expectancy. Neither statute imposes liability for the losses of any other person for whom the defendant would have provided support, or for the sums the decedent would have earned and spent on himself during his lifetime. Partly for this reason, the grotesque adage that a defendant is better off killing than badly maiming a victim tends to remain true, even in states that have enacted both types of statutes. Since dangerous behavior is just as likely to result in serious injury as in death, however, this apparent gap in the amount of deterrence created by the law governing recovery of damages in death cases may be more theoretical than real. Nonetheless, it is worth noting that despite all the apparent concern of modern tort theory with deterrence in personal injury cases, the law governing the damages that are recoverable in the most serious of all such cases—those involving death—is at least theoretically flawed as a means of deterring wrongful conduct.

IV. Punitive Damages

In exceptional cases the plaintiff is entitled not only to recover compensatory damages, but also to an award of damages designed to punish the defendant. These are known as "punitive" or "exemplary" damages. Punitive damages are awarded in only a small percentage of all cases, but the threat that they may be awarded probably has more impact than the small percentage of awards reflects.

The states vary in their descriptions of the behavior that warrants an award of punitive damages, but almost always behavior more blameworthy even than gross negligence is often necessary. In addition to punishment, punitive damages often are said to be designed to deter extremely blameworthy behavior. Presumably the defendant who has acted with something approaching knowledge that his behavior was highly likely to cause harm has been insufficiently deterred by the threat of liability for compensatory damages. This might be because the defendant knows that potential plaintiffs face difficulty in proving causation and therefore does not expect them to sue, because the defendant wishes to harm the plaintiff and is willing to pay compensatory damages to be able to do so, or simply because the defendant has been paying insufficient attention to the threat of liability for compensatory damages. The threat of liability for punitive damages in such cases puts a thumb on the scale, so to speak, in an effort to alter the defendant's cost-benefit calculations and get his attention.

The controversy over the size and unpredictability of pain and suffering awards has been paralleled in recent years by criticism of punitive damage awards on the same ground. In an effort to respond to this criticism, a number of the state statutes that have placed ceilings on awards of pain and suffering damages apply to punitive damages as well. In addition, over the past two decades the U.S. Supreme Court has reviewed punitive damages awards in a variety of cases in response to defendants' claims that excessive awards violate the Constitutional requirement of due process of law. In a series of decisions the Court has articulated three factors to be used in evaluating the constitutionality of a punitive damages award: 1) the degree of reprehensibility of the defendant's conduct; 2) the disparity or proportion between the harm or potential harm resulting from the defendant's conduct and the amount of compensatory damages awarded; and 3) the difference between this remedy and the civil or criminal penalties authorized to punish defendants in comparable cases.[6] The first and third factors are something of a matter of judgment. But in *State Farm Insurance Company v. Campbell*,[7] the Court quantified the second factor, holding that few awards in which there was more than a single-digit ratio between punitive and compensatory damages would satisfy due process. Thus, punitive damages awards that are more than nine times greater than compensatory damages are, in effect, presumptively unconstitutional. Whether and to what extent this test will limit punitive damages awards in cases where the defendant's act was highly reprehensible and subject to substantial criminal penalties, but resulted in comparatively little loss to the plaintiff, remains to be seen.

6. See, e.g., *BMW of North America v. Gore*, 517 U.S. 559, 116 S.Ct. 1589, 134 L.Ed.2d 809 (1996).

7. 538 U.S. 408, 123 S.Ct. 1513, 155 L.Ed.2d 585 (2003).

11

AFFIRMATIVE AND LIMITED DUTIES

According to the textbooks, including this one, the four elements of a cause of action in tort are duty, breach of duty, damages and causation. The "duty" this statement contemplates is the obligation to take some action or to refrain from taking some action. Without such an obligation, or "duty," there could never be tort liability. Duty is a question of law; it is for the court, not the jury, to decide whether there is or is not a duty. Juries, in contrast, decide whether there has been a breach of duty when a duty exists. In many instances, however, asking separately whether the defendant was under a duty, although logically required, is for practical purposes unnecessary. In the ordinary negligence case involving conduct by the defendant that risks foreseeable physical harm to the plaintiff or his property, the defendant is alleged to have had and to have breached the duty to exercise reasonable care to avoid injuring the plaintiff. Asking whether the defendant had a duty to the plaintiff and whether that duty was breached is therefore just another way of asking whether the defendant was negligent, and whether that negligence was a proximate cause of the plaintiff's harm.

In such cases, analyzing the problem in terms of duty adds nothing, and could lead to the mistaken conclusion that even after the negligence and proximate cause questions have been answered, there is still no liability unless the defendant owed the plaintiff a duty independent of the obligation to exercise reasonable care not to risk foreseeable physical injury to the plaintiff. In the ordinary case this conclusion is mistaken, because the defendant's negligence is precisely the breach of duty that is alleged. In such cases "duty" is a largely question-begging concept that can be safely used only if one is not misled by it. Moreover, in most strict liability cases use of duty language to describe what is going on would be peculiar. We would not say that actors are under a duty not to engage in abnormally dangerous activities. On the contrary, the whole point of this form of liability is that engaging in such activities is acceptable but that they must pay their own way. The essential "duty" in such cases is simply to compensate those who are injured by the activity.

There are important classes of cases, however, in which the existence or non-existence of a duty on the part of the defendant to take or refrain from taking some action is precisely the issue. Here use of duty language is not tautological or redundant, but absolutely essential. These are the classes of cases addressed in this Chapter. Situating these cases within a conceptual framework is not easy, because the duty issue arises in a variety of contexts and is influenced by a variety of factors.

Most conceptual frameworks in this area begin with the distinction between affirmative and limited duties. The first set of cases involves possible *affirmative duty*. Here the defendant's conduct does not negligently *create a risk* of physical harm to the plaintiff. Therefore the defendant has not breached any duty in this respect. As is sometimes said, the defendant is not guilty of "misfeasance." But the plaintiff is independently at risk of suffering physical harm and the defendant might, through the exercise reasonable care, *eliminate or reduce this risk* of harm to the plaintiff. The question is whether the defendant has an affirmative duty to do so—whether the defendant is liable for "nonfeasance." Tort law's default rule is that in general there are no such affirmative duties, but there are exceptions to this rule. All the cases in the affirmative duty category are, in a sense, about the duty to rescue. But the term rescue tends to be reserved for cases involving emergency. The remainder of the cases involve the question whether there is an affirmative duty to exercise reasonable care to protect the plaintiff from the risk of physical harm or to reduce that risk even when there is no imminent emergency. These typically involve special relationships between plaintiff and defendant, or subsequent wrongdoing by a third party that the defendant might have prevented. This Chapter addresses the cases in these categories and the policies underlying the extension of, and limits on, affirmative duty.

In the second set of cases the defendant's conduct foreseeably creates an unreasonable risk of harming the plaintiff. The defendant has committed misfeasance rather than mere nonfeasance. But in several categories of cases negligence law places limits on the duty to exercise reasonable care not to risk such harm. These are cases of *limited duty*. These include premises liability involving the manner in which a landowner maintained his property, "pure" emotional harm, and "pure" economic harm. These are cases in which, as a matter of law, there is no liability or only limited liability for negligently causing harm. In these cases there is no duty or only a limited duty, so to speak, not to be negligent. As with affirmative duty, this Chapter addresses the cases in these categories, examining the situations in which there is and is not a duty to exercise reasonable care, and the policies underlying these limits.

It is natural to seek some general formula to use in predicting when the courts hold, or will hold, that there is an affirmative duty, or that there are limits on duty, or that there is no duty. But there is no such formula, at least not one that is operationally useful. The best that can be done is to provide a list of factors that the courts tend to take into account, but whose weight may vary enormously in a particular context. These include (1) the foreseeability of harm; (2) the closeness of the connection between the defendant's conduct and the harm suffered by the plaintiff; (3) the moral blame attached to the defendant's conduct; (4) the extent of the burden on the defendant and the consequences for the community if a duty is imposed; (5) the policy of preventing future harm; and (6) the availability and prevalence of insurance that is or would be available if a duty is imposed.[1]

The main lesson of this Chapter, however, goes beyond these particulars. The lesson is that there is no general duty not to be negligent, no general duty to exercise reasonable care. There are only particular duties to exercise reasonable care, and however broad some of these duties are, there must always be a duty before the question of negligence—breach of duty—arises.

I. Rescue

The traditional rule, still almost universally in force, is that in the absence of special circumstances or a special relationship, one person has no affirmative duty to rescue another person from a position of danger, either by action or by warning. The distinction here is between the defendant who negligently created a risk of harm (misfeasance) and the defendant who did not remove a risk of harm created by someone or something else (nonfeasance). Tort law classically has been willing to impose liability for misfeasance, whether through act or omission, but not for nonfeasance. This rule holds even if the cost or risk to the defendant of rescuing the plaintiff is small or non-existent, and the danger to the plaintiff is great. I have no duty to rescue a drowning person, even if I need not enter the water to do so, but could easily throw him a life preserver or extend a nearby pole to help him.

It is easy enough to explain the principle underlying this rule, though often it is very hard to stomach the rule itself. As a matter

---

1. *See* W. Page Keeton *et al.*, Prosser and Keeton on the Law of Torts, § 358 (5th ed. 1984) (" 'Duty' is simply an expression of the sum total of those considerations of policy which lead the law to say that a particular plaintiff is entitled to protection.").

of principle, the common law cares enough about individual liberty that typically it does not ask people to do more than mind their own business. If I have done nothing to put someone in a position of danger, I have no duty to rescue him from that position. And as a practical matter, it would not be easy to develop rules about *who* would be liable when more than one individual could have accomplished a rescue but no one did. These considerations have led the law of torts to bite the bullet, so to speak, and to continue to decline to impose a duty to rescue even in the pure one-person to one-person rescue situation in which there would be no question as to which party might have accomplished a rescue. The courts seem to see tort law's adherence to this no-duty stance in one-person to one-person cases as a defense against stepping onto a slippery slope of permitting liability for the failure to rescue that would be imposed under a reasonable behavior under-all-the-circumstances standard. Thus, although permitting recovery in the one-to-one, low-cost, low-risk rescue kind of case alone would be very appealing, they abide by the bright-line no-duty rule that has long been drawn.

Importantly, this is a rule that there is no "affirmative" duty to rescue, not a rule that there is never a duty to rescue. Sometimes a defendant who does have a duty to exercise reasonable care can best do so by rescuing. For example, a defendant who has negligently placed the plaintiff in a position of danger may be held liable for negligently failing to rescue him from that danger. Here the distinction is drawn between mere failure to rescue the plaintiff—nonfeasance—for which liability ordinarily is not imposed, and negligently placing the plaintiff in danger to begin with—misfeasance—which may give rise to liability for negligent failure to rescue. Further, even when I am under no duty to rescue, if I decide to undertake a rescue nevertheless, I am liable for conducting the rescue itself negligently. Having waived my right to be left alone by attempting a rescue, and possibly having prevented rescue by others, my liberty is not unduly infringed by the rule that I have a duty to rescue carefully if I rescue at all.

Finally, under certain circumstances one who non-negligently creates a danger to another person may have a duty to warn the other person of that danger, and perhaps even to undertake a more active rescue. In *Montgomery v. National Convoy & Trucking Company*,[2] for instance, the defendant's truck stalled on an icy highway. This was not the result of any negligence by the defendant. A hill then prevented the plaintiff from seeing the stalled

---

2. 186 S.C. 167, 195 S.E. 247 (1938).

truck until it was too late, and the plaintiff collided with the truck. The defendant was held liable for injury to the plaintiff resulting from the negligent failure to warn approaching drivers of the danger created by the stalled truck on the other side of the hill.

Exactly how to distinguish cases like this from those in which there is no duty to rescue is unclear. It is true that the defendant in *Montgomery* was guilty of more than nonfeasance, since its operation of the truck affirmatively created the danger to the plaintiff. But because this was non-negligent operation, it was what might be called "feasance" rather than misfeasance. Morally it can be argued that the defendant is no more blameworthy, and no more waived or surrendered its liberty to be left alone merely by non-negligently driving, than the potential rescuer who simply happens along and encounters the plaintiff in a position of danger that the potential rescuer did not create. Holding that non-negligently creating a danger supports the imposition of a duty to rescue, whereas non-negligently merely happening to be present when a rescue could be made does not, requires the fact that there was commission of a non-negligent act to do a lot of work, especially since modern law has been skeptical of the distinction between commission and omission.

Nonetheless, the fact that there are a number of cases like *Montgomery* suggests the willingness of the courts to impose a duty to rescue when they can find what they believe to be a principled basis for doing so. One such principle may be that there is a duty to rescue when one's activity non-negligently creates a risk "characteristic" of the activity. It is a characteristic risk of driving, for example, that one's vehicle may break down. If this were understood to mean not only that this sort of thing can happen, but that the risk of its happening is substantially increased by engaging in the activity, then the principle may be consistent with the protection of liberty at the heart of the no-duty-to-rescue rule. If I mind my own business, I have no such duty. But once I engage in an activity that substantially raises the level of risk to which others are subjected, even if non-negligently, arguably I am no longer minding my own business in the sense that the no-duty rule contemplates.

II. Special Relationships

There is an exception to the general rule that there is no affirmative duty to rescue or to protect the plaintiff from harm more generally, when the plaintiff and defendant are in a "special relationship." Common carriers and innkeepers traditionally had such a relationship with their customers. Parents and those who fall into the category of custodians, such as child-care professionals and probably babysitters, also fall into this category. The idea behind this rule seems to be that, by entering into a special relationship, which ordinarily involves dependence by the plaintiff on the defendant, the defendant has waived its right to mind its own business and has undertaken a duty to protect the plaintiff from harm, the risk of which the defendant did not create.

At the outer reaches of this rationale are the cases in which mental health professionals such as psychiatrists have been held to have a duty to warn persons endangered by their patients after the patient has communicated to the psychiatrist an intention to cause harm to the third person. The seminal case on the issue is *Tarasoff v. Regents of University of California.*[3] *Tarasoff* has come in for much criticism, not only for the obvious reason that the psychiatrist there (and in most similar cases) had no relationship whatsoever with the victim, but also because the threat of liability in such cases forces the therapist to choose between his professional obligation to keep his patients' confidences and the legally-created duty to the third party. The defendant in *Tarasoff* did have a special relationship with his patient, but it is hard to see how that can be the basis of a duty to the third party, at least if dependence is the basis of the duty to the third party, who had no relationship at all with the defendant.

But the rule in *Tarasoff* appears to be otherwise limited. The rule is applied only when a patient has expressed an intention to injure a third party. And it is applied only to cases involving a specifically identified person whose safety is at risk. The duty could, of course, extend further. There is nothing about the concept of a duty in these circumstances that requires it to be so limited. But the courts are cautious about its reach. The duty, in short, is carefully and narrowly circumscribed.

III. Other Affirmative Duties and Policy–Based Limits on Them

An entirely different but analogous category of liability involves landlords, universities, shopping centers and other such proprietors of property, which have sometimes been held liable in negligence for harm foreseeably suffered by tenants, students, or customers because of the misconduct of third parties. This is a

---

3. 17 Cal.3d 425, 131 Cal.Rptr. 14, 551 P.2d 334 (1976).

subset of what have been called "enabling torts."[4] The classic case on this issue is *Kline v. 1500 Massachusetts Avenue Apartment Corp.*,[5] in which the defendant landlord was held liable in negligence for injuries suffered by a tenant who was assaulted in the hallway of the defendant's apartment house. The defendant was alleged to have been negligent in failing to properly maintain locks on the exterior doors of the building, and the court held that the defendant had a duty to the plaintiff to exercise reasonable care to protect the tenant from assault by a third party.

It is not entirely clear whether cases such as this properly are understood as involving affirmative duty. In these cases the defendants did not *negligently* create the risk of harm to the plaintiff—in *Kline*, for example, that risk was created by the third party who committed the assault. But the defendants in *Kline* and similar cases engaged in activities without which the particular risks in question would not have arisen. If the defendant in *Kline* had not operated an apartment house, the risk in question would not have existed. This issue seems not to have expressly arisen in the cases, however. The courts struggle with the question whether the defendants owed the plaintiffs a duty in such cases, but they do not seem to be troubled by the fact that this could be characterized as an affirmative duty and that the defendant is being asked, in effect, to rescue a plaintiff with whom it has an ordinary relationship. Instead, some courts and commentators think of these as special relationship cases, in which (as noted above) a duty to rescue is well established, and others as cases involving premises liability (see Section IV below) to invitees, where a duty is also not controversial.

In these cases several factors usually are present when the courts hold that the property owner or proprietor has a duty to the victim of a third party who commits a tort on the premises. First, although it may not be a "special" relationship involving dependence, there is a pre-existing relationship of some sort between the plaintiff and the defendant proprietor. The relationship may arise out of contract or through an invitation, express or implied, that the plaintiff be on the property. Second, there are circumstances that put the defendant proprietor on notice of the risk of harm to the plaintiff from third parties. There may have been assaults in the hallways in the past, broken locks reported to the landlord, or similar circumstances. If these prerequisites are met, then the defendant may have a "duty" to the plaintiff. Then the question is whether the defendant breached that duty: whether the risk was

4. Robert L. Rabin, *Enabling Torts*, 49 DePaul L. Rev. 435 (1999).
5. 439 F.2d 477 (D.C.Cir.1970).

sufficiently probable, the potential harm sufficiently great, and the cost of reducing that risk sufficiently small, to render the defendant negligent for having enabled the third party to injure the plaintiff by failing to take precautions that would have avoided the harm. These precautions may involve installing better locks, providing emergency telephones, using better lighting, etc. Third, the defendants in these cases are strategically placed to take precautions reducing the risk that third parties will injure victims in the plaintiff's position. Finally, the primary wrongdoer is likely to be judgment proof or at least have limited assets, whereas the enabling defendant is likely to have a deep, or at least a deeper, pocket, or to be covered by substantial amounts of liability insurance.

But these factors certainly are not always determinative. There is also a series of decisions in which the courts have placed limits on the scope of a defendant's duty, despite the obvious foreseeability of harm, seemingly for reasons of policy that sometimes resemble those that operate in proximate cause. For example, a manufacturer of firearms has no duty to the victim of a shooting even when the manufacturer knowingly permits distribution of the firearms under circumstances that promote their illegal sale to third parties who are likely to misuse them.[6] Virtually all courts rule that a social host is not liable in tort for serving alcohol to an obviously drunk guest, even when the host knows that the guest intends to drive shortly thereafter. The social host is said to have no duty to the victim of the guest's subsequent negligent driving. And an electric utility has no duty to the tenant of an apartment building when the tenant is injured in the dark because of the allegedly negligent failure of the utility to provide the building electricity.[7] In short, the evolution of negligence law from the pre–19th century world described in Chapter Three, in which there were few duties, to a pure world in which there is a general duty not to negligently risk foreseeable physical harm, has not completely occurred and probably never will.

IV. Premises Liability

We now turn to cases in which the defendant has created a risk of harm to the plaintiff. These involve limited duty, or no duty, to exercise reasonable care to avoid harming the plaintiff. Our first

6. *See, e.g., Hamilton v. Beretta U.S.A. Corp.*, 96 N.Y.2d 222, 727 N.Y.S.2d 7, 750 N.E.2d 1055 (2001).

7. *Strauss v. Belle Realty Co.*, 65 N.Y.2d 399, 492 N.Y.S.2d 555, 482 N.E.2d 34 (1985)

example of limited duty involves the liability of the owners or occupiers of property for injuries suffered by those who have entered the property. Any statement of the traditional common law rules governing premises liability must begin with the tripartite classification of entrants onto the land of others: invitees, licensees, and trespassers. Owners and occupiers of land (simply called "owners" hereafter) owe a duty to exercise reasonable care to those whom they invite onto their property. Such invitees include anyone on the property for business purposes, i.e., for the benefit of the owner. Somewhat surprisingly, not everyone who is "invited" qualifies as an invitee to whom a duty of reasonable care is owed. Rather, in most states people who are social guests, though of course they have been invited onto the property, are classified as "licensees." Owners and occupiers owe such licensees a lesser duty of care. The courts say that for a licensee the owner must make the premises as safe as he makes them for himself. What this boils down to is that the owner must warn the licensee of hidden dangerous conditions, but need not eliminate these conditions. Finally, to trespassers—those who enter property without express or implied permission—the owner owes only a duty to refrain from wantonly and wilfully injuring them, e.g., by setting hidden traps that will injure trespassers.

Over time some exceptions to these rules developed. For instance, in many states owners owe "discovered trespassers" reasonable care. And the doctrine of "attractive nuisance" has created a qualified but well-recognized exception for actually foreseen (as opposed to merely foreseeable) child trespassers who trespass because of some particularly "attractive" dangerous condition maintained by the owner, such as a railroad turntable or ferris wheel, especially when the danger the condition poses can be eliminated at a comparatively low cost. To these children the owner owes a duty of reasonable care. But these are limited exceptions to what are otherwise fairly rigid, categorical rules.

Notice the effect of this rigidness. The traditional rules governing the duties of owners and the correlative rights of entrants are established at a high level of generality. Whenever it is clear which category an entry falls into—and often that will not be in dispute—the scope of the duty owed to that entrant is also clear. This makes for comparatively high predictability of outcome and comparatively low adjudication costs. This efficiency is tolerable, indeed desirable, as long as the tripartite set of duties to the different entrants onto land reflects widespread agreement about the proper rights of these entrants and the proper obligations of owners. Under such circumstances commonly-held norms and the rigid categories coincide. But as that social and moral consensus breaks down, then rules about these rights and duties set at a high level of generality are seen often to produce inaccurate or undesirable outcomes.

Until a little more than thirty years ago, the tripartite categorization of entrants onto land, and the distinctions among duties owed to them, remained largely intact. But then some courts began to find this categorization unacceptable. The first and still one of the most far-reaching decisions was the Supreme Court of California's wholesale rejection of the categories in *Rowland v. Christian*.[8] In place of the categories, the court determined that a series of factors should be taken into account in determining the scope of the defendant's duty, including the foreseeability of harm, the closeness of the connection between the defendant's conduct and the plaintiff's harm, and the moral blame attached to the plaintiff's conduct. The court reasoned that because there is not necessarily a connection between these and other relevant factors and the classifications of trespasser, licensee, and invitee, the classifications should be rejected in favor of a reasonable-conduct-under-all-the-circumstances test. The entrant's status could still be taken into account in applying this test, but that status could no longer be determinative. In the decades that have followed, about half the states changed their rules. Nine followed *Rowland*, completely abolishing the categories and the bright-line limitations of duty that go with them. An additional fifteen declined to abolish the separate treatment of trespassers, but did abolish the distinction between invitees and licenses. Thus twenty-four states have engaged in substantial reform.

But a wholesale revolution has not occurred. About half the states still adhere to the traditional approach entirely, and over forty still adhere to the trespasser category. The main reason, I think, is not that the courts in half the states still consider the old categories to be entirely satisfactory. On the contrary, I believe that most courts understand the inaccuracy and unfairness that can result in occasional cases from rigid reliance on the categories. These flaws can be mitigated to some extent, though certainly not entirely eliminated, by flexible application of the exceptions to the categories that already exist, such as the duty of reasonable care owed to discovered trespassers and the attractive nuisance doctrine. But most courts also seem to have recognized that an across the board, total shift to a duty of reasonable care under all the circumstances would make results in premises liability cases much less certain. The amount of care expected would vary radically from

8.   69 Cal.2d 108, 70 Cal.Rptr. 97, 443 P.2d 561 (1968).

jury to jury, and prediction of outcomes would be much more difficult. These courts have chosen not to incur these consequences.

The ideal solution might well be a set of rules at an "intermediate" level of generality that are less rigid than the tripartite categorization, but still draw sufficiently bright lines to render duties clear and outcomes reasonably predictable. The THIRD RESTATEMENT attempts to develop such an approach, though it has little basis in existing law, by distinguishing between "flagrant" trespassers (e.g., burglars) and "non-flagrant" trespassers (e.g., someone who enters a well-marked construction area in a shopping mall in order to find a bathroom). To the former only limited duty is owned, but the latter are subject to an "under all the circumstances" standard.[9] The RESTATEMENT thus attempts to capture the moral disapproval of certain forms of trespassing that inhered in the traditional rule, while accommodating modern attitudes to less blameworthy trespassing. It remains to be seen whether any courts will adopt this approach.

But apart from this, no such intermediate approach seems available. So most courts still take the bright-line approach to trespassers. And for half the courts, the bright-line approach has seemed suitable across the board. As a consequence, the courts have had to choose between retaining the tripartite categorization largely intact, and rejecting classification, at least for licensees. Since neither approach is wholly satisfactory, it is no surprise that the states differ as to the proper choice, and that the law is now divided in this field between the states that still wholly accept the traditional approach and those that do not.

V. Negligently Inflicted Emotional Distress: "Pure" Emotional Loss

There is only a limited duty to exercise reasonable care to avoid causing emotional distress. To understand what is and is not at stake here, remember that there is a separate cause of action for *intentional* infliction of emotional distress (see Chapter Two), and that the right to recover damages for emotional distress that results from negligently-caused physical injury—which tort law terms "pain and suffering"—is of course well-established (see Chapter Ten). In contrast, the issue here is whether there is a cause of action for negligently inflicted emotional distress (NIED) that is not the result of negligently-caused physical injury suffered by the plaintiff. This is sometimes called "pure" emotional loss or distress.

---

9. RESTATEMENT (THIRD) OF TORTS: PHYSICAL AND EMOTIONAL HARM § 52.

There are two general categories of cases in which such liability might be imposed. The first involves what might be called an independent duty. In this category are the instances in which the failure to exercise reasonable care (whatever that might mean in this context) simply causes another person emotional distress. The second category involves derivative duty. In this category are the instances in which the failure to exercise reasonable care to avoid causing physical injury does not result in physical injury to the plaintiff, but does result in emotional distress, either because the person whose physical safety was risked by the defendant suffers emotional distress, or some third party suffers such distress.

Note that there is often real suffering resulting in real losses in these cases, but that not all such losses result in liability. If deterrence of negligence or doing justice between the parties were the only things at stake, the argument for imposing broader liability would be stronger. But other matters are at stake, as we will see.

A. *Independent Duty*

Liability in negligence is only rarely imposed for independently causing another person emotional distress. For example, I might negligently forget that a close relative of yours has just died a painful death, but nonetheless pose a gruesome hypothetical that I ask you to address in torts class. This upsets you. Liability could only be imposed in this situation if there were some sort of freestanding duty to exercise reasonable care not to cause others emotional distress, or some specific duty applicable to classrooms. But there is neither. In general there is no independent duty to exercise reasonable care to avoid causing another person emotional distress. The two rather circumscribed traditional exceptions are for emotional loss suffered when the defendant negligently mishandles the corpse of a loved one, and for emotional loss suffered when the defendant negligently sends a telegram to the plaintiff that incorrectly announces the death of a loved one.

There has been very little expansion in the independent duty category. The major addition to the set of exceptions extends the inaccurate telegram exception (which is essentially empty after the disappearance of telegrams) to a limited number of other situations in which the defendant negligently conveys important information, such as the case of the physician who misinforms the plaintiff, and in rare cases the spouse of the plaintiff, that he has a sexually transmitted disease. And it is possible that where the defendant is in a position of power or authority over the plaintiff such a duty also exists—as in the case of a hospital with custody of a newborn infant that allows it to be kidnaped. But beyond these very limited cases, there is no independent duty to exercise reasonable care not to cause others emotional distress.

The reasons given for this general no-duty rule when it was articulated over a century ago were that there was too great an opportunity for fraud in the typical case in which a plaintiff claimed that he or she was frightened or upset by the defendant, and that in any event the "floodgates" of litigation would be opened if a cause of action for negligently-caused pure emotional loss were recognized. These are not exactly unpersuasive reasons, but somehow they don't seem completely convincing. After all, juries often assess the credibility of allegations of emotional suffering when they have to without our being overly concerned about fraud, and the modern view of law is that courts exist in order to enforce rights that are worth acknowledging.

Another possible reason for the general no-duty rule, not often recognized, is that imposing liability for negligently inflicting emotional distress would require the development of standards of reasonable care that do not now exist except in a vague way. There are accepted standards of reasonable care in connection with physical risk—how to drive, shovel snow on a sidewalk, manufacture a product, practice medicine. But to continue the hypothetical from above, we do not have accepted standards regarding the amount of care teachers should use to remember their students' personal problems. These standards could be developed, in jury trials, over time, but they do not exist "out there" in the world in a condition that would make them automatically available, as a matter of common knowledge, to apply in negligence cases.

But I think that the fundamental reason for the very limited duties that have been recognized in this field—and this includes not only independent duty, but the derivative duties discussed in the following Section—is that remedying NIED in tort suits is just beyond what we want the law to devote its limited energies and resources to. This is not just a "floodgates" of litigation argument, though it is partly that. In addition, for practical purposes there is a limited amount of money, however large it may seem, that we are willing to devote to compensating the victims of tortious conduct. The rules governing NIED seem to imply that we are better off devoting that finite sum of money to compensation of those who suffer physical injury than diluting our efforts with a general cause of action for NIED.

B. *Derivative Duty: Emotional Distress Resulting from Fear of Injury to Oneself or Another*

There is a separate and substantial set of cases in which the defendant negligently risks physically injuring someone, and the question is whether the defendant has a duty to that person, or to another person, for emotional distress that results from their awareness of the danger of physical injury. These cases are derivative in the sense that the precondition for considering whether there is a duty not to cause emotional distress is that the defendant have a duty not to risk causing physical injury. This negligence is the basis for considering whether the defendant also has a duty not to risk causing emotional distress.

Interestingly, many of the older cases stating the scope and limits on recovery involved women who suffered emotional loss because of fear for the personal safety of their husbands or children. It is hard to know whether this is because women were thought to be more prone to suffer these kinds of losses than men, women were more likely to be exposed to the risk of seeing their children placed in danger because they were more often with their children, women were simply more prone to bring suit for emotional loss due to the greater sympathy they expected to receive from juries, or there is some other explanation for the seemingly disproportionate number of female plaintiffs in these cases. In any event, many commentators understandably have viewed this early body of law as being anti-feminist, since the rules long placed significant limits on the right to recover for pure emotional loss.[10] On the other hand, it might be argued that over time this body of law relaxed the limits on liability precisely in order to benefit the women who were so typically the plaintiffs in emotional loss cases. Certainly the law today is very different from what it was a century ago, and that change has been for the benefit of the many female plaintiffs in these cases.

The original rule was that there is no duty to exercise reasonable care not to cause emotional distress—no cause of action for pure emotional loss of any sort. This is of course a rule set at a very high level of generality. As I noted earlier, the stated basis for this limitation in the early cases was concern about fraudulent claims and about encouraging large numbers of claims. These concerns gave way little by little, but as we will see, the concerns have nonetheless motivated the courts to fashion rules that take the

---

10. *See, e.g.*, Martha Chamallas with Linda A. Kerber, *Women, Mothers, and the Law of Fright: A History*, 88 Mich. L. Rev. 814 (1990).

concerns into account, even as the courts have recognized, and then expanded, the cause of action for NIED. There has thus been an expansionist tendency, limited not only by these instrumental concerns, but also by the kinds of normative considerations I mentioned above, since in a sense every dollar spent to compensate emotional loss is a dollar that might not be available to compensate physical injury.[11]

1. The Impact Rule

The first major qualification of the general no-duty rule was the *impact* rule, which permitted recovery in negligence for pure emotional loss only if the defendant's conduct resulted in some physical impact on the plaintiff's body. Some especially cautious courts required that the emotional loss resulting from the impact also manifest itself in physical symptoms (e.g., nausea, inability to sleep, stomach trouble, etc.). But there was no requirement that the plaintiff be physically injured by this impact. This rule is a pretty crude way of distinguishing the claims that are likely to be valid from those that are not, as well as limiting the number of cases that may be brought. But that is precisely what the rule was designed to do. The impact rule was anything but a "reasonable-under-all-the-circumstances" test. Either there was an impact and a cause of action was permitted, or there was no impact and no cause of action.

The impact rule could generate very arbitrary results. If you lose control of a car going at a speed of ninety miles per hour and almost collide with my two year-old son on the sidewalk, neither I nor my son have a cause of action, no matter how much fright and emotional suffering we experience, no matter how long that suffering persists. But if you carelessly back out of your driveway and brush me at two miles per hour, then there has been impact and I can sue for my emotional suffering. How much I will recover depends on how much suffering I can prove, and I may not be able to prove that I suffered much, but the law recognizes the possibility in the latter case only. One of the funniest opinions in the history of tort law, Justice Mussmano's concurrence in *Bosley v. Andrews*,[12] pokes fun at this all-or-nothing feature of the impact rule.

2. The Zone of Danger Rule

Over time the courts became increasingly dissatisfied with the arbitrariness of the impact rule and replaced it with a zone of danger rule. But just as the complete bar to recovery was replaced

---

11. *See* Robert L. Rabin, *Emotional Distress in Tort Law: Themes of Constraint*, 44 WAKE FOREST L. REV. 1149 (2009).

12. 393 Pa. 161, 142 A.2d 263 (1958).

with the impact rule permitting some recoveries even while rigidly excluding other claims, so the impact rule was replaced with a rule that was also couched at an intermediate level of generality, albeit one that permitted more recovery. Under the zone of danger rule the plaintiff could recover for NIED even if there was no impact, if the plaintiff was in the "zone" in which physical injury was threatened, and feared for his or her own safety. A number of courts adopting the rule also required that the resulting emotional loss manifest itself in physical symptoms as well. On the other hand, over time some courts relaxed the zone of danger rule a bit, permitting recovery by those in the zone of danger even when their emotional loss resulted partly from fear that another person in the zone (such as one's small child) would be physically injured.

Like the impact rule, the zone of danger rule attempts to reduce the risk of both fraudulent claims and an excessive number of claims, by identifying a limited class of cases in which it is plausible that there will be emotional loss even in the absence of physical injury to the plaintiff. Having to adjudicate any claim by a plaintiff within the zone of danger was something the courts were willing to do under the new rule, in order to circumvent the arbitrariness of the impact rule. By the same token, undoubtedly the courts adopting the zone of danger rule recognized that there would be cases in which a plaintiff who was outside the zone of danger nonetheless suffered emotional loss. But denying recovery in those admittedly "legitimate" cases was the price these courts were willing to pay in order to avoid the prospect of being forced to adjudicate an unlimited number of potentially plausible claims.

3. The *Dillon* Rule

Then the same sort of thing happened again. Like so many of the cases that had preceded it, *Dillon v. Legg*[13] involved a claim by a mother who had witnessed her daughter's injury. In *Dillon* the Supreme Court of California, which in the years between about 1960 and 1985 was a leader in the expansion of tort liability generally, discarded the zone of danger rule. The court held that the plaintiff in an NIED case need not have been in the zone of danger and therefore need not have feared for her own safety in order to recover for her emotional loss. But like the rule it replaced, the new rule did not employ an "under all the circumstances" test. Rather, the court indicated that three factors would have to be taken into account in deciding whether the claim was one that warranted recovery—presumably not only in jury deliberations, but also in the judicial determination of whether a claim could even go to the jury.

---

13. 68 Cal.2d 728, 69 Cal.Rptr. 72, 441 P.2d 912 (1968).

The three factors were proximity, visibility, and relationship. The court indicated that the closer the plaintiff was to the accident, the more visible the accident was to the plaintiff, and the closer the relationship between the plaintiff and the party within the zone of danger, the greater the foreseeability of emotional harm to the plaintiff and the stronger the argument was for recovery of the plaintiff's emotional loss. It would have been possible for these factors to evolve into mere guidelines surrounding what would amount to an "under all the circumstances" test. But that is not what has happened. The courts that have adopted a *Dillon* test— and many have not, preferring to retain the zone of danger approach—have been adamant about drawing bright lines between the kinds of cases that do and do not warrant recovery. Thus, in *Thing v. La Chusa*,[14] the plaintiff was a mother whose child had been injured in an automobile accident. She was told of the accident, rushed to the scene, and saw the child lying on the ground, bloody and unconscious, believing him to be dead. The Supreme Court of California held that there could be no recovery, choosing instead a "bright line" rule requiring that the plaintiff actually be present and witness the accident. For most other courts as well, merely hearing but not seeing an accident typically is insufficient; and a close friend or lover is apparently not in a close enough relationship with the plaintiff to warrant recovery even when the plaintiff witnesses the injury.

In summary, over a period of almost a century there has been a progressive relaxation of the rule that there can be no recovery in negligence for pure emotional loss. But at each stage of that relaxation, one bright-line rule after another was substituted for its predecessor. This evolution contrasts with what happened, for example, in the field of premises liability. There, as we saw above, the courts never were able to identify satisfactory bright-line alternatives to the traditional approach based on the status of entrants onto land. But in the field of pure emotional loss, the courts fashioned a series of such "intermediate" rules that permitted more recovery than in the past and were serviceable for decades at a time, but were couched at a level of generality that prevented their degenerating into an "under all the circumstances" approach to liability.

4. Fear of Future Injury

In a different category of cases, the defendant has negligently exposed the plaintiff to the risk of suffering future injury, such as

---

14.   48 Cal.3d 644, 257 Cal.Rptr. 865, 771 P.2d 814 (1989).

cancer. Some courts permit the plaintiff, under limited circumstances, to recover damages resulting from fearing future injury. In most of these cases there is actual impact between a force set in motion by the defendant, such as asbestos fibers or contaminated drinking water, thus satisfying the impact requirement that used to be applied in derivative cases. In others there is no actual impact, but exposure to x-rays or a similar source of energy. This is something like impact. In virtually all the cases the defendant would be, or at least could be, held liable for the actual injury that the plaintiff fears will occur in the future, when and if it occurs. So in a sense these cases also are derivative of the defendant's duty to exercise reasonable care not to risk causing the plaintiff physical injury.[15]

But many courts simply do not permit recovery for fear of future injury. Formally this stance is not entirely consistent with the NIED cases just discussed, since these cases permit recovery for fear of injury that might have, but did not, occur. Both sets of cases involve emotional distress, yet fear that occurred in the past is more actionable than present fear about the future. One basis for the distinction is likely the general concern that adjudication about the future, even if it is directed at present fears about the future, is inherently speculative. Allegations of past fear about imminent injury may seem more easy to assess than allegations of present fear about the more distant future. The old but continuing concerns about fraudulent claims thus seem operative here. In addition, many potential cases involving fear of future injury arise out of mass exposure, and therefore implicate concerns about preserving scarce dollars for the priority of compensating for actual physical injury, when and if it does occur, that I discussed above. The result may be a reluctance of courts before whom the physical injury cases are being litigated to recognize a duty regarding fear of future injury, because that might consume resources that would otherwise be available for the physical injury claimants.

VI. "Pure" Economic Loss

The last example of a limited duty involves cases of negligently-caused economic harm, occurring in the absence of bodily injury or property damage suffered by the plaintiff. Again it is important to understand what is and is not at stake here. There is a cause of action in tort for *intentional* infliction of economic loss, known as interference with contract rights or prospective advantage (see

---

15. *See, e.g., Potter v. Firestone Tire and Rubber Co.*, 6 Cal.4th 965, 25 Cal. Rptr.2d 550, 863 P.2d 795 (1993).

Chapter Fourteen). In addition, there is of course a right to recover for economic loss that is the consequence of, or as is sometimes said, is "parasitic" on one's own bodily injury or property damage. The out-of-pocket medical expenses and lost wages that injured plaintiffs recover in ordinary *negligence* cases are economic losses, as are lost profits resulting from property damage. Finally, there is a separate body of rules governing the duty to exercise reasonable care to avoid causing economic loss in cases where the defendant has undertaken to provide a service or supply information and does so negligently. Much of the law of professional malpractice by lawyer and accountants, and the law of negligent misrepresentation, discussed in Chapter Fourteen, falls into this category.

In contrast, in the cases with which we are concerned here, physical injury to the person or property of one party also results in purely economic harm to another party. That is, this latter party's losses are not parasitic on any bodily injury or property damage that he suffered. For example, suppose that the defendant's negligent driving causes a collision on a bridge that necessitates the closing of the bridge for half a day. A party whose business is located on the far side of the bridge is deprived of an essential source of supply because the bridge is closed, and suffers economic loss as a result; or a general contractor is prevented from hand-delivering a construction bid to an office on the other side of the bridge by the 12:00 noon deadline, and would have submitted the low bid. Can either of these parties recover from the defendant for the economic losses that they have suffered as a result of the defendant's negligence?

The traditional answer, given by what is often termed the "economic loss rule," has been to deny such recovery outright.[16] Like the traditional prohibition of recovery in negligence for pure emotional loss, this is a rule at a high level of generality. Unlike the law governing recovery for pure emotional loss, however, in this field there has been only very modest evolution away from the bright-line rule denying recovery. Although a few exceptions have been created, the rule as it now stands is very similar to the rule as it stood a century ago.

The reason is that the considerations that supported the rule a century ago still largely support it today. First, notwithstanding that pure economic loss is often a highly foreseeable result of negligent conduct, the amount of liability that could result if there were a cause of action for pure economic loss could be enormous,

---

16. *Robins Dry Dock & Repair Co. v. Flint*, 275 U.S. 303, 48 S.Ct. 134, 72 L.Ed. 290 (1927).

but its scope would be very difficult to predict. This unpredictability would render the sale of insurance against such liability a very risky undertaking. Such liability might therefore be uninsured. The threat of wholly uninsured liability would probably discourage many potential defendants from engaging in valuable activities that, nonetheless, entail a risk of enormous consequential economic loss if the activities are conducted negligently. For example, think of the size of the economic losses that would be suffered by third parties as a result of the negligent repair of an electric line on a busy urban street, or negligently colliding with a utility pole. And in event, for individuals and small businesses, threatening liability whose potential scope far exceeds their assets is pointless. A party whose net worth is $1 million is just as deterred by the threat of liability for $1 million as by the threat of liability for $100 million. Second, although in theory a deterrence shortfall results from the denial of recovery for pure economic loss, the defendant in all such cases is already threatened with substantial liability for the bodily injury or property damage that may result from its negligence. So the defendant ordinarily is not immunized from all liability as a result of the rule. Third, and conversely, often the third-party economic losses that result from negligently-caused bodily injury or property damage, even when sizeable, are distributed among large numbers of people. Given such already-existing broad loss distribution, the loss-distribution rationale for imposing liability on the injurer is weak, especially since many of these losses can be insured by victims through business-interruption insurance.

Finally, the economic losses resulting from an act of negligence could spread far and wide. A pure economic loss suffered by one party may then result in a pure economic loss suffered by someone with whom he deals, and so on *ad infinitum*. If there were to be some recovery for pure economic loss, a workable and fair distinction between the cases in which recovery would and would not be permitted would have to be developed. But no logical "intermediate" rule seems available. If no such rule can be developed, then permitting recovery would require a general foreseeability or under-all-the-circumstances standard that in every case would threaten unlimited liability, even if that were not always the result. For practical purposes, therefore, the law has chosen to draw the line at no liability rather than to venture into an arena where there would be few if any guidelines for adjudication.

The courts have, however, occasionally created exceptions to the rule. Perhaps the most noteworthy involve cases in which there has been natural-resource damage for which no party seems to have a cause of action. In such cases, liability for economic loss serves as a kind of substitute for a cause of action for physical damage to natural resources. For example, in *Union Oil Co. v. Oppen*,[17] the defendant's negligence caused oil pollution in the Santa Barbara Channel off California. Among other things, this pollution killed fish and resulted in economic loss to the plaintiffs, who were commercial fishermen. Conceivably the State of California could have sued for the overall environmental damage that resulted from the defendant's negligence, but the State made no such effort. The court allowed the plaintiffs to recover, adopting a test which it said was based mainly on foreseeability. But the absence of a proper plaintiff to sue for the physical damage in question, together with the fact that the defendant was a sufficiently large enterprise (a major oil company) to be capable of bearing that liability, probably influenced the result. In a few similar cases recovery has also been permitted by commercial fishermen, but denied to seafood sellers.[18] For the most part, however, common law recovery has been denied even in cases closely analogous to *Union Oil*. Most of the courts faced with the question have subscribed to the traditional rule and have declined to venture onto the potentially slippery slope of permitting some recoveries. Instead, in connection with oils spills, such liability is governed by the Oil Pollution Act of 1990,[19] which creates a cause of action for a variety of those who suffer economic loss, among other things, as a result of damage to natural resources caused by oil spills.

Importantly, even the cases that have permitted common law recovery tend to share one characteristic. In most cases the defendant's negligence is determined by reference to the reasonableness of the defendant's also having risked some other kind of harm—usually physical harm—either to the plaintiff or to a third party.[20] As in liability for negligent infliction of emotional distress, then, this form of liability employs a negligence standard that is anchored in and derivative of the standard that would be applied to the same set of facts if the suit were for physical harm. The cause of action is not for negligently risking economic loss at large, but for negligently risking physical harm to one party or parties that results economic loss to someone else.

17. 501 F.2d 558 (9th Cir.1974).

18. *See, e.g., Pruitt v. Allied Chemical Corp.*, 523 F.Supp. 975 (E.D.Va.1981).

19. 33 U.S.C. § 2701 *et seq.* (2004).

20. *See, e.g., People Express Airlines, Inc. v. Consolidated Rail Corp.*, 100 N.J. 246, 495 A.2d 107 (1985).

12

INSURANCE, TORT REFORM, AND NO-FAULT SYSTEMS

In most tort suits for bodily injury or property damage, a variety of forms of insurance are involved. Any reform of tort implicates insurance, either directly or indirectly. To understand tort reform it is therefore useful to understand the rudiments of insurance. But of course more is required. Most tort law is common law, made by the courts over a period of centuries. In the past several decades, however, the state legislatures have entered the tort law arena, modifying a number of traditional rules of tort law. This Chapter first provides a primer on insurance and a conceptual framework for analyzing any reform. The Chapter then surveys three major tort reforms: statutory modification of tort doctrine, workers compensation, and auto no-fault. The Chapter concludes by examining several targeted no-fault reforms that apply to other areas of liability—including the 9/11 Compensation Fund and the BP Oil Spill Fund—as well as the possibility of extending the no-fault model to medical and product-related injuries. Our purpose here is not to examine every detail of these approaches, but to gain the perspective that an understanding of their structure and function can shed on the nature of tort law itself.

I. A Brief Primer on Insurance and a Conceptual Framework

A. *A Primer on Insurance*

The starting point for any understanding of insurance is the distinction between *first-party* and *third-party* insurance. First-party insurance is victim's insurance. It protects the policyholder or other covered parties against a loss that he or she may suffer. These are the forms of insurance that figure in the collateral source rule discussed in Chapter Ten: health insurance, disability insurance, life insurance, automobile property damage insurance, and fire insurance, among others. We spend nearly a trillion dollars a year in this country for private, first-party insurance, the majority of this sum for health insurance. We spend roughly an additional

$500 billion (half a trillion) on public sources of what amount to first-party insurance: Medicare (health insurance for the elderly), Medicaid (health insurance for the poor),Veteran's benefits, and Social Security Disability insurance, for example.

In contrast, third-party insurance is injurer's insurance, or "liability" insurance. It protects the policyholder or other covered parties against liability, usually tort liability, to others. The defendant has at least some liability insurance in most tort suits alleging bodily injury or property damage. In these suits the typical liability insurance policy not only insures the policyholder against liability, but also provides the right to a defense against such suits. The insurer pays for a defense, and decides whether and when to agree to settle the suit or proceed to trial. Auto liability insurance is by far the most common form of liability insurance, premiums for which exceed $100 billion per year. Homeowners insurance policies also provide some basic liability insurance, the total cost of which is not separately reported, but which is at least several billion dollars per year. Most physicians and hospitals have medical malpractice liability insurance, whose cost is more than $10 billion per year. And most businesses buy Commercial General Liability (CGL) insurance, covering them against liability for bodily injury and property damage, including products liability, at a cost of roughly $40 billion per year.

To be realistic, any discussion of tort reform should take these sources of insurance into account. All told, damages paid in tort suits for bodily injury and property damage in this country are on the order of magnitude of about $150–$200 billion per year, much of which is covered by liability insurance. Most of the deterrent effects of tort liability are not direct, but are likely to be felt indirectly through the threat of changes in premiums paid for liability insurance. Expanding tort liability will tend to raise the cost of liability insurance; reducing tort liability will tend to decrease the cost of liability insurance. On the other hand, tort liability, whether covered by liability insurance or not, is not the only source of compensation for the victims of bodily injury and property damage. In fact, given the very substantial forms of first-party insurance described above, there would be considerable first-party insurance against the medical expenses and lost wages that are now subject to tort liability even if there were no tort liability. In short, tort is part of a larger insurance and compensation system, and depending on how we characterize that system, tort is not necessarily even the major part of that system. This does not mean that we should or should not retain tort liability as we know it, but it does suggest that the above perspective on where tort fits in the overall system may be worthwhile background to the discussions that follow.

B. *Conceptualizing Reform*

Any injury liability-and-compensation system, including tort law, workers compensation, and no-fault, has three major components: 1) the compensable event; 2) the measure of recovery; and 3) the payment mechanism.

The *compensable event* is the occurrence or injury that activates a right to compensation. This may be an injury resulting from fault, as in most suits for accidentally-caused injury; an injury resulting from a specified type of cause regardless of fault, as in strict liability for abnormally dangerous activities or (as we will see momentarily) any on-the-job injury as in workers compensation; or it may simply be a certain kind of loss, such as a medical expense as in health insurance, or the loss of wages as in disability insurance.

The *measure of recovery* consists of the amount and categories of loss that are compensated when a compensable event has occurred. This may be payment in a lump sum of all losses proximately caused by a tort; periodic payment of all such losses; payment of only out-of-pocket losses, either in a lump sum or periodically; payment of out-of-pocket losses plus pre-specified dollar amounts depending on the severity of injury; or some other measure.

The *payment mechanism* is the method that is used to finance the payment of compensation. This may consist of liability insurance for most liable parties with self-insurance for others; first-party insurance purchased by potential victims; government-provided compensation paid out of general revenues or out of a fund that is raised by taxing potentially responsible parties; or some other arrangement.

Thus, in tort the prevailing compensable event is an injury caused by negligence; the measure of compensation is lump sum, full payment of both tangible and intangible losses; and the payment mechanism is the injurer's liability insurance or (so to speak) self-insurance. But it is obvious from the foregoing paragraphs that tort as we know it is not the only possible arrangement of the three components that comprise and liability-and-compensation system. Indeed, in a sense the modification of one or more features of this arrangement is what tort reform consists of.

II. Statutory Reform of Tort Doctrine

First in the mid–1970s and then again in the mid–1980's, there were tort liability "crises" across the country, involving escalating rates of suit and increasing liability insurance costs. There is still controversy over the causes of these crises, but at least one long-term cause is indisputable. Over time, with the expansion of the scope of tort liability, there were more suits, more settlements and judgments, and more money was paid by liability insurers and their defendant-policyholders. In response to these crises, nearly every state legislature modified its state's tort law in one way or another. It is not possible to capture all the nuances of this legislation with a single sweeping generalization. More than anything else, however, the legislation modified various aspects of the law governing damages in tort cases. A reasonably accurate sense of this common theme can be gleaned simply by noting the three reforms that were most frequently enacted: absolute dollar ceilings on the amount of awards for pain and suffering and punitive damages; limitations on or complete elimination of joint and several liability; and abolition of the collateral source rule.[1] Each of the reforms has been referred to in earlier Chapters.

Interestingly, none of these legislative reforms touches the core of tort liability for bodily injury and property damage. They do not affect the compensable event or the payment mechanism. None affects the standard of care or rules governing proof of causation, for example. And none precludes any plaintiff who could have obtained a judgment against a defendant prior to its enactment from obtaining a judgment thereafter. Those defendants who were liable before the enactment of tort reform continued to be liable after enactment, but often for less. The reform legislation accepted the incidence of tort liability as it stood, but restricted the measure of damages a successful plaintiff is entitled to recover. It modifies, directly or indirectly, the measure of recovery.

This legislation can be viewed in two different ways. One view is that as the frequency of tort suits and the size of average awards increased, the need of potential defendants to be able to predict the scope of their tort liability exposure increased as well. When liability insurance and tort liability were only a tiny percentage of the costs of conducting a business or profession, predictability was less necessary. But as liability insurance and tort costs increased, pre-

---

1. *See* Joseph Sanders & Craig Joyce, *"Off to the Races": The 1980s Tort Crisis and the Law Reform Process*, 27 Hous. L. Rev. 207, 217–23 (1990).

dicting their magnitude came to be more important, because the effect of an unexpected increase in costs would be more substantial. State legislatures responded to this need by enacting legislation that would make awards more predictable, without changing the core rules of tort liability in any way. A more cynical view, however, is that as liability insurance and tort costs increased, potential defendants wanted relief from these costs. And what defendants care about most is the amount of their liability, not whether they are held liable. Consequently, defendants sought and received the relief they wanted in the form of legislation that would decrease— or at least slow the increase in—their liability insurance and tort costs. Moreover, this reasoning goes, if the amount of damages that can be recovered in a tort suit is limited, then potential plaintiffs' incentives to sue will be reduced, and the incidence of tort liability will decline even without any formal change in liability standards.

Whether one takes the former or the latter view, there can be no disputing the fact that the tort reform legislation of the past several decades has been limited and incremental. This legislation has left the basic structure of tort liability untouched, even while tinkering around the edges by modifying the measure of recovery in a variety of ways. To gain an understanding of the possibilities for more fundamental reform, we must look to other developments.

III. Workers Compensation

The nineteenth century was a period of enormous industrialization and urbanization in the United States. It is only a slight exaggeration to say that we went from being a nation of rural farmers to being a nation of city-dwelling factory workers. With all this industrialization came a whole series of problems, one of which was industrial injuries. At the dawn of the twentieth century there was growing recognition that workplace injuries were not merely a legal, but also a social problem. The tort system itself was not providing compensation for such injuries in an adequate way. Legal doctrines restricted workers' rights of recovery on grounds of assumption of risk, contributory negligence, and the "fellow-servant" rule that precluded recovery from an employer for injuries caused by another employee's negligence. In addition, many workplace injuries were not the result of anyone's negligence and therefore were not subject to tort liability, because employers were liable only for negligence. After some years of controversy and, at first, the enactment of partial or optional systems in the years between 1910 and 1920 a new system of "workers compensation" replaced tort liability for workplace injuries in virtually every state.

Today, all states have substituted workers compensation for tort. Workers compensation modified the first two components of any liability-and-compensation system: the compensable event and the measure of recovery. It left the third component, the payment mechanism, in place.

A. *The Compensable Event*

The compensable event in tort was an injury caused by an employer's negligence. In contrast, in workers compensation the compensable event is any non-negligently-caused work-related injury. Workers compensation abolishes the tort liability of the employer and provides compensation to employees through an exclusive remedy within an administrative system for injuries "arising out of or in the course of employment." And the only defense available is that the employee intended to cause his own injury or acted with wanton disregard for his own safety. This is strict liability of a very broad sort. "Fault" has been replaced by "cause" as the basis of liability.

B. *The Measure of Recovery*

Workers compensation also modifies the measure of recovery. Because of the expansion of the compensable event and the elimination of defenses, vastly greater numbers of workers are entitled to receive compensation than in tort. Vastly increased costs could therefore be expected. Some administrative cost savings could be anticipated because of the greatly reduced cost of determining eligibility for compensation. In tort it typically would have taken litigation to determine whether an employer was negligent. But most employees who enter the job uninjured and at the end of the day are injured have incontestably suffered a compensable event—a work-related injury. Indeed, what dispute resolution there is takes place out of court, before an administrative board. Despite these administrative cost savings, if the measure of compensation had not been changed, the new workers compensation system would have cost many times what the tort system did.

Consequently, the amount that an employee could recover was limited. At first, recovery was limited to medical expenses and a portion of several weeks' wages. There was no recovery for pain and suffering at all. Over time the number of weeks' wages that were recoverable has increased to the point where there is no limit in some states and the limit is several years in others. Both wage losses and medical expenses are paid periodically as they are incurred. And there has also developed a rough but restricted substitute for pain and suffering—lump-sum awards for partial and total permanent disability have been enacted. For example, the statutes specify particular recoveries to be awarded for loss of a hand, loss of an eye, paralysis of both legs, and so forth. Often these are specified as a multiple of a particular number of weeks' wages. Loss of an arm may be worth 300 weeks wages and loss of an eye 150 weeks wages, for example. Typically these sums are therefore considerably more limited than the pain and suffering awards that might be obtained in a tort suit for the same loss.

C. *The Payment Mechanism*

The changes that workers compensation made in the compensable event and the measure of compensation are important, but what was not changed also matters. The payment mechanism did not change—that is, the employer remained liable, though on a new basis. The employer might purchase third-party insurance—workers compensation insurance, as it is called—to cover its liability for benefits, or might self-insure. But regardless, because it remained liable, the employer's incentive to compare the cost of workplace accidents (the amount of workers compensation benefits) with the cost of reducing workplace accidents was preserved. Indeed, in a sense that incentive was strengthened, because the employer was now liable for many more claims than in tort, though for a much lower average amount per claim. To put it another way, from the deterrence standpoint workers compensation constituted a shift from negligence to very strict liability, and therefore had the potential to capture many of the advantages of strict liability described in Chapter Eight.

And what the theory of strict liability suggests, the facts confirm. Studies show that despite eliminating the threat of tort liability, workers compensation has generated substantial safety incentive effects. Indeed, no definitive study has shown that workplaces are less safe than they would have been had tort liability been preserved, and many show otherwise. That is not to say that workers compensation is without its critics. Benefit levels are criticized as too low, periodic payment encourages some malingering, and with the rise of claims for work-related stress, for back injuries, and for diseases that may be caused by long-term exposure to hazardous substances, determining whether a workers' loss is or is not work-related has become more complicated and more expensive. But over many decades, workers compensation has remained an effective approach that has achieved its goals by providing swift compensation to injured workers on a no-fault basis.

IV. Auto No–Fault

In the period after World War Two the automobile became an essential feature of American life. As more vehicles and miles were driven, however, there inevitably came more auto accidents. Just as there was a point at which workplace injuries went from being perceived merely as a legal problem to being a social problem, so by the 1960's uncompensated auto-related injuries had become sufficiently frequent and serious to be recognized as a social problem.

One approach to this "compensation gap" was the enactment of legislation in many states requiring all drivers to be covered by liability insurance. Such a requirement was meant to assure that no one who was the victim of negligent driving would be left without a solvent source of recovery. In addition, the insurance industry developed a number of other devices that addressed the problem outside of tort law. "Uninsured motorist insurance" purchased by car owners covers them and their family members in the event that a negligent defendant who injures them is uninsured; and "medical payments coverage" affords small amounts of insurance for the medical costs resulting from auto accidents, whether there was negligence involved or not. But these devices still leave gaps in the fabric of compensation for auto-related injuries: not all drivers comply with the requirement that they purchase liability insurance; uninsured motorists insurance only covers losses caused by the negligence of another driver; and medical payments insurance usually has very low limits of coverage. In short, these devices supplement rather than replace tort law as the principal avenue of recovery for those who suffer auto-related injuries.

Naturally the workers compensation model came under consideration as a possible substitute for tort law's approach to the provision of compensation for auto injuries. But it had been recognized for some time that the auto accident problem did not fit neatly into this model. In the employment situation there are two differently-situated parties, the employer and the employee. It was reasonable to conceive of the employer as the injurer and the employee as the victim, because the employer is generally in the superior position to manage the risk of workplace injuries. Placing liability on the employer on a strict liability, or causal, basis therefore made sense in the workplace context. In the typical auto-accident situation, however, the two parties are similarly situated in a number of respects. Both parties tend to be ordinary individu-

288

als who cannot be identified in advance as injurer and victim; both parties may be injured; and sometimes there is only a single victim without any other party involved as an "injurer" at all. Moreover, even when there are two parties involved in an auto accident and only one suffers injury, it does not follow at all that the uninjured party is an injurer. If am carefully stopped at a red light when another driver runs into my car from behind and is hurt, no one would say that I injured him. In the absence of an inquiry into the negligence of the parties, it is not terribly meaningful to ask whether the party who did not suffer an injury was a cause, or merely was involved in an accident that happened to injure someone else.

For these reasons, the workers compensation model of injurer-based causal liability did not (and still does not) transfer comfortably to the auto-accident situation. It took two law professors, Robert Keeton and Jeffrey O'Connell, to think their way through to a solution of this problem. Where workers compensation had left essentially untouched the third element of any compensation system—the payment mechanism—Keeton and O'Connell proposed a wholesale change.

Keeton and O'Connell's idea was to replace the third-party insurance approach with a first-party approach. Auto injuries would not trigger automatic injurer liability on the model of workers compensation, but automatic victim liability. Instead of imposing liability in tort on those who negligently caused auto-related injuries, victims would bear their own injury costs by purchasing first-party insurance against their losses.[2] Thus, auto no-fault consists of two prongs: the abolition of tort liability and the mandatory purchase of insurance directly protecting victims. While this may seem at first to reject the strict liability approach of workers compensation, in a sense this approach does not reject strict liability. Rather, auto no-fault adopts strict liability on the part of the victim, not the injurer, even when there is an injurer. To put it another way, once the element of negligence is removed from the equation, it is just as accurate to think of the victim as causing his own injuries as it is to think of the other party involved in the accident (who may also be a victim) as the cause.

Soon after this idea emerged, it began to be debated in the state legislatures. In the 1970s a somewhat modified version of the idea was enacted in more than a dozen states, and a number of other states have borrowed selected features of the no-fault idea

2. *See* Robert E. Keeton & Jeffrey O'Connell, BASIC PROTECTION FOR THE AUTO VICTIM (1965).

and enacted them into law. For purposes of exposition, I will refer to the theoretical idea of abolishing tort and replacing it with first-party insurance as *pure no-fault*, the modified version that Keeton and O'Connell proposed and that was adopted by statute as *real no-fault*, a third version that operates in a number of states and contains only the first-party insurance prong as *add-on no-fault*, and a version that leaves drivers the option of selecting fault or no-fault and that has been enacted in three states as *choice no-fault*.

A. *"Pure" No–Fault*

Pure no-fault—though not enacted in any state—is an ideal type that is worth analyzing as a baseline against which actual auto no-fault can be compared. Pure auto no-fault would modify all three elements of the tort system. First, tort liability for auto-related injuries would be abolished. Instead, no-fault compensation would be provided to the those who suffered auto-related injuries. The compensable event under this system would be cause-based—an injury "arising out of or in the course of" the operation, maintenance, or use of a motor vehicle,

Second, as under workers compensation, the measure of recovery would be reduced. Compensation for pain and suffering damages would be eliminated. Compensation for a percentage of wage loss and medical expenses would be afforded, however, at least up to a comparatively high (e.g., $50,000) automatic minimum, but drivers would be entitled at their option to purchase coverage in excess of this minimum.

Third, the payment mechanism would be insurance purchased by potential victims rather than by potential injurers. In the language of insurance, compensation would be paid by first-party rather than by third-party (i.e., liability) insurance. To make this insurance automatically available to victims, no motor vehicle could be registered or legally driven in a state adopting this regime unless the owner had purchased insurance covering any driver of or passenger in the vehicle, or pedestrian in an accident involving the vehicle.

One of the principal reasons this system would never be enacted in any state is deep disagreement about whether it would be sensible and fair to eliminate all recovery of damages for pain and suffering. As in workers compensation, a system that afforded compensation for pain and suffering on a no-fault basis would be enormously expensive, and therefore impossible to enact as a practical matter. Consequently, whether to preclude no-fault compensation for pain and suffering is not merely a question about one feature of the system, but goes to the heart of the auto no-fault idea. Critics of no-fault, including pure no-fault, argue that eliminating or restricting tort liability, especially for pain and suffering damages, will cause an increase in the accident rate, because drivers will no longer face the threat of tort liability for negligent driving. In addition, the critics argue, in cases involving serious injury resulting from negligent driving, justice between the parties requires that the injurer be made to compensate the victim. No-fault would relieve injurers of this obligation. In recent years there have been some empirical studies confirming this effect in states that have adopted auto no-fault, although there are other studies suggesting otherwise.

Proponents of no-fault respond to these generic criticisms as follows. First, as to the possible loss of deterrence resulting from the abolition of tort liability for negligent driving, any driver who is not already sufficiently concerned for his own safety to drive carefully will not drive any less carefully once the threat of tort liability is eliminated. As for the justice argument, most acts of negligent driving are momentary lapses of attention. Typical drivers commonly commit acts of negligence, and whether their negligence causes serious injury or none at all depends more on luck than on the degree of blame that can be ascribed to them. Moreover, liability insurance protecting drivers from the financial consequences of their own negligence is very prevalent, and in virtually all states is required. Victims and injurers both pay into the same liability insurance pool, and premiums are only very roughly calibrated to the individual driver's accident record. Justice between injurer and victim in this situation is therefore attenuated at best. Finally, because of the administrative cost savings it would achieve and the reduced need for attorneys, pure no-fault would put more money into the pockets of accident victims and less into the pockets of attorneys and insurance companies.

Whether an impartial observer would assess these arguments to weigh more heavily in favor of or against no-fault, pure no-fault turns out to be just an idea that has no prospect of being enacted in a single state.

B. *"Real" No–Fault*

In about a dozen states a system modeled on the Keeton and O'Connell proposal that includes only a partial abolition of tort liability was fashioned. This alternative, which I shall call "real" no-fault, garnered enough support to be enacted in some states and to remain in force today in most of the states that enacted it. Like pure no-fault, real no-fault also has both tort-abolition and victim-insurance prong. Under the first prong, drivers buy first-party insurance, often termed Personal Injury Protection (PIP) protecting themselves, their passengers, and pedestrians whom they injure, insuring these parties for medical expenses and lost wages "arising out of" the operation of a motor vehicle. But under the second prong of real no-fault, tort liability is abolished only for less serious injuries. Thus, the obstacle that stands firmly in the way of the enactment of pure no-fault on both political and principled grounds—concern over abolition of tort liability for injuries involving substantial pain and suffering—is partly removed.

The reasons even this compromise has had only limited success vary to a degree from state to state, but certainly one major factor has been the opposition of attorneys who regularly represent plaintiffs in auto cases, who have lobbied strenuously against no-fault. A second major factor has been the principled concern of many legislators, who have proved reluctant to support even a limited abolition of tort liability for auto-related injuries, because of their concern for victims' recovery of pain and suffering damages.

In real no-fault the distinction between injuries that are compensable only on a no-fault basis and injuries for which a cause of action in tort is preserved is drawn through the use of a "threshold." Claimants whose injuries surpass the threshold may bring tort actions; claimants whose injuries do not surpass the threshold have no cause of action in tort. There are two types of thresholds. A *monetary threshold* specifies the dollar amount of medical expenses that a claimant must incur in order to preserve her cause of action in tort. A *verbal threshold* lists the various "serious" injuries that qualify for recovery in tort regardless of the medical expenses incurred to treat them. Other than soft tissue injuries and simple fractures, most injuries of any seriousness typically qualify. But since the vast majority of auto-related injuries are not "serious" in this sense, the size of the monetary threshold is critically important. There is considerable variation. These thresholds are as low as a few hundred dollars in some states and as high as several thousand dollars in others.

The result is that in low-threshold states only the most modest tort claims are precluded, while in other states only the most serious are permitted. The effect of this difference, however, depends in part on how the second, mandatory-insurance prong of no-fault is handled. If the minimal level of insurance is high (e.g., $50,000) then most victims are automatically entitled to recover most of their out-of-pocket losses from their own insurance company and typically do so. Since no-fault statutes normally offset tort recoveries by the amount of prior insurance payments (i.e, reverse the collateral source rule with respect to no-fault benefits), for these victims the major effect of preserving their cause of action is that they may recover damages for pain and suffering. In contrast, in states with low minimum levels of mandatory no-fault insurance (e.g., $2000), many victims do not have enough of their own insurance to cover all of their out-of-pocket losses. The preservation of a cause of action permits full recovery of out-of-pocket losses by these victims.

Beyond these general differences lie more subtle, though significant, choices embodied by the distinctions between approaches. The states adopting low thresholds have removed "nuisance" claims from the tort system and assured all victims quick, automatic compensation for their losses. But since the bulk of tort actions are preserved in these states, this form of no-fault looks a lot more like mandatory first-party insurance than like tort reform. By contrast, high thresholds that are difficult to surpass have the potential to shrink the tort system in a significant way. In these states the two prongs of no-fault—mandatory insurance and partial abolition of tort liability—bear an important relation to each other. The higher the insurance-benefit levels that a particular state's no-fault statute mandates, the higher the threshold can comfortably be, for a high threshold will tend to assure full or near-full payment of victims' out-of-pocket losses without the need for tort recoveries.

The shape of the system adopted also affects one of the key questions about no-fault: how much it costs. The disappointingly high cost of no-fault actually has caused several states that originally adopted the approach to repeal it. Critics often charge that no-fault is not cheaper than the tort system, and point to changes in insurance costs after the adoption of no-fault to prove their point. But the comparison of before-and-after costs can be simplistic and misleading. When there is tort liability alone, then drivers must purchase liability insurance only. After no-fault with only partial abolition of tort liability is enacted, however, drivers must purchase both liability insurance protecting them against the liability for "serious" injuries that has been preserved, and first-party insurance covering themselves and their passengers for all out-of-pocket injury costs up to the mandated benefit level. If that benefit level is high, then of course the total cost of real no-fault (tort plus no-fault) will exceed the former cost of tort liability alone. Under the new system the most expensive part of the old system (liability for serious injuries) has been preserved, while another system (mandatory first-party insurance) has been added onto it. The only appropriate cost comparison would be between tort liability and pure no-fault. But that is a comparison that cannot be made in practice, because pure no-fault has never been enacted.[3]

Nonetheless, one feature of auto no-fault seems to have been responsible for a considerable portion of the increasing cost of auto no-fault: medical expense payments. The reason is that, in contrast to modern health insurance, the medical expense component of auto no-fault insurance typically is not subject to deductibles or co-insurance and is not controlled by managed care guidelines. Physicians and hospitals treating accident victims in no-fault states therefore have an incentive to ignore typical health insurance managed care guidelines and bill auto insurers for their charges. In the absence of statutory standards that either prevent this stratagem or impose managed care guidelines for auto insurance, this "hole in the dyke" is another reason that auto no-fault is likely to continue to be more expensive than it might otherwise be expected to be.

C. *"Add-on" No–Fault*

The third version of no-fault is the most prevalent but least significant. This version has one prong only. Under this version no-fault insurance is an "add-on" to the tort system. Tort liability remains untouched, but there is mandatory purchase of no-fault medical-expense and lost-wage insurance.

Formally, this add-on form of no-fault is merely auto-insurance reform without any tort reform whatsoever. But informally, even add-on no-fault may have some impact on the incidence of tort liability. By providing an automatic source of recovery for at least a portion of every victim's out-of-pocket losses, add-on no-fault eliminates the need to sue for these losses. Some victims still will wish to bring suit, especially in cases of severe pain and suffering. But for victims with comparatively small claims and modest injuries, suit is not necessary in order to obtain compensation, and some may decline to sue because their out-of-pocket losses have been paid. In this way even a reform that has no direct control of the incidence of tort suits may have an indirect effect on them. It may be that over time, as the scope of add-on benefits increases, the attractiveness of retaining the right to sue in tort will decline. But at present in most states the legislatures show no particular inclination to move beyond the add-on approach by abolishing any portion of tort

---

3. For a detailed assessment, *see* Gary Schwartz, *Auto No–Fault and First–Party Insurance*, 73 S. CAL. L. REV. 611 (2000).

liability for auto injuries. Instead, tort liability and add-on no-fault peacefully co-exist.

D. *"Choice" No–Fault*

A final model allows drivers to choose whether to participate in no-fault. Those who choose not to participate retain all their tort rights and all their tort liabilities to other drivers who have chosen tort. Those who choose to participate in no-fault partially lose the right to sue in tort (for injuries below the applicable threshold) but receive the same immunity from tort liability. Allowing this choice neutralizes some of the objections to mandatory no-fault, since potential victims are allowed to decide for themselves how valuable their right to sue is to them. Kentucky, New Jersey, and Pennsylvania have enacted versions of this choice approach.

The knotty problem for choice states is how to deal with accidents between those who have chosen different options. In theory the way to handle this issue would be to deny the plaintiff who has chosen no-fault a tort cause of action (in below-threshold situations) against a driver who has chosen fault, and to permit a plaintiff who has chosen fault a full cause of action against a driver who has chosen no-fault. Drivers' liability insurance and no-fault insurance would then make adequate provision for these possibilities. In practice, however, the solutions the states that have enacted vary from these theoretically optimal approaches. Interested readers are directed to the laws governing choice no-fault in these states for details.

V.   Targeted No–Fault in Other Fields

A few no-fault approaches have been adopted in other fields, either by legislation or unilateral establishment. In addition, there continues to be consideration of the adoption of no-fault in the medical and product areas. This Section considers both topics.

A.   *Actually Enacted or Adopted Approaches*

At the federal level the National Childhood Vaccine Injury Act provides no-fault benefits to children who suffer specified side effects of childhood vaccinations.[4] And the September 11 Victim Compensation Fund provided no-fault benefits to the victims of

---

4.   42 U.S.C. §§ 300aa–1 to 300aa–34.

9/11 and their families.[5] At the state level, Florida[6] and Virginia[7] provide no-fault compensation for birth-related neurological injury. And in the wake of the 2010 explosion of its drilling rig in the Gulf of Mexico and the massive oil spill that resulted, BP voluntarily established the Gulf Coast Claims Facility to provide victims with a no-fault alternative to bringing suit to obtain compensation for their losses.

These targeted approaches define and apply to only a narrow compensable event or set of compensable events. Whether a targeted compensable event has occurred is for the most part easy and inexpensive to determine. And these schemes are elective for the victim. That is, they give victims the option of receiving no-fault compensation, or rejecting it and suing in tort instead. Although targeted schemes have not proliferated, there are enough of them to raise significant questions of horizontal equity. Why do those who are beneficiaries of these targeted schemes receive the benefits of access to no-fault compensation, while other victims are left to whatever tort rights they are able to vindicate in lawsuits? The answer, of course, is at least partly political: childhood vaccine litigation was inhibiting the development and manufacture of these vaccines; the airlines sought to avoid tort liability resulting from 9/11, and so forth. But even in the face of these political considerations, targeted no-fault could not be automatically adopted. Rather, the losses in question had to be susceptible to workable no-fault definitions, or (in the case of the 9/11 and BP Funds) the discretion of a Special Master administering them according to guidelines he promulgated. And that may be at least part of the explanation for the limited number of such schemes that exist at present. It takes not only substantial political support for a targeted no-fault scheme before it can be enacted. In addition, a targeted approach is unlikely to be enacted unless it is technically feasible to define a workable compensable event that targets losses on a no-fault basis.

B.   *The Future of No–Fault*

The no-fault revolution is largely at a standstill. No state has enacted real auto no-fault in two decades, although California voters came within a percentage point of doing so in 1996. Nonetheless, long after workers compensation had been put in place it inspired auto no-fault. Is it possible that these two no-fault systems

5.   49 U.S.C. § 40101 note (Supp. I 2001).

6.   Fla. Stat. Ann. §§ 766.301–316.

7.   Va. Code Ann. §§ 38.2–5000 to 5021.

could now serve as models for reform of other aspects of the tort system?

The prospects are not rosy, but it is highly instructive to understand why. The central problem is how to define the compensable event in a suitable way. In the employment and auto settings, defining the compensable event is straightforward and simple: an injury "arising out of or in the course of" employment or motoring. Such a definition works because people virtually always go to work or get into a car uninjured. If they emerge from work or driving injured, it is highly likely that they have suffered a work-related or auto-related injury. Using so straightforward a compensable event, however, is not feasible in such other settings as medical or product-related injuries.

By analogy to workers compensation and auto no-fault, could no-fault benefits easily be made available to anyone suffering an injury "arising out of or in the course of medical treatment?" Unfortunately, determining whether the claimant had suffered a compensable event would require complex fact-finding in a large percentage of such claims. Many people seek medical treatment because they are already ill or injured. In such cases there would have to be a fact-finder who could distinguish injuries or illnesses that were caused by medical treatment from conditions associated with the patient's underlying injury or illness. Whether the physician had committed malpractice would no longer be at issue. But the causation question under medical no-fault—"did the patient suffer an injury arising out of medical treatment?"—would still be at issue in many cases. The swift and certain compensation of victims that is so characteristic of and so much an important part of workers compensation and auto no-fault would therefore often be unavailable. Nonetheless, some research has been undertaken in an effort to assess the feasibility of making medical no-fault determinations, and the results are mildly encouraging.[8] Although these efforts have as yet not gone beyond the research stage, limited experiments in medical no-fault compensation may eventually be undertaken.

A somewhat different problem, also involving the compensable event, would plague efforts to develop product no-fault. No one would want a system of insurance against all product-related injuries. If you fall off a perfectly suitable ladder or cut yourself with a high quality steak knife, I do not want to pay into an insurance pool that will cover you against the losses you suffer as a result of

---

8. See Paul C. Weiler et al., A Measure of Malpractice: Medical Injury, Malpractice Litigation, and Patient Compensation (1993).

these products doing exactly what they are supposed to do. I would rather take care of myself and not pay for your careless climbing or cutting. Consequently, the product no-fault compensable event would have to be limited to something like injuries "arising out of the use of defective products." But of course the difficulty of determining whether a product is "defective" is precisely what so troubles current product liability law, and precisely what makes finding some alternative outside of tort attractive. There would be little point in adopting a no-fault system that replicated the problems it was designed to avoid.

One approach that might avoid some of these problems would be to authorize elective, contractual no-fault for medical and/or product injuries. If legal theorists cannot collectively define a compensable event that is suitable for general use in product no-fault, it may still be possible for individual companies or industry groups to develop more focused alternatives that will work in more limited settings. For example, chain saw manufacturers might want to fashion their own no-fault system for their purchasers. Standing in the way of this alternative, however, is the courts' extreme reluctance to permit contractual disclaimers of tort liability. Potential defendants are therefore reluctant to invest in the development of no-fault alternatives when they know that their investment may be lost when the courts invalidate the approach they have tried to use. Without advance validation there is not much incentive to develop a no-fault alternative to tort liability.

Thus, ideally, legislation would authorize the adoption of such alternatives in advance. Ironically, however, authorizing legislation is unlikely to be enacted until a particular scheme has been developed. The result is a chicken-and-egg problem in which a particular scheme is unlikely to be developed in the absence of authorizing legislation, and authorizing legislation is unlikely to be enacted before a particular scheme is developed. Partly for this reason elective no-fault has not yet gotten off the ground, although at least in theory it is an attractive approach.

13

REPUTATIONAL AND DIGNITARY HARMS: DEFAMATION AND INVASION OF PRIVACY

Virtually everything in the first twelve chapters of this book has been concerned with liability for bodily injury and property damage, or for the consequences of risking such harm. In this Chapter and the next one we take up very different forms of liability involving intangible rather than physical harms. This Chapter concerns causes of action that protect reputation and personal dignity: defamation and invasion of privacy.

I. Defamation

For most of tort law over the past one hundred years, progressive expansion of liability has been the principal story. This is not true, however, of liability for defamation, which is the only major field of tort law that has undergone a major reduction in its scope during the modern era. Until 1964 the law of defamation had remained largely unchanged for a very long time. Beginning in that year the U.S. Supreme Court entered the field and began a still-continuing effort to define and elaborate the limitations on the scope of the law of defamation required by the First Amendment to the U.S. Constitution. Since those limitations are only partial, however, the challenge in this field is both to understand the common law of defamation and to identify the features of this body of law that have been modified by constitutional dictate.

A. *The Core Principles of the Common Law of Defamation*

Defamation is the making of a statement to a third party ("publication") that injures a person's reputation. Reputation itself is not one thing, but a cluster of values. Sometimes reputation is much like property—one's creditworthiness, for example, has monetary value. On the other hand, sometimes reputation is a form of honor, built up over time through accomplishment or good behavior. Finally, sometimes reputation is more closely akin to dignity, which can be lost through ridicule or satire. The law of defamation is designed to protect each of these forms of reputation.

A defamatory statement may be oral, in which case it is *slander*, or it may be made in writing or otherwise more "permanent" form in which case it is *libel*. In a leading case, the Supreme Court of California has held that defamation on the internet constitutes libel.[1] Because libelous statements are permanent and therefore often are capable of doing more damage than slander, the common law of defamation made them more easily actionable, in the ways noted below.

The common law of defamation reflected a particular set of values, placing much more emphasis on the protection of reputation than on freedom of speech. There was strict liability for making a defamatory statement—or for republishing someone else's statement with knowledge that it was defamatory. There are two major exceptions to the rule that republishing a defamatory statement is actionable. First, a federal law protects internet service providers from liability for republication.[2] Second, in some states there is "neutral reporting privilege" that protects media against liability for republication of a defamatory statement made by a "responsible, prominent organization" against a "public figure" if the reporting is "accurate and disinterested."

At common law there also was no requirement that the defendant intend to harm the plaintiff, have been negligent, or that the defendant know that the statement was false. This amounted to strict liability. Indeed, technically speaking, falsity was not even a *prima facie* element of the tort. To be defamatory the statement merely had to injure the plaintiff's reputation. The truth of the statement could in fact be relevant, because truth was a defense. But it was just that—a defense that the defendant had to plead and prove in order to avoid liability.

1. The *Prima Facie* Case

In general a libel was actionable without proof of special damages—i.e., out-of-pocket loss resulting from damage to the plaintiff's reputation. Some states applied this rule only to libel "per se," defined as a statement that was defamatory on its face and therefore required no extrinsic evidence to explain its defamatory character. The great advantage to the plaintiff in a libel per se action was that he could recover compensation for "presumed" damage to his reputation and for consequent emotional loss without

---

1. *Varian Medical Systems, Inc. v. Delfino*, 35 Cal.4th 180, 25 Cal.Rptr.3d 298, 106 P.3d 958 (2005).

2. 47 U.S.C. § 230 (c)(1). For application of the statute's protections to an internet service provider, with respect both to its "publisher" and "distributor" roles, *see Blumenthal v. Drudge*, 992 F.Supp. 44 (D. D.C. 1998).

proving that damage. In contrast, slander was not actionable per se—i.e., there could be no presumption of damage—unless it was defamatory in one of four ways: by accusing the plaintiff of committing a major crime, having a sexually transmitted or other "loathsome" disease, conducting himself in a way that made him unsuited for his business or profession, or engaging in infidelity or other serious sexual misconduct.

Thus, simply by showing that the defendant had made a statement to a third party that was damaging to the plaintiff's reputation, a plaintiff could prove a *prima facie* case of defamation. In a broad variety of libel and slander per se cases, this showing would trigger a presumption that the defamation had caused compensable damage. Among other things this meant that the plaintiff could survive the defendant's motion for a directed verdict by making this simple showing, and that unless the defendant could make out a defense as a matter of law, the plaintiff's case would go to the jury. The message sent by this structure was clear. Any person who considered making a statement damaging to someone else's reputation was putting himself at risk of liability. As between the interest in one's reputation and the right to speak freely, the common law seemed clearly to favor the former at the expense of the latter.

2. Defenses

When the available defenses are added to this mix, the picture becomes somewhat cloudier, but the overall emphasis remains the same. As I noted above, truth was an absolute defense. There was also a series of privileges, some absolute and some conditional. Aside from consent, there was an *absolute privilege* to make defamatory statements in legal proceedings of one sort or another—legislative, judicial, or administrative. And high officials of government had an absolute privilege for any statement made as part of their conduct of office, whether or not the statement was made in a formal proceeding. A *conditional privilege* was one that protected the maker of a defamatory statement from liability unless the statement was made with knowledge that the statement was false or with reckless disregard for the truth or falsity of the statement. This standard was sometimes referred to as "actual malice," a term that the Supreme Court was later to employ.

The conditional privileges to make defamatory statements applied in a variety of contexts. What linked them together was they applied to the kind of statements that had to be made in order for ordinary business and important family matters to be conducted. For example, there were conditional privileges for making defamatory statements in letters of recommendation, in reports to proper authorities about the commission of crimes, and in communications to family members about the character of people with whom they were dealing or had personal relationships—such as prospective spouses. And lower governmental officials enjoyed a conditional privilege to make defamatory statements as part of the conduct of their office. Finally, there was a conditional privilege to engage in "fair comment" on artistic, literary, and other public matters, including public officials. But in the majority of states the fair comment privilege applied only to the expression of opinions, not to assertions of fact.

The effect of the privileges was to give those who held them some room for making false statements that reflected negatively on another person's reputation without facing liability for defamation. If only the defense of truth were available, then any false statement could result in liability. Armed with a conditional privilege, however, the maker of a statement who had an honest belief that it was true would be protected against liability. And if the maker happened to enjoy an absolute privilege, even an honest belief in the truth of a defamatory statement was not necessary. So the common law privileges created some "breathing space" for speech under circumstances where the fear of liability for making a false statement might otherwise have discouraged—"chilled"—the making of valuable true statements.

Since it was the defendant's burden to prove defenses and privileges, however, the law of defamation encouraged even a defendant who believed he was privileged to make a defamatory statement to think twice before he made it. Nonetheless, at least on paper, potential defendants had protection against liability for a wide variety of negative statements about other people that they might make in the ordinary course of business or personal life. For making volunteered, gratuitous, wholly optional statements, however, there was less likely to be a conditional privilege and much more likely to be liability. Two such non-privileged categories of statements stand out especially. Ordinary gossip was unprotected at common law and is unprotected now. The private individual, newspaper, or television station that makes or repeats a defamatory statement about an ordinary individual who is uninvolved in public issues faces strict liability and has only the defense of truth as protection. Similarly unprotected at common law was political speech, broadly conceived, with the exception of the assertion of opinions subject to the fair comment privilege. Those who made false factual statements about government officials, candidates for office, or people involved in public issues enjoyed no privileges and had only the defense of truth to protect them. In contrast to ordinary gossip, however, political speech was about to receive powerful constitutional protection.

B. *Defamation Law and the Constitution*

Beginning in 1964, the U.S. Supreme Court entered the field. There can be no doubt that the Supreme Court's rulings regarding the constitutional limits on the scope of liability for defamation have had great significance. Once utterly untouched by constitutional limitations, defamation law today cannot be properly understood without appreciating these limitations. On the other hand, important as the so-called "constitutionalization" of defamation law is, what has actually happened should not be exaggerated. After a half-century of constitutional elaboration, it is only a modest oversimplification to say that the major development has merely been the establishment of new constitutional conditional privileges for political speech and speech about public issues.

1. *New York Times v. Sullivan*

The most important of the Supreme Court's decisions in this field was its first, *New York Times Co. v. Sullivan*.[3] The plaintiff in that case, Sullivan, was one of three elected City Commissioners of Montgomery, Alabama in 1960. The individual defendants signed a political advertisement published in the New York Times containing a series of accusations regarding the City of Montgomery's conduct toward civil rights demonstrators, some of which were false. The plaintiff was not mentioned by name, but he sued the Times and those who signed the ad for libel. Under Alabama law, if the jury found the statement to be "of and concerning" the plaintiff, the statements were actionable without proof of special damages because the statements were libelous per se and not privileged. Punitive damages also could be awarded if malice were proved, because a retraction the defendant had demanded was not published.

The jury awarded Sullivan $500,000 in compensatory and punitive damages. But the U.S. Supreme Court overturned the verdict, holding that the First Amendment guarantee of freedom of speech (applied to the states through the Fourteenth Amendment) requires that the makers of statements about public officials be afforded a conditional privilege to make those statements. To defeat the privilege, the Court held, a public official suing for defamation

---

3. 376 U.S. 254, 84 S.Ct. 710, 11 L.Ed.2d 686 (1964).

had to prove with "convincing clarity" that the statement was made with "actual malice"—i.e., with knowledge that the statement was false or with reckless disregard for its truth or falsity. In addition, to be actionable there had to be sufficient proof that the statements were "of and concerning" the plaintiff to assure the required constitutional freedom to criticize the government.

In one sense the decision in *New York Times v. Sullivan* is unremarkable. If the existing common-law privileges were designed to afford "breathing space" for speech necessary to the ordinary functioning of business and family affairs, then surely the functioning of a democracy requires that there be at least a similar amount of breathing space for political speech. For example, all that *Sullivan* did substantively was to create a conditional privilege to make defamatory statements about public officials equivalent to the privilege that employers and teachers have when writing letters of recommendation. That can hardly be controversial.

On the other hand, for nearly two hundred years the state courts had operated without any federally-set limits on the scope of defamation law. Now, suddenly, there was a potential federal "presence" in every defamation suit brought by a public official. The context in which *Sullivan* was decided helps to explain how the Supreme Court could have made a decision with the potential to so intrude on the traditional province of the state courts. A civil rights dispute gave rise to Sullivan's lawsuit. The defamatory statements made in a northern newspaper—the New York Times—were technically false in certain respects but were not misleading overall. The plaintiff's suit was then tried in the still-segregated south. And the Alabama jury awarded Sullivan one-half a million dollars without proof that the statements had caused Sullivan any monetary loss at all.

Moreover, the record before the Supreme Court showed that the trial judge in the case had insisted on segregated seating in the courtroom, and had introduced the case with the statement that the Fourteenth Amendment (which guarantees due process of law) is a "pariah and an outcast," indicating also his belief that "the white man's justice * * * will give the parties * * * equal justice under law."[4] Add to this inflammatory setting the fact that the civil rights movement, which by 1964 was at a fever pitch, drew much of its political support from the North, through the mechanism of media coverage. It was therefore understandable for the Supreme Court to be concerned that the threat of large judgments imposing strict liability for defamatory statements made in the course of the

---

4. *See* Rodney A. Smolla, SUING THE PRESS 32–33 (1986).

public controversy over civil rights would be used as a segregation-ist weapon against those who favored civil rights. Viewed in this light, the Supreme Court's willingness to begin creating a whole new constitutional jurisprudence of defamation is somewhat more understandable, especially since the 1960s were a period of venture-some lawmaking by the Supreme Court in other areas as well.

2. Beyond *Sullivan*

Once established, however, the new regime automatically had a life of its own beyond civil rights disputes. In short order the rule in *Sullivan* was applied to not only to public officials, but also to what the Court called public "figures"—individuals who were not elected or appointed officials, but whose prominence in politics, entertain-ment, sports, or other pursuits made them a subject of public interest. Eventually it also became clear that the Constitution required the plaintiff to prove falsity, rather than putting the burden of proving truth on the defendant. And in *Gertz v. Robert Welch, Inc.,*[5] the Court was confronted with the inevitable question of how the law of defamation could be squared with constitutional requirements when the plaintiff was neither a public official nor figure, but the defamatory statement about the plaintiff concerned a matter of public interest.

The Court responded with two rules. First, *Gertz* held that the Constitution does not permit the imposition of strict liability for defamation in cases involving matters of public interest, but that the states were free to adopt any other standard as long as the plaintiff was required to show at least negligence on the part of the defendant. In effect, in cases involving matters of public interest where the plaintiff was not a public official or public figure, the states could adopt a conditional privilege that would be defeated either by a showing of negligence, or, if a state so chose, only by showing actual malice. Second, the Court ruled that in any of these cases now subject to constitutional limits, "presumed" damages were not permissible in the absence of a showing of actual malice. Thus, when the plaintiff had shown only that the defendant was negligent but still was permitted to recover, there could be no recovery without proof of actual loss, though this could be emotion-al loss rather than out-of-pocket economic loss.

For a time it was unclear whether *Gertz* had constitutionalized all or only that part of the law of defamation dealing with matters of public interest, since some of its language was very broad. But in

5. 418 U.S. 323, 94 S.Ct. 2997, 41 L.Ed.2d 789 (1974).

Dun & Bradstreet, Inc. v. Greenmoss Builders, Inc.,[6] the Court ruled that the states were permitted to continue imposing strict liability in cases that do not involve matters of public interest, and apparently free to continue the practice of awarding "presumed" damages in such cases as well. Clearly this rule applies in cases involving private plaintiffs suing non-media defendants. To what extent the rule can coherently apply when a private plaintiff sues a media defendant is unclear, however, since defamatory statements published by the media are likely almost by definition to have somewhat more public "interest" than utterly private statements. Over a period of decades a series of other rules governing important but "subsidiary" issues also has evolved.

The upshot of all this is that there is now a whole set of constitutional limits on the scope of defamation liability. There are now two separate constitutionally-required standards (actual malice and negligence) in cases involving public officials and figures and matters of public interest, respectively. But the states are still free to apply the old strict liability standard in other cases. There is a set of cases in which damages cannot be presumed (when proof of at least negligence is required but actual malice has not been proved). There is a new allocation of the burden of proof regarding falsity. There is a heightened scope of review in cases where the "of and concerning" the plaintiff issue is raised. And there is residual uncertainty about whether different standards apply in some of the cases involving media as distinguished from non-media defendants.

This legal framework is not only complicated, but has produced unanticipated side effects. For example, the actual malice requirement in public official and public figure cases has obviously made it harder for plaintiffs to recover; but because so much blame on the part of the defendant is required for a recovery in such cases, defendants have a tendency to fight defamation suits more strongly than they did in the past, when a finding of liability did not necessarily imply fault or professional misconduct on the part of a newspaper, magazine, or T.V. program. Moreover, what had once been a simple strict liability issue is often transformed into a complicated and costly inquiry into the nature of the defendant's publication and fact-verification process, because constitutional malice or fault must be proved. And if the plaintiff does succeed in proving actual malice, the judgment awarded is likely to be much larger than in the past, because the defendant has been proved to have been highly blameworthy. For this reason also, defendants have an increased incentive to invest whatever it takes to defeat a

---

6. 472 U.S. 749, 105 S.Ct. 2939, 86 L.Ed.2d 593 (1985).

defamation suit. The result is that litigation is more complicated than in the past. Finally, studies have shown that for many plaintiffs, merely bringing suit and proving falsity constitutes vindication, even if they lose because they cannot show actual malice. Many plaintiffs win by suing, even if they do not win by winning.

3. Assessment

At this point the Supreme Court cannot turn back the clock, and might not wish to do so even if it could. But in retrospect it appears that some of the concerns with which the Court began—the threat of liability for large sums in cases involving minor factual inaccuracies, for example—might have been addressed in another way. Conceivably the Court might have focused on the threat of "presumed" damages to the constitutional guarantee of free speech, and limited its intervention in state defamation law to the regulation of presumed damages. Strict liability might then have been permitted to continue in cases in which the plaintiff—typically a public official or figure—wished to vindicate his or her reputation but was not seeking to bankrupt or intimidate the plaintiff.[7] A few states now have enacted statutes permitting such name-clearing actions through proof of falsity alone, but the statutes might not have been necessary had the Court chosen to pursue the damages route in order to assure that the necessary constitutional protections were available.

Nor is the increased protection that media enterprises have come to enjoy entirely consonant with the other legal and economic developments of the past thirty years. At the same time that the rest of tort law was moving closer to enterprise-based forms of liability, such as strict products liability and relaxed rules governing proof of causation in toxic harm cases, defamation law moved in the other direction. One of the principal changes in the world of print and electronic media during this period has been the recognition that "news" is a "product." Yet whereas other product defects now result in more liability, the media's main product results in less liability than in the past, not more.

Finally, although at some level *New York Times v. Sullivan* was intended to take at least some of defamation law out of politics, many of the most noteworthy defamation trials of the post-*Sullivan* period carried into the courtroom the very political struggles that were the subject of the defendant's reporting. A widely-publicized suit against the television program "Sixty Minutes" by the com-

---

7. *See* Pierre Leval, *The No–Money, No–Fault Libel Suit: Keeping* Sullivan *in its Proper Place*, 101 HARV. L. REV. 1287 (1988).

mander of the United States forces during much of the Vietnam War, General William Westmoreland, was only the most celebrated example of many.[8] Ironically, then, not only does the constitutionalization of defamation law run somewhat against the grain of the rest of modern tort law; in addition, much of what that constitutionalization has brought probably has not been anything like what the Supreme Court may have expected. Unanticipated side effects that make litigation more complicated and costly rather than simply creating additional breathing space for political speech now figure in virtually every major defamation suit.

II. Invasion of Privacy

The first principle of the tort of invasion of privacy has been repeated so often that it is almost a cliche. Invasion of privacy is not one tort, but four: 1) appropriation of the plaintiff's name or likeness; 2) unreasonable public disclosure of private facts; 3) intrusion on the plaintiff's solitude or privacy; and 4) portrayal of the plaintiff in a false light. Although these categories are now well-established, all four causes of action emerged clearly only in the twentieth century.

Each privacy tort is concerned with a different form of invasion and, to some extent, a different form of loss. What links the four torts together is not simply the umbrella term "privacy," but their general concern for the protection of personal dignity. In keeping with this concern, none of the four torts requires proof of out-of-pocket damages in order to be actionable. Rather, although (unlike common law libel and slander per se) damages are not "presumed" in invasion of privacy actions, the plaintiff is entitled to recover for the rather abstract non-monetary harm to dignity suffered from the invasion, as well as for resulting mental distress suffered. Given the requirements of the privacy torts described below, the conduct that gives rise to the invasion very often also warrants imposition of liability on the defendant for punitive damages.

As the four privacy causes of action emerged, the courts had not only to decide whether an invasion ever was actionable, but (when it was actionable) under what conditions. Because the privacy torts are of comparatively recent vintage and are not the frequent subject of litigation, their contours still are not clear in every detail. The need for continued clarification of the interests they protect, the basis upon which liability for each form of intrusion may be imposed, and the countervailing concerns that limit the

8. *See Westmoreland v. CBS Inc.*, 596 F.Supp. 1170 (S.D.N.Y.1984).

scope of liability, make the privacy torts open-ended and subject to evolving modification.

A. *Appropriation*

A person's name and the way he or she looks are a central part of his or her identity. For this reason it is tortious for the defendant to appropriate the plaintiff's name or likeness for commercial purposes, and in many states for non-commercial purposes. When the benefit the defendant obtains from appropriation is commercial, the main interest the tort of appropriation protects is the economic value of one's name or likeness. In this sense the interest is much like property, and the defendant's wrong is much like taking property without consent. But even if the plaintiff's name or likeness is not used for commercial purposes the appropriation is a wrong. For example, using the plaintiff's name without permission to publicize a charity ball would also be actionable in many states.

The limits on the tort of appropriation derive from what in a very rough sense can be understood as waiver assumption of risk by the plaintiff. Anyone who attends a public gathering or even goes out onto the street ought to recognize that her photograph may be taken and used as an exemplar by the news media or even by a private person. Thus a fan cheering at a sporting event has no claim against the magazine that publishes his picture, and a person passing by a gruesome accident is not protected against publication of his picture in the background of a newspaper photograph of the scene. The First Amendment probably also exercises some gravitational pull in this field, though there are few decisions actually applying it. Because for the news and entertainment media commercial profit and free speech are inextricably linked, it is not always possible to distinguish a purely commercial appropriation of the plaintiff's likeness from legitimate reporting of matters of public interest. Thus the tort of appropriation may provide less protection for plaintiffs who are public figures and especially entertainers, who must tolerate use of their names and likenesses when publicity is given to their exploits. Nonetheless, simply employing a celebrity's image for commercial purposes is an appropriation, except when the defendant subjects the image to artistic or expressive "transformation," in which case the expression may have First Amendment protection.[9] It is worth noting, however, that since celebrities are the very people whose names and likenesses will help to sell products, the damages they recover when they are successful in an appropriation suit may be substantial.

9. *Winter v. DC Comics*, 30 Cal.4th 881, 134 Cal.Rptr.2d 634, 69 P.3d 473 (2003).

B. *Disclosure*

In general people have a right to be left alone. It is an intrusion on my privacy—on my right to be left alone—if you disclose private facts about me to a third person or persons and under the circumstances your disclosure is "offensive." But because some people have voluntarily placed themselves in the public eye, they have a right to expect less protection against the disclosure of private facts about them than do private individuals. And occasionally the rights of someone who has involuntarily become a subject of publicity must be balanced against the public's legitimate, though not necessarily admirable, interest in them.

One of the leading cases on this score is *Sidis v. F-R Publishing Corp.*,[10] in which the New Yorker magazine profiled a reclusive genius who had received publicity as a child prodigy many years before. The plaintiff had become an "insignificant clerk," was living in a rooming house, and had gone to some lengths to avoid public attention. Nonetheless, the court held that he had no cause of action, on the ground that the facts about the plaintiff, though embarrassing to him, were in an attenuated sense "newsworthy." Apparently the newsworthiness of the facts about the plaintiff influenced the determination that the disclosure was not offensive. Other courts have let the issue whether the plaintiff's fame (or infamy)[11] has faded sufficiently to render the disclosure offensive go to the jury. The U.S. Supreme Court has ruled that the First Amendment precludes the imposition of liability for the disclosure of the name of a rape victim obtained from public records,[12] though subsequent decisions have left unclear exactly how "public" a record must be in order to afford the defendant this protection. But some state courts have permitted the imposition of liability for disclosure in certain cases involving breach of confidence—for example, by a physician who discloses the name of a birth mother to an adopted child.[13]

The lesson of these decisions is that, regardless of the precise point at which the line is drawn, the right to be free from offensive public disclosures of private facts must at some point yield to the

10. 113 F.2d 806 (2d Cir.1940).

11. *See Briscoe v. Reader's Digest Ass'n*, 4 Cal.3d 529, 93 Cal.Rptr. 866, 483 P.2d 34 (1971).

12. *Cox Broadcasting Corp. v. Cohn*, 420 U.S. 469, 95 S.Ct. 1029, 43 L.Ed.2d 328 (1975).

13. *Humphers v. First Interstate Bank of Oregon*, 298 Or. 706, 696 P.2d 527 (1985).

public's right to know about matters of public interest. Whether a disclosure is actionable will tend to be a highly context-dependent decision, taking into account the extent to which the plaintiff has or has not voluntarily subjected himself to publicity in the past, the character of the information disclosed, the manner in which the defendant came into possession of the information, and the legitimacy of the public interest in the information disclosed.

C. *Intrusion*

Nothing comes closer to invading the core of what we think of as "privacy" than physical or electronic invasion of a place or space from which the plaintiff has a right to exclude others. The bedroom is the classic venue, but a physician's examination room, and even a cell phone conversation or one's mail or email also qualify. The intrusion need not literally be physical—visual or auditory surveillance from afar may also be actionable. The only requirements are that the invasion be highly offensive to a reasonable person and that it be into a place or space in which the plaintiff has a reasonable expectation of privacy. Even an ambulance may be a private space for some purposes.[14] In contrast to the other privacy torts, there is usually no countervailing interest that the defendant can point to in order to justify intrusive conduct. The invasion must be sufficiently offensive, however, to warrant the law's intervention. Most allegedly actionable invasions can be resolved with an "I know it when I see it" test that takes the entire context into account. After all, although one can articulate why an intrusion does or does not seem "offensive," ultimately offensiveness is more a matter of common indignation than logic.

One difficult problem involves "stalking" and other persistent intrusions that take place in public spaces rather than on private property. Even on the street, in a park, or at a museum, one's personal space may be offensively invaded by the repeated, harassing presence of the defendant. The plaintiff may not be entitled to maintain that space against intrusion by multiple, nameless individuals; but a single individual day after day may be said to invade the "moving circle" of privacy that follows everyone around, even in public spaces. Celebrities as well as private individuals have a right to protection against this kind of invasion, once it becomes harassment. Unfortunately, however, although the threat of civil liability and even punitive damages may deter business enterprises

---

14. *See Shulman v. Group W Productions, Inc.*, 18 Cal.4th 200, 74 Cal.Rptr.2d 843, 955 P.2d 469 (1998).

from becoming involved in such harassment,[15] a mentally disturbed individual is less easily deterred by conventional means. Here tort law reaches the limits of its capacities, and injunctions or statutorily prescribed criminal penalties become necessary to curtail the ongoing invasion of the plaintiff's privacy.[16]

D. *False Light*

Finally, it is an invasion of the plaintiff's privacy to portray him in a false light if that is done with actual malice (in the constitutional sense)[17] and the portrayal is highly offensive. Often a portrayal in a false light will also constitute defamation, but conceivably a portrayal can be in a false light without injuring the plaintiff's reputation or otherwise defaming him. The interests protected by false light and defamation are extremely close if not identical, however, and indeed in some cases only a narrow definition of the interest in "reputation" protected by the tort of defamation seems to qualify as a portrayal in a false light without its also being defamatory.

15. *See, e.g., Nader v. General Motors Corp.*, 25 N.Y.2d 560, 307 N.Y.S.2d 647, 255 N.E.2d 765 (1970).

16. *See, e.g., Galella v. Onassis*, 487 F.2d 986 (2d Cir.1973).

17. See *Time, Inc. v. Hill*, 385 U.S. 374, 87 S.Ct. 534, 17 L.Ed.2d 456 (1967).

14

ECONOMIC HARMS: MISREPRESENTA-
TION AND INTERFERENCE WITH CON-
TRACT OR PROSPECTIVE CONTRACTUAL
ADVANTAGE

This last Chapter concerns torts that typically arise out of contractual or commercial relations and result mainly in economic losses rather than physical harm. These torts reflect business customs and ethics, and therefore have evolved over time in response both to economic change and new business practices.

I. Misrepresentation

The classic form of misrepresentation is intentional: fraud. But under limited circumstances liability may also be imposed for economic losses caused by negligent misrepresentation, and sometimes even for innocent misrepresentation. Although there is liability for fraud outside of business and commercial settings, most of the litigation involving this cause of action arises out of economic dealings rather than personal relations. For this reason, and before we address the elements of a cause of action for misrepresentation, it is useful to begin by considering what the tort is all about.

A misrepresentation is a false statement of fact. The tort of misrepresentation is therefore intended to redress harm caused by the communication of false information, mainly in the course of business and commercial relations. Not all false statements are actionable, however, because the degree of care that is expected of the party making a statement of fact varies. In virtually every setting—though even here there are a few exceptions—it is expected that one party will not lie to another. On the other hand, there probably is no firm expectation among business people that they will exercise reasonable care that the statements they make to each other in the course of transacting business are true. Only in settings where information is transferred as part of a service purchased—such as legal or accounting advice—is such an expectation commonly held. And still less is there an expectation that the accuracy of statements made in commercial relations is guaranteed to be true, in the absence of an express guarantee of accuracy.

The law governing liability for misrepresentation pretty well coincides with these expectations. There is liability for fraud almost without regard to the business setting in which a lie causes economic harm to its recipient. But liability for merely negligent misrepresentation is not imposed in ordinary commercial settings, being reserved mainly for professional and fiduciary relationships where the parties expect that reasonable care to ensure that statements are accurate will be exercised. And although the scope of liability for innocent misrepresentation varies somewhat between jurisdictions, in general tort liability for innocent misrepresentation (as distinguished from the right to rescind a contract based on it) is imposed only when the defendant has warranted the truth of his statement.

A. *Fraud*

There are five elements to a cause of action for fraud. 1) The defendant must have made a false statement of fact; 2) with knowledge that the statement is false or with reckless disregard of the truth or falsity of the statement (*"scienter"*); 3) intending the plaintiff to rely on the statement; 4) the plaintiff must have justifiably relied; and 5) the plaintiff must have suffered damage as a result. In addition, something like a proximate cause requirement limits the scope of liability for fraud.

1. False Statement of Fact: Misrepresentation and Nondisclosure

There can be no false statements of fact about the future, and there are no false opinions. Typically, therefore, fraud consists of a false statement about a present (or occasionally a past) state of affairs. On the other hand, a person's present state of mind is as much a present fact as anything else. It is therefore possible to make a false statement about one's intention regarding the future or about one's opinion, if the statement misrepresents the defendant's present state of mind. For example, if I say that I intend to pay your way through college if you give up smoking, never intending to do so, my statement is a false representation of my state of mind. Similarly, if I say that I believe that John Doe is to be trusted when I have no such belief, I have misrepresented my opinion.

The failure to disclose a material fact may also constitute fraud. But the law's longstanding reluctance to impose tort liability for nonfeasance, and the norm of *caveat emptor* that animated much of the common law of contract, together meant that traditionally there was little such liability. The general attitude of the law still is that it is incumbent on the interested party to ask about material information. A false answer to a question about a material matter would result in liability for fraud, and a party's expressed unwillingness to give any answer at all would tell the inquirer a lot about the subject of the question. There are some exceptions in which the law imposes an affirmative duty to disclose information not asked for, but most involve unusual situations rather than straightforward withholding of information: for example, for incomplete statements that are half-truths; and for statements that are not knowingly false when made but which the defendant later learns were false. In recent years, however, there has been something of a move toward imposing liability for fraud when the defendant has failed to disclose facts that are "basic" to the transaction. Partly such liability reflects changing norms regarding proper business behavior. But some decisions are an effort to lead rather than follow business ethics.

One of the problems associated with liability for nondisclosure is that neither the case law nor ordinary norms are clear about the situations in which affirmative disclosure is and is not expected. A failure by the seller of a home to disclose that it is infested with termites is often actionable;[1] but a buyer's failure to disclose his belief to the seller of land that it contains deposits of oil is not. Some of this difference in treatment reflects the differences between buyers and sellers, since buyers are often uninformed consumers, whereas sellers are at least sometimes sophisticated and informed repeat players in the market. But that is not always the case, and in any event much of the case law cannot be explained on this basis.

One interesting effort to explain the scope of liability for nondisclosure argues that there is no duty to disclose when the information in question was obtained through a costly search, whether by the buyer or seller.[2] On the other hand, when the information was not the result of a costly investment or search and is basic to the transaction, liability for fraudulent failure to disclose is more likely to be imposed. Thus, the seller of a house infested with termites has come into possession of that information without making a costly effort to do so, whereas the buyer of land under which there may be oil often has invested in geological research. Imposing liability for the former's failure to disclose will create

---

1. *See* RESTATEMENT (SECOND) OF TORTS § 551.

2. *See* Anthony T. Kronman, *Mistake, Disclosure, Information, and the Law of Contracts*, 7 J. LEGAL STUD. 1 (1978).

little if any disincentive to acquire useful information, whereas liability for the latter's failure to disclose would do exactly that.

2. *Scienter*

The defendant must make the false statement of fact with actual knowledge of its falsity or with reckless disregard of its truth or falsity. This state-of-mind requirement is termed "*scienter*." The ordinary expectation in business is that statements of fact will be made with an honest belief that they are true. A statement that is knowingly false or made with disregard of its truth or falsity contains a false implication that the maker believes it to be true, when in fact he does not, or has no belief one way or the other. The requirement that disregard be "reckless" adds an element of blame that would be absent from merely casual or inadvertent disregard for the truth or falsity of what one is said.

3. Intent That the Plaintiff Rely

The defendant has not committed fraud unless he intends that the plaintiff rely on his false statement. This requirement is sometimes called an "intent to deceive," but this latter way of describing the requirement can be misleading. A defendant who knowingly makes a false statement and intends the plaintiff to rely on it automatically intends to deceive. On the other hand, a defendant who acts only with reckless disregard may intend the plaintiff to rely, but does not necessarily intend to deceive the plaintiff. It could be argued that if such a defendant intends the plaintiff to rely on the statement, he must also intend to give the plaintiff the mistaken impression that he (the defendant) has an honest belief that the statement is true. But it seems just as possible that a defendant who disregards whether what he says is true or false is at the same time simply disregarding whether the plaintiff will suppose that the defendant believes the statement to be true. Admittedly, however, the two situations are very close, and any defendant who has an actual intent that the plaintiff rely normally also has an actual intent to deceive the plaintiff about his (the defendant's) state of mind.

4. Justifiable Reliance

This element adds the necessary causation requirement to a claim for fraud. If the plaintiff did not rely on the defendant's false statement, then the statement did not cause the plaintiff's loss and there can be no recovery. That reliance also must be justifiable, however, which means both that a) the statement must be material—i.e., would be of substantial importance to a person involved in the transaction in question—and b) is not so preposterous or otherwise lacking in credibility that the plaintiff should not have relied on it.

The materiality and credibility criteria thus require weighing the importance and character of the statement, in context. A false statement that a house being sold is not infested with termites will virtually always be material, whereas a statement that the house has a dry basement when in fact small puddles appear twice per year probably is not material in the absence of special circumstances. As to credibility, the plaintiff is not justified in relying on the defendant's statement that his fifty-year old house is in "perfect condition" and "is strong enough to stand up in a tornado." An exaggerated statement of high quality is the kind of "puffing" that so often takes place in the course of negotiation that people must learn to discount it. It may be justifiable, however, to rely on more precise assertions made under circumstances in which exaggeration is not to be expected. For instance, it is *not* mere puffing for a defendant who has applied for credit to exaggerate the amount of money he has in a bank account.

5. Damages

This element raises more complicated issues than might be supposed in the first instance. Ordinarily the measure of damages in tort is designed to make the plaintiff "whole"—that is, to put him in the same position he would have been in had his loss not occurred. In fraud, compensation for the plaintiff's *out-of-pocket* losses would accomplish this goal. For example, suppose that defendant represents his house to have copper plumbing and new wiring when in fact it has neither. If these statements were true, the house would be worth $100,000, but in fact it is worth only $85,000 in its actual condition. The plaintiff buys the house for $90,000. His out-of-pocket loss is $5000—the difference between what he paid and what the house is actually worth. Note that if the plaintiff had paid only $85,000 for the house then he would have no out-of-pocket damages and would recover nothing.

However, the defendant's statement caused another form of harm that the out-of-pocket measure does not capture: it deprived the plaintiff of the *benefit-of-the-bargain* he had made. Had the property been in the condition represented by the defendant, the plaintiff would have purchased a $100,000 house for $90,000. His loss in this respect was $10,000. In fact, therefore, the plaintiff has lost a $10,000 bargain and has suffered a $5000 "out-of-pocket" loss. Courts and commentators occasionally also describe this total ($15,000) loss as the benefit-of-the-bargain, on the theory that what

317

the plaintiff should recover is the difference between the value of what he bargained for ($100,000) and the value of what he received ($85,000). This measure of damages puts the plaintiff in a better position than he would have been in had the misrepresentation never occurred—something tort law does not typically do. But that is precisely what contract law does when it awards expectation damages for breach of contract, measured by the difference between the value of what was promised and what was delivered. The benefit-of-the-bargain measure simply recognizes that even in an action that is brought in tort (perhaps because the plaintiff is also seeking punitive damages), fraudulent misrepresentations made in the course of contractual negotiations may have a promissory character that warrants an award of damages for loss of the promisee's benefit of the bargain.

Many courts permit the plaintiff to choose his preferred measure of damages, because there are times when the benefit-of-the-bargain measure does not maximize the plaintiff's recovery.[3] Of course, where there was no contract between the plaintiff and the defendant, the plaintiff's out-of-pocket or consequential loss is the only measure of damages available. But suppose that the values stated in the earlier hypothetical case were that the same except that the plaintiff paid $110,000 for the house. The plaintiff's out-of-pocket loss would be $25,000. Of course, one might question whether the plaintiff should receive such an award, since in effect it disregards the fact that he would have lost money had the defendant's statement been true. But the courts permitting such a recovery have subscribed to the principle that the defendant who commits fraud should not be heard to complain that part of the plaintiff's loss results from his poor bargain. In effect this is simply a rejection of contributory negligence as a defense to fraud.

6. The Scope of Liability

Something like a proximate cause requirement applies in fraud, and serves to limit the right of recovery to those persons whom the defendant actually knows will rely on his false statement or whose reliance is highly foreseeable. When the fraud occurs in the course of contractual dealings, of course, the other party is known. But sometimes third parties can be expected to rely either on representations made to a contracting party or otherwise. For example, potential investors can be expected to rely on statements made by auditors, future creditors can be expected to rely bank references, etc. There is naturally a concern that the threat of liability to a large number of unidentified parties will deter desirable involve-

---

3. *See, e.g., Selman v. Shirley*, 161 Or. 582, 91 P.2d 312 (1939).

ment in these activities. The law has therefore tended to draw the line short of liability to all foreseeable plaintiffs, though there is liability to plaintiffs who are actually foreseen and to those who are "highly" foreseeable.

B. *Negligent Misrepresentation*

There may of course be liability for negligent misrepresentation that foreseeably causes bodily injury or property damage. If you ask me whether it is safe to stand on a ladder that I have carelessly inspected and I answer the ladder is safe, I am liable for any injuries that you suffer when the ladder collapses. This is ordinary negligence. In Chapter Eleven, however, we saw that in general there is no liability in negligence for pure economic loss. That rule applies to negligent misrepresentation as well, for in business and personal relationships there is no generally established expectation that people will exercise reasonable care that their statements are true before they speak. Rather, people are expected only to be honest—i.e., not to make knowingly false statements. In certain settings, however, reasonable care is expected, and in these settings there is liability for economic loss caused by negligent misrepresentation.

With the obvious exception of knowledge of falsity, proof of the other elements of a cause of action for fraud (falsity, intent that the plaintiff rely, justifiable reliance, and damages) is also required for negligent misrepresentation. Two other important issues do arise in connection with negligent misrepresentation: 1) the incidence of liability—when there can be any such liability at all; and 2) the scope of liability, or duty, issue—when there can be such liability, to whom the defendant may be held liable.

1. The Incidence of Liability

The principal example of liability for negligent misrepresentation involves what amounts to malpractice by professionals and other providers of expert or fiduciary services. Accountants, attorneys, weighers, surveyors, real estate agents, and other similarly situated experts are liable for negligently inflicted economic loss because they are expected to exercise reasonable care in accordance with the standards of their callings. And most often that negligence is memorialized in the form of some advice, information, opinion or conclusion that is negligently inaccurate. Holding these parties liable to their clients or customers for negligent misrepresentation is unremarkable. Such liability also is sometimes imposed on certain non-professional fiduciaries who stand in a "special relationship" of trust and confidence to those whom a negligent misrepresentation harms, such as the directors of a corporation to investors, or a bailee to a bailor.

Liability for pure economic loss resulting from negligent misrepresentation is rare, though not unheard of, in situations that do not fall into one of these two categories. For example, if a non-professional, non-fiduciary defendant supplies information to the plaintiff and reasonably appears to invite the plaintiff to rely on the information, then there may be liability. Thus, a health insurer who inaccurately certifies to a hospital that a patient has coverage may be liable to the hospital for negligent misrepresentation. In addition, of course, if the parties to an ordinary business relationship actually expect each other to exercise reasonable care in the transmission of information, then they are always free to provide by contract that one or both parties promise that they have exercised or will exercise reasonable care that their statements are accurate and that they will be liable for the harm that results if they were negligent. In the absence of such agreement, however, the law assumes that they expect to be held liable only for fraud.

In fact, in practice, contractual provisions requiring the exercise of reasonable care are rare, for two reasons. First, when parties in a commercial transaction want more than honesty, they tend to want guaranteed accuracy, not just reasonable care. As a consequence, the typical contract provision representing a fact to be true is a warranty whose breach results in liability automatically—i.e., on a strict liability basis. Second, outside the professional services context, what constitutes a "reasonable" degree of care to assure the accuracy of representations is difficult to inform by reference to independent norms. Professionals and other "experts" tend to follow common practices and to comply with common standards. They impliedly hold themselves out as following these practices and complying with these standards. The failure to do so is at least some evidence of their negligence. In contrast, non-professional and non-expert pursuits tend not to be governed or even "ordered" by common practices or standards regarding the transmission of accurate information. For example, it is unclear how meaningful it would be even to talk about whether a clerk in a movie-supply business had exercised "reasonable" care to assure that the descriptions of the movies in its catalogue were accurately matched-up with the movie titles. For this reason, neither the law of misrepresentation nor the parties acting for themselves by contract tend to find a negligence standard appealing in such settings.

2. The Scope of Liability: Duty

Supposing that the defendant has made an actionable negligent misrepresentation, to whom may he be held liable? Here, what amounts to duty or proximate cause becomes central. The courts have long been concerned about the scope of various forms of liability for negligence that does not cause bodily injury or property damage, because of the unpredictable and potentially unlimited extent of pure economic losses. As a consequence, although the defendant may be held liable in appropriate cases to his client or customer for negligent misrepresentation, liability has reached only a little beyond those with whom the defendant is in privity of contract.

In the paradigm case in this field, *Ultramares Corporation v. Touche*, then Chief Judge Cardozo expressed in often-repeated terms this concern about the dangers of "liability in an indeterminate amount for an indeterminate time to an indeterminate class."[4] Although the law may have all three of these concerns, in practice the focus has been on the last. *Ultramares* and other similar cases involve the common situation in which independent auditors are paid to inspect and then to certify the financial condition of a business. The owner or manager of the business misleads the auditors by overstating assets or understating liabilities in some way that the auditors do not detect. The auditors know that third parties will see and rely on their certification—that is its purpose. Of course, the primary wrong is committed by the party being audited, who committed fraud. But typically he or his business is completely or partly judgment-proof. The auditors are likely to be certified public accountants covered by malpractice liability insurance and with assets of their own.

The plaintiffs seeking a deep-pocketed defendant are third parties such as investors or creditors who have lost money by relying on the certification provided by the auditors. So they sue the auditors for negligent misrepresentation. This is in effect another of the "enabling torts" that were discussed in prior chapters. Fairly early it was settled that if a defendant such as the auditor had actual knowledge of the specific identity of a party who would rely on its statement, then that party could recover even in the absence of privity of contract. Since then the scope of liability has expanded, but not very much. In most jurisdictions there can be liability to more than one person who is not in privity with the defendant, but only if that person is a member of a "limited group" of "actually foreseen" individuals, though their specific identities

4. 255 N.Y. 170, 174 N.E. 441, 444 (1931).

ordinarily need not be known by the defendant. In some jurisdictions that group may in theory be larger, if only one individual in the group (such a future owner in the chain of title to real property) is ultimately likely to rely on and be injured by the misrepresentation. This state of affairs is to be contrasted with claims for actual fraud, in which liability extends further: to anyone whose reliance was highly foreseeable.

There is no deep explanation for this limitation on liability for negligent misrepresentation, any more than there is a deep explanation for the limitations on liability for negligently-caused emotional distress discussed in Chapter Eleven. The explanation is largely practical. The courts' objective is to permit the imposition of liability to those beyond the boundary of privity, but to contain the scope of that liability within manageable proportions under a rule with sufficient texture to make results predictable. The rule extending liability to a "limited number of actually foreseen" individuals does this. But if history is any guide, if over time the limits of this rule erode it will have to be replaced with another more expansive rule that also has sufficient texture to make results predictable.

C. *Innocent Misrepresentation*

Typically there is no liability for innocent misrepresentation outside the contracting context. However, when one contracting party has expressly or impliedly warranted to the other the truth of a fact material to the transaction, then liability for breach of warranty amounts to strict liability for innocent misrepresentation. Benefit-of-the-bargain damages sometimes are awarded in such cases. In contrast, when an innocent misrepresentation does not amount to a warranty, the law is far less clear. Suppose that in negotiations for the sale of my house I innocently misrepresent it to be free of termites. In some jurisdictions the statement is not actionable at all. In others the statement is actionable, but only the equitable remedy of rescission or its legal equivalent, liability for out-of-pocket loss, is available. Indeed, under some circumstances the plaintiff in such a transaction may not obtain rescission but may only recover the cost of repair.

These rules are unsettled largely because the expectations on which they must be based if they are to work effectively also are unsettled. We simply do not have uniform and firm standards about responsibility for innocent misrepresentations. What is perceived as a "warranty" or a guarantee will vary from individual to individual, as will moral intuitions about what an innocent misrepresenter ought to be required to do, if anything, to make things right. As long as these intuitions vary so much from setting to setting, the tort law rules governing liability for innocent misrepresentation will remain unsettled, and will have to be specified by contract or litigated on a case by case basis.

II. Intentional Interference with Contract

It is a tort to interfere *intentionally* with a contract between two other parties or to induce breach of such a contract. On the other hand, *negligent* interference with contract rights ordinarily is not actionable, as we saw in the Chapter Eleven's discussion of negligent infliction of pure economic loss. Of course, other torts—such as fraud, or false imprisonment, or others—may be committed with the intent of causing a breach of contract. But the cause of action for intentional interference exists even if the means of interference is not itself an independent tort.

The modern tort of intentional interference derives from the English case of *Lumley v. Gye*,[5] in which the defendant induced an opera singer to breach her contract to sing at the Queens Theater. The complaint in *Lumley* alleged that the interference was done with malice, and for some time it was unclear whether maliciousness was an element of the tort. It is now well-established that maliciousness is not required. On the other hand, not every interference is tortious. To be tortious, the interference must be for an "improper" purpose. However, most interferences—including those intended merely for the defendant's economic benefit—are held to be improper. Indeed, it would be more accurate to say that there is liability unless the defendant had an especially "proper" purpose, except that this way of putting the matter inaccurately suggests that defendant always bears the burden of proof on this issue. Some of the purposes that are "proper" and that therefore exempt an interfering defendant from liability have included preventing immoral behavior, and influencing a child not to marry the "wrong" person. On the other hand, a boycott in service of the desire to pressure a contracting party to take some collateral action—such as settling a labor dispute—ordinarily is not a "proper" purpose.

In recent years the commentators have disagreed about whether the tort of intentional interference should exist at all. On the one hand, the theory of "efficient breach of contract" suggests that sometimes it is value-enhancing for a contract to be breached and for the breaching party to pay damages. On this view the tort should not exist, since it inhibits efficient breach, for which the

5. 2 El. & Bl. 216, 118 Eng.Rep. 749 (Q.B.1853).

plaintiff will be compensated by the breaching party anyway.[6] On the other hand, the kinds of on-going "relational" contracts (employment, commercial requirements or supply arrangements, etc.) that are involved in the typical intentional interference action may be best served by promoting cooperation rather than efficient breach.[7] Neither view has clearly prevailed or exercised much influence on the courts.

III. Intentional Interference with Prospective Advantage

It is not only a tort to interfere with contract, but also to interfere intentionally with prospective economic advantage. Typically, though not always, such economic advantage is a possible but not executed contract. In fact, prospective contractual advantage (as distinguished, for example, from advantage that could be gained from an inheritance or gift) is the typical interest protected by this tort.

The major difference between this tort and intentional interference with contract is that it is emphatically not a tort to engage in "fair" economic competition that is designed to deprive a competitor of a *prospective* contract and garner that advantage for oneself. Thus, as in intentional interference with contract, whether the interference is done for a "proper" purpose is key, but ordinary competition is proper in the absence of an existing contract that will be interfered with. As the Supreme Court of California put it, the test is whether the defendant's action was "wrongful by some measure beyond the fact of interference itself."[8] Some forms of improper interference have crystallized into categories of "unfair competition" that have developed to the point that they are separate "sub-torts" whose contours are beyond the scope of this book: trademark infringement, false advertising, misappropriation of intellectual creations, industrial espionage, and boycott, as well as a catch-all category that is called *prima facie* tort in the State of New York. The entire area is further complicated by the existence of causes of action based on federal statutory protections for trademarks, copyrights, and patents. As various forms of intellectual property such as computer software become an increasingly important part of our economy, the scope of protection afforded to their

6. Harvey S. Perlman, *Interference with Contract and Other Economic Expectancies: A Clash of Tort and Contract Doctrine*, 49 U.Chi. L.Rev. 61 (1982).

7. Lillian R. BeVier, *Reconsidering Inducement*, 76 Va. L.Rev. 877 (1990).

8. *Della Penna v. Toyota Motor Sales, USA, Inc.*, 11 Cal.4th 376, 45 Cal.Rptr.2d 436, 902 P.2d 740, 751 (1995).

creators will be increasingly litigated, but almost certainly any common law protection will be provided in the shadow of the statutory schemes that expressly address the problem.

TABLE OF CASES

References are to Pages

INDEX

331

†